Explaining Cameron's coalition

Explaining Cameron's coalition

How it came about
An analysis of the 2010 British General Election

Robert Worcester, Roger Mortimore,
Paul Baines and Mark Gill

biteback

First published in Great Britain in 2011 by

Biteback Publishing Ltd

Westminster Tower

3 Albert Embankment

London

SE1 7SP

ISBN 978-1-84954-133-6

10 9 8 7 6 5 4 3 2 1

A CIP catalogue record for this book is available from the British Library.

Printed and bound in Great Britain by

TJ International, Padstow, Cornwall

Table of contents

Table of contents...ii
Lists of tables, figures and cartoons...iv

Acknowledgements viii

Foreword ix

Preface 1
Elections and opinion polls 1

The 2010 election 5
Introduction 5
Why Labour lost and the Tories didn't win 17

1. How Labour lost it 28
Tony Blair digs a hole 28
Gordon Brown and Labour's double-dip recession.............................49
Could Labour have won with a different leader?.................................77
When did Labour lose? 95

2. How the Conservatives failed to win it 98
The mountain the Tories had to climb..98
The political task 99
The electoral task...110
How the Tories made progress...123
Targeting the marginals 141
Tory standing on the eve of the election...155

3. The new presidentialism in British politics...................... 158
Issues or image? Why people vote as they do 158
The issue agenda in 2010 169

4. The campaign: how the voters dithered 191
The tactical battle: overview 191

The Liberal Democrats enter the story...198
The debates 210
The campaign away from the debates...224

5. One year on and the future electoral battle.................... 250
'Out of power for a generation'...250
(Cameron's) coalition succeeds in 2010..255
Equalising constituency sizes 264
Towards 2015?..270

Appendix 1: Polls and polling 290
The polls in 2010..290
How is a poll conducted?..300
How well the polls are reported..310
If not the polls, then what?..316

Appendix 2: Editorial cartoons and the 2010 election
by Kent Worcester.. 326

Index 345

Lists of tables, figures and cartoons

List of tables

Table 1: British general election result 2010, compared with 2005 13
Table 2: Key events, 2005-6 31
Table 3: Key events in 2007 up to the retirement of Tony Blair 32
Table 4: Local elections, 2006-9 – on-the-night gains and losses 34
Table 5: Mirror, mirror... who is the sleaziest of them all? 39
Table 6: Perceived trustworthiness of Blair, Brown and Cameron, 2006 40
Table 7: Vote swings, 1997-2005 and 2005-10 48
Table 8: Most capable Prime Minister – Brown or Blair? 51
Table 9: 'Like him, like his party?' – Blair, Brown and Cameron 54
Table 10: Hypothetical voting intentions if Brown were Leader, January-May 2007 56
Table 11: Key events, June-December 2007 61
Table 12: Key events, January 2008-April 2009 70
Table 13: Brown and Blair in tricky times 74
Table 14: Brown the world leader 76
Table 15: A good job in difficult circumstances? 76
Table 16: Most capable Prime Minister 78
Table 17: 'Like him, like his party?' – Brown and the Labour Party 80
Table 18: Like him/her? Like his/her policies? 1990-2010 81
Table 19: Image attributes of the leaders, April 2010 82
Table 20: Perceived trustworthiness of the leaders, 2007 and 2010 84
Table 21: Leader image, May 2010 85
Table 22: Leader image, Gordon Brown compared with Tony Blair 88
Table 23: Party image – the Labour Party, 1997-2010 90
Table 24: Party image, May 2010 91
Table 25: If Brown had stepped down 94
Table 26: Party image – the Conservative Party, 1992-2005 105
Table 27: Evolution in the nature of Tory support, 1992-2009 117
Table 28: David Cameron's image, September 2006 and May 2010 125
Table 29: 'Like him, like his party?' – Cameron and the Conservatives 126
Table 30: Improvement in Conservative Party image, 2005-10 127
Table 31: London Mayoral elections, 2004 and 2008 130
Table 32: Key events, May 2009-April 2010 133
Table 33: British elections to the European Parliament, 2004 & 2009 137
Table 34: Best party on key issues – Marginal Seats 143
Table 35: Leader image – Marginal Seats 144
Table 36: Cameron's readiness to govern – Marginal Seats 145
Table 37: Reported impact of the debates – Marginal Seats 146
Table 38: Volatility of the vote – Marginal Seats 147
Table 39: Vote share changes by constituency type, 2005-10 151
Table 40: The public's policy (il)literacy 168
Table 41: Most important issues facing Britain today. quarterly averages 173
Table 42: The issue agenda: 'very important' election issues 175
Table 43: Cut fast or cut slow? 186

Table 44: Election campaign timeline, 6 April-6 May 2010 195
Table 45: Who won the debates? 196
Table 46: If the Liberal Democrats could win 204
Table 47: Sympathy with Liberal Democrat values 208
Table 48: Preferences in a hung parliament 210
Table 49: Will the LibDem surge last? 219
Table 50: Interest in election news 225
Table 51: Standard of campaigning 232
Table 52: Key demographic voter segments in 2010 233
Table 53: Social media engagement with party election broadcasts 238
Table 54: 'Bullygate' 241
Table 55: Is Gordon Brown two-faced? 242
Table 56: Voting by newspaper readership, 2010 244
Table 57: Voting intentions of *Sun* readers, 2005-10 245
Table 58: Declining media interest in the election debates 247
Table 59: Positive/negative media coverage of the leaders 248
Table 60: Party expenditure at the 2010 British general election 249
Table 61: Change in LibDem support, 2010 election to Jan/Feb 2011 252
Table 62: Like Nick Clegg/like the Liberal Democrats, January 2011 253
Table 63: Government policies and the economy 258
Table 64: Government policies and public services 259
Table 65: The 'Big Society' 260
Table 66: Like David Cameron/the Conservative Party, January 2011 261
Table 67: Satisfaction with David Cameron and the Government, 2010-11 262
Table 68: Image of Miliband, Cameron and Clegg 263
Table 69: Variation in constituency size and vote 268
Table 70: Like Ed Miliband/like the Labour Party 272
Table 71: Like/not like opposition leaders, 1984-2011 273
Table 72: How Britain voted, 2010 278
Table 73: Voting by region 279
Table 74: Self-Assessed Social Class 283
Table 75: Self-assessed social class compared to social grade 284
Table 76: Voting by 'Mumsnetters' (ABC1 women aged 25-44) 287
Table 77: Change in party support, 2010 election to Jan/Feb 2011 288
Table 78: Final pre-election polls in 2010 292
Table 79: The record of the British exit polls, 1997-2010 294
Table 80: Ipsos MORI polls before and during the 2010 election campaign 296
Table 81: Published voting intention polls before the first debate 297
Table 82: Polls between the first and third debates 297
Table 83: Polls after the third debate 299
Table 84: Average voting intention poll results by company, 2009 299
Table 85: Calculating the voting 'prediction' in Ipsos MORI's final poll 307
Table 86: The proof of the pudding 310
Table 87: Polls published on 7 March 2010 312
Table 88: Banning polls and other election coverage 316

List of figures

Figure 1: The general election result: votes and seats (UK) 5
Figure 2: Turnout in general elections in Great Britain, 1945-2010..............................16
Figure 3: Voting intentions 2005-7 (poll of polls)...............................29
Figure 4: Local election and general election vote shares, 1998-2010.........................35
Figure 5: Do you now or did you ever...? The Iraq war.............................42
Figure 6: Tony Blair's and Gordon Brown's public standing, 1997-2010 45
Figure 7: The public view of the Blair government's record, May 2007........................47
Figure 8: Net satisfaction with Chancellors, 1979-2007 52
Figure 9: Voting intentions 2007-8 (Poll of Polls) 59
Figure 10: How the polls suddenly turned in Autumn 2007..........................66
Figure 11: Gordon Brown's 'double-dip recession', 2007-10 72
Figure 12: Leader image, May 2010 87
Figure 13: Party image, May 2010 – perceptual map 92
Figure 14: The decline of the 'working class' 1969-2009...........................116
Figure 15: Satisfaction with PM and government, 1978-9 and 2009-10 120
Figure 16: Average net satisfaction ratings of opposition leaders 1955-2010.............124
Figure 17: Voting intentions, 2009-10 (poll of polls).............................135
Figure 18: Trust in professions to tell the truth, 2009 136
Figure 19: Potential impact of the expenses scandal on voting 138
Figure 20: Trust in MPs.............................140
Figure 21: Net satisfaction with opposition leaders – Blair v Cameron 141
Figure 22: The scale of variation in constituency results, 2001-10 149
Figure 23: Swing to Conservatives in Labour-held targets 1-75 152
Figure 24: Swing to Conservatives in Labour-held targets 76-150 153
Figure 25: Swing to Conservatives in LibDem-competing seats.............................154
Figure 26: Parties' perceived readiness to govern 157
Figure 27: The Political Triangle©, 2010.............................163
Figure 28: The Political Triangle: Trends 165
Figure 29: Most important issues facing Britain, 2005-10 172
Figure 30: Best party on key issues 178
Figure 31: Economic policies – the gap between desire and expectation.................185
Figure 32: Economic optimism and Labour voting intention share, 2008-10 187
Figure 33: Economic optimism and general election results 189
Figure 34: Electoral volatility since 1983.............................192
Figure 35: Late decisions on how to vote.............................193
Figure 36: The course of the campaign – all published polls 197
Figure 37: Reported tactical voting by party supported, 2010.............................206
Figure 38: The course of the campaign (poll of polls) 216
Figure 39: Impact of the first debate (self-assessed by the public).............................217
Figure 40: Impact of the first debate on poll findings.............................218
Figure 41: Impact of the second debate (self-assessed by the public) 222
Figure 42: Labour campaign poster (1).............................226
Figure 43: Labour campaign poster (2).............................227
Figure 44: Conservative campaign poster (1) 228
Figure 45: Conservative campaign poster (2) 228
Figure 46: Liberal Democrat poster campaign (1).............................229
Figure 47: Liberal Democrat poster campaign (2).............................230
Figure 48: Real-time tracking of message persuasiveness.............................231

Figure 49: Reported general election canvassing levels, 1979-2010..........................236
Figure 50: Seats to votes: the bias...266
Figure 51: The class shift in Labour's vote, 1992-2010...281
Figure 52: The gender gap, 1974-2010..286
Figure 53: Watch the money watch the polls 319

List of cartoons

Cartoon 1: Martin Rowson, *Guardian*, 19 April 2010..328
Cartoon 2: Marf, *Political Betting*, 28 September 2009 332
Cartoon 3: Three Matt cartoons from the *Daily Telegraph* 336
Cartoon 4: Peter Brookes, *The Times*, 28 April 2010..338
Cartoon 5: Scott, *Daily Star*, 27 April 2010..340
Cartoon 6: Steve Bell, *Guardian*, 30 April 2010 342

Acknowledgements

The three cartoons by Matt on page 336 are copyright by Telegraph Media Group Limited, and are reproduced by kind permission.

The cartoon by Peter Brookes on page 338 is copyright by Peter Brookes/The Times/NI Syndication, and is reproduced by kind permission.

The cartoons by Martin Rowson (page 328), Marf (page 332), Scott (page 340) and Steve Bell (page 342) are copyright by the artists, and are reproduced by kind permission.

Foreword

This is our fourth book on British general elections to examine recent contests between the principal political parties in Great Britain as they compete for victory in the protracted and expensive (and to many, exciting) exercise in democracy. We view them from the standpoint not of the players, the politicians and their closest observers, the media, but from the vox populi, the people, for whom after all it's all about.

This book is substantially different from its three predecessors, *Explaining Labour's Landslide* (1997 General Election), *Explaining Labour's Second Landslide* (2001) and *Explaining Labour's Landslip* (2005) – most importantly because of the outcome, a hung parliament with no political party having an overall majority. In the first-past-the-post system of electing Members of Parliament from a single-member constituency, the candidate with the most votes, even one vote more than any other candidate, becomes the Member of Parliament for that constituency. There have been contests, called three-way marginals, where the three largest parties, Conservatives, Labour and Liberal Democrats, have each had between them 34% against 33% and 33%, and the winner and MP is the one with the most, 34%.

There have been hung parliaments before. In February 1974, Labour was four seats ahead of the Conservatives but 17 short of 318 (one over half the parliamentary seats at the time), close enough so that on the Monday – after a fraught weekend when the sitting Conservative Prime Minister, Edward Heath, frantically attempted to forge alliances with the Liberals, Ulster MPs and others to stay in power – Harold Wilson, the Labour leader, went to the Palace and then took office at Number Ten. But this one was different. Again in 2010, after the fraught weekend and just into the following week, Labour's Prime Minister appropriately stayed in office despite a 30% share of the vote to the Conservatives' 37%. (The Liberal Democrats had 24% and others 10% of the Great Britain vote). But the total number of votes across the nation isn't the criterion by which elections in Britain are decided. The number of MPs, including the 18 Northern Ireland MPs, is 650. Thus 326 are required to form a majority. In 2010, the Conservatives elected 306, 20 short of an overall majority. Labour elected 258, the Liberal Democrats 57, and others 29. This gave the Liberal Democrats the 'swing vote', as their 57 could in a coalition with the Conservatives have a majority of 76. Alternatively, if the Liberal

Democrats supported Labour, the combined number would be 315, 11 short of the necessary 326, thus requiring some other parties' MPs to join a 'rainbow coalition', much more fragile than the two-party agreement which is just what happened.

In the chapters that follow, and in the appendices, we begin by reviewing the 'long campaign', which starts with the day following the previous (in this case 2005) general election. We track the opinion poll question 'How would you vote if there were a general election tomorrow?'. But in addition, every month since 1979 (making MORI/Ipsos MORI the longest consistent trend line of the British public's voting intention) our surveys have also measured satisfaction with the government of the day, with the Prime Minister, the Leader of the Opposition and the leader of the third party, recently the Liberal Democrats, the result of the 1988 merger of the Liberals and the Social Democrat Party. They have measured the 'Economic Optimism Index' (EOI), and, less frequently but still consistently, they have measured many other trends in political opinion.

In one way this election is especially curious, as everyone lost – the Tories because they didn't get quite enough seats to form the required majority over all other parties to govern without the help of any other parties' MPs, Labour because it ran a poor second, losing 97 seats, and the Liberal Democrats because they lost five seats despite their leader, Nick Clegg, and all, without exception, of its MPs believing that they would gain seats, not lose them, a belief shared by nearly every pundit, political editor and punter in the land. It was also a let down for the independent candidates, of whom a record number were standing. Before the election was called, I chaired a day-long workshop sponsored *pro bono* by GovNet (I am a member of its Advisory Board) and around 100 came, mostly independent candidates as the major parties had their own workshops. Some were standing completely alone, others as part of the ill-fated 'Jury Team', many of whom thought they were in with a chance (a view not shared at the time by me). We try in separate chapters to explain why in our view each of the three major parties 'lost' the election.

In another way, also covered in these chapters, this was a curious election as for the first time in over thirty years all three party leaders were untested in a previous general election, Brown having succeeded Tony Blair in 2007 as leader of the Labour Party and therefore PM, Cameron following after

Michael Howard and Nick Clegg replacing Sir Menzies Campbell (who had replaced Charles Kennedy) as leader of the Liberal Democrats.

Also covered in detail is the impact of the leaders' debates, a first for Britain. They electrified the campaign and raised the hopes of the Liberal Democrats, while not doing much for Cameron of whom much was expected, and disappointing Gordon Brown. He thought, going into the debates, that his 13 years experience at the top of government, first as Chancellor and then as Prime Minister, would shine through – it didn't, overtaken by his lack of appeal to the electorate and weighed down by the 'time for a change' syndrome of decade-long government occupancy and the state of the economy.

And in yet another way it was curious by not being the 'internet election', as anticipated. It was at one level, that of the 'players', politicians, pundits, news media and election nerds, but by and large, the hype was far bigger than the action on the part of the electorate. The principal means by which people took part in the election was by watching the TV, being aware of (if not reading) the leaflets, which contrasts with the 'new media', with just about one in six of the potential voters in key marginal seats utilising the internet to get information about the election.

This book would not be possible without the indispensible data arising from the many polls – 91 during the period between 6 April 2010 and election day, 6 May – carried out by a clutch of polling organisations all determined to do the best job they could with the tools they have, the techniques of survey research, assisted by qualitative research, but in all cases with the individual elector centre stage. But elections are not just about the final act in the Great Play of a British General Election. The determination of their values in early life forms many people's life-long decision-making as to even whether they believe it is their duty to vote in general elections (86% of the British public said they thought it was in 2010), and if they do vote, how they will vote.

From a theoretical base derived during the 1970s that voting decisions among floating voters determine not only the outcome but the margin of victory in every general election, we have examined the mood of the electorate around a 'political triangle' of the perceptions of our respondents as to the importance ('salience') of the issues facing the country and their perceptions of which political party has the best policies to solve these problems, if any. The second 'face' of the political triangle is their perceptions of the effectiveness of the party leaders who are plausible candidates to become Prime Minister, and the third their perceptions of the political parties fighting the election. (For a detailed description of how this model was initially derived and developed see pp 6-10 in our earlier book, *Explaining Labour's Second Landslide.*)

In some recent elections, the Conservative and Labour Parties have been heading for a landslide on a date pretty certain, e.g., in 1979 when Callaghan had to go to the wire to give Thatcher her landslide, as did Major in 1997 to give way gracefully to Tony Blair. Sometimes they come as a complete surprise, as did Harold Wilson's 1970 election and as didn't Brown's missed opportunity in 2007. There is also a 'typical' four-year cycle as in 1974 (February), 1983, 1987, 2001 and 2005.

The outcome of the election is also sometimes predictable, at least to everyone other than those so blinded by party loyalty that they can't see it coming, such as in 1979 and 1997.

In 1997 there were three examples of this I recall. I addressed the Conservative Peers' group a month or so before the election, and despite the Blair tsunami roaring down towards the beach, a former Tory Party chairman stood up to challenge my confident assessment that there was likely to be a defeat for their party on election day, saying that the electorate was sure to reward his party for the excellence of its economic performance and return them with a workable majority. Sadly, he died before the electorate gave Labour its 179 majority, and so never knew how wrong he'd been.

And in the same election, at a dinner party when a Tory peer and a City grandee were singing William Hague's praises and saying what a good Prime Minister he'd make, the hostess said 'What does Bob think?' I replied that I thought they were talking nonsense. Challenged by the City gent to make a spread and he'd say whether he'd buy or sell, I said a Labour majority of '82 to 102'; he said, as I'd hoped, that he would sell Labour at 82. He then asked 'How much a seat?' and I responded '£100 a seat'. He lost and paid nearly £9,000, on the nail.

Then on the day before the election, addressing the Carlton Club's political committee, I had deliberately ducked making a forecast, thinking they must know what election day would bring. However, during questions I was pressed to make a prediction. Wanting to be kind, I said 'It could be over a hundred' which was greeted with sharp intakes of breath and vigorous shaking of heads and much muttering that it was not what they were finding on the ground.

At this election, we like nearly all the other polls with remarkable consistency pointed towards a hung parliament. It was on this basis that so much advance preparation was made, by the Cabinet Secretary and the Institute for Government (IfG) in collaboration with the Palace, on what should happen in the event the polls were right and the electorate did make the Conservatives the largest party and left the Liberal Democrats with the swing vote. In addition, it dictated the strategy of the Liberal Democrats' Campaign Manager, John Sharkey, formerly of Saatchi's, to rehearse all the permutations and scenarios they could conceive of in anticipation of their being – for them the opportunity, literally, of a lifetime (and more), the prospect of being in government, which prepared them for the negotiations which took place immediately following the result. The Tories, I have been told, were half prepared for the negotiations, Labour not at all.

Not many saw it coming, but in *Kent on Sunday*, which serves the county in which I live, the Sunday four days before the election my interview carried the headline 'Clegg will hold balance of power', and in the text was '...it is highly unlikely that either Labour or the Conservatives will improve enough before the election... it is highly likely that Mr Clegg will hold the balance of power and will have to decide which of the main parties to form a coalition with.'

Even despite our record (see page 294), there are those who still won't believe the exit poll. In fact, this election it seemed nobody did when at 10 pm all three election night broadcasts announced the result of the exit poll they had, BBC, ITV and Sky collectively, sponsored from a consortium of Ipsos MORI and Gfk NOP. While we took stick on the night, we kept thinking that the one who laughs last, laughs best. Why, one well-known blogger even said if the exit poll was right he'd run naked down Whitehall. After the election, he said he didn't say when.

This book on our view of the people's view of the election, the fourth in the series, has been co-authored by political analyst Dr Roger Mortimore and myself[1]. In 2005, we added the political expertise of Dr Paul Baines of Cranfield University. Paul is that rare breed of a political pragmatic academic with whom I have now co-authored four or five academic articles. This year, we welcome to our co-authorship my colleague before as head of the political team at MORI and now for some four years working with me on international projects, including for the Government of Trinidad & Tobago, Mark Gill. It has truly been a wonderfully cooperative and collegiate collaboration, but the crucial core work is mostly that of the redoubtable Roger once more. Any errors are ours, collectively!

I also pay tribute to my son, Professor Kenton Worcester, who has authored an Appendix to this book on the editorial cartoons during the election, heretofore a relatively unresearched area of political marketing. While there have often been cartoons sprinkled about other British election books, none that we know of has to date focused on this aspect of a general election, and yet such cartoons are part of the political communications during elections. One need but look back now to see that Matt's 'pocket' cartoons in the *Telegraph* must have caused great amusement among *Telegraph* readers while doing the Liberal Democrats' leader Nick Clegg no good at all.

There are many others to thank: Ipsos MORI's country manager and the star of radio and television coverage during the 2010 election, Ben Page; Bobby Duffy, who heads up Ipsos MORI's Social Research Institute, within which the political team operates under Gideon Skinner, business manager for the political team; team leader Helen Cleary; our link person with Reuters; Tom Mludzinski and Jerry Latter, key members of election team; Chris Phillips, who ran the final poll, helped by Simon Atkinson and Brian Gosschalk, another former head of the political team; Graham Keilloh, Rob Melvill and George Margesson, the exit poll team; Sara Butler and Anna Pierce, who directed the Ipsos MORI 'worm' for the broadcasters' coverage of the debates, and Fiona Nolan and David Kingsmill, who were in charge of recruiting those focus groups; Daniel

[1] The other series I started with *Political Communications and the British General Election of 1979* lives on, and is now in its eighth volume with Dr Roger Mortimore as a co-editor in 2010.

Cameron, who ran our polling for the *Economist*; the former head of the political unit, Julia Clark, for coming back from the US Ipsos office in Washington to help in election week; another former head of the political team Simon Braunholtz, who now heads the Ipsos MORI Scotland office; Joe Broughton, Duncan Peskett, Liam Carroll and Denis Winterburn for working all hours on the data processing; the exit poll field team, led by Rebekah Joseph, Mette Turay, Toni Whitehead, Gemma Rowden, Alastair Townend and Samantha Irving, together with all the interviewers; Joe Stead and the team at MTS, and *their* interviewers; Matt Flanders, for working with the media coverage, our secretaries, Charlotte Mackintosh and Kerry Colville; and not least our loyal and hardworking receptionists at Borough Road, Jenny Palmer, Salli Barnard and Lyn West.

And tributes to our clients, without whose support we would not have been able to write this book as we would not have had the data: Jodie Ginsberg at Reuters; David Wooding at *News of the World*; Hilary O'Neill at BBC *News at Ten*; Merril Stevenson at the *Economist*; and my pals and continuing clients before and during the 2010 election, Joe Murphy at the *Evening Standard*, Bob Roberts then at the *Mirror*, and Paul Webster, Toby Helm, Anushka Asthana and the graphics genius at the *Observer*, Pete Guest. And to the exit poll clients: Sue Inglish, David Cowling (BBC), Jonathan Munro (ITV News) and John McAndrew (Sky), plus John Curtice, Colin Rallings, Michael Thrasher, Nick Moon and their teams, all integral parts of the exit poll.

Our sincere thanks to them all, collectively and individually.

Sir Robert Worcester

Founder, MORI

March 2011

Preface

Elections and opinion polls

The 2010 election ended by producing a hung Parliament, the Conservatives the largest party but well short of an overall majority and forced to negotiate a coalition with the Liberal Democrats to take power. But, although it was the first indecisive general election for a third of a century, it took few people unawares: though many of the participants no doubt hoped for a different result, most of the commentators in the media (and surely, privately, most of the politicians) had considered a hung Parliament to be the most likely outcome for weeks if not months. Why? Because the opinion polls, consistently and almost unanimously from beginning to end, indicated that support for the parties was at levels that made a hung Parliament likely.

The 2010 election saw more polls of voting intention from more polling companies than any British election since polling began.[2] There were a dozen companies publishing polls, nearly a hundred national polls and scores of regional and local polls published between the announcement of the election and polling day. The eventual outcome showed that their message had been broadly accurate (almost completely so in indicating the most important measurement, the Conservative lead over Labour, perhaps less so in showing how far the dramatic ten-point surge in Liberal Democrat support immediately after the first of the three leaders' debates had faded by the time voters went to cast their votes on election day).

Despite the media's desire to use polls to forecast elections, the laws of statistics and the progress of the campaign will not allow them to predict anything, except perhaps in the last 24 hours before the election (as the horses near the finish line) – polls take 'snapshot' measurements of public opinion at a single point in time in the same way that the sports announcer reports the state of the race as it rounds the track.

To mix metaphors, polls are like barometers – while not predictive in themselves, they measure something that is very useful in enabling pundits

---

[2] See Tables 79 and 81– 83 in Appendix 1 for the full list.

1

to make their predictions, and the best of these use polling data in anticipating the result of an election weeks or months away, but only if they bear in mind the limitations of people's intention to vote, and their current voting intentions (their *opinion*) as a predictor of future voting *behaviour*.

But tracking voting intentions is far from the only function of opinion polls, nor their most useful function. Polls give a much broader range of information which helps understand elections – and, yes, to predict their results, perhaps far in advance – on a more sophisticated basis than succumbing to the obsession with the 'horserace' (which is, after all, no more than the guesses of the might-votes how they might vote). Polls can measure the public perceptions of the parties and their leaders, their reactions to events and to proposed policies, and the interaction between all these factors in influencing voting behaviour. They serve, too, between elections, to measure public attitudes to the government and its policies – so, at the moment, they offer a measurement of the progress being made by the Coalition, not as some vague foreshadowing of voting in 2015 but as a matter of interest in itself. They can help us understand who votes, and which way, and why, and what the parties and candidates might do to change that, why some governments succeed and others fail. Above all, they help us to understand voters, to get into their minds and see what makes them tick.

It is this that is, ultimately, the purpose of this book and of the series to which it belongs.[3] Elections are for voters; they are the embodiment and enforcement of Lincoln's principle of 'government of the people, by the people, for the people'.

British elections now produce a plethora of books, both popular and academic, many first rate in achieving what they set out to do; but nearly all approach the election first and foremost from the perspective of the politicians competing for power, what they did and what they hoped to achieve. That is an important consideration, of course, but it is not the whole story. By concentrating on what the opinion polls can tell us about

---

[3] The previous books in the series are Robert Worcester and Roger Mortimore, *Explaining Labour's Landslide* (London: Politico's Publishing, 1999); Robert Worcester and Roger Mortimore, *Explaining Labour's Second Landslide* (London: Politico's Publishing, 2001); Robert Worcester, Roger Mortimore and Paul Baines, *Explaining Labour's Landslip* (London: Politico's Publishing, 2005).

the election, and the government of the UK in the five years leading up to it, we put the spotlight firmly on public opinion and on what the voters and non-voters themselves thought about it. And, taken together with more recent soundings, they put the new government's performance in its proper context.

The opinion polls we use are mainly those conducted by Ipsos MORI, the company for which most of us work or have worked, although we cite evidence from the other polling companies whenever it seems to us to shine light on some question that our own polls have not fully covered.

Ipsos MORI is now the UK arm of the Paris-based Ipsos research group, and is the second largest market and social research agency in the UK and the third largest in Europe. Its history is distinguished. Over the past 60 years, the UK market research industry has grown in stature and in global influence. The companies that formed what is now Ipsos MORI were there almost from the beginning, and political polling has always been a part of their work.

Robert M Worcester (now Sir Robert) came to the UK in 1969 to set up MORI (Market & Opinion Research International), ultimately aiming to found a company providing research 'at the heart of business and public life'. MORI first conducted private polls for the Labour Party at the 1970 and two 1974 general elections for Prime Minister and then Leader of the Opposition and yet again Prime Minister Harold Wilson, and for Prime Minister James Callaghan in 1979, and has published polls at every general election since 1979. During the 1980s and 1990s, MORI continued to grow its reputation and capabilities in large-scale central and local government research studies.

Ipsos was founded in France in 1975 to serve a select client base that sought high quality research. In 1991, Ipsos purchased the UK-based Research Services Ltd (RSL), founded by Dr Mark Abrams, one of the founding fathers of social and market research in Britain and a co-founder of the Market Research Society, who worked for Harold Wilson in the 1964 and 1966 elections (and for Hugh Gaitskell before that). RSL published polls at both the general elections in the 1960s as well as, memorably, 1979. First as RSL under Mark Abrams and later Dawn Mitchell, and then as Ipsos UK, the company experienced rapid growth and became a recognised brand, known in particular for their media research.

Ipsos MORI is the merger of these two successful research companies. Ipsos UK and MORI joined together the October after the 2005 election. Increasingly the Ipsos Group has been doing election polling in many of its nearly 70 countries around the world, and Ipsos MORI has been involved in advising and conducting political polls in other Ipsos companies.

Although political polling is only a small part of Ipsos's wider research business, and a small part of Ipsos MORI's, it is probably the most visible part. This is appropriate, since it explores questions of importance to all of the public who take any interest in the political life of their nation. How and why did the 2010 election turn out as it did? What did the voters want from it? And what does this mean for the new government that has resulted from it, and the policies they are now trying to pursue? These are the questions this book tries to answer, Explaining Cameron's Coalition.

The 2010 election

Introduction

The British General Election held on 6 May 2010 came at the end of a five-year Parliament, delayed until the last practicable date on which it could be held. The Labour government, which had been re-elected in 2005 under Tony Blair's premiership, had been led since Blair's retirement in 2007 by his Chancellor of the Exchequer, Gordon Brown. It went down to a resounding defeat, with under 30% of the vote, losing almost a hundred seats. That defeat had long seemed inevitable. It was the natural consequence of government unpopularity over the wars in Iraq and Afghanistan, dissatisfaction with the state of public services, distrust of government immigration policy and anger over a string of revelations that threw into question the integrity of the entire political class, coupled with an uncharismatic Prime Minister who was unable to turn public opinion around. But all was eventually completely overshadowed by the banking collapse in 2008 and the wider economic and public spending crisis which that precipitated.

Figure 1: The general election result: votes and seats (UK)

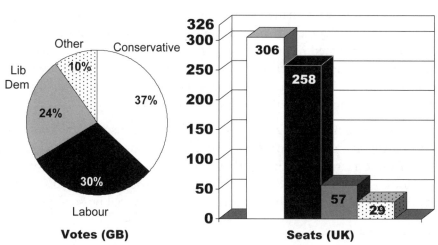

Source: Election results as published in the House of Commons Library Research Paper 10/36 (8 July 2010)

Yet the result was a huge disappointment to the opposition Conservatives: given the deep unpopularity of the Labour government, which had been in office thirteen years, they felt entitled to nothing less than a sweeping victory. But the Conservatives won only 36% of the United Kingdom vote (37% excluding Northern Ireland[4]) and finished 20 seats short of a majority in the House of Commons. After a tense weekend of negotiations following Election Day, it was not the electorate, but the leader of the third-placed Liberal Democrats, Nick Clegg, who had the final say. He chose to align his 57 MPs with the Conservatives rather than Labour to form a government, and hand the premiership to the Conservative leader, David Cameron.

After protracted discussions following a more or less open offer of 'anything' from David Cameron, the Liberal Democrats were given five places in the coalition cabinet, including the Deputy Prime Minister title for Nick Clegg with responsibility for reforming Parliament, and the promise of a referendum on an alternative voting system to the traditional first-past-the-post system. It was the centre party's first peacetime involvement in government for almost ninety years, and arguably the first British coalition government to be formed solely in response to an indecisive election result since the 18th century. The Liberal Democrats achieved a share of power despite managing only a small increase in their share of the vote and a net loss of seats.

It was an election with many fascinating and unusual features. All three major parties had changed their leaders during the Parliament (indeed, the Liberal Democrats had done so twice), so all the candidates for Downing Street were fighting an election in that capacity for the first time, a rare event in itself. The eventual victor, David Cameron, became the youngest Prime Minister since before the Reform Act of 1832.

There were more new candidates than usual at the constituency level, too. An extraordinary number of MPs had decided not to seek re-election, many of these fearing they had little chance of success after controversial revelations of their expenses claims (and perhaps mindful that redundancy-style payments for departing MPs might well be scrapped after

---

[4] As there are different political parties in Northern Ireland, all 'national' opinion polls are representative of the adult population of Great Britain (England, Scotland and Wales).

the election), though others of course were simply retiring in the normal way. More MPs stood down in 2010 than did so at the 1945 election (which on account of the extraordinary wartime circumstances came ten years after the preceding election), 149 in all.[5] Moreover, more independent and minor party candidates stood for election than ever before.

Furthermore, there were boundary changes, with only 73 of the 573 constituencies in England and Wales being unaltered. Expert analysis[6] suggested that this would produce a small benefit (around 12 seats) to the Conservatives, slightly offsetting the bias to Labour in the operation of the electoral system. But perhaps more significant was the widespread uncertainty that any boundary revision causes, and the inconvenience (to say the least) suffered by sitting MPs dislodged from their strongholds and forced to campaign in pastures new among unfamiliar voters.

So many voters faced unfamiliar choices on all fronts – local candidates who had not represented them before and party leaders about whom their impressions were probably vaguer than usual. Many had no clear opinions of the leaders at all, while others were learning more and modifying their impressions as time went by. Further, the dominant issue of the day was the economic crisis: all the alternative remedies being proposed by the parties were painful and, not unnaturally, the public did not relish any of them. Most were essentially unqualified to make such economic judgments themselves, and knew it. Therefore, even more so than usual, they were dependent on deciding which leader's word and which leader's judgment they could trust to make the decisions for them. All these factors may have contributed to causing an election in which the public mood reached unprecedented levels of volatility.

Less well publicised but potentially as significant in changing the way elections are fought were newly-tightened spending restrictions on candidates, which regulated the amount they could spend on their

---

[5] 100 Labour, 35 Conservatives, 7 Liberal Democrats, 2 Independents, 1 Independent Conservative and 1 member each from Plaid Cymru, the SNP, the DUP, and the SDLP. (House of Commons Library Research Paper RP10-036).
[6] Colin Rallings & Michael Thrasher, 'The Electoral Impact of the New Parliamentary Constituency Boundaries – Great Britain', p 5, in *Media Guide to the New Parliamentary Constituencies* (Plymouth: Local Government Chronicle Elections Centre, 2007).

campaign from the turn of the year rather than only from the moment they were formally adopted as a candidate, as had previously been the case. However, this change had no effect on spending before the end of 2009, and hence did not apply to one much-discussed pre-campaign element, Lord Ashcroft's spending of several million pounds to help Conservative candidates in 'marginal' constituencies.

The volatility of support during the election campaign only reflected the experience of the years since Gordon Brown's elevation to the premiership, a period in which voting intentions swung wildly, from a Labour lead at one extreme to the makings of a Conservative landslide at the other, then back towards parity. According to many accounts, the election was nearly held in October or November 2007 rather than May 2010. After taking over from Tony Blair, Gordon Brown saw a sharp improvement in Labour's poll ratings, and, even though this was widely interpreted as the 'honeymoon' effect that almost any new Prime Minister can expect, by time of the party conferences there was much talk about the possibility of Brown calling a snap election. Then the Labour 'bounce' suddenly stalled.

The turn in fortunes seems to have come after the Conservatives announced that they would exempt properties worth less than £1m from inheritance tax, and was apparently first detected in Labour's private polls, a couple of days before published polls showed the same trend. Brown confirmed in a television interview that there would be no immediate election on the same day as polls came out showing Labour behind for the first time, both nationally and in the marginal constituencies.

Of course, we will never know now whether that Tory upturn was only a blip that would have melted away again in the heat of an election campaign – Brown ensured that it lasted by the way he handled the situation. It seems certain that by seeming to dither over whether to risk an early election and then by publicly stating that the opinion polls played no part in his decision (which was plainly untrue), Gordon Brown lost face and credibility. What would have happened if Brown had, in fact, visited the Palace to secure a dissolution in 2007? We can only speculate. (Harold Wilson had the nerve to try to exploit good opinion poll standings, backed up by unexpectedly favourable local election results, and called an election for June 1970. He lost, narrowly and much to his surprise.)

From that point in the autumn of 2007, when it seemed to some at least (if not to us) that Labour had the opportunity to call the election and win it, the government's popularity spiralled rapidly downwards until by the middle of 2008 it appeared a certainty that an immediate election could only result in a Conservative landslide. Then, as suddenly, the gap narrowed again. Then it widened once more. As the banking crisis rumbled on, Gordon Brown's standing waxed and waned with the vicissitudes of the markets. Labour was, by turns, four-square behind its leader and enmeshed in abortive plots to topple him. In December 2008, Labour was only five points behind; in early 2009, the Conservatives were enjoying consistent double-figure leads in the voting intention polls.

As curtain to the final act, in the summer of 2009 the *Daily Telegraph*'s revelations on MPs' expenses besmirched and humiliated all the major parties equally, so much so that the UK Independence Party (UKIP) could finish second in the European elections of that year, with Labour reduced to less than 16% of the vote and the Conservatives able only to celebrate a hollow victory with under 28% themselves. At this point, the Conservative lead in the 'general election tomorrow' polls was still enough for outright victory, but by the turn of the year the gap was down to single figures. It then hardly moved before the campaign proper, which began with the Conservatives on 38%, Labour on 30% and the Liberal Democrats on 16% in the 'poll of polls', a 5% swing to the Tories when they needed about 7% for outright victory. Similarly, from before the start of the year Gordon Brown's satisfaction ratings were slowly rising while David Cameron's were slowly declining, and although Mr Cameron retained a slender lead as the 'most capable Prime Minister', on many other crucial characteristics such as 'understanding world problems' and being 'best in a crisis' it was Mr Brown who had the advantage.

One key reason the election was so finely balanced was simply that none of the parties ever succeeded in establishing a clear lead on any of the issues that mattered most to the voters. Most important of these was managing the economy. But those 40% of the public who said that the economy or unemployment was an important issue for them in deciding how to cast their ballot were almost evenly split over which party had the best economic policies, 31% saying that the Conservatives did and 28% Labour, whereas 23% either thought that none of the political parties had the best policies or that they didn't know. Not surprising, perhaps, given that they rejected all the suggested solutions to the country's economic crisis: by substantial majorities the public opposed increasing income tax, increasing national insurance, increasing VAT and cutting spending on public services. (Yet 55% continued to name the economy as one of the most important issues facing Britain – way ahead of the second most important issue, race relations/immigration, picked by 29%.)

Perhaps as a consequence, this was an election in which the voters' views of the leaders mattered much more than what they thought about the parties or their policies. *Even before the leadership debates*, we found that for the first time in our experience people were saying that the leaders were as important as policies to their vote, a 7% swing since 2005 in electors' allocation of what they felt was important to them in their voting decision.

But it was the introduction, for the first time, of televised leaders' debates during the election campaign which will be the abiding memory of the 2010 election. The broadcasters, naturally, have been eager for many years to establish these, a staple of the election contest in many other countries, most obviously in the United States since the 1960 Kennedy/Nixon debates. Always, until now at least, one of the leaders – usually the Prime Minister but in 1979 the Leader of the Opposition[7] – refused to take part, and the idea has never come to fruition until this election. In 2010, there was a Prime Minister who reportedly held a low opinion of his principal opponent and was convinced that the knowledge derived from his 13 years as Chancellor and then Prime Minister would stand him in good stead. The Leader of the Opposition, on the other hand, was convinced *he* would shine, and both were sufficiently confident to accede to the Liberal Democrats' demand for equal inclusion without, apparently, too many misgivings. The LibDem leader, Nick Clegg, was a comparatively anonymous figure, who entered the election with almost a third of the public unable to give an opinion on whether they were satisfied with the job he was doing or not; the debates would give him a chance to change that.

The debates exceeded not only the LibDems' expectations but the expectations of virtually every pundit, politician and pollster, being by far

---

[7] In 1997, both John Major and Tony Blair claimed to be in favour, but each side blamed the other for the eventual failure to get the idea off the ground.

the most memorable events of an otherwise rather dull campaign. The first debate was a watershed event, provoking the most dramatic swing in party support during any British election since opinion polls were first introduced just before the War. Nearly ten million people watched the first debate at its peak viewing, and the *average* viewing figure was just over nine million, confounding assumptions that an hour and a half of closely controlled three-way debate would prove a turn off. Nearly half of the public said it had had some effect on their voting intentions (if only to strengthen their determination to vote for the party they already supported), and in the key marginal constituencies four in five felt the debates had helped to get more people interested in the election campaign.

As a direct result of the first debate – in which the previously little-noticed Liberal Democrat leader excelled – the polls swung dramatically with Liberal Democrat support rising from around 20% to 30%, literally overnight. But as the impact of that first impression wore off and the media attention focused more critically on them, vote share began to drift away from the Liberal Democrats and back to the Conservatives and Labour. Nevertheless, the scale of the short-term swing was unprecedented.

The result was, for the first time in many years, a general election where the outcome seemed in doubt almost to the last moment. True, the Conservatives were ahead in terms of votes throughout the campaign. But would their lead be big enough to deliver a majority?

Interpreting the position was complicated by the bias in the operation of the electoral system, which has dictated in recent years that for a given share of the votes the Conservatives win substantially fewer seats than Labour does. Even with the beneficial effect of the most recent boundary changes, the Conservatives needed to achieve a 7% swing in their target seats to win an overall majority. Projected nationally, this was equivalent to an 11-percentage-point lead over Labour (whereas in 2005 Labour had had a comfortable overall majority with only a 3-point lead).

But the Conservatives did not *need* to do that well nationally: they only needed to do that well in their target seats. Millions of Lord Ashcroft's money had reportedly been spent, concentrated where it should do most good, before the election spending restrictions came into effect at the start of 2010. This offered the Tories the hope that even if they fell short of an

11-point lead in the national vote they might do better in the marginals and grasp a narrow majority anyway. The question of whether the national vote shares, and the assumption of uniform swing, were underplaying Conservative prospects was, therefore, one of the most important and unpredictable questions of the election. But the polls in the marginal constituencies said the Tories were not doing significantly better there than anywhere else.

The final polls left the outcome on a knife-edge. If they were right, it would be a hung Parliament with the Conservatives the largest party and highly likely to lead the new government, but hamstrung by the need to form a coalition or negotiate as a minority government. Yet a slightly stronger performance would give the Conservatives the overall majority they yearned for. A slightly weaker performance would leave Labour and the Tories equal and give the Liberal Democrats a freer choice of who they should put in power. A little worse still, and Labour would be safe in government even if they had to depose Gordon Brown as a condition of retaining power.

The final polls *were* right (and the exit poll spectacularly so).

Who won and who lost

In the final voting, the Conservatives took 37% of the vote in Great Britain (nowhere near the hoped for 40%-plus) and Labour 30% (their bare 'core vote' and only a point-and-a-half better than the disastrous 1983 defeat), almost exactly where they had when the election was called. Meanwhile the Liberal Democrats managed only 24%. This came as a shock to the media and a surprise to everyone, so much so that there was almost universal disbelief of the exit poll prediction showing the Liberal Democrats losing rather than gaining seats; but the exit poll rather than the pundits turned out to be correct. Far from challenging for second or even first place, as seemed possible at the height of 'Cleggmania', the LibDems found their share of the popular vote was only a little higher than it had been in 2005, and they did indeed end up with five fewer MPs.

Table 1: British general election result 2010, compared with 2005

	SEATS (n)			SHARE OF VOTE (% - GB only)			VOTES (millions - GB only)		
	2005	2010	Chg	2005	2010	Chg	2005	2010	Chg
Conservative	198	306	+108	33.2	36.9	+3.7	8.78	10.68	+1.90
Labour	355	258	−97	36.1	29.7	−6.4	9.55	8.60	−0.95
Liberal Democrat	62	57	−5	22.6	23.6	+1.0	5.99	6.83	+0.84
Scottish National Party	6	6	0	1.6	1.7	+0.1	0.41	0.49	+0.08
Plaid Cymru	3	3	0	0.7	0.6	−0.1	0.17	0.17	0.00
UK Independence Party	0	0	0	2.3	3.2	+0.9	0.60	0.92	+0.32
British National Party	0	0	0	0.7	1.9	+1.2	0.19	0.56	+0.37
Green	0	1	+1	1.1	1.0	−0.1	0.28	0.28	0.00
The Speaker	1	1	0	0.1	0.1	0.0	0.02	0.02	0.00
Other (GB)	3	0	−3	1.6	1.4	−0.2	0.43	0.42	−0.01
Other (NI)	18	18	0						
TOTAL	646	650	+4	100	100	0	26.44	28.98	+2.54

Source: Calculated from election results as published by the House of Commons Library in Research Paper 10/36 (8 July 2010)

The polls in the last weeks before the election had already shown that LibDem support had begun to drain away from their peak immediately after the first debate. Perhaps everybody should have doubted from the start how much of that surge in support would survive all the way to the polling station three weeks later. There were plenty of signs in an unusually volatile election that LibDem support might be even softer than that for the other parties, and was disproportionately concentrated among those who had not voted before or who had not felt sure before the first debate whether they intended to vote or not. Post-election polling discovered that more people than ever reported deciding whether or not to vote, and for whom to vote, in the final 24 hours of the election campaign, and over a quarter of voters said they decided in the final week.

However, while the Liberal Democrats may have lost the battle, they won the war. As the third party, their chance of power depends not only on their own strength but on how closely balanced the fight between the two bigger parties is: only if neither has a majority can the Liberal Democrats hold the balance of power. At most general elections, it is only the performance of the two biggest parties that is of real significance to the outcome: one or the other will win a working majority of the available seats, enabling it to form a government and to stay in office until it chooses to call the next election. In 2010, however, the contest between the Conservatives and Labour ended indecisively, with the result that almost every seat won and lost could, in theory, be weighed in the balance towards forming a post-election government. The Conservatives increased their strength by 1.9 million votes and a 3.7% share in Great Britain, and consequently won an overall increase of 108 seats[8], bringing them to 306;. Labour, conversely, saw their vote fall by almost a million, reducing them to 29.7% of the vote outside Northern Ireland and made a net loss of 97 seats. But dramatic though this swing in fortunes was, it left the Conservatives 20 short of an overall majority and Labour a further 48 seats behind. This meant that the Liberal Democrats, with a slightly reduced 57 seats, could easily put the Conservatives in power on their own, but to form a coalition with Labour or to prop up a Labour minority government would need the help of several other parties. Meanwhile no two other parties combined would be big enough to give the Conservatives a majority if the Liberal Democrats would not co-operate.

Of the smaller parties in Great Britain, the Scottish National Party and Plaid Cymru both held their own, the SNP share of the vote marginally up and Plaid Cymru's marginally down, but winning an unchanged 6 and 3 seats respectively. The Green Party's national vote was also steady, but better concentrated in their target constituencies, and the party won its first-ever Westminster seat at Brighton Pavilion; this helped offset the recapture by the major parties of the three seats that had been won by minor party or independent MPs in 2005.[9] Both UKIP and the BNP also significantly increased their national vote without winning any seats, so that the total 'other' share of the vote, that withheld from all three of the main parties, was up from 8% to 10%. But it was well short of the unprecedented level that had some had expected a few months before the election, when the minor parties were riding high in the opinion polls as they benefited from discontent over the expenses scandal, from right-wing Tories flirting with UKIP, and disillusioned Labour supporters flirting with the Greens, to say nothing of those attracted from all parties towards the BNP over immigration policy.

---

[8] Because of the boundary changes since the last election, this was not the same as the number of seats they 'gained': on the basis of the 'notional results' of the 2005 election calculated by Professors Rallings and Thrasher, the Conservatives started with 12 seats more than they had held in the just-dissolved Parliament, and made a further 96 net gains.
[9] Wyre Forest by Richard Taylor of Kidderminster Hospital and Health Concern, Bethnal Green & Bow by George Galloway for Respect and Blaenau Gwent by Peter Law as (to all intents and purposes) Independent Labour and (held in the same interest by Dai Davies at a by-election after Law's death).

14

In Northern Ireland, as usual, the election was a separate one, with only the Conservatives of the bigger mainland parties running candidates, having effected a merger with the Ulster Unionists, and getting nowhere. (The united party lost the only seat it held, convincingly defeated by its former MP, Sylvia Hermon, running as an independent after rejecting the party merger.) Sinn Fein held their five seats and the SDLP their three, while the Democratic Unionists (DUP) won eight but lost East Belfast to the Alliance, another party recording its first victory at Westminster after decades of trying, in one of the election's most unexpected results.

For once the Northern Irish results might have been significant to the national picture, since the continued refusal of Sinn Fein's MPs to take their seats reduces the effective threshold for a majority, while the support of the SDLP and Alliance would certainly have been needed in any 'rainbow' coalition to sustain Labour in government. Similarly, had the Tories done rather better in England than they did, they might have been able to consider a pact with the DUP as an alternative to making concessions to the Liberal Democrats.

But it was not to be: the Conservatives and Liberal Democrats managed to find sufficient common ground to justify joining in the most obviously manageable coalition, and Northern Ireland's results receded once more into the background. Because the political debate in Northern Ireland is so far removed from that in Great Britain, the Province is rarely included in political opinion polls, and that is true of virtually all the polls discussed in this book. From this point onwards, therefore, our discussion concerns only England, Scotland and Wales, and omits Northern Ireland.

Beyond the party make-up of the House of Commons, the 2010 election was also responsible for some other changes in the characteristics of its membership. Many more members than is usual after an election – 227 of the 650, more than a third – were new members with no previous Parliamentary experience. More than ever before were women (143, 22% of the total), and there were 27 members of minority ethnic groups (16 Labour and 11 Conservative), including the first three Muslim women MPs.[10] Furthermore, the outcome possibly has even more profound

---

[10] These figures are all as published by the House of Commons Library in Research Paper 10/36 (8 July 2010).

implications for the future of the Commons, with the coalition agreement committing the government to reducing the total number of MPs (to 600, in the Act passed in February 2011) and to a referendum that could replace the centuries old first-past-the-post electoral system with the Alternative Vote. (As we write, the outcome of the referendum is unknown.) The House of Lords, too, may find itself elected in the not-too-distant future. But we've been promised that before, by governments with a much more obvious ideological reason to want it to happen.

Figure 2: Turnout in general elections in Great Britain, 1945-2010

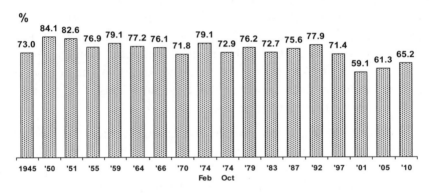

Source: 2010 from election results as published by the House of Commons Library in Research Paper 10/36 (8 July 2010); for previous elections calculated from figures at www.politicsresources.net
Note: Figures given are for turnout in Great Britain only, excluding Northern Ireland

The turnout can be damned with faint praise by lauding it as the highest so far this century. Despite the uncertainty of the outcome and the respectable viewing figures achieved by the leaders' debates, only 65% of those on the register voted, the third lowest figure since the War. True, this is a small improvement on the derisory 59% and 61% of the last two general elections, but still a full six percentage points lower – 1.5 million votes fewer – than at Tony Blair's first victory in 1997, even though the result of that election was rightly seen as a foregone conclusion and resulted in a majority of 179 for Labour. By comparison with the 76% average turnout at the 15 general elections between 1945 and 1997, this is a poor performance indeed. (See Figure 2). The last time a British election seemed as close as this one, in 1992, as many as 78% of the registered electorate went to the polls – and that was without the facility for postal votes on demand that now exists. In fact, the single highest constituency turnout in 2010[11] was lower than the *national* turnout had been in 1992.

The 2010 election was closer – in seats if not in votes – than any for years. That should have been no surprise. The election began with the final pre-election polls showing a 5.5% Tory swing nationally, suggesting that a hung parliament was a distinct possibility. There were 91 polls during the election, triple the number five years earlier. The average of all 91, with fieldwork from 7 April to 6 May, was a 4.9% swing. The final result showed a 5% swing to the Tories and, as the polls in marginals had indicated, they did not perform substantially better there than nationally: needing 326 seats for a minimal overall majority, they won only 306 – a sandwich short of a picnic.

Why Labour lost and the Tories didn't win

The 2010 election, then, was in many ways a dramatic one, with a big shift in votes and a government thrown out of power, despite what was in many ways an indecisive result. But why did it happen? What was it in the parties' records, their personnel or their promises, that produced this change? In short, what did the voters themselves think?

It is not difficult, of course, to suggest reasons why Labour lost. A once-popular government had far outstayed its welcome; it had replaced the leader who had won the previous three elections with another who, whatever his other qualities, completely lacked the appealing charisma which plays such an important part in most modern politics; and, although it was arguable whether this could be considered in any way the government's fault, it had been in office during the biggest economic collapse in decades.

The real question is why Labour didn't lose much more convincingly than they did, given the hole they found themselves in. Judging by the popularity of the government and Prime Minister, defeat at the next election looked a virtual certainty even before Tony Blair handed over the reins to Gordon Brown. Under Brown, things went from bad to worse,

---

[11] 77.3% in East Renfrewshire – the national turnout (for Great Britain) in 1992 was 77.7%.

the gap in the polls widening to improbable proportions and this verdict being confirmed regularly by catastrophic defeats in by-elections, local elections and European elections. Labour had hoped that Brown could turn his apparent failings into a virtue, portraying himself as highly competent rather than showy ('Not flash, just Gordon', to quote the Labour Party's astonishing advertising theme used in 2007, which seemed to be a critique of his predecessor and a lack of confidence in himself). But this hope collapsed under the weight of evidence to the contrary as the government stumbled from one disaster to another and was flayed for it in the press.

Yet what appeared a foregone conclusion a year before the election was suddenly less clear-cut by the dawn of 2010. In 2009 the Tory average lead was 14%; in January of 2010, it was 10%, then 7% in February, then 6% in March. Partly, this reflected a steady fading by David Cameron, though with no obvious single reason to explain it. Perhaps it was simply that almost any new leader can only count on the indulgence of the public and the benefit of the doubt for so long, and sooner or later they begin to slip from their peak of popularity; it happened to Tony Blair as well, even before he was first elected Prime Minister, but he had made his hay while the sun was shining and could afford some slippage in his lead without endangering his victory. Cameron's peak of popularity was lower, the cards were more stacked against him because of the bias in the electoral system, and so perhaps the landslide victory that seemed possible in 2009 was always a pipe dream unless the election came immediately. The way the political agenda over most of the final year was dominated by the expenses scandal probably contributed to Cameron's problems. It may also have reminded some wavering voters about residual doubts they had about the Conservatives. Certainly, it made it difficult for Cameron to secure his position by seizing the initiative with a more positive message, and the controversy about the apparently airbrushed posters of Cameron that were unveiled across a range of marginal seats at the turn of the year did little to reassure those floating voters that the would-be Prime Minister was more concerned with substance than style.

But the story was not just a decline in David Cameron's star. At the same time, something turned around Labour's fortunes. Gordon Brown's satisfaction ratings were climbing slowly but steadily from mid-2009, perhaps a sign that the Prime Minister was gaining some credit for the survival of the British economy, parlous as its state still was, and his final pre-election satisfaction rating was actually better than Blair's final pre-election rating in 2005 (though Brown didn't have the good luck of running against a leader whose rating was even worse, as Tony Blair had done.) By the time the election was called, the Tories were still ahead but the polls were now firmly in hung Parliament territory, where they stayed throughout the campaign.

Then came the election campaign proper. The first ten days were unremarkable, but then the Liberal Democrats suddenly entered the picture with the first of the three leader debates. It always looked possible that the Liberal Democrats might be more than a side-show, since a hung Parliament would almost certainly offer them the balance of power in some way. This likelihood would surely turn the spotlight on them before polling day however low key their campaign. Nor was there any reason to suppose their campaign *would* be low key – with the state of the economy overwhelmingly the most important issue facing the public, the LibDems could almost claim to enter the contest on equal terms, such had been the effectiveness and popularity of their 'shadow Chancellor' Vince Cable. But their role turned out to be much more central than that, with Nick Clegg seizing the opportunity offered to him by his platform in the leaders' debates and taking the whole campaign by the scruff of the neck.

The size of the swings in the polls during the campaign suggest that, far from being already decided, with a month to go the election was still to be won and lost – either David Cameron or Gordon Brown might, had things gone otherwise, have still been able to produce a very different outcome. Another 2% of the vote for the Tories would probably have given them an overall majority; another 2% for Labour would not have saved Gordon Brown, but it would probably have allowed the Liberal Democrats to choose between a coalition with the Conservatives and with Labour.

Yet in the end Labour neither gained nor lost ground during the election campaign – they started on 30% and they got 30%. The Tories started with enough votes to oust Labour but too few for an overall majority, and ended up that way. The Liberal Democrats gained over the campaign, but only from the minor parties. The debates certainly stirred things up a lot, but most of the effect had evaporated by polling day. What may have been important was that Clegg made Cameron look poor by comparison, so that instead of being able to annihilate Brown, the Tory leader ended up as an equal loser. Could Labour have realistically made gains during the campaign with a more effective leader? Possibly, although criticism of Brown's performance in the TV debates ignores the underlying problem that he was trying to make bricks without straw – the public was fundamentally dissatisfied with the government's record and, as both David Cameron and Nick Clegg pointed out in discussing reform of the House of Lords, a government could hardly expect credit for newly embracing a popular policy when they had already failed to implement it in thirteen years in government.

Since the election, things have moved on. Labour's progress in the first ten months or so since the election has been encouraging, to some degree. The party regained a lead over the Conservatives in the regular voting intention polls and the broad appeal of the party is in better shape than the last time it lost in 1992 or when compared to the Conservatives in 1997. Yet, by the early months of 2011, Labour's new leader, Ed Miliband, had not made a strong impression with the public. At this stage, it is too early to write him off as a potential Prime Minister, but, in our view, his satisfaction scores and public image will need to improve if he is seen to be a credible alternative to David Cameron.

The Conservatives also had a relatively good 2010 after the election – seemingly convincing enough of the public that reducing the nation's debt was an urgent priority and that this would involve spending cuts. At the end of 2010, the Tories' poll numbers were actually higher than their vote at the general election. However, 2011 and the second year of the coalition government looks set to be much tougher. Public opinion turned negative towards the government as a whole in 2010 and with the Prime Minister specifically in 2011; explained perhaps by the growing economic worries. As we write this chapter we also see fresh evidence that shows the majority of the public still thinks that the necessary public spending cuts can mainly be achieved through efficiency savings rather than on the frontline. Many may be in for a shock in 2011 and beyond.

It is undoubtedly the LibDems that have, to date, paid the biggest price since the election. Their support has halved since the election, falling even further among their core young vote. Nick Clegg's personal ratings have plummeted also from the high point of the election campaign (at one point reaching levels not seen since the heyday of Tony Blair's first term as

Prime Minister) to being ranked the most unpopular of the three main party leaders.

But before we consider further where we are going next, we must begin by understanding how we got here.

Understanding election results

In one sense, fighting elections is simple. Whoever is most popular gets most votes, so if you want more votes, do something to make yourself more popular.

But how does a candidate become or remain popular? In recent years, there has been much academic analysis of Tony Blair's success in reaching office and his first few years in power from the perspective of 'political marketing'. The core of much of this discussion has been the question of whether 'New Labour' was a 'market-oriented party', one whose offering to the electorate is driven by what the voters want rather than by what the party wants to persuade the voters to accept. Partly because these arguments have been misunderstood and partly because any descriptive model set up to allow the study of a real situation is inevitably a simplification, this has been taken by some as arguing that such a party entirely abandons ideological considerations in favour of purely pragmatic short-term grubbing for votes, and further that this is a formula for electoral success. In other words, as BBC *Newsnight* presenter Jeremy Paxman put it on one occasion, a party would 'commission polling evidence and focus groups to find out what people wanted. And then to offer it to them.' [12]

Real life is not that easy, of course, and thank goodness for that. Raw populism is unlikely to work in British elections, and voters do not just vote en masse for whichever party offers the most appealing list of promises. In the first place, neither election campaigns nor the varying fortunes of government and opposition between them have the least effect on most people: the majority of voters still vote for the same party at election after election. In the past we have estimated that this almost

---

[12] James MacTaggart Memorial Lecture, 2007, http://image.guardian.co.uk/sys-files/Media/documents/2007/08/24/MacTaggartLecture.pdf.

completely solid 'core vote' for the parties may amount to 80% of the total vote (30% for the Conservatives, 30% for Labour and 20% for various other parties), with only the most catastrophic circumstances likely to weaken any of the parties below this level, and therefore leaving just one voter in five who is a 'floating voter'. Perhaps these days, with party loyalty weakened by various factors, the core votes are slightly lower and the floating vote slightly larger. Certainly, with turnouts much lower than they used to be, there is more scope for swing simply from one party's voters getting to the polls while another's stays at home. But the fundamental picture is still true – only a minority of votes are up for grabs even in the most dramatic elections.

But considering those votes that can be swung, how can the parties attract them? Voters do not judge the alternatives simply on the basis of the most attractive list of policy promises. They naturally take into account whether they trust the party to deliver on those promises, which requires the promises both to seem realistic and to have been made by a party in whose integrity they have faith. Further, they need to trust the people involved, most importantly the party's leader (as candidate for Prime Minister), and to feel confident in his competence. Even a party with a perfect list of policy promises cannot cover all eventualities in advance, and the floating voters will naturally prefer a government they believe will cope best with the unexpected. A leader, therefore, and his team, must give the impression that they would be good in a crisis, and also espouse political principles that the voters support – some will prefer that a government should deal with the questions not covered in its manifesto from a socialist perspective, others from a conservative or liberal one.

Consequently the image of a leader and of his party are important factors in their own right. Understand, though, that by 'image' we are not talking about their hair styles and the cut of their suits, but such meaningful and important characteristics as the public's view of their competence, belief in their understanding of the problems facing the country and the world, and confidence that they listen to the views of ordinary people.

But, further, these three factors – party image, leader image and policies on important issues – interact with each other. On an issue where voters have no clear opinions of their own, they may prefer to take a lead from the politicians they trust. On complex matters such as economics, to take one example, many voters may well feel unqualified to make their own decisions. Conversely, they may come to decide which politicians they trust from their record in government or opposition, the policies they pursue and their success in pursuing them. And their first impressions of either a policy or a politician may be moulded by preconceptions about the party from which it or he/she arises.

All three of these factors act separately and differently on each floating voter, and on each hitherto core voter who might become detached from his or her party loyalty. This may be affected by demographic factors, of course – younger voters, for example, may want something different from the election to what is wanted by their older counterparts. But numerous other factors, not all measurable and including simple psychological disposition, will also play their part: some people are just more pre-disposed to be moved by what they think of the people involved while for others hard policy issues or ideology are more decisive. Further, depending on the circumstances of an election, the relative importance of these factors may vary considerably.

Nor is it enough in the case of a British election to understand how the votes will be won. We must also understand the operation of the electoral system, how votes are translated into seats in Parliament, because in truth some votes are more valuable than others. The aim of the Conservative and Labour parties in an election is not to maximise their votes but to maximise the number of seats they win, with the hope of securing a majority in the House of Commons. Meanwhile, the rational aim of the Liberal Democrats, albeit a generally unstated one, should be not to maximise either their own seats or their votes as such, but to achieve an equilibrium between their two bigger rivals so that neither has a majority and the Liberal Democrats hold the balance of power.

In other words, understanding an election result and understanding how to win an election is a complex business. Taking all in all, we have isolated five answers to the question of why the 2010 election turned out the way it did, and what happens next.

1. **The government's performance in its first four years after re-election in 2005 was dreadful,** ensuring that Labour had almost certainly lost the election a year in advance of election day. Victory was already virtually hopeless for Labour by mid-2009, quite possibly by mid-2007, given everything we know from past British politics. It is not clear whether

a better leader than Gordon Brown could have helped, but it wasn't really his fault in the first place. Almost all governments steadily lose support, whether over a short period or a long period, until they slide from victory to defeat. No British government since the 1950s has succeeded in increasing its share of the vote after a full term in office. Maybe the steady decay of government popularity is becoming an inevitable process in British politics; certainly, there is evidence that this Labour government's popularity was on the wane almost from the moment when it took office in 1997, so perhaps the only question was when it would finally slip into the red, not whether it could recover the lost ground. Probably nothing could have stopped them losing their majority; Labour could only hope that the electorate might view the opposition as unelectable, winning then by default.

2. **David Cameron was unable to 'seal the deal' with the voters**, as the leader of a still unpopular party. A once-impressive Tory lead driven by Labour's unpopular leader, unpopular policies, and the feeling that it was 'time for a change' slipped until it was no longer big enough to secure a parliamentary majority. The operation of the electoral system made a crucial contribution to this – the Conservatives needed a much bigger lead in votes than did Labour to ensure an overall majority. (In fact Cameron's margin of victory in votes was more than double Tony Blair's margin in 2005, which delivered Labour a third term.) Nevertheless, this was understood in advance, and the task was possible: had the election been held in 2009, Cameron might well have secured a landslide. But his lead slipped, and he failed to over-perform in the marginal seats as many Tories had confidently expected.

3. **Once the campaign began** it quickly became evident that it could be the most volatile election in the two-thirds of a century that polls have tracked their course, which meant that perhaps the 'impossible' was possible after all and **nothing was yet a foregone conclusion**. But even the record numbers of potential voters who warned us that they had not yet made up their minds hardly prepared us for the seismic shifts in voting intention that followed the first televised leaders' debate. Yet despite all the excitement, the campaign made *little net difference* in the end – Labour and the Conservatives ended up with the same support as they had had a month before, and although the Liberal Democrats recovered some lost ground from minor parties it was too thinly spread to have a pay-off in

seats. Indeed, because the final polls over-estimated Liberal Democrat strength, some commentators supposed that the whole reaction was a mirage and that the LibDem 'surge' never really happened. Nonsense. We don't believe that for a minute. The LibDem surge was real. However, it was a surge concentrated disproportionately among those people who were never likely to turn out in the end anyway – principally the young, only 44% of whom bothered to vote on the day. So the apparent volatility of the electorate may never have been a real opportunity for the parties to achieve a radical change in their fortunes.

4. **The election turned out to be much more about the leaders than the parties' policies**. In trying to explain most British election results, most analysts start with the main policy issues and how they divided the parties or the public's perceptions of them. Our research in the past has found that when voters balanced the various factors as they made up their minds, they felt they gave a weight of around 45% to the parties' policy positions, while leader image contributed about 33% and party image 22%. But 2010 was different.

While the leadership debates contributed to this, beginning with the cool performance of Nick Clegg in the first of the three debates in mid-April, the electorate asserted the importance of what they thought of the leaders long before the debates took place. As early as February, the public was telling us that this time they were giving equal weight to leaders and policies. In fact, it may be that it was the fact that the leaders were already seen as the decisive factor that threw such a spotlight on the debates.

Is this evidence of increasing prominence of the images of the leaders, as some think, of a steadily increasing 'presidentialisation' of British elections? If so, Gordon Brown's choice as Labour leader was a major factor in Labour's defeat, for he was always likely to be at a grave disadvantage in an election fought on those terms, however convincingly he could portray himself as a competent technocrat with the best policies. But arguably, it was the circumstances of the election, rather than any long-term evolution in the nature of British politics, that determined that this would be a contest in which leadership was the decisive factor.

The most important policy issue, by far, was the economy, on which both major parties had been unable to establish any advantage, not least because the electorate seemed mostly in denial about the depth of the economic crisis and not prepared to support any of the offered solutions, from the left or from the right. Furthermore, in so many other policy fields the stances of the parties had so converged that it was difficult to distinguish one from another. This may have been an election where there was too little differentiation between the parties' relative competence to deal with the issues of concern for a choice between them to be made. As we have observed before, there are four hurdles an issue must jump with a swing voter before it can 'bite' sufficiently to convince him or her to move from one party to another: first, the issue must be salient to the voter; second, the prospective switcher must be able to differentiate between the parties on the issue; third, they must believe that the party if in power could implement their policy, and fourth, that it *would* do so. Not enough issues jumped these hurdles for enough voters in 2010 to make it an 'issues election'.

These four points, we believe, are the key to understanding the result of the 2010 election. But equally important in understanding the implications of the result and in looking towards the future is a fifth:

5. **The nature of electoral support in Britain has changed, probably permanently**. This is not a new phenomenon, only the culmination of years of steady change, but it must affect how we interpret the 2010 election and how we look to the future. British voters are not only less committed to the political parties than they used to be, but they are less tribal – or, at least, their tribalism manifests itself in different ways – and less polarised. Where once the electoral battle centred largely on demographic characteristics, social class, council house tenancy, and age, the class distinctions are now much less clearly drawn. When Labour last lost, in 1992, three-quarters of their votes were drawn from the 'working class'; in 2010, they won more 'middle class' votes than 'working class ones'. Meanwhile, age distinctions between the parties have been largely eroded and the 'gender gap' has actually flipped its direction. On the other hand, regional divisions have hardened, to the extent that a Conservative government has been elected with just one seat in Scotland and none in the major cities of the North, inconceivable even thirty years ago.

These changes may cement for the future a system where elections are more dependent on personalities rather than politics, since the less that parties' vote bases are demographically distinct from each other the less likely that they will have distinct policy needs to form the basis of an appeal to their interests. Is this inevitable, or could one of the parties find a policy offering or ideological stance that would once more mark out for them a distinctive constituency, and one big enough to win elections from? This was the assumption of the rival camps within the Labour Party, conducting their post-mortems as they prepared to elect a new leader. We are agnostic as to whether Labour can find a way along these lines to redefine itself and secure future election victories; but we are unconvinced that there was any ideological realignment that could have saved Labour in 2010, or made any real impression on an election where almost everyone agreed on the single most important issue and no party could offer them a solution that satisfied them.

Let us consider these five points in turn.

1. How Labour lost it

Tony Blair digs a hole

It is an old adage that 'oppositions don't win elections, governments lose them'. Having started a Parliament with sufficient support to put them or keep them in power, if a government disappoints enough of its erstwhile voters by its record in office they will ensure it is booted out at the next opportunity; do well enough to hang onto that support, and there will be nothing the opposition can do to dislodge it.

This proposition is, of course, a great simplification, but there is truth in it. Certainly, one cannot understand the 2010 election only by reference to what happened from 6 April 2010 onwards. The unavoidable foundation on which the rest of the story of the election must be constructed was that Labour went into the election trailing in support and expected to lose, and that the reason for that was mostly the way in which the voters viewed their record in office since 2005, and perhaps indeed since 1997. Once again, the 'long election', not just the intensive month-long formal campaign, helped determined the outcome.

There is a strong argument that Labour was already doomed well before the Parliament had run its term. By 2008, the polls were consistently showing the lowest Labour share of voting support in the 70-year history of polling – 26% on average for four successive months. It got worse. As the MPs' expenses scandal engulfed the media in May 2009, Labour support plummeted still further. In the eleven polls published between the first revelations in the *Daily Telegraph* and the ignominious cabinet reshuffle following local election humiliation three weeks later, Labour averaged a 22% share and in the worst single poll (Ipsos MORI's, which take account of falling certainty of voting among a party's supporters as well as active switching) bottomed out on an all-time low of 18%. The lowest poll rating ever previously recorded by a government that eventually won re-election was 23%.[13]

---

[13] This was the Conservative rating in a single Gallup poll in December 1981

The nadir of the government's popularity came with Gordon Brown in Downing Street. But all was hardly rosy before Tony Blair stepped down – indeed, many in the Labour Party had hoped his departure would be similar to that of Margaret Thatcher, the ousting of a leader heading for certain defeat and a last-gasp chance to turn the corner under new management and win a fourth term. It is plainly with Tony Blair's time in Downing Street that our analysis must begin.

In 2005, Tony Blair was re-elected for a third term as Prime Minister, although he had already made it clear that he intended to serve only for part of the Parliament, and that he expected Gordon Brown to succeed him in Number Ten. In May 2007, he announced that he would step down at the end of the following month, and Brown was elected unopposed to succeed him.

Figure 3: Voting intentions, 2005-7 (poll of polls)

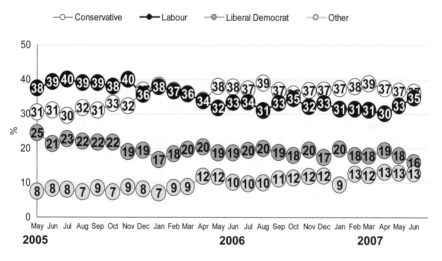

Source: Ipsos MORI analysis of data reported by pollingreport.co.uk.
Note: Figures given are the averages of polls conducted each month by the six established polling companies

We can track the progression of the government's popularity and credibility by considering the monthly polls between the 2005 election and Blair's retirement. Here we are helped by the fact that the polls of all the major companies were in line with each other for almost the whole of the

2005-10 Parliament[14], so we can rely on the 'poll of polls' in tracking the parties' popularity, giving us a much greater frequency of measurement than any single poll series could do and a much reduced 'margin of error' (allowing a finer understanding of the short-term movement of opinion and protection from being misled by occasional rogue polls). Figure 3 shows the monthly averages of the published voting intention polls over the two year period, giving a very clear picture of the public's reaction to political and other events.

Labour stayed in the lead throughout 2005, boosted perhaps (as in 2001) by satisfaction with the government's handling of a terrorist threat, in this case the 7 July 2005 bombings on the London transport system. By the end of 2005, however, when David Cameron took over the Conservative leadership, the parties were neck-and-neck, and the Tories edged into a lead from May 2006 which they then retained for the rest of the Blair premiership.

The final two years of the Blair premiership were not comfortable ones for the Labour party, even if things were to be worse under his successor. Increasing internal dissent over Iraq and the extension of police anti-terrorism powers led to the government's first Commons defeat in November 2005, when 49 Labour MPs voted against the proposal to increase the period that terrorist suspects could legally be held without charge to 90 days. The change was one that the police had asked for[15], and Blair described the Commons vote as 'deeply irresponsible'; ministers attempted at first to salvage their proposals, but the bill eventually became law (as the Terrorism Act 2006) with provisions for only 28 days' detention (which was, nevertheless, double the previous limit). Civil libertarians had also confronted the police over the death of Jean Charles de Menezes, mistaken for a terrorist suspect and shot dead by anti-terrorist

---

[14] See Appendix 1. Throughout, where we use the 'poll of polls' to graph changes in public opinion, we restrict inclusion in the averages to the 'established pollsters' (ComRes, Harris Interactive, ICM, Ipsos MORI, Populus and YouGov), the six companies who polled during both the 2005 and 2010 elections. This allows us to take a single consistent measurement of the trend throughout 2005-10 without the risk of its being distorted by including pollsters with different methodologies who published polls in the last few months before the election.
[15] In a public letter to the Prime Minister from Andy Hayman, Assistant Commissioner of the Metropolitan Police.

Table 2: Key events, 2005-6

Date	Event
2005	
5 May	Labour government re-elected with majority of 66
29 May	France votes against EU constitution in referendum
1 June	Netherlands votes against EU constitution in referendum
1 July	UK's six-month Presidency of the EU begins
6 July	G8 summit opens at Gleneagles
6 July	Announcement that London will host the 2012 Olympic Games
7 July	Terrorist attacks on London Transport kill 56 people during the morning rush hour
22 July	Metropolitan Police shoot Brazilian Jean Charles de Menezes, mistaking him for a terrorist suspect
2 November	David Blunkett resigns
9 November	Government defeated in Commons over 90-day detention for terrorist suspects: 49 Labour MPs vote against
5 December	First Civil Partnership ceremony
6 December	David Cameron elected Conservative Party leader
2006	
7 January	Charles Kennedy resigns as Liberal Democrat leader
9 February	Dunfermline & West Fife by-election – LibDem gain from Labour, 16.4% swing
14 February	Commons vote to ban smoking in pubs and other public places in England
2 March	Sir Menzies Campbell elected Liberal Democrat leader
26 March	Ban on smoking in pubs and public buildings comes into effect in Scotland
24 April	Patricia Hewitt heckled at UNISON conference
25 April	Home Office admits more than 1,000 foreign criminals were released between 1999 and March 2006 without being considered for deportation
26 April	Patricia Hewitt heckled at Royal College of Nursing conference
26 April	John Prescott admits an affair with his diary secretary
4 May	Local government elections: major Labour losses
5 May	Cabinet reshuffle: Charles Clarke sacked, Jack Straw sidelined
29 June	Blaenau Gwent by-election – Labour fails to recapture a once-safe seat from Independents
12 July	Lord Levy arrested over 'cash for honours'
30 July	Blair reported to have agreed £4m publishing deal for his diaries with Murdoch-owned HarperCollins
10 August	24 arrests over alleged plot to blow up planes with liquid explosives
5 September	Publication of a letter signed by 17 Labour MPs calling on Blair to resign
7 September	Blair announces that the 2006 Labour Party conference would be his last as leader
23 November	Alexander Litvinenko poisoned in London with radioactive polonium
30 December	Execution of Saddam Hussein

officers on an underground train in July 2005. In fact, the indications are that public opinion was probably on the side of the government and the police rather than the rebels at this period (only 15% of Londoners said in September they were dissatisfied with the way the police were handling the response to the terrorist attacks)[16], but the plain disunity among Labour was damaging to the government's longer-term image.

Table 3: Key events in 2007 up to the retirement of Tony Blair

Date	Event
19 January	Downing Street official Ruth Turner arrested over 'cash for honours'
26 January	Blair re-interviewed by Police over 'cash for honours' (News of this withheld until 1 February)
February	Cull of 160,000 turkeys after bird flu is discovered in Suffolk
21 March	Budget: Brown announces abolition of 10% starting rate of income tax
23 March	Iran seizes 15 Royal Navy personnel in the Persian Gulf
4 April	Naval hostages released
2 May	Blair confirms he will stand down within weeks
3 May	Scottish Parliament, Welsh Assembly and local government elections: substantial Labour losses, but Blair calls them 'a good springboard' to win the next election
10 May	Blair announces he will step down on 27 June; John Prescott announces he will retire as deputy leader on the same date
11 May	Gordon Brown confirms he will stand as leader
14 May	John McDonnell announces he will stand against Brown
16 May	Brown reaches 308 nominations, leaving too few for McDonnell to qualify as a candidate. Brown therefore sure to be elected unopposed

An even more inflammatory issue, and one only exacerbated by the effect of the terrorist situation on race relations, was immigration and asylum. It is essential to understand, of course, that the vast majority of the public take a hard anti-immigration line, and that the policies of the major parties have all moved to the right without successfully winning the public's confidence on the issue. In an April 2005 poll, we offered the public five options, and more than two-thirds said either that immigration should be stopped altogether (11%) or that laws on immigration should be 'much tougher' (58%); one in five (19%) thought laws on immigration should remain as they are, and only one in ten that they should be relaxed (8%) or abolished altogether (2%). Although Labour in particular might feel ideologically uncomfortable in taking an anti-immigration line, they cannot ignore what is in effect a cross-party consensus. Not only among the

---

[16] MORI poll for the GLA, 22-26 September 2005. Also, of the two-thirds of Londoners who said they had seen more police patrols in London since the July bombings, 49% said this made them feel safer and only 4% that they felt less safe, although in a separate MORI poll for BBC London at almost the same time, only 45% of Londoners felt that 'Allowing the police to have a policy of 'shoot to kill' a suspected terrorist' was acceptable while 51% felt it was unacceptable.

floating voters, but even among their own core vote, there is a strong majority in favour of further restrictions on immigration. (Nor should this strand of public opinion be thought to be driven wholly or mainly by racism – in fact even polls of members of ethnic minorities generally find majority support for the proposition that 'There are too many immigrants in Britain'. The issue has been further complicated in recent years by significant white immigration from Eastern Europe, notably Poland, which has stirred up just as much opposition and controversy.)

No recent government has really been in a position to lose the public's trust on the issue, since they have never commanded it in the first place, but Labour has certainly been in a weaker position than the Conservatives, and the events which ended with the sacking of Charles Clarke as Home Secretary in May 2006 – although, strictly speaking, not a matter of either immigration or asylum – represented another damaging episode for the government. It emerged, a few weeks before the local elections, that over a period of some time more than a thousand foreign prisoners had been released from jail in Britain without being considered for deportation as should normally occur; these included a number convicted of violent or sexual offences, and many could now not be traced even if it was thought desirable to deport them. Further, it seemed that the issue had first been raised with the government by the National Audit Office in 2005, but that the uncontrolled release of foreign prisoners had continued.

The episode of the foreign prisoners was by no means the only damaging incident as Labour faced its first national electoral test since the 2005 general election. At almost exactly the same time, Health Secretary Patricia Hewitt was being heckled by delegates at the UNISON conference, another sign of discontent among Labour's most natural support base, while Deputy Prime Minister John Prescott was caught up in a sex scandal. In fact all three stories broke over the same three-day period. The local elections on 4 May, covering almost 4,500 seats on English district and unitary councils, including the London and metropolitan boroughs, as well as four Mayoral elections, were only a fortnight later and delivered the expected drubbing. Labour was relegated to third place in terms of the 'estimated national equivalent vote share' (the generally accepted measure of the major parties' local election performance), with only 26% of the vote. It made a net loss of more than three hundred seats, and controlled 17 fewer councils than it had before the elections. There was a minor measure of comfort in the knowledge that this was not Labour's worst-ever local election performance – in fact, the 26% share was the same as in 2004, from which they had recovered to win the 2005 general election – but it was a very poor one nonetheless.

Table 4: Local elections, 2006-9 – on-the-night gains and losses

	2006	2007	2008*	2009	Total 2006-9
Councils controlled (net change)					
Conservative	+11	+39	+12	+7	+69
Labour	−17	−16	−9	−4	−46
Liberal Democrat	+1	−5	+1	−2	−5
Others	0	−4	−1	0	−5
No overall control	+5	−14	−3	−1	−13
Council seats (net change)					
Conservative	+317	+927	+257	+244	+1745
Labour	−320	−642	−334	−291	−1587
Liberal Democrat	+1	−257	+33	−2	−225
Estimated national equivalent vote					
Conservative	39%	40%	43%	35%	
Labour	26%	26%	24%	22%	
Liberal Democrat	25%	24%	23%	25%	
Others	10%	10%	10%	18%	
Approximate turnout	37%	38%	36%	35%	

Sources: House of Commons Library Research Papers 06/26, 07/47, 08/48, 09/54 and 10/44 (which include national equivalent vote calculations by Colin Rallings & Michael Thrasher).
Table refers only to gains/losses in the annual local elections and makes no attempt to include by-elections or to correct for boundary changes
*In 2008, figures refer only to council elections, not to elections of the London Mayor and Assembly

A particularly ominous feature for Labour – but perhaps also disappointing for the Conservatives – was the strong performance of the minor parties, who seemed to be picking up Labour's protest votes. The Greens gained 21 council seats, Respect 13, and most alarmingly the British National Party (BNP) gained 27 and took over the mantle of official opposition in the London Borough of Barking & Dagenham. Presumably the BNP in particular found the foreign prisoners issue a useful one.

But local election results often have a direct result on the political narrative as well as functioning as a measurement of it. On the night, the BBC's national vote share estimates put the Conservatives on the psychologically important 40% of the vote[17] for only the second time since 1982. (The previous occasion was in 1992, in the immediate after-glow of John Major's unexpected general election victory.) Perhaps more significantly, the results gave signs of the Tories having re-established themselves throughout much of England as the default alternative to Labour. Although some way short of the support they would probably need to win a majority at a general election, it was unquestionably a result with which they had reason to be pleased.

Figure 4: Local election and general election vote shares, 1998-2010

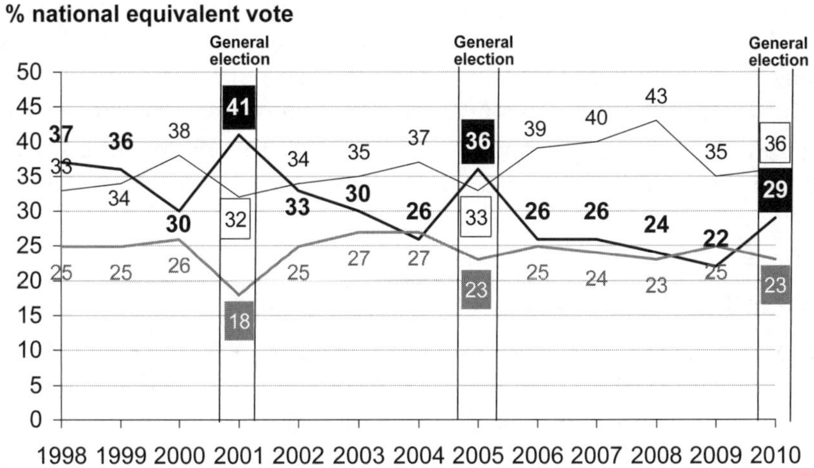

% national equivalent vote

Source: Calculations by Colin Rallings & Michael Thrasher, quoted in House of Commons Library Research Paper 10/44

Probably just as damaging to the government's image, though, would have been the appearance of division in their own ranks. David Blunkett, the former Home Secretary, had already called for heads to roll over the

---

[17] Estimates broadcast on the night are based for practical reasons on only a sample of wards. The eventual Rallings and Thrasher estimate, once all the data was in and long after the dust had settled, revised this down to 39%.

foreign prisoners' mix-up. Frank Dobson, a former Health Secretary, publicly blamed Blair for Labour's defeat in Camden. A radical cabinet reshuffle – rather than a slower, face-saving evolution – may have given a further impression of panic. Clarke was sacked; Prescott, though keeping his post, was effectively relieved of all departmental duties by the shifting of his responsibilities to a new Department of Communities and Local Government. Margaret Beckett took over as Foreign Secretary from Jack Straw, who became Leader of the House of Commons, while John Reid became Home Secretary (his ninth different cabinet post in nine years). With various other changes at lower levels, more than half the cabinet found themselves in new posts.

Predictably, this did little in the short term to restore the government's popularity. The 'general election tomorrow' polls during May showed Labour down to 32% support, with David Cameron's Tories establishing a significant lead for the first time, and Tony Blair hitting his then-lowest Prime Ministerial satisfaction rating of 26%. Tellingly, both 'race relations/asylum/immigration' and 'crime/law and order' rose significantly over the month in our unprompted poll on the 'most important issues facing the country', suggesting that it was the foreign prisoners fiasco which had most public resonance of the government's various travails.

Sleaze and party funding

The most damaging issue over the next year was probably the stream of allegations of illegalities in Labour party funding. The question of financial 'sleaze' was a running sore throughout the 2005-10 Parliament – and indeed an issue that had dogged Blair on and off since he took office, and for that matter John Major before him. This eventually became subsumed into the much clearer scandal surrounding MPs' expenses, which broke in earnest during the Brown premiership, and this mitigated the damage to the government since many of the most newsworthy cases involved Conservative MPs. But under Blair, the government was intermittently shaken by a series of embarrassing incidents. In the first of these, in November 2005, David Blunkett resigned from the cabinet (for the second time), after being criticised by the Committee on Standards in Public Life (CSPL) for breaching the ministerial code on shareholding and company directorships.

Soon afterwards came the first 'Cash for Honours' accusations. Early in 2006, apparent leaks to the press suggested that the House of Lords Appointments Commission was considering rejecting some nominations for working peerages because they were of people who had made substantial donations to the political parties that had nominated them, and in March an SNP MP referred rumours to the Metropolitan Police that Labour nominees had donated or made loans to the party in the expectation of receiving peerages. Over the next year-and-a-half the police investigation continued, intermittently hitting the front pages, with Tony Blair himself being interviewed by police officers in Downing Street and his close friend Lord Levy, who had responsibilities for Labour Party fundraising, being among those who were arrested. An extra complication and source of controversy was that the Attorney General, Lord Goldsmith – not in any way personally implicated, but a political appointee and already a controversial figure because his official advice had paved the way for the invasion of Iraq – would have to consent to any prosecution. In the end, however, no charges were brought against anybody (the decision being taken by the Crown Prosecution Service, with no involvement from the Attorney General).

However, the investigation highlighted other controversial aspects of Labour fundraising, including the accusation that restrictions on donations were frequently evaded by making long-term loans, to which different rules applied. In March 2006, the party treasurer Jack Dromey (husband of the cabinet minister Harriet Harman) stated that neither he nor the chairman of the National Executive Committee had any knowledge of certain major loans to the party. Two days later, it was disclosed that the party had received £14m of secret loans to fund its campaign in the 2005 election. Small wonder that 54% of the public, in a survey by Ipsos MORI for the CSPL conducted between December 2005 and April 2006, felt 'not confident' that the authorities would generally uncover wrongdoing by those in public office. Unsurprising, too, that politicians are consistently among the groups the public trust least, and have been since our first 'Veracity test' survey in 1983. (See Figure 18 on page 136).

Yet in that same CSPL survey, covering the trustworthiness of politicians and civil servants as well as confidence in their regulation, 57% of the public said that no recent event had influenced their opinions. Among the remaining 43%, the most frequently cited influences were the War in Iraq

(12%), the Hutton Enquiry (3%) or simply 'Tony Blair' (7%), rather than anything more directly relevant to the questions asked. This survey reaffirmed our evidence that there is always a high level of generalised distrust towards politicians ('they are guilty until proven innocent'), often fed by controversial policy decisions or issues such as Iraq, and that specific incidents of corruption probably do little more for most of the public than reinforce already negative attitudes. The David Blunkett case, mentioned by 11% in the CSPL survey, was the only frequently mentioned event influencing opinions that involved any allegations of monetary gain; the Cash for Peerages allegations, even though they were breaking in the newspapers as the survey was being conducted, were mentioned by just 1%.

Nevertheless, many of the public took the allegations over Labour's funding as evidence of the government's disreputability. This was all jam for the Conservatives. Undoubtedly, part of the handicap that they had gone under at the past three elections was the memory of the Major government, in which the impression of sleaze was an integral part, putting off waverers who might otherwise have considered voting Tory. Now the boot was on the other foot. According to our poll conducted for the *Sun* on 9-11 February 2007, shortly after news emerged that the police had interviewed the Prime Minister, a quarter of the public considered the Blair government to be 'more sleazy' than the Conservative government under John Major which had preceded it; only 14% thought the Major government more sleazy (Table 5). This is a question we asked several times over the years, but this was the first time that those who thought the Blair government was the sleazier had outnumbered those who thought the Major government had been worse.

Of course there is nothing very surprising in this finding, which owes little to the credibility or otherwise of the allegations. Few are as vulnerable as politicians to the specious argument that there is no smoke without fire, because the public have long since stopped allowing them the benefit of the doubt. But the public's generally low opinion of politicians limited the damage to Blair, as the Tories' gain was mostly limited to achieving a feeling that they were 'all as bad as each other', rather than establishing themselves as the 'whiter than white' alternative (as Tony Blair once fleetingly did).

Table 5: Mirror, mirror… who is the sleaziest of them all?

Q. The previous Conservative Government under John Major was accused of sleaze. Do you think the current Labour Government is more or less sleazy than the previous Conservative Government, or is there no difference between the two?

	25-26 January 2001	15 May 2001	21-26 February 2002	9-11 February 2007
	%	%	%	%
More sleazy	12	10	18	24
Less sleazy	30	27	22	14
No difference between the two governments	54	56	54	50
Neither is/was sleazy	1	1	1	1
Don't know	2	6	4	11

Source: Ipsos MORI

Base: c. 1,000 GB residents aged 18+ in each survey

However, the same phenomenon also limited the impact of changing the Prime Minister and any advantage that Gordon Brown could hope to gain from a fresh start with a clean slate; just because Brown had not been personally implicated in any of the allegations did not mean the public would assume he was more reputable than his opponent. Asked in February 2007 to judge whether a Brown government or a Cameron government would be least sleazy, more than half the public said there would be no difference; a minority felt there would be a difference, but they were equally split, 17% expecting Brown and 15% Cameron would lead the less sleazy government, no significant advantage either way. Similarly, direct measures of trust in the three men showed that while Brown was substantially more trusted than Tony Blair (42% said they would describe Brown as trustworthy compared to 29% saying this about Blair), the then Chancellor had more people describing him than Cameron as 'not trustworthy', meaning that the Conservative leader's net trustworthy score was statistically no different from Brown's (+7 and +3, respectively).

This lack of public differentiation in the trustworthiness of Brown and Cameron remained even up to the month that Brown became Prime Minister. In a survey conducted on 8-10 June 2007, we found that both Brown's and Cameron's 'net trustworthy' scores both stood at −12.

Table 6: Perceived trustworthiness of Blair, Brown and Cameron, 2006

Q. In general would you describe each of the following politicians as trustworthy or not?

	Trustworthy	Not trustworthy	Net
	%	%	%
Tony Blair	29	60	−31
Gordon Brown	42	39	+3
David Cameron	36	29	+7

Base: 988 GB residents aged 18+, 31 August-6 September 2006
Source: Ipsos MORI

Labour's crumbling electoral performance

Blair announced at the Labour Party's annual conference in September 2006 that it would be his last as leader. The gap in the polls closed briefly at the end of that year, but had re-opened by the following May's elections. Labour was perhaps pulled down by Gordon Brown's budget, in which he had announced the abolition of the 10p tax band – a surprisingly regressive move for a Labour chancellor. The elections this time included those for the Scottish Parliament and Welsh Assembly as well as for a swathe of English and Scottish councils, and once again ended in a sound thrashing for the government. At 26% once more in the national equivalent vote share (but estimated at 27% on the night by the BBC), the best that could be said was that Labour's position did not seem to have deteriorated further – but there was also ever-present the knowledge that Blair was in his final few weeks in office (which he had publicly confirmed just before the elections), and hence the suspicion that this was little more than a 'phoney war' – the real situation could not be judged until his successor, universally assumed to be Gordon Brown, was installed.

But, once again, the elections in reality were important in themselves, not just as an indicator of political mood. Most dramatically, Labour's poor performance in Scotland put an SNP administration into power at Holyrood for the first time. Also significant was the disappointing result for the Liberal Democrats: although their vote share held up at 26%, they made a net loss of almost 250 seats, many in the areas where the Conservatives needed to regain Westminster seats for a realistic hope of an overall majority in the forthcoming general election. It was the party's second successive failure to capitalise on Labour's unpopularity (in 2006 they had made a net gain nationally of a single council seat), and was undoubtedly a factor in Sir Menzies Campbell's resignation as Liberal Democrat leader later that year.

Iraq and Afghanistan

Beyond the issues which arose anew after the 2005 election, Blair left Brown with one highly problematic ongoing commitment, British involvement in the wars in Iraq and Afghanistan. The Iraq War had briefly, at the time of the invasion, enjoyed majority support (though it is arguable that even then this represented only the public's acceptance of a fait accompli and support for British troops in the position in which they had been put, rather than whole-hearted support for the government's war aims and its expectation of achieving them.[18] Before the invasion, two-thirds had said they would support military action with a new UN resolution to back it, but two-thirds were opposed if there was no new UN resolution, as of course was eventually the case.) At any rate, by 2005 public opinion was already running against the war by two to one, and inevitably the issue was much raised during the general election, though in our opinion it had only a very minor direct effect on the outcome.

But over the next two years, the war still dragged on, with regular British casualties and little apparent hope of successfully concluding the original mission of leaving a stable democratic regime in control in Baghdad. Opinion hardened further. By May 2007, as Figure 5 shows, just 14% of the public still supported the war while 82% were opposed. Perhaps more significantly, though, the proportion admitting that they themselves had once supported the war was also shrinking. This was ominous in its implications for the level of blame that voters would place on those who had taken the decision to invade. The myth of a Blair decision taken in defiance of unanimous public opposition was becoming an increasingly solid hurdle to Labour re-election.

---

[18] We discussed this question in more detail in our book *Explaining Labour's Landslip* (London: Politico's Publishing, 2005). In 2008, we found only 18% of the public thought that the troops being withdrawn from Basra had successfully completed their mission; 69% felt 'there is little chance of our being successful in restoring peace to the area'. (Survey for the BBC: Ipsos MORI interviewed 1,070 UK adults aged 16+ by telephone on 3-6 January 2008.)

Figure 5: Do you now or did you ever...? The Iraq war

Q. Which, if any, of the following statements comes closest to your own view about the war in Iraq?

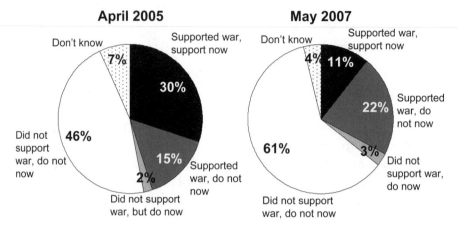

Source: Ipsos MORI
Base: 1,007 GB residents aged 18+, 28-29 April 2005; 961 GB residents aged 18+, 11-13 May 2007

But might Brown, not part of the inner circle that took the decisions, be seen as less personally implicated? Iraq and Afghanistan apparently offered an opportunity. Handled adroitly, they had the potential to be to Brown what the poll tax had been to John Major, an unpopular policy that could be reversed as a demonstration that the new regime in Number Ten offered a genuinely new start and a policy change around which his party could rally towards winning the coming election. But the politically easy option of immediate withdrawal once he took over from Blair he judged to be militarily irresponsible. (And though this was apparently the preferred option of most of the public[19], Brown would have to deal with the consequences of any miscalculation.)

In fact, by the time of the election, Brown's opponents had found a way to use the issue against him without needing to blame him for the original decision to go to war. In March 2010, after Brown had appeared before

[19] A ComRes poll for the *Independent on Sunday* in July 2008 found 74% of the public agreed that 'British troops should be withdrawn from Iraq as soon as possible', http://www.comres.co.uk/page19042410.aspx, accessed 31 January 2011.

the Chilcot Enquiry into the war, YouGov asked several questions on the public's perception of the position, prefacing them with a reminder that 'some retired generals and civil servants' had accused him of 'starving' the armed forces of needed money before the War. They found that 39% of the public agreed and 41% disagreed that 'By depriving our armed forces of some of the equipment and protective clothing they asked for, Mr Brown is personally responsible for some of the deaths of British troops in Iraq and Afghanistan'[20]; but it is not clear how many, when not prompted by YouGov's question, would have carried this hostility into the polling booths. None of the polls suggested that either Iraq or Afghanistan remained leading issues at the general election. But in any case, by 2010, hostility to Brown on other grounds probably made him vulnerable to uncharitable interpretations of his record over Iraq which might have been less accepted had he retained his popularity in other fields. Also had the economic crisis not so completely rewritten the issue agenda, we cannot tell whether Iraq and Afghanistan might have featured .more prominently in the election campaign.

The 'political legacy' that Blair left to Brown

How should we assess the prospects with which Gordon Brown was faced once Tony Blair had handed over the reins of power? Was the government a going concern in June 2007, suffering from routine mid-term blues but with every chance of securing a fourth term eventually, or was it already inevitably on the road to ruin?

In terms purely of the voting intention polls, it is plain that the situation under Blair was not nearly as parlous as it was to become under Brown. At Labour's lowest point in the 2005-7 period, the monthly average Tory lead reached 8 points, in August 2006 and again in March 2007; under Brown,

---

[20] YouGov poll for the *Sun*, conducted 20 March 2010, from http://today.yougov.co.uk/ sites/today.yougov.co.uk/files/YG-Archives-Pol-Suntopical-100310.pdf, accessed 12 January 2011. YouGov's question (in a self-completion internet survey) was prefaced with the statement 'Last week Gordon Brown was questioned by the Chilcot Inquiry into the war with Iraq seven years ago. He said that, when he was Chancellor, he agreed to every request from the armed forces at the time of the war for spending on equipment needed to fight the war. Some retired generals and civil servants have said that he starved the armed forces of much-needed money in the years leading up to the war. Do you agree or disagree with the following statements?'

within a year of his taking over, the gap had hit 20 points. But it is worth noting that the difference in the ratings of the government and of the Prime Ministers[21] was not nearly so dramatic. Satisfaction with the government fell to 22% three times between 2005 and 2007, while satisfaction with Blair himself bottomed out at 23% in a single poll and touched 25% or 26% several times. The low point in satisfaction with Brown's government was 16%, recorded once; otherwise it was 18% on three occasions, and satisfaction with Brown himself was only once as low as 21%. So a 12-point difference in the voting intention gap reflects only a difference of between two and six points in satisfaction ratings.

In fact, largely unnoticed, Blair underwent a steady reduction in popularity that began almost as soon as he was elected. As Figure 6 shows, he began with high satisfaction ratings, but these began to fall almost immediately and in fact, smoothing out the occasional peaks and troughs that events impose on the longer-term pattern, the deterioration in the underlying trend was faster in his first term than in his second or third.

It is a myth, which seems to be particularly pervasive among New Labour sympathisers, that the invasion of Iraq was the sole major political error of Tony Blair's term in office and as such the turning point in his public standing — all was perfect in his relationship with the voting public until that fatal day, is the impression conveyed, all sharply downhill afterwards. Yet in fact almost the opposite is the case. As can be clearly seen from the graph, the trend in decline was consistent, starting early in his first term in power. His peak of popularity for his handling of the crisis after 9/11 concealed the trend at the time, but in retrospect this can be seen as no more than a short-lived blip in the general course of decline.

In fact the invasion of Iraq has no perceptible effect on the trend. The decline in Blair's standing was actually slower in the latter part of his premiership than in the first few years when it was declining from the impressive and unlikely heights at which it began (perhaps because a Prime Minister easily loses the support of the floating voters that he has attracted in his first successful run for office but his core vote, the natural

---

[21] These are often referred to as 'approval ratings', which reflects the preferred question wording for similar polls in the USA, but in fact our question asks respondents whether they are satisfied or dissatisfied with the way each leader is doing their job – as Prime Minister, as Leader of the Opposition or as leader of the Liberal Democrats.

supporters of his own party, are harder to dislodge). And, as the graph makes just as plain, Brown's satisfaction ratings – despite the dramatic 'honeymoon' peak and equally dramatic trough which once again, taken together, served to disguise the underlying trend – fit neatly into the continuation of the course started under Blair. If we had to predict what Tony Blair's ratings would have been had he still been Prime Minister in 2010, we might in fact have expected them to be very close to those actually achieved by Brown.

Figure 6: Tony Blair's and Gordon Brown's public standing, 1997-2010

Q. Are you satisfied or dissatisfied with the way Tony Blair/Gordon Brown is doing his job as ...Prime Minister?

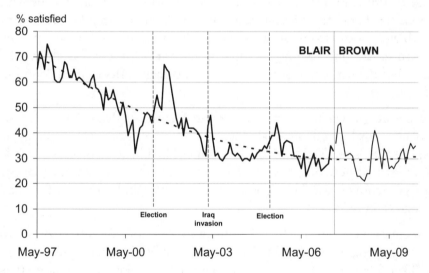

Source: Ipsos MORI
Base: c. 1,000-2000 GB residents aged 18+ each survey

So why, if Blair had been doing as poorly as Brown did, did he win his last election while Brown lost? The missing element, obviously, is that satisfaction scores are absolute measures while voting intentions are comparative and zero-sum. At its nadir, Tony Blair's government was not much less unpopular than Gordon Brown's, but David Cameron's ratings were substantially more impressive during Brown's premiership than Blair's. Cameron's satisfaction rating the first time we measured it, only a few weeks into his leadership, was 31%. This was a relatively respectable starting point, but then he made no significant improvement during the whole of the next 18 months before Blair's retirement, touching 33% satisfied just once and otherwise completely becalmed around 30%. Worse, the 17% who were dissatisfied in that first poll grew quickly until they stood steadily at double the figure: in each of the three polls in the second quarter of 2007, there were 33% of the public declaring themselves dissatisfied with the leader of the opposition's performance, giving Cameron a negative net score. But he improved markedly from October 2007.

But there is another factor of political perception rather than governmental substance to consider, the very fact of there having been a change of Prime Minister. At first, this worked to Labour's advantage with the polls turning in their favour as soon as Blair announced his retirement and a bigger boost from Brown's inevitable 'honeymoon' effect once he took office. But once the novelty began to wear off, there was always the danger that Brown would suffer from the 'nostalgia effect' often found in the polls.

Even before Brown took over, we found a surprisingly positive view of the Blair record given his shaky standing in the voting intention polls. True, only 28% believed that the government had kept its promises, while 64% felt it had not. But, nevertheless, 46% thought that ten years of Mr Blair's government had been good for the country and 43% that they had been bad (Figure 7).

The sceptics were fewer when they were asked about the effect on them personally: here, 46% thought that the Blair effect has been positive and only 35% felt it had been negative, with 19% having no opinion. It is striking how much higher this positive rating of the Blair government's performance was than the public's assessment had been at the time. Compared to this 46% who felt Blair's government had been good for the country, the government's average monthly satisfaction rating over its ten years of office had been only 36%. The monthly rating had not once been above 30% satisfied since January 2006, and had not been as high as 46% in three consecutive months since the start of 2002. As Gordon Brown took over, far more of the public thought Tony Blair had done a good job overall than had ever voted for him, more than for years had thought he was doing a good job at the time, far more than thought he was still doing a good job in 2007.

Figure 7: The public view of the Blair government's record, May 2007

Q. On balance, do you think that ten years of Mr Blair's Government have been good or bad for the country?
Q. On balance, do you think that ten years of Mr Blair's Government have been good or bad for you personally?

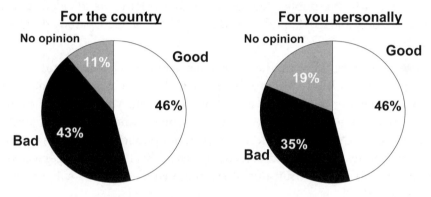

Source: Ipsos MORI
Base: 961 GB residents aged 18+, 11-13 May 2007

There was an obvious danger that this rosy view of the past might reflect badly on Gordon Brown's premiership by comparison once things started to go wrong. Moreover, it was an open secret long before 2007 that Blair and Brown had fallen out on a personal level, and it seemed to many that Blair's procrastination over resigning was as much driven by wishing to deny Brown power as by his own reluctance to relinquish office. When Blair jocularly suggested his successor would be a 'big clunking fist' in opposition to a lightweight Cameron, it was very much a two-edged compliment.

But, more important, the personal divisions between Blair and Brown had crystallised into opposing factions, 'Blairites' and 'Brownites', within the Labour Party. This had two consequences. At Brown's takeover, those ministers and advisers who were seen as 'Blairite' were immediately suspect; yet after ten years in office, Labour could hardly afford to marginalise all its most experienced figures. Further, the media and perhaps many in the Labour Party saw the division as an ideological one, with Brown seen as being further to the left and his premiership a step away from the 'New Labour' orthodoxy that had held since 1994. Yet this was probably always a myth. Brown was as much one of the architects of New Labour as Blair had been, and his accession was never likely to mark a significant shift in policy. So those preferring to remain in the centre-ground were put unnecessarily on the defensive, those hoping for a shift leftwards found their hopes disappointed, and the division between the two became a quite unnecessary focus of internal dissension. The proportion of the public seeing the Labour Party as divided trebled between 2005 and 2010; and, as we always say, divided parties don't win elections.

Labour's poor standing under Brown as compared to that under Blair, then, may owe at least a little to there having been a change of leader at all, and to Cameron's maturing as a credible opponent. We should be careful, also, not to over-estimate the extent to which Labour's existing decline accelerated under Brown's leadership. The public's view of the Blair government by 2007 seems already to have been of a once-successful administration that had run out of steam, even if there was still a residual level of goodwill.

Table 7: Vote swings, 1997-2005 and 2005-10

	1997	2005	Change 1997-2005	2010	Change 2005-10
	%	%		%	
Conservative	31	33	+2	37	+4
Labour	44	36	−8	30	−6
Liberal Democrats	17	23	+6	24	+1
Others	8	8	0	10	+2
Lab-Con swing			**5%**		**5%**

The 2010 election was a convincing defeat for Labour and the scale of the party's loss of support, though not unexpected, sent a shockwave through the upper echelons of the party and moulded the battle to choose Gordon Brown's successor. Yet Labour's loss of support between 1997 and 2005 was bigger than its loss between 2005 and 2010! It was only less obvious, perhaps, because in the earlier period (under Blair) it was LibDems rather than Tories who benefited, so that the swing[22] in each period was 5%, but of the 44% share of the vote that Blair had amassed in 1997, it was Blair who lost 8% over the next two elections, and Brown lost only a further 6%.

This is not to argue that Labour's performance in 2010 was satisfactory – of course it wasn't. Yet it was merely the continuance of an existing decline, not a new phenomenon. The Labour government's vote base was already decaying, saved perhaps only by the unelectability of the Conservative opposition in 2005. Nor did any single incident or policy apparently cause that decline to set in: there was no turning point, only a continuing loss of popularity over 13 years, which the occasional sudden upticks such as those after the death of Diana, Princess of Wales and the 9/11 attacks served to disguise but never to halt. Blair's legacy to Brown was a government already in its death throes; the question was not whether Labour would hit the buffers, but when.

Gordon Brown and Labour's double-dip recession

Gordon Brown replaced Tony Blair as Prime Minister in June 2007, just under three years before the latest possible date at which he could choose to hold the next general election. He began with an immediate 'bounce' in the government's ratings, Labour was suddenly ahead once more in the polls and for a couple of weeks in the autumn it looked as if the election would be held before the end of the year. But Brown drew back from the brink – sensible caution or a loss of nerve, according to interpretation. A year on, some of the polls were showing the lowest Labour share in the 70-year history of polling.

There was plenty to drive the government's popularity downwards. The unpopular war in Afghanistan rumbled on with no end in sight while on the domestic front the government stumbled from blunder to blunder. But the most far-reaching problem was the mortgage crisis in the banking system – much more a result of the misjudgments of the American banks than the British ones, but sparked by a run on a minor British bank,

---

[22] We explain how swing is calculated and what the figures mean on page 112.

Northern Rock, and later requiring the government to invest billions of pounds in the major British banks to prevent their collapse. The banks survived but the culture of easy credit could not, and this plunged Britain and much of the rest of the world into recession. Brown won foreign plaudits for the way he handled the crisis – a Freudian slip in the Commons when he claimed to have 'saved the world' might not have seemed too far fetched outside the UK, and even many British voters gave him credit for performing well in the circumstances. By the end of 2008 his ratings were recovering and the Tories seemed almost within touching distance.

Then, as quickly as it had come, Brown's recovery faded again. The government's ratings plunged once more and the Tory lead was back to landslide proportions. Brown's popularity had undergone its own double-dip recession.

By now it was clear that Brown would not be 'going to the country' four years into the parliament, the normal course for all but governments in crisis. Then, in early 2009, the crisis took on a new dimension with the public revelation of MPs' expenses claims, making the political class seem by turns grasping, out-of-touch, ridiculous and in a few cases apparently downright fraudulent. The European elections followed a few weeks after the main flood of revelations in the *Daily Telegraph*, and produced unprecedented levels of votes for all the minor parties, with the Conservatives and Liberal Democrats apparently as much damaged by the impact as Labour. Yet, notwithstanding this, the Conservatives' lead over Labour was still so commanding as to translate into an easy victory if there was an immediate election.

But there was not an immediate election, and yet another twist in the government's fortunes was waiting as the epilogue.

Brown's standing before he became leader

For many years before it became clear when Tony Blair would eventually relinquish the premiership, it was widely believed that Gordon Brown's public image was an asset to the Labour party. This was evident at the previous General Election in 2005, with polling both before and after that election showing that, on balance, people felt Brown would make a more capable Prime Minister than Blair.

Table 8: Most capable Prime Minister – Brown or Blair?

Q. Who do you think would make the most capable Prime Minister – Tony Blair or Gordon Brown?

	Blair %	Brown %	Don't know %
20-24 January 2005	35	39	25
7-11 April 2005	33	41	26
29-30 September 2005	39	42	20

Source: Ipsos MORI
Base: c. 500-1,000 GB residents aged 18+ each survey

In fact the popularity of Brown was a major strength to Labour's election strategy in 2005. The Conservatives had launched a poster campaign warning the public they would 'vote Blair, get Brown', which was soon withdrawn as the message apparently backfired: many voters angry or sceptical about voting Labour again felt reassured that Blair would be stepping down at some point during the 2005-10 Parliament.

Brown's popularity and growing impatience for the top job were key factors in Tony Blair's forced announcement in September 2006 that he would step down from office at some point in the next twelve months. And the fact that Brown then enjoyed a smooth transition into Number Ten, without a formal ballot of the party's membership, can largely be seen as being built on his reputation as one of the country's most successful Chancellors of the Exchequer, not least in terms of public approval of his performance in the job over the previous decade.

Ipsos MORI measured public perceptions of Gordon Brown as Chancellor on 25 occasions between July 1997 and April 2007; and in only three of these surveys did we find more people dissatisfied than satisfied with Brown's performance. (This was a much stronger endorsement than that achieved by any of his Conservative predecessors – see Figure 8.) The first 'crisis of confidence' happened in the autumn of 2000 when the country was held almost hostage by the fuel protests in September. Brown's approval ratings moved from a net +14 in July 2000 to −21 by September, a swing of 17.5% in just two months. But this rebounded quickly as the crisis was overcome, so that by the following March more than half the public were satisfied with Brown's performance as Chancellor and fewer than three in ten dissatisfied. This net approval rating of +23 was a solid position from which New Labour fought and won its second landslide election.

Figure 8: Net satisfaction with Chancellors, 1979-2007

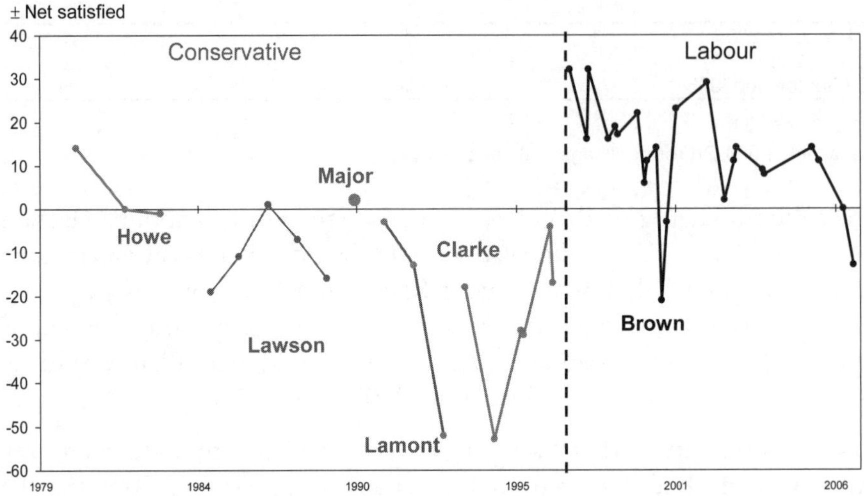

± Net satisfied

Base: c. 1,000 GB residents aged 18+ each survey
Source: Ipsos MORI Political Monitor

But, significantly for Brown as the future Prime Minister in 2010, his public image as a successful Chancellor had started to slip several months before Tony Blair departed from office. By the end of 2006, as many people were reporting dissatisfaction with Brown's performance as satisfaction after his last Budget; and in April 2007, just a third of the public (32%) expressed satisfaction as opposed to 45% being dissatisfied, giving Brown a −13 approval rating – a low not recorded since the fuel crisis at the start of the decade. The Chancellor's decision to cut the main rate of income tax and to pay for this by abolishing the 10p starting rate was designed to provide headlines to attract the 'Middle England' voters that Blair as Prime Minister and Brown as Chancellor had won over in their transformation of Labour into New Labour. But the immediate effect on his ratings was not what he would have wanted, and within a year the implications of the scrapping of the 10p rate would rebound. By April 2008, Brown was already struggling politically when the time came to pass the finance bill that would bring the tax changes into effect: backbench Labour rebels joined forces with the Conservatives, forcing the new Chancellor, Alistair Darling, to provide transitional relief to those on lower incomes who were worst affected. Brown had misjudged the mood of the party and his 'core supporters', not for the last time.

Nevertheless, weeks before he took over as Prime Minister, Brown's reputation for running a sound economy was broadly intact, with three in five (59%) people saying the Government had done a good job at managing the economy, and only 32% that he had done a bad job.[23] (Even two in five, 39%, of those intending to vote Tory admitted this, though 53% took the contrary opinion; of Labour voters, 83% felt their government had done a good job.)

The factors that the public use to rate their Chancellor will always be somewhat different to those applied to a Prime Minister; and there was never any guarantee that positive approval ratings for stewardship of the economy would translate seamlessly into positive approval ratings for leading the country. A key element in David Cameron's strategy when he became leader was to associate himself more with the character and 'radical' policies pursued by Tony Blair, for example in March 2006 providing Conservative parliamentary support on foundation schools which allowed Blair to survive what otherwise would have been one of his only parliamentary defeats as Prime Minister.[24] At the same time, and anticipating that his opponent would most likely be Gordon Brown at the next General Election, Cameron and the Tory leadership were happy to be seen to be much more hostile towards Brown, in particular arguing that he supported policies that were frustrating the 'New Labour' agenda and that his personality made him a poor choice for leader.

This Conservative strategy involved a certain degree of risk, if it allowed Brown to paint himself as the anti-spin leader (i.e. different from both Blair and Cameron). But the Conservatives realised that while Brown was likely to inherit Number 10 with a more positive image than Blair, he was

---

[23] Ipsos MORI interviewed 961 GB residents aged 18+ by telephone on 11-13 May 2007.
[24] http://news.bbc.co.uk/1/hi/uk_politics/4810898.stm, accessed 18 October 2010.

certainly not going to be seen as a fresh, new leader, without political or reputational 'baggage'.

In January 2007, we explored the public's attitudes to Brown – as well as to Blair and Cameron – in more detail, asking whether the public liked them and whether they liked their parties. Brown's 'likeability' score was only two points higher than that of Blair (36% to 34%). The difference between the two was that slightly fewer said they did not like Gordon Brown than did not like Tony Blair (49% against 55%). The net likeability score gave Tony Blair a minus 21 against Gordon Brown's net likeability score of minus 13, though the fact that half the electorate were then saying they 'did not like' Gordon Brown should perhaps have raised some questions about the future Prime Minister's ability to connect with voters. It was also instructive that asking about Gordon Brown rather than Tony Blair made no impact as to how people felt about the Labour party: in both versions of the question the net likeability score of the Labour party was minus 9.

Table 9: 'Like him, like his party?' – Blair, Brown and Cameron

Q. Which of these statements comes closest to your views of [LEADER] and [PARTY]?

	Blair/ Labour	Brown/ Labour	Cameron/ Conservative
	%	%	%
I like (leader) and I like the ... Party	23	25	19
I like (leader) but I do not like the ... Party	11	11	17
I do not like (leader) but I like the ... Party	17	13	10
I do not like (leader) and I do not like the ... Party	38	36	34
Don't know	11	15	20
Total like (leader)	34	36	36
Total do not like (leader)	55	49	44
Net like (leader)	–21	–13	–8
Total like the ... Party	40	38	29
Total do not like the ... Party	49	47	51
Net like the ... Party	–9	–9	–22

Base: 973 GB residents aged 18+, 12-14 January 2007
Source: Ipsos MORI/The *Sun*

There was little to separate Brown and Cameron in terms of likeability in mid June 2007 – both had 36% of the public saying they liked them, though Cameron had slightly fewer expressing dislike for him (44% against

49%); and, as we shall see, the two were also evenly matched in their image for trustworthiness. The really significant differentiator was the image of their political parties with the Conservatives receiving a net likeability score of minus 22 (29% like and 51% did not like), a much worse rating than that of the Labour party on minus 9 (38% like and 47% did not like).

This implies that while a Brown bounce was almost inevitable, as virtually all new Prime Ministers benefit from one and given the poor public ratings for Tony Blair, the extent to which this bounce would provide a fundamental and lasting shift in favour of Labour was less certain.

Journalists often want to know how people would vote if a political party was led by someone other than the current party leader. Most often the request is to ask a question such as 'Would you be more likely to vote Labour if Gordon Brown was Prime Minister rather than Tony Blair?'. This is a bad polling question wording which a reputable polling organisation should refuse to ask, as the results are at worst misleading and at best useless, for without further questioning and analysis it is impossible to determine how many people actually have moved from supporting one party to another. If the question above had found 40% of the public saying they would be more likely to vote Labour with a different leader (in this case Gordon Brown) we would not know whether this simply represented current Labour supporters simply reaffirming their support for the party of their choice or even being more solidly behind their party. It clearly doesn't tell us if Labour would pick up additional support from voters who otherwise would have voted for another party. The additional danger in these types of 'more or less' questions is that it can exaggerate the saliency of an issue or event in influencing people's attitudes or intended behaviour.

One method polling organisations use instead to try to explore these situations is to ask the voting intentions question in exactly the same way as they would for their standard voting intentions question but to replace the name of the leader. This gives us a much better sense of the net movement in voting intenders when comparing different leadership scenarios.

Regular surveys were conducted by several polling companies between the 2005 election and Brown's accession to office, asking people how they would vote in a General Election if Gordon Brown were leader of the

Labour party instead of Tony Blair. Table 10 compares the results of the standard voting intentions questions with those of the hypothetical voting intentions question in the same survey, for each of the surveys conducted in 2007.

Table 10: Hypothetical voting intentions if Brown were Leader, January-May 2007

Survey end date	Company/client	Con %	Lab %	LD %	Con lead %
7 January 2007	Brown	39	34	15	+5
Populus/Times	Blair (standard question)	39	32	18	+7
	Difference	0	+2	−3	−2
4 February 2007	Brown	35	34	16	+1
Populus/Times	Blair (standard question)	36	33	19	+3
	Difference	−1	+1	−3	−2
4 March 2007	Brown	42	29	18	+13
Populus/Times	Blair (standard question)	38	30	18	+8
	Difference	+4	−1	0	+5
16 March 2007	Brown	41	31	13	+10
YouGov/S. Times	Blair (standard question)	38	32	16	+6
	Difference	+3	−1	−3	+4
18 March 2007	Brown	43	28	18	+15
ICM/Guardian	Blair (standard question)	41	31	18	+10
	Difference	+2	−3	0	+5
15 April 2007	Brown	41	30	19	+11
Populus/Times	Blair (standard question)	37	29	20	+8
	Difference	+4	+1	−1	+3
22 April 2007	Brown	40	28	20	+12
ICM/Guardian	Blair (standard question)	37	30	21	+7
	Difference	+3	−2	−1	+5
13 May 2007	Brown	42	32	15	+10
Populus/Times	Blair (standard question)	37	33	17	+4
	Difference	+5	−1	−2	+6
20 May 2007	Brown	38	30	20	+8
ICM/Guardian	Blair (standard question)	34	32	21	+2
	Difference	+4	−2	−1	+6

Source: Data from www.pollingreport.co.uk

While the difference in voting intentions between the two questions was rarely substantial, the difference in the Conservative lead when there was one was almost invariably in Tony Blair's favour.

Oddly, the difference in Conservative support if Brown were leader was almost always bigger than the difference in Labour support, which while not impossible is unlikely, and suggests that what these surveys were registering was not simply the impact of replacing Blair with Brown but other extraneous factors as well.[25] Their value may therefore be limited. Nevertheless, in so far as they are useful they suggested that the change of leader would have a negative rather than a positive effect on the Labour position.

Whatever else the polling showed before Gordon Brown became leader, it did not show that he was likely to transform Labour's political fortunes – or at least the public did not expect him to do so. Of course, these were all hypothetical questions: the real test would come when the public saw Gordon Brown as Prime Minister for real.

The 'unelected' leader

Gordon Brown was declared Labour leader on 24 June 2007 and, as the leader of a party with a stable majority in the House of Commons, he was formally appointed Prime Minister by the Queen three days later. Constitutionally, it was always nonsense to complain that Gordon Brown was an 'unelected Prime Minister', an accusation which was to be raised again and again by opponents (both within the party and outside it) once his star had waned. In the British parliamentary system as in most others, new Prime Ministers frequently take over in mid-term on their predecessors' retirement, and it has always been accepted that constitutionally this raises no requirement for a new general election. In the 20th century, 14 Prime Ministers entered Number 10 following the resignation or retirement of their predecessor; and two of the previous four Prime Ministers (Callaghan and Major) succeeded mid-term.

---

[25] The three companies used different question wordings for their hypothetical questions, but all reminded respondents of the leaders of the other two parties as well as asking them to consider Gordon Brown as Labour leader.

Indeed, Brown's elevation was even more unassailable than that of many of his predecessors since, far from coming out of the blue, it must have been clear to any intelligent voter at the 2005 election that if Labour won Tony Blair would be replaced by Gordon Brown at some point during the subsequent Parliament. In fact, as previously discussed, Labour's 2005 General Election campaign was partly built on this 'promise'. In this case, nobody could reasonably claim that Brown lacked a legitimate mandate. No Prime Minister is directly elected by the voters, and a vote for a Labour MP in 2005 was as much a vote for Brown as PM later in the Parliament as it was a vote for Blair in the immediate future.

Nor is it true that Brown was given the leadership of the party unopposed. Brown did have an opponent, John McDonnell, who declared himself a candidate but was not able to gather enough nominations from MPs to trigger a formal contest and take the decision to a ballot. The reality is that through their nominations Labour MPs voted by 313 to 29 for Brown as leader.

In the short term, the avoidance of an internal Labour leadership election was politically beneficial to the party. Not only did it save it money (though the incremental costs would probably not have been so important, given that the party *did* hold a full contest for the deputy leader position), it allowed Labour to avoid the potentially damaging splits that a full vote of the party membership and affiliated institutions might have provided. To this extent, Brown' succession to the top – together with Tony Blair's endorsement – was a symbolic moment for the movement, apparently showing a reconciliation of the 'Blairite' and 'Brownite' factions that had so damaged the party in power over the previous decade.

These events helped the party to present the change of leader as part of a smooth transition of leadership, rather than the reaction to deep internal splits as the election of John Major as Conservative Party leader in 1990 most certainly was. And the political consequences of party unity should not be underestimated.

In the longer term, perhaps there are arguments that it would have been better for a grassroots campaign and vote for a new party leader. But this argument is made with hindsight and based on Brown's performance as Prime Minister rather than based on the method of his selection. And while the opposition were able to make continuing criticisms of Brown's apparent lack of any 'democratic legitimacy' to be Prime Minister, this only had resonance with the public to the extent it reinforced their other perceptions, which were based on how they rated his actual performance as Prime Minister rather than how he was selected. The trajectory of Labour's popularity from July 2007 makes quite clear that the problems the government eventually had owed little if anything to immediate misgivings about the principle of Brown's succession.

First few weeks: the Honeymoon

The effect of Gordon Brown becoming Prime Minister, indeed of the anticipation among the public that this was soon to happen, was certainly dramatic – as witnessed by the movements in voting intentions shares during 2007. In the 26 months between the 2005 General Election and Blair's resignation, the Conservatives had been ahead in the published polls in 15 months and behind in only 7; moreover, they had been consistently ahead for the previous 14 months. (See Figure 3 on page 29.)

Figure 9: Voting intentions 2007-8 (Poll of Polls)

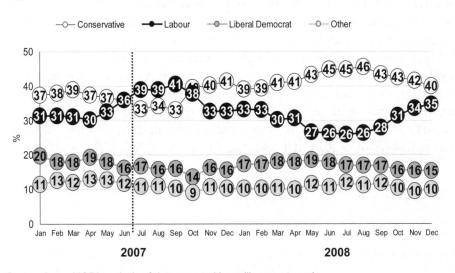

Source: Ipsos MORI analysis of data reported by pollingreport.co.uk.
Note: Figures given are the averages of polls conducted each month by the six established polling companies

In the first quarter of 2007, the Conservatives were close to 40% support while Labour was reduced to the low thirties: in March the gap peaked at 8 points, 39% Conservative to Labour's 31%.

Thereafter, Labour fortunes began to improve – not, it should be noted, from the point at which Gordon Brown moved into Number Ten but from the moment when Tony Blair announced the date on which he would move out. The final Ipsos MORI voting intention poll while Tony Blair was Prime Minister (conducted 14-20 June 2007) showed the Labour government recovering its lead over the Opposition, with 39% of those saying they were absolutely certain to vote at a general election indicating their preference for Labour, three points above the support for the Conservatives, on 36%. This was the clearest sign of the potential impact of the Brown bounce which continued to be evident over the next several weeks.

This continued when Brown took office. From a low point of 30% in April, Labour's voting intention share had reached 41% (and touching 44% in two polls) by the time of their conference in late September. The positive public reaction to the Brown government was reflected – and probably partly caused – by the almost universal media acclaim, passing positive judgments on how he and his government handled a range of unforeseen and potentially devastating events such as flooding, attempted terrorist attacks and a foot and mouth outbreak. Several surveys found the public satisfied on balance with the government's handling of crises as diverse as the Foot and Mouth outbreak[26] and a run on the Northern Rock bank.[27] Brown's smooth handling of these crises was underlined by an uncharacteristic gaffe by David Cameron, who decided to continue with a two-day fact-finding trip to Africa despite flooding in Witney, and was wrong-footed by a Rwandan journalist's question 'What do you have to

---

[26] According to an Ipsos MORI survey for the *Sun*, 72% of the public were satisfied with the way the government was handling the foot and mouth outbreak. (Ipsos MORI interviewed 1,010 GB residents aged 18+ by telephone on 8-9 August 2007.)

[27] Ipsos MORI survey for the *Sun*, 42% were satisfied and 25% dissatisfied with the way the government had handled the problems with the Northern Rock bank. (Ipsos MORI interviewed 1,009 GB residents aged 18+ by telephone on 20-22 September 2007.)

say about continuing with your visit to Rwanda when part of your constituency is completely devastated by floods?'[28]

Table 11: Key events, June-December 2007

Date	Event
24 June	Brown becomes leader of the Labour Party
27 June	Brown accepts the Queen's invitation to become Prime Minister
27 June	Brown rescinds the order in council that allows Special Advisers to give orders to civil servants
28 June	Brown reshuffles the cabinet: Alistair Darling Chancellor, Jacqui Smith Home Secretary, David Miliband Foreign Secretary
29 June	Two car bombs in London discovered and made safe
30 June	Apparent terrorist attack on Glasgow Airport foiled
7 July	Brown announces £14m aid package for areas hit by flooding
20 July	BBC reports CPS decision that no charges will be brought over the 'Cash for Honours' allegations
23 July	David Cameron continues trip to Rwanda despite flooding in his Witney constituency
3 August	Brown delays holiday to deal with Foot and Mouth Disease outbreak in Surrey
12 September	Northern Rock announces liquidity problems following the US sub-prime mortgage crisis, and asks Bank of England for help
14 September	Run on Northern Rock begins, with queues to withdraw deposits; Bank of England grants Northern Rock liquidity support
17 September	Darling guarantees all Northern Rock deposits
2 October	Brown visits troops in Iraq
3 October	Conservatives at party conference promise Inheritance Tax cuts
8 October	Brown announces there will be no general election in 2007
15 October	Sir Menzies Campbell resigns as Liberal Democrat leader
20 November	Government admits loss of HMRC data disks
27 November	Brown admits Labour had accepted illegal donations by proxy
27 November	Vince Cable mocks Brown as having turned from Stalin into Mr Bean
13 December	David Miliband stands in for Brown at signing of Lisbon Treaty; Brown later signs in private
18 December	Nick Clegg elected as Liberal Democrat leader

Media hype about the first few weeks of Brown's premiership was epitomised by a *Guardian* article on 6 August 2007, which asked its readers 'Has any PM had a more difficult first month?'. (Mike Smithson, editor of the politicalbetting.com blog, perhaps answered the headline best when he pointed out that Churchill's first few weeks in office saw the fall of France in May 1940 followed by Dunkirk and the evacuation of the British

---

[28] Mike Pflanz, 'Rwandan press quiz Cameron on floods', *Daily Telegraph*, 25 July 2007, http://www.telegraph.co.uk/news/worldnews/1558492/Rwandan-press-quiz-Cameron-on-floods.html, accessed 9 September 2010.

Expeditionary Force, probably a greater national challenge than those faced by Britain's new Prime Minister in 2007![29])

What did seem to be unusual was Brown's level of direct involvement in overseeing the responses to all these problems, arguably storing up trouble for when the press turned against him and preferred to portray him as an incompetent control freak. By the following March, the Tories were making political capital of the fact that Brown had convened the emergency crisis committee Cobra twenty times since taking office, an average of once a fortnight.[30]

Within the first few weeks of Brown taking over as Prime Minister, more detailed 'character assessment' polling demonstrated the positive attributes Brown was seen to be able to bring to the job. In August 2007, seven in ten people (69%) felt that he was the leader who would be 'best in a crisis' – far ahead of those picking either David Cameron (10%) or Ming Campbell (8%). Brown also dominated his two rivals in terms of being seen as the best person to 'understand the problems facing Britain' with half the public (51%) selecting this attribute for Brown rather than Cameron (17%) or Campbell (8%). Labour's advertising at this point, using the slogan 'Not Flash, just Gordon' to position Brown as distinctly different from both Blair and Cameron, putting the emphasis on experience and policy competence, was harping on these same perceptions.

This was a theme to which Brown was to return in a later brief period of ascendancy when he argued his case to be preferred over Cameron as custodian of an economy threatened by crisis in the memorable phrase 'This is no time for a novice'. As we shall see, and perhaps surprisingly in the light of the way the media portrayed him, vestiges of this image of competence were to survive to the election, with Brown still narrowly leading Cameron on some of these key perceptions. It is possible that his advisers missed a trick in not hammering this message harder even when

---

[29] http://www2.politicalbetting.com/index.php/archives/2007/08/page/13/

[30] 'Panic stations! Gordon Brown has convened crisis committee Cobra once a fortnight since becoming PM', *London Evening Standard*, 25 March 2008, http://www.thisislondon.co.uk/news/article-23463428-panic-stations-gordon-brown-has-convened-crisis-committee-cobra-once-a-fortnight-since-becoming-pm.do, accessed 9 September 2010).

events perhaps suggested that the public would be unlikely to take Brown's claim to competence seriously.

For even at the height of his honeymoon period, further analysis of Brown's public image presented some cause for concern, particularly given that it was unlikely the honeymoon would last forever. In the modern media age, 'style' does matter. The same August survey revealed that Cameron trumped Brown in terms of which was seen to have 'the most personality' (42% and 31%, respectively). Once this became the main focus of comparison, Brown's position was far more precarious.

The Brown bounce was virtually inevitable – he had received no more than the boost that is customary for new Prime Ministers. The bounce in particular became a big story because it put Labour back ahead after trailing the Conservatives for so much of the time Cameron had been their party leader. The length of the honeymoon can be measured and contextualised through an analysis of Ipsos MORI's monthly tracking data on public satisfaction with the party leaders, which provides trend data going back to the late 1970s.

The first few months are especially important as they show the opinion of those who at first refrain from making a judgment on a new Prime Minister. In our first satisfaction rating measure for Gordon Brown (fieldwork conducted 12-17 July), we found 44% saying they did not know whether or not they were satisfied with the job he was doing (giving 36% satisfied and 20% dissatisfied); while this seems high compared to the 7% of 'don't knows' in Blair's last rating, or even the 34% who didn't know what they thought of David Cameron at that time, it was lower than for any recent leader of any major party in his first month. Another month onwards, and Brown's 'don't know' rating was already down to 34%, and those who had made up their minds split two to one in his favour (43% satisfied against 23% dissatisfied).

One excellent measure of a new Prime Minister's honeymoon's future is the length of time he or she survives with more of the public satisfied than dissatisfied with his or her performance. Gordon Brown's was remarkably short, ending sometime in October, approximately four months into the job. In our monthly Political Monitor, the survey conducted on 18-23 October found that 37% of the public were satisfied with Brown's performance and 38% dissatisfied, giving a 'net satisfied' rating of minus one.

This compares unfavourably with the three years or so of honeymoon enjoyed by Tony Blair, which ended in June 2000; and for John Major a honeymoon that lasted throughout his first short term in office from the end of 1990 to the General Election in 1992, though ending dramatically during the Autumn of 1992 with the events of Black Wednesday. However, we can overplay the importance of an early honeymoon period to the eventual success – or at least duration – in power. Mrs Thatcher had no discernable honeymoon after becoming Prime Minister in 1979.

John Major successfully faced a defining moment for his premiership within weeks of taking office, British involvement in the (popular) first Gulf War. In the same way, when Tony Blair took over after winning the 1997 election, he had to handle the crisis caused by the death of the Princess of Wales before the novelty of his government had had time to fade, and the positive public reaction to his approach helped cement approval of his leadership at a high level. Thus, for Brown's two predecessors, events outside their direct control in the early months of their premierships helped them to solidify their positive public image. For Brown, perhaps the single biggest cause of the ending of his honeymoon period and the reversal of the positive public reaction to the first weeks of his premiership was wholly within his control; and his control alone.

The honeymoon effect looked less dramatic, too, when we examined the sources of Labour's increased support. Although the increase in Labour support saw a draining away from the Tories over these first few months, the net changes since the previous election showed a different story. The average of the voting intentions surveys conducted in September 2007, at the peak of the Brown bounce, had Labour on 41% – a five-point gain since the 2005 election – but the Conservatives were no lower down than in 2005, averaging 33%. The Brown bounce therefore apparently did not attract committed Tories; rather it was more successful in attracting voters who had supported the LibDems in 2005 and quite likely (if they were old enough to vote) voted Labour in 2001 and 1997 – people who had merely flirted with the idea of voting Conservative in the previous few years without yet having had the chance to put it into practice.

The Brown bounce may simply have been the reconvening of the New Labour coalition which was splintered in 2005 by loss of trust in Blair and the Iraq invasion, bringing temporary 'deserters' back into the fold. The Liberal Democrats were clearly suffering the most from the change of Prime Minister, with their average September support at 16%; not only was this down from its 20% peak of that year in January, it was down seven points from the General Election. There were also some dramatic demographic differences in the impact of Brown's honeymoon, with men swinging far more sharply to Labour than women, and the middle-aged moving much more than younger or older voters; but as the bounce faded, these distinctions corrected themselves.[31]

The 'election that never was', and the backlash

The tide seems to have turned in the week of the Conservative conference, strengthened a few days later when Mr Brown announced that there would be no snap election. It is not clear whether this decision had a direct effect on voting intentions or not. (Once the announcement had been made, the country was divided: 47% felt the PM was right not to call an election and 42% that he was wrong.)

It was not a decision that surprised us, or anybody else with up-to-date information. On the Thursday, 4 October, as press speculation built to a frenzy, there was a meeting of the Media Group at the Reform Club, at which one of us (Bob Worcester) was asked to speak at the end of the evening about the likelihood of an election being called that weekend. He got on the phone to Ben Page at around 9:30 pm, to get the results of the three polls we knew were coming out the next morning. When asked about 10:15 pm to speak, he asked for a hands-up on whether or not an election would be called and about half the assembled journalists, pundits and guests indicated that they thought an election would indeed be called that very weekend. He then announced the three polls' results: a 4-point

---

[31] In Ipsos MORI's voting intention polls, aggregating two monthly measures to achieve a more robust sample size, men swung 9.5% from Conservative to Labour between April/May and July/August, while women swung only 2.0%. Similarly, 18-34 year olds swung 4.5%, 35-54 year olds 9.5% and 55-and-overs 2.5%. However, there was no significant difference in the swing by social class, in stark contrast to the eventual pattern of swings between the 2005 and 2010 elections.

Labour lead (YouGov), a 3-point lead (Populus) and dead level (ICM). He then asked the 80 or so diners how many *now* thought there would be an immediate election. One hand was raised.

The next two polls to come out, in the Sunday papers, both showed the Tories ahead; but by then Brown had pulled the plug, telling Andrew Marr in an exclusive interview on the Saturday that there would be no election. Figure 10 shows the poll findings published in the three-week period in which speculation was most rife: it shows the polls by publication date rather than by fieldwork date, and the 'gap' rather than vote shares, two practices we normally deplore; but in this case, as illustrating the impression created by the polls rather than the reality they were measuring, they are perhaps for once justified.)

Figure 10: How the polls suddenly turned in Autumn 2007

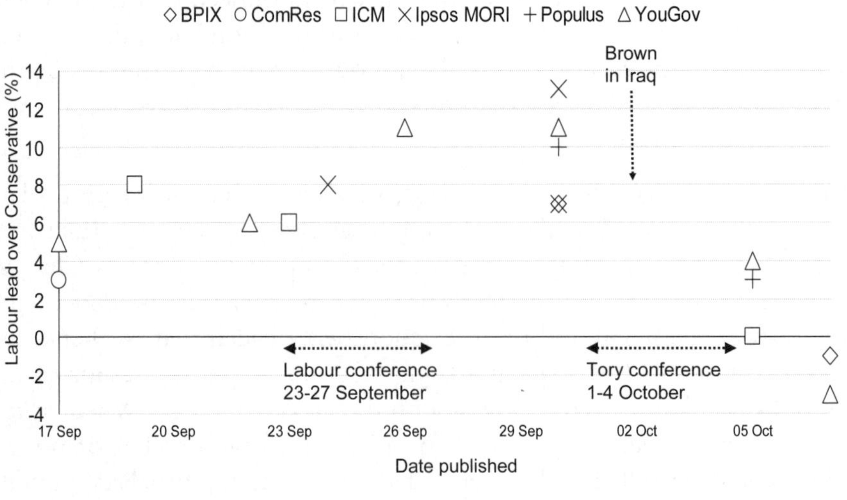

◇ BPIX ○ ComRes □ ICM ✕ Ipsos MORI + Populus △ YouGov

Source: Ipsos MORI analysis of data from published polls

Brown himself, of course, denied that his decision not to hold an election was in any way related to the opinion polls, a statement few can have believed and which cannot have enhanced his credibility at what might have been a pivotal moment. For that matter, another newspaper poll in marginal constituencies (and, reportedly, Labour's own private polls) suggested even greater weakness there, so that Brown could not expect so strong an electoral performance in seats as was implied by the vote shares in the published national polls.

But if it was the downturn in the polls that frightened Brown off from calling an early election, why had the polls turned down? The impression at the time, certainly, was that a favourable reception for Conservative proposals on inheritance tax was a decisive factor, though this may well have been exaggerated. Brown's visit to troops in Iraq, attacked by his opponents as a cynical attempt to exploit an unpopular war for electoral advantage, may also have been counter-productive. But we think it is not unlikely that an equally important factor was the very prospect of an immediate election and the discussion surrounding it. To understand this, we need to consider the nature of public opinion, and what it is that is measured by mid-term voting intention opinion polls.

As we have seen, there was nothing unexpected in the 'Brown bounce'. But how 'real' is such a rise in popularity in terms of the possibility of translating it directly into votes at the ballot box? Almost every new PM since regular polling began has had some sort of a 'honeymoon' or bounce, but none of them has ever called an election to test whether it would hold firm through an election campaign.

As we consistently tell anybody who will listen, opinion poll findings on propensity to vote and voting intention are no more than a snapshot of what a representative sample of the electorate say they would do if there were a general election tomorrow. But there is not a general election tomorrow. Members of the public are perfectly well aware that they are still making up their minds about the leaders, and that they have no need yet to commit themselves to one party or another – time enough to worry about that once the election is called, if they have not already reached a natural conclusion by then. So when they answer opinion polls at this stage, they are often not telling the interviewer about a settled and reasoned decision they have already reached, and they certainly don't agonise over their answers and come up with a considered opinion on the spot; many will give a snap reaction, their top-of-the-mind impression, an instant answer. Even after an election has been called and we are asking them 'How will you vote?' on a specific day a few weeks in the future, we know that they may not be able to predict their own behaviour perfectly, however honestly they try to answer. How much less reliance, then, should we place on a question about an election that is not going to happen anyway?

In fact there is no mystery about what is going on. You probably do it every day yourself, whether or not you have ever been polled. How often do you get frustrated by bad service or a dodgy product and tell yourself, and anybody else who will listen, that you will never, NEVER, NEVER buy that brand again? And how often do you find when it comes to the point that you choose the same brand as usual after all? But what would you have told a market researcher if you had been interviewed before your anger wore off? It applies just as much to politics, and it can just as well cause upwards as downward bounces.

Nor is it confined to opinion polls, of course – by-elections, local elections, European elections, they are all affected by protest voting and the public making a gesture that they would not make at a general election because it exaggerates their real depth of feeling and has much more meaningful consequences.

The media and some commentators love to project these elections to what-would-happen-if-this-result-had-occurred-in-a-general-election. So what's their record? The worst 'predictor' is the by-election, the next worst is a Euro-election, next worst are local government elections. And the best? Opinion polls of the nation's electorate are, in election after election. But even so, we should not be tempted to take mid-term voting intentions as literal 'what would happen now' projections, let alone assume a five-point lead in the polls equates to a five-point victory at an election a month away if the PM asks for an immediate dissolution any more than today's weather predicts the weather a month away.

That does not mean that the voting intention measures are useless. They are a real indicator of public mood, and the best one we have. That Gordon Brown got his bounce was an indication that the public were genuinely better disposed to the Labour Party than they had been earlier in the year. Part of that, no doubt, was a routine honeymoon effect, people being prepared to suspend judgment and allow the new man the benefit of the doubt until they had had some evidence on which to make up their minds, but that did not make the good will any less real. Nevertheless, it fell far short of an unconditional change in opinion. More likely it was a pledge that would eventually have to be redeemed by a more satisfactory performance in government than that of his predecessor. Solidifying the goodwill into votes is another step entirely.

All of which makes it perfectly possible that it was the speculation surrounding a possible snap election which caused the public to reassess. By the time of the Labour conference in the last week of September 2007, the clear media consensus was that an election within a few weeks was more likely than not. Suddenly, for the public, voting intention was not a hypothetical question about an event which was not going to happen, in which they could express their willingness to give Gordon Brown a chance before deciding whether to condemn him, but a meaningful and concrete choice about how they might vote in a few weeks' time. And, for a significant minority of 'swing voters', the answers to those two questions were different. So Labour's apparent lead seemed suddenly to evaporate and the election was off.

Brown stumbles on

Brown had done himself real damage by the way in which he handled his TV announcement that there would be no election, and events conspired to create the impression that the new Premier had, at best, lost control of his government and, at worst, misused the office of the Prime Minister for political advantage – playing games with the announcement of the election and timing a visit to a war zone during the Tory party conference. Things then immediately went from bad to worse. Of course, not all of the events that led to Labour's problems starting in the autumn of 2007 can be blamed on Gordon Brown. HMRC's loss of discs containing data on millions of child benefit claimants can hardly be seen as the direct responsibility of the Prime Minister.

But as Napoleon is supposed to have pointed out, a leader needs to be lucky as well as able. The all-pervasive atmosphere of governmental incompetence which suddenly descended was very reminiscent of that in the dying years of John Major's administration. As Vince Cable memorably put it, Gordon Brown had gone in a few weeks from being Stalin to Mr Bean – and while a politician may be strengthened by being feared, nothing is more damaging than for him to be laughed at.

Table 12: Key events, January 2008-April 2009

Date	Event
2008	
22 February	Northern Rock nationalised
17 March	Brown announces an Inquiry into the Iraq War will be held, but not immediately
5 April	Abolition of 10% rate of income tax comes into effect
1 May	Local elections. Boris Johnson ousts Ken Livingstone as Mayor of London
22 May	Crewe & Nantwich by-election: Conservative gain from Labour, 17.6% swing, the party's first by-election gain since 1982
11 June	Commons votes narrowly for a 42-day terrorist detention limit
12 June	David Davis announces he will resign to force a by-election in protest at proposed new anti-terrorist provisions
26 June	Wendy Alexander resigns as Labour leader in Scotland after being suspended from the Scottish Parliament over breaches of donation rules
11 July	Haltemprice & Howden by-election: David Davis re-elected
24 July	Glasgow East by-election: SNP gain of Labour's 3rd safest seat in Scotland, 17.3% swing
30 July	David Miliband denies plotting against Brown after an article he writes in the *Guardian* is interpreted as a leadership bid
12 September	Siobhain McDonagh sacked as junior government whip after calling for a Labour leadership election
23 September	Brown speech at Labour Conference – 'No time for a novice'
2 October	Metropolitan Police Commissioner Ian Blair announces his resignation after disagreements with London Mayor Boris Johnson
3 October	Congress approves emergency bail-out of US banks by Treasury
6 October	Biggest one-day fall in the FTSE100 since 1987
8 October	Government announces bank rescue package totalling around £500bn
13 October	42-day detention defeated in Lords, and dropped from the government bill
4 November	Barack Obama elected US President
27 November	Police enter Commons offices and arrest Conservative frontbencher Damian Green over Home Office leaks
24 November	Pre-Budget Report
17 December	Brown makes surprise visit to Iraq, where he announces all British military operations in the country will end by 31 May
21 December	Police Assistant Commissioner Bob Quick accuses Conservative Party of involvement in a *Mail on Sunday* article that he considered endangered his family.
2009	
21 January	Government forced to drop motion that would exempt MPs' expenses claims from Freedom of Information provisions
23 January	Figures officially put UK in recession
8 February	Press reports of Jacqui Smith's expenses claims
25 February	Sudden death of David Cameron's six-year-old son, Ivan
5 March	Bank base rates at lowest ever level (0.5%)
1 April	Ian Tomlinson dies during Police 'kettling' of anti-capitalist demonstrators
9 April	Bob Quick resigns as Police Anti-Terrorism chief after inadvertently revealing details of a counter-terrorist raid
11 April	'Smeargate': Brown's special adviser, Damian McBride, resigns after the publication of emails showing McBride discussing fabricating smears about the private lives of opposition MPs
29 April	Government defeated in Commons over residence rights for Gurkha veterans

From that point onwards, the story was one of Conservative ascendancy. The Tories had a lead once more in October 2007, and never lost it again, while the tide of news stories about the government's performance turned inexorably from positive to negative.

The impact of the events in the final three months of 2007 came to define the image of Gordon Brown as Prime Minister, from which he never really recovered and which overturned most of the gains he had achieved in the first few weeks of his premiership. For example, instead of the continuing lead he had enjoyed over David Cameron in mid September as being seen as the leader 'best able to deal with the challenges of the 21st century' where four times as many people thought this of Brown than Cameron (50% against 12%) by the start of 2008, the Leader of the Opposition had gained the upper hand (37% Cameron compared to 34% Brown).[32] These events also affected the wider image of the Labour Government and its perceived competency to govern. In mid September four times as many people felt that Gordon Brown rather than David Cameron 'led the most united team' (54% to 12%), but by the following January the proportion of the public still thinking this of Brown had halved (to 27%) and those ascribing this attribute to Cameron trebled (to 34%).

Similarly, by January 2008, there was very little difference in the public's mind about which of these two leaders was most capable, with 33% choosing Cameron and 37% Brown; which again demonstrated a big reversal of fortunes for the Prime Minister from the towering lead he had had over Cameron back in mid September (58% to 17%).

Analysis shows that March to September 2008 was a low point for Brown – not only did his personal satisfaction ratings slump to record lows, but also the difference between his net score and that of the Government was almost wiped out (Figure 11).

The local elections on 1 May 2008 – Brown's first as leader – emphasised Labour's travails. Boris Johnson's defeat of Ken Livingstone in London made most headlines, but in fact the swing was comparatively small and was a blow Labour could afford. Less so the Tories' gains on councils across England: had those votes been cast at a general election rather than

---

[32]Survey for the *Sun*. Ipsos MORI interviewed 1,006 GB residents aged 18+ by telephone on 9-10 January 2008.

at local elections, David Cameron would have become Prime Minister with the working majority he missed in 2010. The BBC projection of the 'estimated national equivalent vote share' put the Conservatives' share of the vote at 43%, their best level since 1992. Labour slipped to third place on just 24%, worse than at any of the elections under Tony Blair's leadership. (The party was steady on a 26% share in 2004, 2006 and 2007.) Even allowing for the way that local elections always flatter the Conservatives because they benefit from the lower turnout, a lead of this scale would translate to a Tory General Election victory with plenty of room to spare.

Figure 11: Gordon Brown's 'double-dip recession', 2007-10

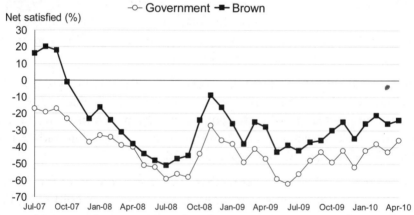

Q. How satisfied are you with the way...
...the government is running the country?
...Gordon Brown is doing his job as Prime Minister?

Base: c. 1,000 GB residents aged 18+ each month
Source: Ipsos MORI Political Monitor

As bleak a view for Labour was given by the roll-call of councils won and lost. Labour controlled 9 fewer councils afterwards than it had before the elections, and made a net loss of more than 300 seats, which seems to have exceeded the leadership's worst nightmares; the Tories gained around 250 councillors and 12 councils. The Conservative gains spoke of advances in the marginal-rich urban North (Bury) and in some of Labour's remaining footholds in the South (Southampton). Labour's losses seemed to show a party in deep trouble, even in its own heartlands (Blaenau Gwent, Torfaen, Caerphilly, Merthyr Tydfil, Hartlepool).

Of course, local election defeats were nothing new — indeed, they are the almost invariable rule for all governments. In fact Labour had made a net loss of council seats every year since Tony Blair reached Downing Street. But a government can only afford the steady drip of constant losses for so long. The effects are cumulative. When Tony Blair was first elected, Labour had well over 10,000 councillors. After 2008, the figure was barely half that.[33] Even if these votes against Labour were no guarantee that the voters would repeat their verdict at the general election, their impact on party morale can hardly be over-estimated.

That, naturally, goes for the Tories as well. Symbolically particularly important was that the 19-point margin of victory in the 2008 local elections almost equalled Labour's biggest under Tony Blair (a 22-point lead, 47% to 35%, in his first year as leader, 1995), and was considerably more convincing than Labour's 14-point win in 1996, the last before Blair's first general election landslide. It was not wholly fanciful, therefore, for Cameron to feel that the solid evidence of votes cast was putting him into the same victorious bracket as Blair. Three weeks later, at the Crewe & Nantwich by-election, Tory hearts were further lifted by the capture of Gwyneth Dunwoody's former constituency on a 17.6% swing, the party's first by-election gain since 1982, despite Dunwoody's daughter being the candidate defending her popular mother's seat. The Cameron magic, it seemed, was working at parliamentary as well as council level.

The campaign was notable for the first appearance of Brown's preferred class-war rhetoric, branding the Conservative candidate, Edward Timpson, as 'The Tarporley Toff' and 'Lord Snooty', with Labour campaigners in top hats and tails following him around to ram home the point.[34] Daniel Finkelstein in *The Times* compared[35] the stunt to the equally childish one in

---

[33] The number fell further at the 2009 elections to around 4,700. See House of Commons Library Research Paper RP09-054, p 14.

[34] Ben Macintyre, 'Attempts to stir class war backfire for Labour in Crewe & Nantwich', *The Times*, 21 May 2008, http://www.timesonline.co.uk/tol/news/politics/article3972727.ece, accessed 8 September 2010.

[35] Daniel Finkelstein, 'Toff stunt is the end for New Labour', *The Times*, 21 May 2008, http://www.timesonline.co.uk/tol/comment/columnists/daniel_finkelstein/article3972268.ece, accessed 8 September 2010.

the 1997 general election when the Tories hired a man dressed as a chicken to follow Tony Blair about – he judged the Labour effort to be even stupider than the chicken, and concluded 'New Labour is dead. Gordon Brown has killed it'. Meanwhile, the *Daily Telegraph* reported Tory claims that 'Labour activists have been posing as Tories and calling voters at 4am. They are said to have told residents that Tories have been campaigning in Bentley cars.'[36] Even this claim would have been a spectacular own goal in a constituency where Bentley is one of the main employers.

By mid-July 2008, Brown's standing was lower than Blair's had been in his post-Iraq slump, with two-thirds of the public disappointed that he had 'not lived up to expectations' and half saying that he should resign (Table 13).

Table 13: Brown and Blair in tricky times

Q. For each of the following statements, please tell me whether you agree or disagree.
'Gordon Brown has lived up to my expectations'
'It's time for Gordon Brown to resign and hand over to someone else'

	Lived up to expectations		Time to resign	
	Blair (June 2003) %	Brown (July 2008) %	Blair (June 2003) %	Brown (July 2008) %
Strongly agree	12	11	31	36
Tend to agree	20	15	15	14
Neither agree nor disagree	7	7	8	8
Tend to disagree	23	19	20	20
Strongly disagree	36	45	25	19
Don't know	2	3	1	3

Base: 1,007 GB residents aged 18+, 26-27 June 2003; 1,016 GB residents aged 18+, 18-20 July 2008
Source: Ipsos MORI

But this proved to be Brown's lowest ebb. The global financial crisis that had been steadily bubbling since his first weeks in office suddenly boiled over, and the political landscape was changed.

---

[36] Andrew Porter, 'David Cameron attacks 'Old Labour class war'', *Daily Telegraph*, 20 May 2008, http://www.telegraph.co.uk/news/1991207/Tory-leader-David-Cameron-attacks-Old-Labour-class-war.html, accessed 8 September 2010.

The banks and the economic crisis

From this point onwards the escalating economic crisis, following the collapse or near collapse of major banks both in Britain and around the world, was naturally the government's main preoccupation and soon that of the voters as well. The first domino to fall had been the medium-sized British bank, Northern Rock, in September 2007. Brown's Chancellor, Alistair Darling, had acted quickly to head off a panic by guaranteeing deposits at the bank within a few days, and on 22 February 2008 he formally nationalised it. The initial handling of the crisis, at the height of the Brown honeymoon, had been well received by the public, but once it came to appear that the government was spending billions of public money to prop up the entire British banking industry, this was doing little to prop up support for Brown. The situation was not helped by the extraordinary ignorance of basic economics displayed by many of the journalists covering the story, nor by the misconception that the government investment was being lost for ever rather than paid out in exchange for assets that might eventually prove profitable and allow the public money to be recovered, with interest.

But perhaps the public were right to be concerned, for while the problem at Northern Rock was essentially a liquidity crisis (the Bank of England accepted that Northern Rock's assets had always been sufficient to cover its liabilities), it had been sparked by the 'toxic debt' problem of the American banks which had lent against effectively worthless security. During 2008, all five of the biggest US investment banks were either bailed out by Washington, bought up by other companies or, in the case of Lehman Brothers, allowed to go bankrupt, while the government-sponsored agencies 'Fannie Mae' and 'Freddie Mac' were placed in receivership. These seven institutions had a combined liability of $9 trillion, hardly less than the entire US National Debt of $10 trillion.

In Britain, stock market speculation in banking shares became rampant and HBOS almost collapsed in September 2008. It was hurriedly bought out by Lloyds TSB, the government suspending normal competition law restrictions to allow the takeover to go ahead. On 8 October, Darling announced a broad bank rescue package totalling some £500 billion, available to bail out British banks or for short-term liquidity loans, to restore confidence in the sector. In fact, two of the 'big five', Barclays and HSBC, accepted no funding from the scheme and supported themselves from their own resources. But the impression left on the public was that all the banks were being entirely propped up with public money having wasted their own. Brown, who as well as overseeing this rescue of the entire British financial system from fatal collapse had reportedly played a major role in the international discussions that helped mitigate the wider chaos, got in return a sharp boost in his poll ratings.

Table 14: Brown the world leader

Q. Please tell me whether you agree or disagree with the following statement: 'Gordon Brown's response to the current economic crisis shows that he is a true world leader'.

	%
Agree	41
Disagree	53
Don't know	6

Base: 1,004 GB residents aged 18+, 17-19 October 2008
Source: Ipsos MORI

Only a minority of the public agreed that his handling of the crisis showed that he was a 'true world leader' (Table 14), but the majority were briefly prepared to agree in September that he was doing a good job in difficult circumstances (Table 15), a 16% swing in his favour since July.

Table 15: A good job in difficult circumstances?

Q. To what extent do you agree or disagree that Gordon Brown is doing a reasonable job in difficult circumstances?

	18-20 July 2008 %	12-14 September 2008 %
Strongly agree	14	15
Tend to agree	21	36
Neither agree nor disagree	6	5
Tend to disagree	20	16
Strongly disagree	38	26
Don't know	1	1

Base: c. 1,000 GB residents aged 18+ each survey
Source: Ipsos MORI

The political recovery peaked in November 2008, when Brown's net satisfaction rating almost moved into the black and one poll[37] put Labour voting intentions within a point of the Conservatives. Meanwhile, on the other side of the Atlantic, Barack Obama had been elected President. But was that an omen for the candidate of the left, or for the candidate who was young and charismatic? As Christmas came and went with no lightening of the economic mood, it was the younger, more charismatic British leader who was looking increasingly comfortable once more. By the end of January, Britain was officially in recession and, ominously, the government had failed in its attempt to exempt MPs' expenses claims from Freedom of Information provisions. Brown's figures, and Labour's figures, slipped backwards: the Tories had a double-figure lead in the voting polls again, and seemingly were romping to victory. It didn't turn out quite like that, for there were yet more twists to come in which the uncustomary volatility of public opinion would again play its part, but the foundations for Labour's certain defeat had surely been laid by the start of 2009 with the failure of Brown's last chance to parlay credibility as an economic leader into a robust case for re-election as Prime Minister.

Could Labour have won with a different leader?

Given how comparatively close the final election result was, in seats if not in votes, the question inevitably rises as to whether, if only Labour had had a more inspiring leader than Gordon Brown, they might have added those last few hundred thousand votes and been able to keep the Tories out. Or alternatively, given the scale of Labour's recovery between mid-2009 and the election, might there be a case for regarding Gordon Brown as much maligned, the unheralded leader who came tantalisingly close to pulling off a political miracle? (Tony Blair, in his memoirs published soon after the election, had no doubts, though he explained the difference as one of policy rather than personality: 'Labour won when it was New Labour. It lost because it stopped being New Labour.'[38] But this comes from the

---

[37] A ComRes poll for the *Independent*, conducted on 28-30 November and published 2 December 2008.
[38] Quoted in the *Guardian*, 31 August 2010, http://www.guardian.co.uk/politics/2010/aug/31/tony-blair-gordon-brown-disaster.

same man who was so convinced that Ken Livingstone and Rhodri Morgan would be disastrous leaders that he blocked both from being Labour candidates.)

Gordon Brown's image

To answer this question more objectively, we need to look in much greater detail at the public's perceptions of Brown himself. A natural place to start is their view of who would make the best Prime Minister, which we tested at regular intervals up to the election. Naturally, the trend of these findings tends to be not too far removed from that of voting intentions, since a choice of party is in large part also a choice of Prime Minister. As Table 16 shows, Gordon Brown began with a substantial lead over David Cameron, but Cameron had reversed this and Brown trailed badly by September 2009.[39]

Table 16: Most capable Prime Minister

Q. Who do you think would make the most capable Prime Minister, Gordon Brown, David Cameron or Sir Menzies Campbell/Nick Clegg?

	14-20 June 2007	25-27 September 2009	19-22 February 2010	23 April 2010	5 May 2010
	%	%	%	%	%
Gordon Brown	40	24	29	28	29
David Cameron	22	41	38	32	33
Menzies Campbell/Nick Clegg*	5	16	12	17	19
None/don't know	33	19	20	23	19

Source: Ipsos MORI
Base: c. 1,000-1,500 GB residents aged 18+ in each survey
* Campbell in 2007, Clegg in 2009-10

Yet from this point onwards, Brown staged a recovery much as his party's voting intention ratings did (though never returning to his 'honeymoon' popularity of 2007). In fact by the final eve-of-election poll Brown was

---

[39] Other Ipsos MORI polls between June 2007 and September 2009, which make only a head-to-head comparison between Brown and Cameron, omitting the LibDem leader, show the same picture, with Brown well ahead up to the time of the 'election that never was' but Cameron drawing level at the start of 2008.

trailing Cameron by a smaller margin than Labour trailed the Conservatives, and the increase in Nick Clegg's score following the first leadership debate seems to have come entirely at Cameron's expense rather than Brown's.

However, the best Prime Minister ratings are comparative and 'zero-sum' – a respondent cannot express increased approval of one leader without shifting his or her preference from one of the others. More revealing, perhaps, are Brown's satisfaction ratings as Prime Minister, which we can compare with the ratings of David Cameron and Nick Clegg – each of these is an absolute rather than a relative rating, since respondents can approve of as many or as few of the leaders as they choose.

By March 2010, our last poll before the election was called, Brown's net ratings were lower than the incumbent Prime Minister in any election since 1979, at the same stage of the campaign, and also lower than those of any party leader who has gone on to win an election, in line with approval of John Major in 1997, and William Hague in 2001. Brown scored 34% satisfied but 60% dissatisfied, a net −26. Nevertheless, Tony Blair's rating in 2005 had not been substantially better, at −22. Indeed, viewing only the satisfaction ratings and ignoring dissatisfaction, Brown's position in 2010 was as good as Blair's: Blair's final three monthly ratings before the 2005 election were 33%, 35% and 34% satisfied, and Brown's in 2010 were 33%, 36% and 34%. The difference was in the perceived quality of the alternative: only 31% were satisfied with Michael Howard in March 2005, while 42% approved Cameron's performance in March 2010.

It should perhaps be noted that satisfaction with Gordon Brown's performance was, in most months, several points ahead of satisfaction with 'the way the government is running the country'. (Figure 11 on page 72). But this is not a new phenomenon. For every Prime Minister whose public standing we have measured, back to James Callaghan in the 1970s, his or her personal ratings were consistently better than those of the government.

On the other hand, Brown undoubtedly had a problem: he was not widely liked. Another of Ipsos MORI's regular polling measures asked the public to say whether they liked Brown and whether they liked the Labour Party (Table 17), and on this criterion – unlike David Cameron, when we tested his image in the same way (see the table on page 126) – Brown invariably was liked by fewer respondents than liked his party. Even as Chancellor, more people said they disliked him than liked him, and from 2008 three in five or more were saying they did not like the Prime Minister. Of course, this is not necessarily an insuperable barrier to re-election (Margaret Thatcher overcame levels of dislike little lower than this)[40], but it was clearly a weakness, and one which was perhaps more relevant than usual in an election which came to be so dominated by the battle of personalities. In April 2010, only 11% of those who said they did not like Brown were intending to vote Labour despite their feelings about him personally.

Table 17: 'Like him, like his party?' – Brown and the Labour Party

Q. Which of these statements comes closest to your views of Gordon Brown and the Labour Party?

	12-14 January 2007	18-20 July 2008	26-28 January 2010	18-19 April 2010
	%	%	%	%
I like Gordon Brown and I like the Labour Party	25	18	20	24
I like Gordon Brown but I do not like the Labour Party	11	11	15	13
I do not like Gordon Brown but I like the Labour Party	13	21	19	19
I do not like Gordon Brown and I do not like the Labour Party	36	44	42	41
Don't know	15	5	5	4
Total like Gordon Brown	36	29	35	37
Total do not like Gordon Brown	49	65	61	60
Net like Gordon Brown	−13	−36	−26	−23
Total like the Labour Party	38	39	39	43
Total do not like the Labour Party	47	55	57	54
Net like the Labour Party	−9	−16	−18	−11

Source: Ipsos MORI
Base: c. 600-1,000 GB residents aged 18+ in each survey

With which voters was Brown's unpopularity most particularly a handicap? Those who said in April 2010 that they liked the Labour Party but disliked Gordon Brown were concentrated particularly among the young, and were

---

[40] In 1985, we found that 56% disliked Mrs Thatcher while only 39% disliked Labour leader Neil Kinnock, but she nevertheless defeated him convincingly at the 1987 general election.

rare among DEs, Labour's natural constituency. (This was not because Brown was well liked by DEs – half of them said they disliked him – but because the vast majority of DEs who disliked Brown also disliked the Labour Party.) This reaction was also more common in the South of England, especially in London, than elsewhere. But, again, the difference in London was not in reactions to Gordon Brown as such, but that far fewer than in other parts of the country disliked the Labour Party.

We can give the public's dislike of Brown slightly more context by considering a slightly different polling question (Table 18), which we asked about Brown during the election campaign and which we had previously also asked about Margaret Thatcher, John Major and Tony Blair close to the end of their premierships. Respondents are asked to contrast the leader and his or her policies rather than the party, but again it gives a direct measurement of whether the leader was liked or disliked.

Table 18: Like him/her? Like his/her policies? 1990-2010

Q Which of these statements comes closest to your views of [LEADER]?

	Thatcher	Major	Blair	Brown
	26 November 1990 %	24-27 January 1997 %	11-13 May 2007 %	18-19 April 2010 %
I like him/her and I like his/her policies	20	19	27	24
I like him/her but I dislike his/her policies	19	32	30	21
I dislike him/her but I like his/her policies	8	8	6	13
I dislike him/her and I dislike his/her policies	52	32	31	39
No opinion	1	9	6	3
Like him/her	39	51	57	45
Dislike him/her	60	40	37	52
Net	–21	+11	+20	–7
Like his/her policies	28	27	33	37
Dislike his/her policies	71	64	61	60
Net	–43	–37	–28	–23

Source: Ipsos MORI
Base: c. 600-1,700 GB residents aged 18+ in each survey

Few will be surprised to see that by the end of her term of office, Margaret Thatcher was more disliked than any of the other three, although even more of the public said they disliked her policies than disliked her personally. But both John Major and Tony Blair were liked by more than half the public even at these low points of their careers, while Brown was more disliked than liked.

Brown's answer to this would presumably have been that his claim to re-election was always based on competence in office rather than personality, and here he was on more solid ground – much more so than was widely recognised by commentators who had already decided that Brown's inadequacies were the defining story of the election.

Table 19: Image attributes of the leaders, April 2010

Q. In choosing between Gordon Brown, David Cameron or Nick Clegg, which leader do you think...?

		Gordon Brown	David Cameron	Nick Clegg	None	Don't know
...best understands the problems facing Britain	%	33	26	26	6	8
...would be best in a crisis	%	40	28	14	8	10
...best understands world problems	%	45	22	14	8	12
...is most out of touch with ordinary people	%	42	39	6	4	8
...is most capable	%	33	30	21	7	9
...is most likely to promise anything to win votes	%	36	43	9	4	8
...best understands the fine details of policies	%	38	23	18	7	13

Source: Ipsos MORI Political Monitor
Base: 1,253 GB residents aged 18+, 18-20 April 2010

Q I am going to read out some things both favourable and unfavourable that have been said about various politicians. Which of these, if any, do you think apply to...?

		Gordon Brown	David Cameron	Nick Clegg
Good in a crisis	%	46	38	29
Has sound judgment	%	40	47	47
More honest than most politicians	%	32	37	49
Patriotic	%	64	73	62
Rather inexperienced	%	14	61	76
Out of touch with ordinary people	%	55	46	25

Source: Ipsos MORI/*News of the World*
Base: 1,245 GB residents aged 18+, 23 April 2010

During the campaign, we tested leader image in two slightly different ways. In the first, we asked the public to choose between the three leaders on a number of criteria, both in our national polls and in those in the key marginal seats. But, as a second test, we also read the public a number of different descriptions and asked to them to say whether they felt each description fitted each leader or not, with no limits on how many leaders they could pick for each description. All the descriptions were chosen as being attributes that we have found in the past are viewed as important by voters in making their choice. Table 19 shows the findings of the two surveys, both conducted in mid-campaign – the first was carried out over the weekend after the first of the three leaders' debates, the other the day after the second debate.

What comes across clearly from both surveys is how well Brown was rated by the public on attributes that might be broadly described as relating to 'competence'. In the comparative survey, he was slightly ahead of Cameron at understanding domestic problems and well ahead on understanding international ones and on understanding the fine details of policy.

Both surveys gave Brown a clear lead on being 'good in a crisis'; with the yes/no formulation, almost half the voting public saw this as a description that applied to him. The supposition that Brown might have entirely squandered the good impression he had made in his early handling of the banking crisis by his subsequent failure to produce any solid good news from the situation proved to be mistaken. This was only slightly weakened by his being placed third on having sound judgment, said by 40% to apply to Brown but by 47% to fit Cameron and Clegg – the deficit was a narrow one and 40% a respectable score. In a separate follow-up question, in which Clegg's name was not included, Brown beat Cameron as 'the best person to lead the country out of the current economic crisis' by 44% to 41%.

Brown was also rated reasonably well in terms of the more cynical assumptions about politicians. Though Cameron scored a little better than him, and Clegg much better, on being 'more honest than most politicians', Cameron's lead was slim, and of the two it was Cameron who was felt most likely to 'promise anything to win votes'. On trustworthiness (Table 20), Clegg was again well ahead of Brown and Cameron. Cameron had a slight lead over Brown, but both were significantly more likely to be seen as 'not trustworthy' than they had been in October 2007; however, given the extent to which the overall image of politicians' integrity had been dented by the expenses scandal and other incidents in the intervening period, that is probably not surprising.

Table 20: Perceived trustworthiness of the leaders, 2007 and 2010

Q. In general, would you describe each of the following politicians as trustworthy or not?

	8-10 June 2007 %	8-9 August 2007 %	10 October 2007 %	18-19 April 2010 %
Gordon Brown				
Trustworthy	37	54	48	41
Not trustworthy	49	37	43	55
Don't know	14	9	9	3
David Cameron				
Trustworthy	34	36	44	43
Not trustworthy	46	50	40	51
Don't know	21	14	16	5
Sir Menzies Campbell				
Trustworthy	34	41	45	
Not trustworthy	33	34	29	
Don't know	33	25	25	
Nick Clegg				
Trustworthy				66
Not trustworthy				24
Don't know				10

Source: Ipsos MORI
Base: c. 1,000 -1,250 GB residents aged 18+ in each survey

Brown's greatest weakness as revealed by the image questions was that he was seen as the most out of touch with ordinary people, by a narrow margin over Cameron in the comparative test and slightly more convincingly under the yes/no format. But it was Clegg rather than Cameron who was least seen as out of touch, and the accusation is a familiar one against any unpopular politician, even if it seems somewhat incredible that any Labour leader could be seen as less in touch with 'ordinary people' than an Old Etonian millionaire.

Clearly, then, the least that can be said for Brown is that he had strengths as well as weaknesses in the way the public perceived him. Avoiding double counting of the attributes tested in both surveys, of the eleven leader image attributes tested Gordon Brown was ahead of David Cameron on seven (though one of these was the comparatively unimportant factor of inexperience).

But we can go a little further by making some historical comparisons to put Brown's image into context. After the election dust had settled, in the third week of May, we wrapped up our election polling programme with a more detailed view of the public's perceptions of the leaders and parties, using the full list of leader image and party image measurements that we have employed at previous elections. (The party image results are discussed below, pages 89-94). In these surveys we show respondents a list of possible descriptions of politicians, and ask them to pick as many or as few as they feel fit each of the three party leaders. The descriptions were chosen a number of years ago, following extensive work in focus groups to identify the characteristics that voters found most important in judging the leaders, and have proved their worth many times since. For both parties and leaders, there are nine positive and five negative descriptions; but there is no particular magic to that ratio, it merely represents the way that voters found most comfortable in expressing each characteristic or issue.

Table 21: Leader image, May 2010

Q. Here is a list of things both favourable and unfavourable that have been said about various politicians. I would like you to pick out all those statements that you feel fit [Mr Brown/Cameron/Clegg].

Attributes	Brown %	Cameron %	Clegg %
A capable leader	22	28	15
Good in a crisis	21	9	4
Understands world problems	28	17	12
Has sound judgement	12	13	10
More honest than most politicians	15	14	18
Down-to-earth	14	12	14
Understands the problems facing Britain	30	33	19
Patriotic	20	22	13
Has got a lot of personality	3	24	19
Average positive	*18.3*	*19.1*	*13.8*
Tends to talk down to people	22	12	4
Rather narrow minded	16	6	5
Too inflexible	21	5	5
Rather inexperienced	3	22	39
Out of touch with ordinary people	28	21	8
Average negative	*18.0*	*13.2*	*12.2*
No opinion	15	21	30
Net index (positive minus negative)	*+0.3*	*+5.9*	*+1.6*

Source: Ipsos MORI
Base: 975 GB residents aged 18+, 13-18 May 2010

Table 21 shows the number applying each description to each candidate for the premiership; to derive an overall summary figure we have separated the positive descriptions from the negative and calculated an average score for each, but the list shown to respondents was not divided in this way.

One fact which immediately jumps out from the table is how well Gordon Brown scores given that he had just lost the election, confirming the pre-election findings (with separate samples of the public, of course).[41] Overall, Brown averaged 18.3% on the positive attributes and 18.0% on the negative ones, for a positive net index, albeit of only +0.3. David Cameron's net score was +5.9, having scored barely higher than Brown on the positive descriptions but with many fewer people applying the negative ones.

We can go a step further by using a technique that reduces the comparative images of the leaders to graphical form. A statistical technique, correspondence analysis, allows us to reduce this complex data set to an easily comprehensible and accessible visual format, a 'perceptual map'.[42] Conceptually, a perceptual map is a diagram of 'image space' based on differences between perceptions of, in this case, the party leaders. It produces a picture of relative image – how the leaders are viewed by comparison with each other, and to which leader particular attributes are most strongly seen as applying or not applying. Figure 12 shows the perceptual map of leader image, arising from the matrix of data in Table 21. Ellipses have been added round each of the leaders to aid visual comparison. Broadly speaking, the map can be read on the basis that the

---

[41] It should be noted that, for comparability with previous years, this survey was conducted face to face with respondents shown a list of descriptions, while the pre-election surveys involved reading out the list of descriptions over the telephone. The face-to-face method normally produces lower proportions of respondents picking each description, positive or negative, and the two should not be compared directly as indicating any change in opinions between the times of the two surveys.

[42] We discuss perceptual maps and correspondence analysis in more detail in the previous volumes in this series (e.g. Robert Worcester, Roger Mortimore and Paul Baines, *Explaining Labour's Landslip* (London: Politico's Publishing, 2005), pp 34-6), and in Robert Worcester and Roger Mortimore, 'Political Triangulation: Measuring and Reporting the Key Aspects of Party and Leader Standing Before and During Elections', *Journal of Political Marketing*, Volume 4 (2005), 45-72. For an explanation of the statistical theories underlying correspondence analysis and the technicalities of how to carry it out and interpret the results, see Joseph F Hair Jr, Ralph E Anderson, Ronald L Tatham and William C Black, *Multivariate Data Analysis with Readings,* 4th edition (Englewood Cliffs, NJ: Prentice-Hall, 1995), p 516-27 and Brian S Everitt and Graham Dunn, *Applied Multivariate Data Analysis*, 2nd edition (London: Arnold, 2001), pp 74-91.

nearer an attribute is plotted to a leader, the more strongly it is seen as applying to him (relative to the others).[43]

Figure 12: Leader image, May 2010

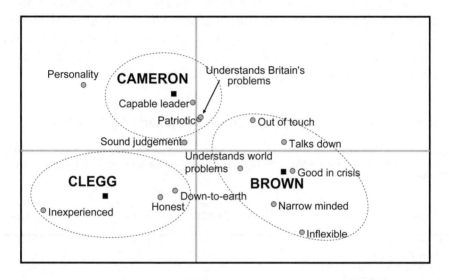

Base: 975 GB residents aged 18+, 13-18 May 2010
Source: Ipsos MORI Public Affairs Monitor

The perceptual map perhaps makes a little clearer why an apparently strong defensive hand still left Gordon Brown in a losing position. Four of the six descriptions that seemed most distinctive of Brown were negative ones, outweighing the otherwise powerful advantages as being thought to be best in a crisis and (less distinctively) understanding world problems. The descriptions that define the clearest distinctions between the leaders (those furthest from the centre) show Brown as narrow-minded and inflexible and Clegg as inexperienced. Clegg's inexperience went without

---

[43] Strictly, this is a simplification. To read the perceptual map precisely, a line should be drawn from the attribute's position through the origin, and a perpendicular dropped to that line from the position of each of the three leaders: the attribute applies more strongly the nearer the intersection of that perpendicular with the original line is to the attribute itself. But, in practice, simple proximity tends to provide broadly the same interpretation, and does so in this example.

saying, and might even have been an asset in the 2010 context. But a narrow-minded, inflexible leader is likely to be an unpopular one.

Nevertheless, we must emphasise that Brown's standing was not impossibly poor. At both the last two general elections, using exactly the same questions, the beaten Conservative leaders had substantially negative net indices, William Hague scoring −13.2 in 2001 and Michael Howard −7.1 in 2005. Gordon Brown, then, was much better regarded than either of them. But, even more surprisingly, Tony Blair also had (just) negative scores at both those elections, −0.4 in 2001 and −0.5 in 2005.

Table 22: Leader image, Gordon Brown compared with Tony Blair

Q. Here is a list of things both favourable and unfavourable that have been said about various politicians. I would like you to pick out all those statements that you feel fit [Mr Brown/Blair].

Attributes	Blair April 2001 %	Brown May 2010 %	Brown advantage
A capable leader	33	22	−11
Good in a crisis	15	21	+6
Understands world problems	22	28	+6
Has sound judgement	13	12	−1
More honest than most politicians	17	15	−2
Down-to-earth	18	14	−4
Understands the problems facing Britain	25	30	+5
Patriotic	15	20	+5
Has got a lot of personality	24	3	−21
Average positive	*20.2*	*18.3*	*−1.9*
Tends to talk down to people	25	22	+3
Rather narrow minded	15	16	−1
Too inflexible	16	21	−5
Rather inexperienced	11	3	+8
Out of touch with ordinary people	36	28	+8
Average negative	*20.6*	*18.0*	*+2.6*
Net index (positive minus negative)	*−0.4*	*+0.3*	*+0.7*

Source: Ipsos MORI
Base: c. 1,000 GB residents aged 18+ in each survey

Table 22 makes a direct comparison of Brown's ratings with those of Tony Blair a few weeks before the 2001 election. (Blair's 2005 ratings are not too dissimilar, but the comparison with 2001 is preferred to avoid any contamination of the figures by opposition to the war in Iraq: here we see the public's view of Labour's most successful election leader in his prime, just before being re-elected with a second landslide majority.) As would be expected, Blair far outshines Brown on 'has got a lot of personality' and also as a 'capable leader', but on other positive descriptions there is much less difference, with Brown having the clear advantage as being 'good in a crisis' and understanding both 'world problems' and the 'problems facing Britain'. Similarly, Brown was much less seen than Blair as being 'out of touch with ordinary people'. Nor did many feel Brown was inexperienced, as some still felt of Blair even after four years in Downing Street. (By 2005, Blair had rid himself of the inexperience tag but also, among other changes, had lost much of the perception that he was 'more honest than most politicians'.)

These findings put into real doubt the assumption, which seems to be widely held in both media and political circles, that Gordon Brown was Labour's biggest handicap in the election. Certainly, he was not widely liked, and his very low score on 'has a lot of personality' reflects an uncharismatic leader who was probably not well qualified to deal with and draw any advantage from the leaders' debates. But he certainly gives the impression of being in most respects a leader that the voters would have been prepared to tolerate if the other factors were in place. In the comparisons that should have mattered, those with David Cameron, he was still after the election well ahead on being good in a crisis, understanding world problems and, of course, on not having Cameron's inexperience. His greatest faults, that he was seen as talking down to people and being narrow-minded and inflexible, were ones that Blair had survived against weaker opponents. Only the lack of personality singled him out, but with the novelty of the debates dominating the election it was perhaps the most dangerous dimension in which to be weak.

How the public saw Labour under Brown

It is also worth considering how the Labour's Party image had changed between 2005 and 2010, using a party image measure similar to the leader image one. Table 23 provides an insight into the public's changing perceptions of the Labour Party. Naturally, there is a risk that the interpretation of these is to some extent ambiguous as it relates to Gordon Brown – however much we think of a party's image as distinct from that of its leader, the one cannot be entirely separated from the other.

But, in fact, we find that many of these ambiguities resolve themselves when we look at the figures. Just as Brown's image score was better than that of Blair in 2005, so we find that the Labour Party was less unpopular at the end of this election that they lost than they had been in 2005 when they won. (Of course, it must be borne in mind that the 2010 survey was post-election, but given that Brown's own image scores were respectable the improvement cannot simply be attributed to the knowledge that he would soon step down.) But much the biggest changes in the public's perceptions between 2005 and 2010 were on the two items related to the leadership – there was a collapse in the number feeling Labour had a good team of leaders (from 23% to 7%), but also a corresponding fall in those feeling it was 'too dominated by its leader' (from 37% to 18%), showing both a positive and negative aspect of Blair's replacement by Brown.

Table 23: Party image – the Labour Party, 1997-2010

Q. Read through the list slowly keeping the Labour Party in mind. Every time you come to a statement that fits your ideas or impressions of the Labour Party just tell me the letter next to it. You may pick as many or as few as you like. You don't have to be certain, just pick the letters next to the statements you feel fit the Labour Party.

	April 1997 %	May 2001 %	April 2005 %	May 2010 %	Change 2005-10 %
Concerned about the people in real need in Britain	36	21	20	21	+1
Has a good team of leaders	25	25	23	7	−16
Has sensible policies	27	27	18	15	−3
Keeps its promises	9	9	6	5	−1
Looks after the interests of people like us	30	21	16	15	−1
Moderate	15	20	16	14	−2
Professional in its approach	21	19	17	11	−6
Represents all classes	31	24	23	18	−5
Understands the problems facing Britain	37	28	26	28	+2
Average positive	*25.7*	*21.6*	*18.3*	*14.9*	*−3.4*
Divided	12	11	22	25	+3
Extreme	5	3	6	4	−2
Out of touch with ordinary people	7	24	27	24	−3
Too dominated by its leader	15	26	37	18	−19
Will promise anything to win votes	31	35	40	30	−10
Average negative	*14.0*	*19.8*	*26.4*	*20.2*	*−6.2*
Net index (positive minus negative)	*+11.7*	*+1.8*	*−8.1*	*−5.3*	*+2.8*

Source: Ipsos MORI
Base: c. 1,000 GB residents aged 18+ in each survey

Only one other aspect of Labour's image was significantly changed: the party was less likely to be seen as being prepared to promise anything to win votes, though this was still the single most widely applied description in the entire list. Arguably this was a stereotypical criticism of 'New Labour' and might indicate that post-Blair some of its negative image remained; but perhaps more likely, given the high numbers picking the same attribute to describe the Conservatives and Liberal Democrats as well, it is probably part of a wider cynicism about the nature of all politicians. At any rate, it seems that this significant lessening of the cynicism around Labour's sincerity was the sole real change in the way the public viewed Labour beyond their reaction to the difference in the leaders.

Table 24: Party image, May 2010

Q. Read through the list slowly keeping the ... Party in mind. Every time you come to a statement that fits your ideas or impressions of the ...Party just tell me the letter next to it. You may pick as many or as few as you like. You don't have to be certain, just pick the letters next to the statements you feel fit the ... Party.

Attributes	Labour %	Conservative %	Liberal Democrat %
Understands the problems facing Britain	28	32	22
Concerned about the people in real need in Britain	21	16	22
Has sensible policies	15	20	20
Represents all classes	18	10	22
Moderate	14	13	23
Professional in its approach	11	24	12
Looks after the interests of people like us	15	13	13
Has a good team of leaders	7	16	8
Keeps its promises	5	6	5
Average positive	*14.9*	*16.7*	*16.3*
Will promise anything to win votes	30	29	21
Out of touch with ordinary people	24	25	7
Too dominated by its leader	18	10	7
Extreme	4	7	3
Divided	25	13	15
Average negative	*20.2*	*16.8*	*10.6*
Net index (positive minus negative)	*−5.3*	*−0.1*	*+5.7*
No opinion	14	17	24

Source: Ipsos MORI Public Affairs Monitor
Base: 975 GB residents aged 18+, 13-18 May 2010

Of course, a party's image does not exist in isolation: to understand how Labour was really viewed we also need to see how the public's feelings about the other major parties compared. Viewed simply in terms of the summary index, while Labour were viewed on the whole negatively (with a score of −5.3), the Liberal Democrats had a similarly sized positive score (+5.7), and the Tories broke almost exactly even.

As with leader image (above, on page 87), we can understand party image more clearly by reducing the data to a 'perceptual map'. Figure 13 shows the perceptual map of party image, arising from the matrix of data in Table 24. (The ellipses have been added to aid visual comparison, and are not part of the statistical output). Again, broadly speaking, the map can be read on the basis that the nearer an attribute is plotted to a party, the more strongly it is seen as applying to them (relative to the others: those descriptions that are much nearer to one party than another are the particularly distinctive parts of a party's image, while those between two parties may be shared by both. Those descriptions mapped near the origin (the centre of the graph where the axes cross) are the weakest discriminators, least effective at distinguishing between the parties, while those mapped furthest out represent the most obvious or apparent differences.

Figure 13: Party image, May 2010 – perceptual map

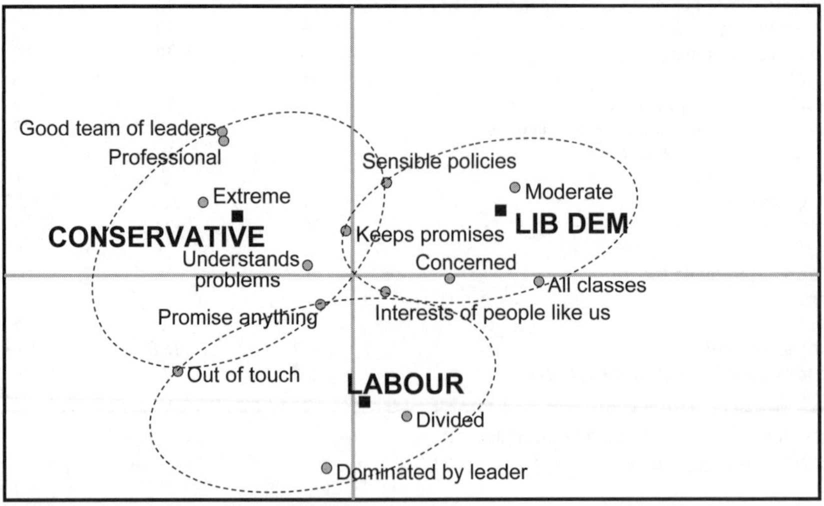

Base: 975 GB residents aged 18+, 13-18 May 2010
Source: Ipsos MORI Public Affairs Monitor

Neither Labour nor the Liberal Democrats are seen as embodying two key characteristics that the voting public applies to the Tories – being professional and having a good team of leaders. Nor, however, are either Labour or the LibDems seen as extreme, another description the public finds most appositely applied to the Conservatives. (This demonstrates also how the correspondence analysis technique picks up even the very rarely applied descriptions. Only 7% of the public in 2010 said they thought that the Conservatives were extreme, but that was nevertheless significantly more than the 4% who said that of Labour or the 3% who thought it of the LibDems. None of the parties was widely viewed as extreme, but if the public *had* to name an extreme party, the cap fitted the Conservatives the best.) But the analysis also shows that despite the Tories outgunning Labour in being seen as professional they retained the air of elitism (only the Liberal Democrats were perceived as representing all classes) – given the backgrounds of the leader, his new Chancellor of the Exchequer and for that matter the best-known Tory outside the government, Boris Johnson, perhaps the public had a point.

Probably the real weakness in Labour's image was being seen as being divided: as we have argued for several decades, 'divided parties don't win elections', and although the number of people thinking this was a fair description of Labour was not significantly higher in 2010 than in 2005, the number seeing the Conservatives as divided was barely half what it had been five years before. For the first time in a generation the Conservatives rather than Labour were able to appear the more united party, and that surely had an impact on people's evaluation of their fitness for office – and, again, who can blame the public for believing Labour were divided (even if the division was more about who the leader should be rather than a fundamental policy argument).

The clearest impression of Labour was as 'too dominated by its leader', but this could be explained by a certain proportion of the public simply disliking Gordon Brown, rather than being about the balance of power within the party as such – and in any case, many fewer people felt Brown was too dominating a leader than had felt the same about Blair five years earlier.

It is clear that the difference between defeat and survival for Labour in 2010 was not solely to be found in its new failures since 2005. Whatever the public's view of the government's record in office, their perception of

93

the party as a whole was not entirely a negative one and certainly not incompatible with election victory, as 2005 showed. But 2005 was victory by default, when Labour's poor image score was nevertheless higher than the Tories' dreadful one.

And, certainly, even if Gordon Brown was the wrong choice as leader in 2007, there was no salvation to be had by staging a last-minute leadership coup. This should be evident from the comparison of all the various ratings of party and leader in 2005 and 2010 which, as we have seen, show Brown performing worse than Blair in few respects except actual voting support. But there is further evidence from the direct verdict of the voting public themselves. Just after the start of the election campaign, YouGov asked[44] whether people felt they would have been more or less likely to vote Labour if Brown had stepped down before the election was called (Table 25).

Table 25: If Brown had stepped down

Q. Would you be more or less likely to vote Labour if Gordon Brown had resigned as prime minister and handed over to a new Labour leader BEFORE the current election?

	All %	Con %	Lab %	LD %
More likely	16	19	6	21
Less likely	7	2	13	7
No difference – I would vote Labour anyway	22	1	77	8
No difference – I would NOT vote Labour anyway	43	73	0	54
Don't know	12	6	3	10

Source: YouGov/*Sunday Times*
Base: 1,431 GB residents aged 18+, 9-10 April 2010

The majority said it would have made no difference; and in such polls it is worthless simply to take at face value the net score of those who say they would be more or less likely to vote in a particular way because this gives no reliable indication *how much* more or less likely they would be – how many would actually do one thing in one situation and another in the other? But in this case we can legitimately note that of those who were intending to vote Labour, twice as many said it would have made them *less*

---

[44] http://today.yougov.co.uk/sites/today.yougov.co.uk/files/YG-Archives-Pol-STResults-100410.pdf, accessed 12 January 2011.

likely rather than more likely to support the party. If we can take these answers literally, Labour under a fresh-faced new leader might have been at risk of losing as many votes from their existing support as they could have hoped to pick up from the other parties.

When did Labour lose?

So, had Labour definitely already lost the coming election by the autumn of 2009? As already noted, no previous government had ever fallen so low in the voting intention ratings and recovered to win re-election. But because much of Labour's lost support had moved to the Liberal Democrats or the smaller parties than to the Conservatives, the size of the gap between the two major parties was not quite as big as Labour's support in isolation might imply. Normally, we are assiduous in telling the followers of opinion polls to *watch the share, not the lead* – it is share that the polls measure directly, the margin of error on the measurement of lead is double that on the share, and concentrating on the lead can sometimes exaggerate and sometimes underplay both the volatility of the public mood and the differences between individual polls. But in these particular circumstances the lead was the crucial factor politically, for all that the polls are not ideally placed to measure it. Lead translates directly into swing, and is much more closely related to the number of seats a party will win than is share alone; the fact that the Conservatives as well as Labour were leaking support to the third parties in 2009 offered Labour a glimmer of hope.

Certainly Labour was trailing the Tories by a daunting margin, and little in the political landscape seemed to offer them an immediate prospect of recovery. Yet, notwithstanding Bismarck's famous definition that 'politics is the art of the possible', very little in politics is literally impossible. When we talk of the impossibility a man running a three-minute mile, we are referring to a real physical barrier. But there is no physical effort involved in a politician achieving a 20% swing in public opinion – all that is involved is people changing their minds. Apparently improbable swings in public opinion do take place every now and then – one thinks, for example, of the 1993 Canadian election where the sitting Progressive Conservative government was reduced to two seats.

Of course, it is much easier to lose the public's trust than to gain it, and many of these sudden turnarounds in opinion therefore consist of plummeting support for a government after some disastrous incident or, less frequently, of sudden alienation from an opposition that previously looked electable. But this is not the only way that such swings can occur. Two of the biggest recorded swings in British public opinion involved MORI's first political client, the Harold Wilson Labour government, and in both cases were a swing in the government's favour. In December 1968, after more than four years in office, Labour trailed the Conservatives on voting intention by 25½ percentage points. In July the following year, only eleven months before the eventual election, the lead was still 23½ points, yet Wilson was able to call the election in May having moved back into a 7½ point lead, a national swing of 15.5% achieved in well under a year. Because Wilson lost that election after all, the scale of his recovery has often been forgotten. It was a recovery achieved more by increasing popularity of the government than falling faith in the opposition (between July 1969 and June 1970, Wilson's Prime Ministerial satisfaction rating rose from 30% to 51% – in fact a bigger swing than the swing in voting intention – while satisfaction with Edward Heath as Conservative leader over the same period fell, but not quite so sharply and by less than the voting intention swing, from 40% to 28%).[45]

But Wilson's government, albeit assisted by the opposition, achieved an even more dramatic turnaround in public opinion during the run-up to the referendum in 1975: a 22% swing in favour of the Common Market (as it then was) in just six months, relying on the public's confidence in the government and its assurances that the renegotiated terms of membership represented a good deal for Britain.

Viewed in these terms, Gordon Brown's task looked improbable but perhaps not impossible, and not quite unprecedented – especially as it was likely that Labour could afford to trail narrowly in voters and still expect to remain in office. At least three individual polls in 2009 put Labour 22 points behind the Tories, though the monthly averages of all the polls never put the gap higher than 16. As far as we have been able to trace, the worst single poll finding from which any British Prime Minister has

---

[45] All these figures are from Gallup's polls, recorded in Anthony King and Robert Wybrow, *British Political Opinion 1937-2000 – The Gallup Polls* (London: Politicos Publishing 2001).

recovered to win a further term in office since polling began was an 18½-point deficit, the margin by which Hugh Gaitskell's Labour led Harold Macmillan's Conservatives in Gallup's monthly poll of September 1957.[46] More impressively, the Conservative government was 28 points behind in the March 1990 Harris poll, yet won a general election in April 1992 – but that involved a change of Prime Minister, Margaret Thatcher's replacement by John Major, in the interim.[47]

But there is always a reason for such dramatic shifts in opinion. The problem for Gordon Brown was that in May 2010, unlike Harold Macmillan in 1959, he couldn't tell the voters they had never had it so good. If only Brown had been able to achieve a miraculous economic recovery, satisfying the voters on the issues they considered most important and demonstrating his own and his government's competence, he might well have hoped for re-election. Failing that, failing a successful replacement of Brown by another leader, and failing some quite spectacular gaffe by the opposition that demolished their own claim to electability, it is probably true that Labour really was already doomed by the autumn of 2009.

---

[46] Anthony King and Robert Wybrow, *British Political Opinion 1937-2000 – The Gallup Polls* (London: Politicos Publishing 2001), p 5. According to MORI's polls, Margaret Thatcher trailed Labour by 16 points in October 1980 and the newly-minted Alliance by 17 points in November 1981, but never by quite as much as Gaitskell's lead over Macmillan. However, the swing in her favour by the time of the 1983 election, from a 16-point Labour lead to a 16-point Conservative one, was even bigger than that which Macmillan managed.

[47] The Harris finding does not seem to have been a rogue poll – ICM put the lead around the same time as 27 points and MORI as 24. Nevertheless, the comparison with the eventual election result is complicated by the polls' over-estimation of Labour's strength at the 1992 election, having been accurate in their measurements in 1987. It is impossible to tell at which point during the Parliament the polling figures and real voting intentions began to diverge – if the exaggeration of Labour's lead was as big this early as it was in the final election polls, then it could be argued that the Tories in reality only recovered from a significantly smaller deficit.

2. How the Conservatives failed to win it

The mountain the Tories had to climb

With a consistent lead over Labour of around 15 points in the polls for most of 2009, the Conservatives looked to be sitting pretty, and may have felt they only needed to avoid appalling gaffes to see a landslide fall into their laps. But it never looked that simple to cautious observers. Just as Gordon Brown in 2007 could not assume that he could translate his honeymoon bounce into real votes if he called an election, so the Tories needed to be aware that landslide leads in mid-term polls can melt away when voters have the imminent prospect of a real election to concentrate their minds.

'Mid-term blues' are an almost universal affliction of governments everywhere. Sometimes they never fully recover, sometimes they do, but governments almost never perform as badly at the general election as their mid-term fortunes might suggest – and this applies just as much to the 'real votes in real ballot boxes' of which poll-sceptics sometimes speak as it does to opinion poll answers. Government performance in by-elections and at second order elections – European, local or devolved – is almost invariably much worse than at the subsequent general election.

So it was always our guess (frequently expressed in public) that the Labour Party would do better at the general election than their 2009 average, which had the party even lower than in 1983 when with the least popular party leader, unpopular policies, and a shambles of a campaign (Bob knows, he was in the centre of it, doing the Labour Party's private polling), they still got 28.5%. Gordon Brown was not so unpopular as was Michael Foot, their policies were better attuned to the public's priorities, and (as it emerged at the start of 2010) their campaign strategy was to be led by the 'Prince of Darkness,' Peter Mandelson (who apparently added campaign manager to his long list of titles and duties).

The reason all this mattered was that the apparently-commanding 15-point Conservative lead in share of the vote was much less impressive when viewed in the context of the operation of the electoral system. For some years, the arbitrary way in which the British first-past-the-post electoral system has translated votes into seats has been tilted to Labour's advantage: for a given share of the vote, Labour would expect to win more seats than the Conservatives, and the Conservatives needed a much bigger lead in votes than Labour did to secure a House of Commons majority.[48] On the assumption of a simple national uniform swing – in other words, if everybody across the country had moved towards the Conservatives since the last election at exactly the same rate – the Conservatives needed a clear lead of 11% of the vote over Labour to expect a wafer-thin overall majority. So a 15-point lead left the Tories very little scope for slippage (unless they could find some way to falsify the uniform swing assumption and reduce the bias, to which they were giving close attention with Lord Ashcroft's help).

The task facing the Conservatives, then, was a considerable one. Starting from 2005, off the back of three convincing general election defeats, they needed to achieve a 7 per cent swing in votes, a feat surpassed in modern history only by Tony Blair in 1997 (and before him, after a ten-year Parliament and the disruption of a world war, by Clement Attlee in 1945).

With a popular new leader and a vigorous 'decontamination of the brand', they had by 2009 succeeded in convincing the majority of voters that they were electable and of getting the swing as registered in the polls up to 9 percent on average. But was this enough? Could they find some counter to the laws of political gravity to prevent there being sufficient swing back to Labour to deny them their outright majority? As it transpired, it was not, and they could not.

The political task

We can divide the task facing the Conservatives in 2005 into two parts, the political and the electoral. Politically, they had to find a leader towards whom the voters could warm, to transform the image of the party so that

---

[48] The Liberal Democrats are much more disadvantaged still, because their votes are the most evenly spread – at one point during the election campaign, when it seemed just conceivable that they might end up with more votes than either of the other two parties, we calculated that this would still have left them a bad third in terms of seats.

it was seen as a credible alternative by enough of the voters to be electable, and to put together a package of proposed policies for government which could take them over the final hurdle. Ideally, they also needed to solve each of these problems in a way that made it possible to govern well if elected, so that they had some chance of surviving in office more than a single term. Electorally, they had to translate these improvements into votes, and in such a way that it secured them enough parliamentary seats to win the election.

Choosing the right leader

Given the importance within the Conservative Party of the leader, who still has a much greater influence over the party's policy direction and management than his counterparts in the other major parties, the choice of leader was the first and most critical of the questions to be solved.

Party leadership candidates must be able to appeal to at least two different constituencies of voters to reach Downing Street: they must win the leadership by appealing to their own party, but must then also be able to convince the electorate at large that they are a better choice as Prime Minister than the other parties' leaders. The problem arises in that these two constituencies usually want different things: what appeals to a party's core voters, who make up the paid-up rank-and-file membership, is often very different from what will appeal to the floating voters who decide a general election. The stances and statements that were successful in differentiating the candidate from other rivals of the same party and convincing their supporters that they will best represent their partisan hopes and fears may prove to be liabilities once the general election has to be fought. There is usually a tendency to be more radical in issue stances in these leadership campaigns, to differentiate oneself from the other candidates. Of course, the party members are sometimes responsible enough to consider what type of leader will appeal to the wider electorate rather than concentrating purely on their own preferences, especially after a long period out of power when compromising on a less-than-ideal but electable leader may seem more attractive. But there are no guarantees, and of course they may judge the public mood incorrectly in any case.

The campaigning medium may well also be different. The party membership is essentially a narrowcast audience, likely to be paying attention to the contest, and can be reached by direct mail and speech-making. By contrast, to reach the millions of potential voters at a general election requires a broadcast appeal, using varied means such as appearing on popular radio and television programmes, giving interviews and writing articles for newspapers and other political PR, debates, party election broadcasts and billboard advertising as well as through direct marketing tools to hit targeted voters in key constituencies. (Many more members of the public are reached by printed leaflets through the letterbox than by other campaigning medium, but these are still locally produced and in general neither party headquarters nor the leader has much control over their contents. It is by no means unknown for discontented local candidates to conspicuously avoid any mention of their party leader in their literature, or even to make a point of being photographed with other senior party figures to emphasise that they are distancing themselves from the leadership.) A candidate strong at campaigning in one medium may prove to be so weak in the other as to be a liability.

Of course, this problem is not unique to Britain. In the United States, for example, a presidential candidate first has to win the party's nomination by appealing to its registered supporters in primary elections or caucuses, but must then turn his or her attention to appealing to the wider electorate.[49] The candidate will then often choose a vice-Presidential candidate with the specific intention of broadening their ticket's appeal rather than with regard to their suitability to be vice-President. (Not that this is necessarily successful, as John McCain demonstrated by his choice of Sarah Palin as running mate in 2008).

For the British Conservative party under its current election rules, the problem is to satisfy not two but three separate constituencies. First, Conservative MPs vote in successive ballots to reduce the field of candidates to two. Then the national membership of the party, roughly a

---

[49] For a fuller consideration of how British and American political campaigning mechanisms operate and their differences, see Paul Baines, 'Marketing and Political Campaigning in the US and the UK: What Can the UK Political Parties Learn for the Development of a Campaign Management Process Model?', Unpublished PhD Thesis (Manchester: The University of Manchester, 2001).

quarter of a million in 2005, choose between these two in a postal vote. Only then can the victor put his or her mind to beating Labour and the Liberal Democrats.

The Conservatives had been much handicapped at the last few elections by the ideological divisions within the party and the consequences of this for its choice of leader. In the first place, they had been split between (the majority) Eurosceptics and (minority) Europhiles, a policy division of much more importance to the Conservative party rank and file than to the public at large: it has been almost solely this factor that has prevented the otherwise best-fitted candidate, Kenneth Clarke, from winning the leadership and exploiting his popularity with the public to the party's advantage. Secondly, there is a cross-cutting ideological division, which is not so much between left and right as between traditionalists and modernists, the latter tending to extend their laissez-faire philosophy to social and moral issues as well as economic ones. Before 2005, the membership had never had the chance to vote for a straightforwardly modernist candidate: in 2001, Michael Portillo was eliminated before the final stage by the votes of the Tory MPs, so that Iain Duncan Smith won the leadership by default when the members had to choose between him and the Europhile Clarke.

Michael Howard, defeated at the 2005 general election, delayed his resignation so that the party had time to reflect before making its decision and, crucially, that the leadership election would not begin until after the party's annual conference in October, where all the candidates would have a chance to speak and present their cases. Of the likely candidates only one, the perennially unsuccessful Ken Clarke, was particularly well known to the public, and he was well ahead in the public's preferences for the leadership before the party conference. An Ipsos MORI poll at the end of September[50] found 36% of the public preferring Clarke, with David Davis in second place on 13%; David Cameron was on 8% and Liam Fox on 5%. Clarke was also well ahead in being thought likely to make the most capable Prime Minister of the four, a verdict that supporters of all three of the main political parties agreed with: 46% of Tories put him first, again a three-to-one advantage over his closest rival, Davis. But, tellingly, when

---

[50] For the *Sun*. Ipsos MORI interviewed 504 adults aged 18+ by telephone from 29-30 September 2005

the public were asked how they would vote if the Tories were led by each of the four alternatives, it made virtually no difference, though Fox was very marginally the least popular. Apart from Clarke, the candidates were probably too little known for most of the public to make a considered judgment of them.

However, the youngest and least-experienced of the alternatives, David Cameron – a shadow Cabinet member for only just over a year – had powerful declared support within the Parliamentary party, and would clearly be the standard bearer of the modernists. Following a disappointing platform performance by the apparent likely winner, leading from the right, David Davis, Cameron's impressive speech at the party conference, delivered apparently without notes and demonstrating youthful vigour and charisma that were perhaps reminiscent of Tony Blair at the same stage in his career, propelled him to the head of the race.

One consequence of this was that while there were clear differences in the leadership preferences of the different voting segments Cameron was now strongly placed in all of them. Among the general public, an Ipsos MORI poll[51] on 20-25 October 2005 found a distinct difference between those that would vote Conservative if there were a general election tomorrow (some of whom would be Conservative Party members) and those who would not (who represent voters the Conservatives would like to win over to gain power). Kenneth Clarke was in close contention among non-Conservatives (19% picked him as the best person for the leader's job), just behind David Cameron (22%), but well ahead of David Davis (8%). Among Conservative voters, the picture was different, with 45% selecting Cameron to 18% selecting Clarke, though Davis again was in third position with 8%.

By the time this survey went into field, Ken Clarke had already fallen foul of his primary electorate: in the first ballot of Tory MPs on 18 October 2005, he won only 38 votes to David Davis' 62, David Cameron's 56 and Liam Fox's 42, and he was therefore summarily eliminated from the contest. Meanwhile, in a poll of Conservative party members by YouGov, conducted on 18-19 October, almost three in five (59%) wanted Cameron

---

[51] Ipsos MORI Political Monitor survey, published in the *Observer*. Ipsos MORI interviewed 508 GB residents aged 18+ by telephone on 20-25 October 2005.

to be leader, but more Tory members said they would vote for Liam Fox (18%) than David Davis (15%) as leader, if given the chance. However, they were not given the opportunity, as the second ballot of MPs narrowed the choice to Cameron and Davis – with Cameron now well ahead but Davis only six votes clear of Fox.

In this, they reflected the public's preferences, as our 'trial heats' poll now showed significant differences in voting preferences depending on who was the Conservative leader: on 19 October, we found[52] the Tories received a 36% vote share on the supposition that Cameron was leader, only three points behind Labour, whereas they would be on 33% if led by Davis and 31% if by Fox. The national membership came to the same conclusion, and Cameron won a little over two-thirds of the vote in the postal ballot. On 6 December 2005, he was declared leader.

The existing image problem

Cameron seems to have made a deliberate strategic decision to concentrate first on tackling his party's existing image problem, before developing a programme of serious policy commitments to carry into the general election.

We can gain a first impression of the Conservative Party's image problems by considering the standard measures of party image that MORI has been using at and between elections since the early 1980s. As already explained, the public are shown a list of 14 descriptions and asked which, if any, they feel fit their impressions of the Conservative Party; we then repeat the exercise for Labour and the Liberal Democrats. Usually we tend to concentrate on comparing the parties with each other, noting the similarities and differences between them and what this tells us about their strengths and weaknesses (as we have done above, in Table 24, in discussing the Labour Party). But to understand the situation in which David Cameron found himself when he took over the leadership in 2005 it is instructive just to consider the image of the Conservatives themselves, and how this has changed over the years.

---

[52] Poll for the *Sun*. Ipsos MORI interviewed 508 GB residents aged 18+ by telephone on 19 October 2005.

Table 26: Party image – the Conservative Party, 1987-2005

Q. Read through the list slowly keeping the Conservative Party in mind. Every time you come to a statement that fits your ideas or impressions of the Conservative Party just tell me the letter next to it. You may pick as many or as few as you like. You don't have to be certain, just pick the letters next to the statements you feel fit the Conservative Party.

	June 1987 %	March 1992 %	April 1997 %	May 2001 %	April 2005 %
Concerned about the people in real need in Britain	20	18	8	9	14
Has a good team of leaders	43	35	10	7	8
Has sensible policies	37	31	14	15	17
Keeps its promises	28	20	5	5	3
Looks after the interests of people like us	25	21	9	11	11
Moderate	15	19	11	12	12
Professional in its approach	49	42	13	13	15
Represents all classes	16	20	10	8	9
Understands the problems facing Britain	40	38	20	18	22
Average positive	*30.3*	*27.1*	*11.1*	*10.9*	*12.3*
Divided	7	14	44	30	23
Extreme	15	16	10	12	14
Out of touch with ordinary people	51	51	50	36	32
Too dominated by its leader	56	14	10	13	16
Will promise anything to win votes	40	41	40	46	45
Average negative	*33.8*	*27.2*	*30.8*	*27.4*	*26.0*
Net index (positive minus negative)	*–3.5*	*–0.1*	*–19.7*	*–16.5*	*–13.7*

Source: Ipsos MORI
Base: c. 1,000-2,000 GB residents aged 18+ in each survey

Table 26 shows the public's view of the Tories on the eve of each of the five general elections up to 2005. In 1987 and 1992 they won, in 1997 and 2001 they were beaten easily, and in 2005 they lost more narrowly.

We should begin with the situation as it was in 2005. Well over twice as many of the public on average picked the negative descriptions of the party as picked the positive ones, and on only one positive description ('understands the problems facing Britain') could even one in five potential voters be persuaded that it was an accurate characterisation of the Tories. By contrast, not far short of half, 45%, felt the Tories would 'promise anything to win votes', and 32% felt they were 'out of touch with ordinary people'. These perceptions may be inaccurate or unfair, of course, but it is what the voters themselves believed. This is plainly not the picture of a party that could expect to win a general election.

Furthermore, this image had hardly changed at all since William Hague's landslide defeat in 2001 or even since John Major's, at the head of an incumbent government, in 1997. Throughout, the begrudging admission of one in five that the Tories understood the problems facing Britain was the best that could be said for them. They had made up a small amount of ground in increasing the numbers who felt they were concerned about the people in real need, and more significantly had halved the number who felt they were a divided party and also reduced the number thinking they were out of touch, but the improvement was only the slight softening of an image that still doomed them to certain defeat whenever they went to the polls.

If we compare the situation at these three elections with the party's image in its previous two victories, the scale of the difference is clear. The net score, instead of being deep in negative territory, is at or near parity. But it is possibly an important lesson that almost all of this difference came not from their scores on the negative attributes being lower, but their positive scores being higher. The Conservatives may have been no less disliked, with no fewer obvious weaknesses, under Thatcher or under Major in 1992 than in their later defeats – many more of the public, for example, felt the Tories up to 1997 were out of touch than used that description of the party under either Hague or Howard. But they were able to offset these disadvantages with clear perceived strengths which formed positive reasons to re-elect them. Coupled with the public's scepticism about Labour under Neil Kinnock at both of these elections, it was enough to turn the scale.

What could Cameron hope to achieve, then, in 'detoxifying' the party's image? It would be useful if he could lay the ghost of being a divided party without recreating the impression of being too dominated by its leader, as it was under Thatcher. It would be helpful also to reduce still further the numbers who considered them out of touch with ordinary people (not easy, given that the party had just elected an Old Etonian millionaire as its leader!). While the cynical assumption that the party would promise anything to win votes must be a damaging one, it would probably be far harder to shift, especially for a leader from the moderate wing of his party needing to tread cautiously before espousing any principles that might alienate the party traditionalists; but since this perception did not stop Margaret Thatcher from winning, it was arguably a less urgent problem. The real task in recreating Thatcher's winning formula, though, was to offset the disadvantages by re-establishing the positives, in particular the image of competence that has always been at the heart of a Conservative government's self image. Cameron had to convince the voters that he and his party understood the problems facing Britain, were professional and had sensible policies. Perhaps as important, he needed to win the voters' trust, of which a belief that the party would keep its promises is one manifestation. If he could do this, given a fair wind and a failing government he might persuade the voters to give him a chance.

In fact, the sum total of these various aspects of the party's image can be drawn together with a single poll question that we also put to the public just before the elections in 2001 and 2005. Asked whether they agreed or disagreed that 'the Conservatives are ready to form the next government', only 25% of adults agreed in May 2001 and 35% in April 2005. Cameron's success or failure might be judged by how far he could raise this figure and how quickly: in December 1994, only months after Tony Blair was elected Labour, 66% had agreed that Labour was ready to form the next government.

Blair's experience also had another cautionary message for Cameron. From 66% believing Blair's party was ready to govern in 1994, the figure slipped to 55% by the eve of the election in 1997 – still ample in his case, of course, but a potentially decisive slippage had it happened from a lower peak. Cameron needed not only to repair the Tories' image of electability, but to maintain it once he had done so right up to polling day.

Offering an alternative programme for government

The third element of the Tories' political task was to develop a policy programme to offer to the electorate when the time came. A number of strategic decisions were involved here, not least of which was that of timing. Since the Tories would have no chance to implement any policies until after they had won an election, it was possible to argue on pragmatic grounds that there was little need to make policy decisions until they were needed for the manifesto. In theory this had a number of advantages: government policy could be attacked whenever convenient without the opposition having to defend their alternatives; the risk of splitting the party with decisions that were unpopular with one wing or another could be postponed until Cameron's leadership was more firmly established; and there was no danger of having the rug pulled from under them by the government adopting their most effective proposals as their own. Perhaps the strongest argument in favour of an initial 'policy-lite' approach to leadership, as it came to be described, was that Cameron considered it important to address the party's image first. In the past, policies which might otherwise have proved popular with the public had been tainted by the knowledge that it was the Conservatives that had proposed them[53], and there was a clear case for dealing with this image problem before rushing into policy commitments or ideological declarations.

On the other hand, running the opposition in a policy vacuum had its dangers. Labour were keen to portray Cameron as being 'all style and no substance', especially after Gordon Brown took over from Tony Blair (against whom the same accusation had often been levelled). Further, there was always – at least at first – the danger of the government calling a snap election that would catch the Tories with their trousers down and no manifesto in place. The absence of policy commitments, too, risked their opponents being able to portray the Tories and Cameron as what they were not, perhaps so cementing a misleading image with the public that by the time the Tory manifesto was revealed it would be too late to shift the public's preconceptions. It is possible that a government in a more secure situation than Blair's and Brown's might have been able to make damaging mischief from Cameron's delay in setting out a policy agenda, but as it turned out their own position was so precarious that they could do little. For most of the 2005-10 parliament they were too busy trying to cope with the pressures of governing – or, as often, to cope with having only realised the need for a policy in retrospect, as with the banking collapse and the MPs' expenses debacle.

So Cameron had a relatively free hand. Of course, a new party leader does not start from scratch in deciding his party's policies. A party already has an identifiable ideological orientation and a legacy of policy stances on many issues. These cannot credibly be jettisoned, nor would most leaders want to do so. But it is nevertheless possible on occasion to entirely transform the direction of a party, as Tony Blair did with Labour in 1994,

---

[53] For example, an ICM survey in January 2005 had found that while 82% of the public said they supported 'the idea that immigration should be controlled more strictly', only 65% said they supported 'Conservative policy to control immigration more strictly'.

retaining its position as the more left-wing of the two major parties but moving it firmly towards the centre, and even adopting some trademark Conservative policies.

Despite its convincing defeat in 2005, some elements of the Conservative Party's policy portfolio – or at least the public's attitudes towards the Tory stance on those issues – remained strong; more of a problem was that the issues where the Tories were strong were, for the most part, well down the public's list of election priorities. They had a convincing lead as the party with the best policies on law and order (third in salience to the public and a perennial Tory strength) and a smaller lead on taxation. More powerfully, but more sensitively, they had an overwhelming lead as the party with the best policy on asylum and immigration (but their use of this issue in the 2005 election had, arguably, backfired). Also, much further down the voters' shopping list, they were better rated than Labour on Europe, defence and Iraq. But Labour led on the two most salient issues, healthcare and education, as well as on managing the economy, important to only 35% of voters in 2005 but destined to be of far more potential significance in 2010.

Cameron's approach to the policy question was mostly slow and cautious, and combined the espousal of liberal and moderate principles which pleased the modernists (and later made possible a coalition with the Liberal Democrats) with occasional solid policy commitments rooted more in the party's traditionalist instincts. He declared his social liberalism robustly, together with a type of political libertarianism manifested in opposition to ID cards (once a Tory policy), as well as attacking government incursions on civil liberties in its campaign against terrorism. His party, too, seemed consistently at odds with the police, very much a shift of traditional positioning, although arguably this was more because the police allowed themselves to become identified with the policies of the Labour government than because Cameron had softened the usual Tory commitment to law and order. Cameron was also an uncompromising defender of the National Health Service and, although he made no explicit softening of the party's stance on immigration, nor was it a constant theme in his political rhetoric. Further, he committed his party to the fight against climate change and ambitious environmental policies, under the slogan 'Vote Blue, go Green', with a concurrent rebranding in which the party's campaigning colour was changed from deep blue to a shade bordering on turquoise, and the long-standing flaming torch symbol was replaced by an abstract representation of an oak tree as the party's logo. These symbolic changes survived when the economic crisis swept away any chance that the expensive environmental commitments would reach the election manifesto.

At the same time, Cameron threw sops to the right of the party. The Eurosceptics were mollified by the decision to leave the European People's Party (the Christian Democrat group in the European Parliament to which the Tories had previously belonged), and he maintained the aspiration that the Tories would be a low-tax party, most effectively embodied by the 2007 promise to restrict inheritance tax, which played so well with public that it derailed Gordon Brown's honeymoon.

But he made no attempt to draw the strands together into a single unifying theme that would express the soul of the revamped party until just before the election, by which time tax cuts were no longer a realistic option even to the most bullish of traditionalists. But the 'Big Society' project as a unifying theme was so vague that canvassers on the ground complained they could not explain it on the doorstep, and many would claim it is still not clear what it means, almost a year into its implementation. (See pages 259–60).

The electoral task

The Conservatives' political task was of course only one side of the coin: the election outcome is determined only by concrete votes in the ballot box, and we need to consider how many of these they needed to win, and where.

The theoretical winning post in a British general election is securing an overall majority in the House of Commons: take half the seats or more and a party's leader will automatically be summoned to Buckingham Palace and invited to form a government; fewer than that, and at best there will be negotiations which might put its leader at the head of a coalition or minority government. With the 650-seat house to be elected after the 2010 election, therefore, 326 seats were needed for a theoretical majority; but in practice a fair few more than this would be needed for a working majority likely to last the four or five years to the next election, while the presence of the non-voting Speaker and of several Sinn Fein MPs who never take their seats means that two or three seats short of 326 would in fact deliver a technical majority to begin with, at least.

Let us begin from that theoretical finishing line. At the 2005 general election, the Labour Party won 355 seats and the Conservatives won 198. So Labour would have retained a majority if they had made a net loss of less than 30, whereas the Conservatives faced the daunting task to secure a majority of their own of making a net gain of at least 128 seats.[54]

The good news for the Conservatives was that at least a small part of this task had been done for them already: parliamentary constituency boundaries are periodically updated, and new boundaries came into effect at the 2010 election in England, Wales and Northern Ireland. These changes worked, as they usually do, to the benefit of the Conservatives. To measure the size of this effect, we use the calculations by the experts at Plymouth University, Professors Colin Rallings and Michael Thrasher. Their 'notional results'[55], used by all the major broadcasters and most of the press in the reporting of the election, are estimates of how each new or revised constituency would have voted in 2005 – assuming that everybody had voted in exactly the same way, and all that was different were the boundaries.

According to Rallings and Thrasher's figures, the boundary changes gave the Conservatives 12 notional net gains, while Labour lost 7 seats and Plaid Cymru 1. (The total number of seats increased by 4, which completes the total.) Slightly offsetting this, Labour made a notional gain and the Conservatives a notional loss through the change of Speaker, since Labour could now include Glasgow North East in their column, while the Tories had lost Buckingham from their own. This put the Conservatives on a baseline of 209 and Labour on 349, with the Conservatives needing 117 more gains for an overall majority.

---

[54] By convention, comparisons are generally made from general election to general election, rather than taking account of by-election results which can sometimes be hard to replicate. So we ignore in these calculations the Tories' two by-election gains from Labour, at Crewe & Nantwich and Norwich North, and consider that the Tories had to 'gain' these seats again to hold them in the new parliament.
[55] Colin Rallings & Michael Thrasher, *Media Guide to the New Parliamentary Constituencies* (Plymouth: Local Government Chronicle Elections Centre, 2007)

It don't mean a thing if…

But how does this target in seats translate into votes? The most widely used means of projection, and the one we consider the best starting point even though it is a considerable simplification, is to assume that there will be a uniform national swing.

What does this mean? Swing is a simple summary measure of the way in which votes for a party have changed since the last election (or over any other period). There are several different ways of measuring it, but the simplest and most widely used is that which is sometimes called 'Butler swing' (after the academic Sir David Butler), which simply measures the net movement from one party to another as a percentage of the total vote. For example, if the Conservatives have 33% of the vote at one election and 40% at the next, while Labour's share falls from 36% to 29%, the former have gained 7 points and the latter have lost 7 – exactly as if 7% of the voters have simply switched from one to the other (although it is probably much more complicated than that under the surface, with voters moving in both directions and to and from other parties and non-voting as well). This would be a swing of 7% from Labour to Conservative. Calculated on this basis, the Conservatives needed a 7% (uniform national) swing from their 2005 position to get an overall majority in 2010.

In the same way, we can calculate a swing if one party's gain is not the same as the other's loss, or even if both their votes move in the same direction. Suppose there is a Liberal Democrat surge, so that the Conservative share falls by 1 point but Labour share falls by 5. Even though the Conservatives are weaker overall, they have gained in relation to Labour – their lead over Labour is now 4 points more than it was before, exactly as it would have been if 2% of the voters had moved from Labour to Conservative and everybody else had stayed where they were, so this is a swing of 2%. In fact this is an easy way to calculate swing: it is the change in the percentage point lead divided by two – so if the Conservative lead over Labour falls by 4 points, that is a 2% swing to Labour. 'Uniform national swing' is when the swing in every constituency across the country is the same.[56]

---

[56] These days the term is often used to apply not just to the swing between any two parties, but to uniform movements in vote shares of all the major parties (which therefore guarantees that the

Uniform swing is a helpful assumption in terms of understanding how to interpret a given share of the national vote (and therefore the findings of an opinion poll measuring this). If we know for instance that the Conservatives were 4% behind the Liberal Democrats in a given constituency in 2005, they would need at least a 2% swing there from the Liberal Democrats to capture the seat. (As the swing is half the change in the lead, a 2% swing is enough to take a seat where the lead is 4%.) If the national shares of the vote show the Conservatives up 3 and the LibDems down 2, that is a 2.5% swing, so the Conservatives are doing well enough nationally to win the seat. This, therefore, is what we mean when we say that in 2010 the Conservatives needed a 7% swing from Labour to win an overall majority – if there was a 7% swing to the Conservatives from Labour in every single constituency in the country, and every other party's share of the vote stayed the same, the Conservatives would just make the 117 gains they needed, and would have a majority.

In practice, swing is not entirely uniform – at a minimum there will inevitably be some random variation, and there may be systematic variations as well. Marginal seats may behave differently from safe seats; there may be different regional swings; and individual constituencies may behave individually – this seemed especially a possibility in 2010 when some of the candidates had been tainted by the expenses scandal. At the election of 1997 and again in 2001, Labour did much better in the marginal constituencies than it did in the rest of the country, and gained many more seats than it might have expected under uniform swing. In 2005, by contrast, it was the Conservatives who achieved a higher swing on average in the marginal constituencies than nationally, and therefore won more seats than a uniform swing projection based on the national shares of the vote would have given them.[57]

The key to understanding the electoral task facing the Conservatives in 2010, therefore, is to forget the national swing or national shares of the vote, except as a crude indicator of their progress towards a subtler target.

---

swing will be uniform whichever two parties you consider). For example, if the Conservatives have gained 5% of the vote nationally since 2005, a uniform national swing would mean that these changes also apply in each individual constituency.

[57] Uniform swing would have given the Tories only 184 seats in 2005 instead of the 198 they actually won.

The swing in the 'safe' constituencies is irrelevant to the national outcome – they are (mostly) not going to change hands anyway. What the Conservatives needed to achieve was simply a 7% swing in each *marginal* seat. Even that is a simplification, in fact, because many of their target seats needed a lower swing than this – in a constituency where the Labour lead was 10 points they needed only a 5% swing, and could afford to fall below the 7% line, provided they hit 7% in those constituencies where nothing less would do. Furthermore, of course, given that the swing would never be completely uniform, they could afford to miss a few of their 117 prime targets provided they over-performed in at least as many slightly safer Labour constituencies and captured them with swings of more than 7%.

It is this simple model that underpinned our polling in marginal constituencies, conducted at the 2010 election for Reuters. There were 57 constituencies won by Labour in 2005 where the Conservatives needed a swing of between 5% and 9% to gain the seat (that is, where the Labour lead over the Conservatives was between 10% and 18% of the vote). [58] We did not attempt to poll in each of these constituencies separately – a huge and quite unnecessarily expensive task – but we were able to poll across the whole group. If the Tories could achieve a 7% swing across the whole group, the chances were that they would win just enough for a majority; if more than that, they could hope for a more comfortable majority, if less – as the polls in the event found – they would fall short, as indeed they did.

The Tories, naturally, were fully aware of the special importance of marginal seats and, with funding from Lord Ashcroft, reportedly put disproportionate effort into their campaigning there, starting long before election year. We shall see in due course how well they succeeded.

There is one other important point to be made, however. Talk of a 7% swing is a little abstract; after all, it does rather depend where you start from. We get a much better idea of the mountain facing the Conservatives if we translate this back into votes at the national level. If the Conservatives were to achieve a 7% national swing from Labour, that would mean they led Labour by 11% of the vote – a huge lead. (Assuming

---

[58] This, of course, refers to the 'notional result' allowing for boundary change, not to the real result in a sometimes much-altered constituency.

a turnout of 65%, this would mean getting about 3.2 million more votes than Labour.)

But our electoral system does not normally require the largest party to win by such a margin to achieve a majority, or hung parliaments would be far more frequent than they are. In 2005, Tony Blair's Labour Party beat the Tories by only 3%, yet their reward for that was a very comfortable majority in seats. How can this be? The reason is that the British electoral system is currently biased towards Labour, in the sense that Labour wins more seats for a given percentage of the vote than the Conservatives would win if the situation were reversed. That was true in 2001 and 2005, and was always likely to be true again in 2010. Assuming uniform swing, Labour could have hung on with a wafer-thin overall majority even if the Tories narrowly beat them in votes. With a 5% Tory lead, Labour could still be the largest party in Parliament. (We consider why this is the case later – see pages 264–9.)

Consequently, the Tories had to face this further hurdle of overcoming the bias in the electoral system. But if they could tackle their electoral task in the most efficient way, by getting a bigger swing in the key marginal seats than they achieved nationally, they would at the same time be reducing the bias of the system against them.

Population change

While we are considering the substantial hurdle that the operation of the electoral system put in the Tories' way, we should not lose sight of another factor that worked to their advantage. Population change and developments in patterns of turnout in recent decades have both been in their favour, and should be making it easier for them to gain a given share of the vote than it otherwise would be.

The demographic groups among which the Tories have always been strongest have been growing and, furthermore, their turnout has fallen less than that of Labour's natural supporters, further magnifying the advantage. The parties are competing for votes among an older and more middle class electorate than when the Tories last won in 1992.

Figure 14: The decline of the 'working class', 1969-2009

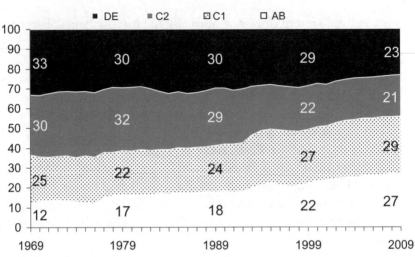

Source: National Readership Survey

Figure 14 shows the startling growth over the last forty years in the 'middle class' (ABC1s) at the expense of the 'working class' (C2DEs), as those groups are measured in market research terms – and what is more both the age and class gaps in turnout are bigger than they were then, giving the party strongest among these groups a double boost.

In fact, this has not worked for the Conservatives quite as strongly as it might have done. The Conservatives are weaker than they used to be both among older voters and those defined as 'middle class', the groups that most strongly support them, and although they have widened their base of support by finding more votes where they have traditionally been weaker, that in itself has not been enough to compensate. It is the increased voting power of the groups where they are strongest which is making up the shortfall.

We can see this most clearly by considering the profile of Conservative supporters in the voting intention polls in 2009. In that year, the Conservative standing in our polls was on average 42% – almost the same as the 43% share of the vote the party had gained when they last won an election, under John Major's leadership in 1992. We can therefore make a fairly straightforward comparison. Table 27 shows the findings of our aggregate of polls for 2009, combining roughly 12,000 interviews conducted during the year as part of our Political Monitor surveys, and enabling us to examine the demographic characteristics of Conservative support in some depth. We can compare these findings directly with our analysis of the vote in 1992 (based on nearly 15,000 interviews during the election campaign, weighted to reflect the final result). As can be seen, although Conservative share of the vote overall was almost as high in 2009 as in 1992, it was dramatically lower among ABs and C1s, with only a partial compensation of a higher share of DE support. Similarly, though to a less marked degree, Tory share was lower among older voters but not in the two younger age bands.

Table 27: Evolution in the nature of Tory support, 1992-2009

	1992 (general election)				2009 (voting intention aggregate)				Con change
	Con %	Lab %	LD %	Oth %	Con %	Lab %	LD %	Oth %	
All	43	35	18	4	42	26	19	13	−1
Men	41	37	18	4	40	28	17	15	−1
Women	44	31	18	7	43	25	20	12	−1
18-24	35	38	19	8	35	29	17	19	0
25-34	40	37	18	5	41	23	23	12	+1
35-54	43	34	19	4	39	27	18	16	−4
55+	46	34	17	3	45	26	18	11	−1
AB	56	19	22	3	45	23	21	11	−11
C1	52	25	20	3	44	25	18	13	−8
C2	39	40	17	4	39	26	17	18	0
DE	31	49	16	4	36	33	17	13	+5

Source: Ipsos MORI
Base: 14,764 GB residents aged 18+, interviewed March-April 1992, data weighted to final election result; 12,076 GB residents aged 18+ interviewed January-December 2009 (of which 6,289 'absolutely certain to vote')

So how could the Conservatives have made big losses among their strongest groups, offset only by much smaller gains among their weaker groups, and yet be breaking even with roughly the same share of the vote as before? Simply because their strongest groups now make up a higher proportion of the vote. That is partly because more of the public these days are middle class and the population is also ageing. But it is also because far fewer people now vote. That fall in turnout has not been evenly spread – the differentials in turnout have widened, so that older voters and the middle class make up a bigger proportion of the vote than they used to.[59]

Despite their loss of vote share among ABC1s and 35+s, the Tories were still the biggest party in both groups, and the increasing voting power of these groups had increased the value of any given lead – a small lead among a large proportion of voters is as valuable as a large lead among a small proportion. Consequently, David Cameron's share of the popular support in 2009 was almost as high as was John Major's in his 1992 election win, despite having a less secure grip on the loyalties of ABC1s.

These demographic changes, therefore, certainly made the Tories' task a little less daunting than it otherwise would be. (Conversely, now the election is over and Labour is licking its wounds, these changes also have profound implications for the future strategy of 'The People's Party'. But that we will discuss in its due place – see pages 281–5.)

The Thatcher precedent

It is all very well to consider the number of seats and votes that the Tories needed to win, but perhaps that does not give a very clear view of how easy or difficult that task actually would be. One way of comprehending more clearly what the Tories' task entailed is to compare their position with previous elections, and the historical perspective offers one obvious parallel. The last time the Tories ousted a Labour government and took office themselves was in 1979, with James Callaghan the beleaguered Prime Minister and Margaret Thatcher his still-untried challenger. Then, a Labour Prime Minister, a former Chancellor of the Exchequer elected without facing the country after his predecessor retired, was challenged by a younger, Oxford-educated Conservative leader who was also a relatively unknown quantity. Economic considerations were to the fore (though it was inflation that was then the most troubling aspect, together with unemployment). Labour trailed the Conservatives in voting intentions for most of the year before the election, though the gap was rather narrower than that faced by Gordon Brown in 2009. Then, as in 2010, the voting

---

[59] Unfortunately, we can only chart these changes in general terms – MORI did not measure turnout by subgroup in 1992.

intention polls were volatile, swinging from almost level in November 1978 (when the Conservatives led by 43% to 42%) to a cavernous 19-point gap (55% to 36%) by the end of January 1979 as the 'Winter of Discontent' began to make itself felt.

But in other respects the circumstances were a little different. To begin with, Mrs Thatcher had less of a mountain to climb than Mr Cameron. At the previous election (October 1974), Labour had achieved a majority of only three seats, which had melted away long before 1979; in 2005, Labour's majority was a solid 66 seats. So Cameron's Conservatives needed to gain many more seats than did Thatcher's for a majority, or even to become the largest party.

Furthermore, whereas these days the operation of the electoral system gives a substantial advantage to Labour, then the bias was slightly in favour of the Conservatives. Moreover, the greater strength of the modern Liberal Democrats and minor parties means that the major parties need a more convincing margin of victory than they once did to avoid a hung Parliament. Mr Callaghan knew that, with uniform swing from the previous election, even a one-point Conservative lead would put Mrs Thatcher within touching distance of an overall majority; that same one-point defeat for Gordon Brown might still have left him his own wafer-thin majority and would certainly have kept him in Downing Street.

Margaret Thatcher's approval ratings fluctuated during the 1977-9 period, but the public were frequently more dissatisfied than satisfied with the way she was doing her job as Leader of the Opposition, and in November 1978 her net rating was a low as −13 (38% satisfied and 51% dissatisfied), much worse than any of David Cameron's poll ratings. (See Figure 15.) But only 11% at that stage did not have an opinion of Mrs Thatcher – partly, no doubt, because she had been on the scene much longer than David Cameron had, having been an MP for twenty years and having already served in Ted Heath's cabinet. No doubt, too, many had an opinion, positive or negative, simply because of the novelty of having a woman as party leader.

But remember also how little public exposure party leaders had in those days. Broadcasting Parliament on the radio had only just been introduced, and TV cameras in the Commons were still years away: voters had to rely for their impressions on occasional staged news events and party political broadcasts, unless they happened to see the leaders at a live meeting (which even in those days applied only to a vanishingly small fraction of the public). At the end of 2009, with the wall-to-wall coverage, constant spin-doctoring and ever-increasing range of communications which make up the modern political campaign, 17% said they didn't know if they were satisfied with David Cameron's performance or not. Modern apathy and disengagement? Or just a leader making less of an impact than his predecessor? Probably both.

Figure 15: Satisfaction with PM and government, 1978-9 and 2009-10

Q. Are you satisfied or dissatisfied with the way ... is doing his/her job as .../the way the government is running the country?

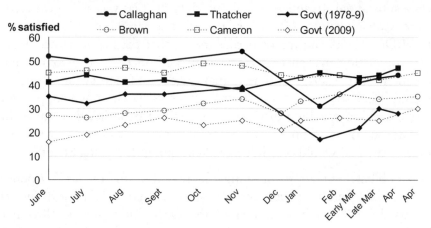

Source: Ipsos MORI
Base: c. 1,000 GB residents aged 18+ in each survey

But there were doubts about Thatcher as about Cameron, though for different reasons. (How fascinating it is to note that, in November 1978, 55% of the public thought that, if the Conservatives were to win the election, Ted Heath would make a better Prime Minister than Margaret Thatcher would.[60]) Being a woman was an issue for Mrs Thatcher: at the start of the campaign, 40% thought that the prospect of a female Prime Minister would hinder the Tories while 25% thought it would help; but

---

[60] MORI poll for the *Daily Express*, conducted 8 November 1978.

only 29%, less than one in three, thought it would make no difference either way.

In fact we can clearly see in retrospect that throughout that campaign Mrs Thatcher was potentially the weak link for the Conservatives, while the well-liked Callaghan was an asset for Labour. Predictably and reasonably, voters were much more likely to feel that Thatcher was 'rather inexperienced' than to say the same of Callaghan. But Thatcher was also much more likely than Callaghan to be seen as tending 'to talk down to people' (31% picked that as a description that fitted Thatcher, only 16% applied it to Callaghan), and more thought that she 'sometimes has rather extreme views' (26% compared to 12%), while Callaghan scored because more people saw him than saw her as understanding the problems facing Britain, being a capable leader and being down to earth. But despite this, when the voters were asked what a Conservative or Labour government would be like, rather than about the leaders, the Tories did much better. Intriguingly, Gordon Brown had a similar advantage over David Cameron in many of these key respects (see page 82).

But the real contrast between 2010 and 1979 was in the standing of the Prime Minister, a difference which looked as if it ought to have redounded to Cameron's advantage. Even with support for his government down, Jim Callaghan remained a relatively popular figure. In November 1978, before the disastrous events of the 'Winter of Discontent' and an iconic but unfair *Sun* headline ('Crisis? What crisis?') applied the *coup de grâce*, 54% of the public were still saying they were satisfied with the way he was doing his job, even though only 39% were satisfied with the government and the Tories had a lead in voting intentions. It was only after the turn of year, when satisfaction with both government and Prime Minister plummeted, that Mrs Thatcher's ratings moved ahead of his for the first time, and by the time the election was approaching he had recovered so that the two were neck-and-neck with satisfaction ratings over 40%. Gordon Brown only achieved 40% satisfied in one monthly poll in the two-and-a-half years after the 'election that never was', while David Cameron never fell below that line after May 2008.

On a related issue, at every election from 1983 onwards, the eventual election winner has had a lead over his or her rival in the public's choice of 'most capable Prime Minister'. (Indeed, some commentators have suggested that in 1992, when John Major had a clear lead over Neil

Kinnock on this measure, it ought to have been taken as a warning that the voting intention polls were misleading.) But the 1979 election shows clearly that this is not necessarily the case: Mr Callaghan was consistently ahead of Mrs Thatcher, and indeed his lead grew through the campaign; yet it didn't stop her replacing him in Downing Street. In 2010 Cameron led, but only narrowly by the time of the election (see Table 16).

One vital difference between the two campaigns, of course, is that Brown and Cameron debated against each other and against Nick Clegg on television. In 1979, Callaghan offered to take part in a televised debate with Thatcher, but she – perhaps feeling she had nothing to gain and everything to lose – ducked the challenge. The public thought – by 43% to 32% – that Callaghan would have come off best had the debate taken place; but they split almost evenly on whether Mrs Thatcher was right or wrong to refuse the invitation[61]. In 2010, it was David Cameron who was expected to perform best in the debates, by a much wider margin than Callaghan had in his favour; in retrospect, how he must wish he had been able to follow his predecessor's example and refused to take part!

In the end, the outcome was different and yet the same. 1979 saw a once-impressive Tory lead evaporating as the polls narrowed, but the gap eventually opened up once more, and Margaret Thatcher won a majority in the end. In 2010, the gap never narrowed so far, but nor did it appreciably re-open: an 8-point lead on average between the start of January and the end of March translated into a 7-point victory on polling day. Cameron had to be content with the need for a deal with the Liberal Democrats to secure the keys to Number Ten; yet that same 7-point margin gave Margaret Thatcher a majority. In judging Cameron's task, and his failure where Margaret Thatcher succeeded, this needs to be borne in mind.

---

[61] MORI poll for the *Daily Express* and *London Evening Standard*, conducted 8-9 April 1979.

How the Tories made progress

We can look for signs of Conservative progress after Cameron's election in several places. The voting intention polls are an obvious indicator, though they will reflect Labour failure as well as Tory success and may for that reason mislead since the possibility of a Labour recovery was outside Cameron's control. The same observation applies to some extent to electoral gains in local government, devolved and European Parliament elections, but whatever their cause these have a solid reality that makes them a valuable success in themselves. More revealingly, though, we can examine opinion polls that directly measure what the public thought of David Cameron and his party, and track their movement as time passed.

Decontamination of the brand

At first Cameron made slow progress towards acceptance, not least among Tories themselves. As we have already seen (page 46), from his election as leader until a couple of months after Brown had moved into Downing Street, Cameron's satisfaction ratings among the general public were unimpressive, and his net score by 2008 was invariably negative, albeit only by a few points.

To put this into historical context, as Figure 16 shows, no opposition leader since Ted Heath in 1970 had succeeded in dislodging the government while recording a significantly negative average satisfaction score.

His ratings were naturally better among those intending to vote Conservative, but even among this group many remained unconvinced: he only topped 60% satisfied once, and there were over 20% dissatisfied in each of the first four months of 2007. In fact Cameron's average ratings among Conservatives up to Brown's accession were significantly weaker than Michael Howard's had been.[62] Of course, this is probably simply a reiteration of the dilemma facing a Conservative leader, in that what appeals to the party's core vote and what appeals to the wider public

---

[62] Howard averaged 54% satisfied and 20% dissatisfied among intending Conservative voters up to the 2005 election, while Cameron averaged 48% satisfied and 31% dissatisfied from January 2006 to June 2007.

(including the 'floating voters') is often very different: Howard's ratings with the public as a whole were considerably weaker than Cameron's even in the pre-Brown period.

Figure 16: Average net satisfaction with opposition leaders 1955-2010

Q. Do you think ... is or is not a good leader of ... Party? (Gallup, Gaitskell to Callaghan))
Q. Are you satisfied or dissatisfied with the way ... is doing his job as Leader of the Opposition? (MORI/Ipsos MORI, Foot onwards)

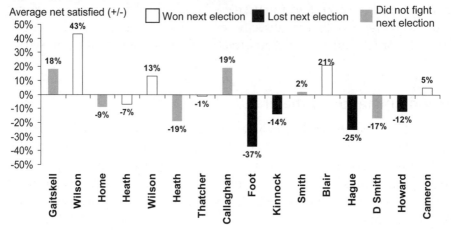

Source: Gallup, MORI/Ipsos MORI

Brown's accession brought a very clear turning point. Cameron's ratings briefly plummeted during the Brown honeymoon, then took a clear upward turn. In September 2007, before the Brown bubble burst, the public as a whole was twice as dissatisfied as satisfied with Cameron, 45% to 23%, and even Tory voters gave him a net negative score. But in October, after the Conservative conference (which was widely credited as playing a major role in scaring off Brown from calling an early election), he was up to a best-ever rating of 36% satisfied, then improved again to 39% at the start of December. In June 2008, he hit 50% satisfied for the first time, and his average score for the next 18 months was 47%.

It is clear that part of Cameron's problem was that he took a long time to make a clear impression on many of the public. His detailed image profile in September 2006 (Table 28) shows no outstanding negative impressions beyond the inevitable judgment that he was inexperienced, but also few of the public convinced of his positive virtues. On almost all of the attributes measured, positive and negative, more of the public saw them as applying to Cameron by the time of our post-election poll in 2010, but the increase was particularly dramatic in the perception that he was a capable leader and that he understood the problems facing Britain, two of the key determinants of suitability for office (and, significantly, two aspects on which Gordon Brown was able to match him in the public's perceptions even after Cameron's image was better established – Cameron might have found himself at a real disadvantage against Brown on these grounds in a snap election during the Brown honeymoon).

Table 28: David Cameron's image, September 2006 and May 2010

Q. Here is a list of things both favourable and unfavourable that have been said about various politicians. I would like you to pick out all those statements that you feel fit Mr Cameron.

Attributes	August-September 2006 %	May 2010 %	Change 2006-10 ±%
Has got a lot of personality	19	24	+5
A capable leader	17	28	+11
Understands the problems facing Britain	16	33	+17
Down-to-earth	14	12	−2
Patriotic	14	22	+8
Understands world problems	12	17	+5
More honest than most politicians	12	14	+2
Has sound judgement	9	13	+4
Good in a crisis	3	9	+6
Average positive	*12.9*	*19.1*	*+6.2*
Rather inexperienced	37	22	−15
Out of touch with ordinary people	14	21	+7
Tends to talk down to people	7	12	+5
Rather narrow minded	6	6	0
Too inflexible	4	5	+1
Average negative	*13.6*	*13.2*	*−0.4*
No opinion	35	21	−14
Net index (positive minus negative)	*−0.7*	*+5.9*	*+6.6*

Source: Ipsos MORI
Base: c. 1,000 GB residents aged 18+ in each survey

A similar story is shown by the 'like him, like his party' measurements we conducted at four points during the parliament (Table 29). In January 2007, more than a year into Cameron's leadership, there were still more of the public who said they did not like him than said they did, although he was nevertheless comfortably outscoring the Conservative Party. But his image, and the party's, had dramatically improved by the middle of 2008.

Table 29: 'Like him, like his party?' – Cameron and the Conservatives

Q Which of these statements comes closest to your views of David Cameron and the Conservative Party?

	12-14 January 2007	18-20 July 2008	26-28 January 2010	18-19 April 2010
	%	%	%	%
I like David Cameron and I like the Conservative Party	19	35	27	31
I like David Cameron but I do not like the Conservative Party	17	19	18	22
I do not like David Cameron but I like the Conservative Party	10	8	12	7
I do not like David Cameron and I do not like the Conservative Party	34	28	34	35
Don't know	20	11	9	5
Total like David Cameron	36	54	45	53
Total do not like David Cameron	44	36	46	42
Net like David Cameron	–8	+18	–1	+11
Total like the Conservative Party	29	43	39	38
Total do not like the Conservative Party	51	47	52	57
Net like the Conservative Party	–22	–4	–13	–19

Source: Ipsos MORI
Base: c. 1,000 GB residents aged 18+ in each survey

In the 2007 poll[63], Cameron appealed equally to all age groups but rather more strongly to broadsheet readers than to tabloid readers and to the middle class than the working class, as might be expected of any Tory leader (43% of ABs and 31% of DEs said they liked him, though the proportion disliking him was almost identical, 46% and 45% respectively.) But again we see unexpected weakness among his core vote: of those who said they voted Conservative on 2005, considerably more liked the party (89%) than liked Cameron (64%). By January 2010, Cameron had won over many working class voters (40% of DEs now said they liked Cameron, compared to 47% of ABs), but still a quarter, 26%, of those

---

[63] Poll for the *Sun*. Ipsos MORI interviewed a representative quota sample of 973 GB residents aged 18+ by telephone on 12-14 January 2007.

who claimed to have voted Conservative in 2005 said they did not like Cameron.

Table 30: Improvement in Conservative Party image, 2005-10

Q. Read through the list slowly keeping the Conservative Party in mind. Every time you come to a statement that fits your ideas or impressions of the Conservative Party just tell me the letter next to it. You may pick as many or as few as you like. You don't have to be certain, just pick the letters next to the statements you feel fit the Conservative Party.

	April 2005 %	May 2010 %	Change 2005-10 %
Concerned about the people in real need in Britain	14	16	+2
Has a good team of leaders	8	16	+8
Has sensible policies	17	20	+3
Keeps its promises	3	6	+3
Looks after the interests of people like us	11	13	+2
Moderate	12	13	+1
Professional in its approach	15	24	+9
Represents all classes	9	10	+1
Understands the problems facing Britain	22	32	+10
Average positive	*12.3*	*16.7*	*+4.4*
Divided	23	13	−10
Extreme	14	7	−7
Out of touch with ordinary people	32	25	−7
Too dominated by its leader	16	10	−6
Will promise anything to win votes	45	29	−16
Average negative	*26.0*	*16.8*	*−9.2*
Net index (positive minus negative)	*−13.7*	*−0.1*	*+13.6*

Source: Ipsos MORI

Base: c. 1,000 GB residents aged 18+ in each survey

Nevertheless, Cameron was polling ahead of his party – with only 39% feeling that they liked the Conservatives and 52% that they did not, they were clearly in a shaky position by the turn of the year. This does not seem to be because the party had entirely failed to 'detoxify' its image. Our post-election measure of party image bears witness to the considerable strides Cameron and his team had made in this direction. But it also points to the weaknesses that had still not been effectively addressed. The Conservative improvement between 2005 and 2010 was the biggest for any of the three main parties[64], but realistically it was not quite good enough.

---

[64] Labour had improved only slightly (see Table 23) and the Liberal Democrats' image had deteriorated.

Most of the improvement stemmed from reducing the negative impressions of the party – the number picking each of the five negative descriptions fell, with 'will promise anything to win votes' falling fastest of all. (Surely something of a surprise, given the criticism of Cameron's 'policy-lite' approach that seemed to some critics to be resurrecting Blair's New Labour populism?) Even so (on this slightly artificial measure of overall image) they achieved only parity, not positive attractiveness, which matches the finding that they were still more disliked than liked. The reasons not to vote Conservative had been diluted, but the party still fell short of the positive attraction that Tony Blair and New Labour had succeeded in projecting in 1997.

What we can't tell, unfortunately, since we have no data from 2008 or 2009, is whether the party might have temporarily reached a stronger image in the middle of the parliament and then subsequently fallen back again as issues such as the expenses scandal intervened. Certainly, more said they liked the party and fewer that they did not in 2008 than was eventually the case by the time of the election, and of course at the same period they held a much more impressive lead in the voting intention polls than they were able to deliver in the end. These positive indicators might have resulted from the public's holding a rosier view of various aspects of the party's image, but equally they might have come about with the public having a much less clear view of the party and being prepared to give it temporarily the benefit of the doubt. If the latter, this might explain the downturn in the months before the election, based not on any particular negatives but merely on the failure to establish the positive impression for which the voters were waiting.

Nevertheless, it is clear that Cameron had succeeded, well before 2010, in making his party a more acceptable alternative for many voters. The next stage was to translate this into a concrete gain of votes.

Progress in the polling booth

An important step towards the hoped-for general election success was to make progress in 'second order elections' (the dismissive jargon some academic theorists use to describe contests such as elections to local government, the European Parliament and the devolved assemblies). This would help to establish a winning habit, bolster morale among the grass-roots membership and energise the party's campaigning machinery at local level. Although, in theory, none of these elections involve voting for the national party, in practice more voters probably vote to express their opinions of national events, to make a protest or 'send a message' to London than consciously choose between the candidates actually listed on their ballot papers or the policies on which they are campaigning. As we have already seen in our analysis of Tony Blair's and Gordon Brown's records, at the local elections up to the end of 2008, David Cameron largely achieved this aim with a series of convincing victories in the national vote and many satisfying alterations in council control. The Tories also did well in the 2007 Welsh Assembly elections, although they made no progress whatsoever in the Scottish Parliament – arguably a worrying sign that they might be succeeding in England only by default, and that where there was another credible alternative to Labour, the SNP in this case, voters still preferred not to back the Tories.

But one Tory victory deserves closer attention here, as its potential significance went beyond the merely symbolic, and its importance to the Tories far outweighed the extent to which the defeat was a blow to Labour. This was the 2008 Mayoral election in London. Certainly London is the sole local election capable of gaining even national attention in its own right, justifiably so if only because of the size of the electorate. (With an electorate of five-and-a-half million, London makes up about an eighth of the population of Great Britain. The Mayoral election involves by far the highest number of voters of any direct election in the UK, and few elsewhere in Europe can compare.) Boris Johnson's defeat of Ken Livingstone would probably have made headlines round the world on this basis alone, but a close contest between two larger-than-life figures made it all the more newsworthy.

Had Johnson lost, it would have been a real blow to Tory hopes but probably one that would have been quickly forgotten by all but the parties' election planners as new events intervened. But Johnson's victory made him immediately the highest profile Tory in office anywhere in Britain, the normal prominence of the post enhanced by the imminence of the 2012 London Olympics. His similarity of age and background to David Cameron made it inevitable that any success or failure would rub off on the public image of his leader. Johnson represented the Conservatives' greatest opportunity to establish their credentials for governing, though at the same time, a big risk should he prove not up the job. In the event he proved a generally safe pair of hands, perhaps surprisingly so.

Table 31: London Mayoral elections, 2004 and 2008

	2004			2008		
	First pref-erences %	After transfer %	Final perc-entages %	First pref-erences %	After transfer %	Final perc-entages %
Labour	36.8	44.4	55.4	37.0	42.6	46.8
Conservative	29.1	35.8	44.6	43.2	48.4	53.2
Liberal Democrat	15.3			9.8		
UK Independence Party	6.2			0.9		
Respect	3.3			-		
British National Party	3.1			2.9		
Green	3.1			3.2		
Christian People's Alliance	2.2			1.6		
Other	0.9			1.4		
Not transferred	-	19.8		-	9.0	
Total	100.0	100.0	100.0	100.0	100.0	100.0

Source: Calculated from figures at londonelects.org

There were electoral lessons too. The importance to Johnson's victory of the high turnout in Tory areas, with a bigger swing since 2004 than nationally, pointed towards the resurrection of an effective Conservative campaigning machine. The Tories, led by Lynton Crosby's firm hand, got their vote out so effectively that Johnson had as many first preference votes in 2008 as his predecessor Steven Norris had mustered in the previous two elections combined. On the other hand, a turnout of 45%, while much better than at previous Mayoral elections, was nevertheless far lower than the likely turnout at a general election – would the Conservative advantage be less marked when 65% were getting to the polls?

Equally important was the anatomy of the victory. For all the talk of an epic head-to-head contest between Ken and Boris, Johnson's victory did not depend on taking Livingstone's votes. Livingstone's share of first preferences in 2008 was 37%, fractionally higher than in 2004, but Johnson's was 43%, a 14-point improvement on the 29% gained by Norris four years earlier. The Tories had proved more attractive than in 2004 at the expense of the smaller parties, and also took more of the second preferences from these parties once their candidates had been knocked out, but they had made no inroads at all into Labour's core vote. If this were to be repeated nationally at the general election, the Tory task might still be impossible. (In the event, it was not – Labour's vote showed much of the same resilience in London as in 2008, and held up even better in Scotland, but plummeted elsewhere in England and Wales.)

The return of sleaze – the lead slips, 2009-10

With a year to go, the Tory project still looked to be well on course. Almost every poll taken in the second half of 2009 projected to a huge Tory majority, almost all with a Tory lead in double figures and the Tory share in the 40s (averaging 40.5% but with only 6 out of 65 polls under a 40% share for the Tories), and Labour languishing in the twenties with only 3 above 30%, averaging 26.5%. The Liberal Democrats were consistently below 20%, averaging 18.8%, with the combined others at an unusually high 13.9% – having hit 20% in June 2009 (of which more later).

But with the election not yet on the horizon, the Tories needed to keep up the momentum. Above all, it was desirable that the political narrative should continue to provide reasons why the voters should eject the government. The last thing the Tories wanted at this point was a switch to a mood that taught the lesson that 'All politicians are as bad as each other'.

Unfortunately for them, by far the most compelling political story of the final year up to the start of the election was the controversy over MPs' expenses, from which many voters plainly drew exactly that moral.

The attention centred around the *Daily Telegraph*'s publication, starting on 9 May 2009, of full details of the expenses claims made by individual MPs in previous years, which had been leaked to the newspaper from The Stationery Office[65]. For days on end the *Telegraph* led with new twists in the story, naming further MPs and new cases on each front page. It should be noted that the vast majority of the abuses alleged were breaches of the

---

[65] Robert Winnett and Gordon Rayner, 'MPs' expenses leaked over failure to equip troops on front line in Afghanistan and Iraq', *Daily Telegraph*, 25 September 2009, http://www.telegraph.co.uk/news/newstopics/mps-expenses/6229051/MPs-expenses-leaked-over-failure-to-equip-troops-on-front-line-in-Afghanistan-and-Iraq.html, accessed 11 October 2009.

spirit rather than the letter of the rules, and many indeed were arguably more matters of taste than honesty. In particular, parliamentary rules allowed for MPs living outside London to reclaim the cost of maintaining a home in London as well as in or near their constituency, including both rent or mortgage interest payments and other expenses such as furnishing and cleaning. In many cases there was a huge gulf between what could be legitimately claimed and what the taxpaying voter was likely to be content to pay for.

The controversial claims were of many types, but the *Telegraph* made much in particular of claims for second home allowances: in a number of cases the choice of which property to designate as the main home and which as the second home seemed to have been manipulated to maximise the amount that could be claimed. The *Telegraph* pointed to these cases as justifying its publication of the leaked information, rather than waiting a few weeks for the official Freedom of Information release of the same claims data, since the official release was to be 'redacted', removing certain details to protect MPs' privacy. Among the details which would be so suppressed would be the addresses for which claims were made, hiding any abuse of the system that depended on identifying the second home. The *Telegraph* detailed cases of 'flipping' – switching which address was designated as the second home at the right moment to get the best of both worlds – and of MPs naming one property as their second home for expenses purposes and another in their capital gains tax returns.

Leaders of all parties reacted with horror to the revelations, and promised action. Gordon Brown called it 'the biggest Parliamentary scandal for two centuries', but was much mocked for a video he posted on YouTube announcing reforms to the expenses system in April 2009, 'his body swaying, a random smile contorting his features' as the *Financial Times* reported it.[66] This was before the publications in the *Daily Telegraph* had escalated the importance of the issue, but David Cameron was widely felt to have handled the issue more effectively once it hit the front pages, promising that he would repay any excessive claims and that all Conservative MPs would be forced to do the same. A former public

---

[66] George Parker, 'YouTube clip turns into video nasty', *Financial Times*, 28 April 2009, http://www.ft.com/cms/s/0/1e863bbe-342a-11de-9eea-00144feabdc0.html#axzz1Dx10hlvi, accessed 14 February 2011.

relations advisor himself, Cameron recognised immediately how badly any association of his MPs with unpopular expenses claims would tarnish his party's image.

Table 32: Key events, May 2009-April 2010

Date	Event
8 May	*Daily Telegraph* begins publishing details of MPs' expenses claims
19 May	Michael Martin announces he will resign as Speaker after a no confidence motion is tabled over his handling of the expenses issue
2 June	Jacqui Smith says she will leave the government at the next reshuffle
3 June	Hazel Blears resigns
4 June	Local elections: Labour loses 4 councils and 291 councillors. The BBC projected national vote share puts Labour in third place on 23%, behind the Liberal Democrats (26%) and Conservatives (38%)
4 June	James Purnell resigns from cabinet and calls for Brown's resignation
5 June	Cabinet reshuffle: Jacqui Smith replaced by Alan Johnson
7 June	European election results announced: Labour third behind UKIP
23 July	Norwich North by-election: Conservative gain from Labour, 16.5% swing
20 August	Lockerbie bomber Abdelbaset Al Megrahi released on health grounds by Scottish government and flies to Libya
30 September	The *Sun* announces it will support the Tories at the election
30 October	Professor David Nutt sacked as government advisor on drugs for publishing a pamphlet disagreeing with government drugs policy. Other advisers resign in protest shortly afterwards
24 November	Brown appears before the Iraq Inquiry
9 December	Pre-Budget Report includes tax on bankers' bonuses
21 December	Announcement that the election will include three leaders' debates on TV
2010	
6 January	Patricia Hewitt and Geoff Hoon call for secret ballot on Brown's leadership
31 January	*Mail on Sunday* serialisation of Andrew Rawnsley's book raises bullying allegations against Brown
5 February	DPP announces intention to charge three Labour MPs and one Conservative peer with criminal offences over their expenses claims
24 March	Final pre-election budget
6 April	Election date officially announced as 6 May

There seemed to be a general assumption at the time that the issue was more likely to damage the government than the opposition, though it was never particularly obvious to us why this should be the case. Even before 2009, there had been a number of widely-reported and embarrassing revelations about the expenses claimed by MPs; the MPs so named included Conservative as well as Labour members, and included senior figures. Among the highest profile cases on the Tory side was that of Party Chairman Caroline Spelman, who was asked to repay money used to hire a nanny earlier in her parliamentary career, though the Privileges Committee ruled that her breach of the rules was inadvertent. On the government side, Ed Balls and Yvette Cooper were accused of exploiting loopholes in the rules surrounding second home allowances to pay for a house in London, and the Home Secretary, Jacqui Smith, was said to have designated a flat where she rarely stayed as her main home so as to maximise her second home allowance; in both cases their actions had clearly been within the letter of the rules, but were nevertheless liable to antagonise the voting public.

In terms of political impact, it was almost certainly the more memorable or ridiculous claims – whether legitimate or not – which resonated most, rather than those which seemed most clearly dishonest. In this, despite Jacqui Smith's sterling single-handed efforts to ensure that Labour's sins were the most egregious, the government was outclassed by the Tories with effortless ease. Smith's contributions included claims for a bathplug and a doormat (though why either of these innocuous items should be considered inappropriate or unnecessary adornments for a second home remains something of a mystery to us) and, most memorably, an inadvertent claim for two pornographic films watched by her husband. But stories on the Tory side of items such as Douglas Hogg's moat clearing, Sir Peter Viggers' duck house (sold after the election because even the ducks didn't like it), Christopher Fraser's row of trees and Anthony Steen's rabbit fence easily put these in the shade. Steen was ordered by Cameron to stand down at the next election after telling Radio 4 that it was the Freedom of Information Act that was the problem and that 'I have done nothing criminal. And you know what it's about? Jealousy. I have got a very, very large house.'.[67] (Note that, again, none of these cases involved the MP in question breaching the rules – indeed, Hogg denied he had ever claimed for the cleaning of his moat, and Viggers' claim had not been allowed in the first place. But that did nothing to soften the effect on public opinion.)

---

[67] Nigel Morris, 'Tory maverick: "You're all just jealous"', *Independent*, 22 May 2009, http://www.independent.co.uk/news/uk/politics/anthony-steen-youre-all-just-jealous-1689211.html

Figure 17: Voting intentions, 2009-10 (poll of polls)

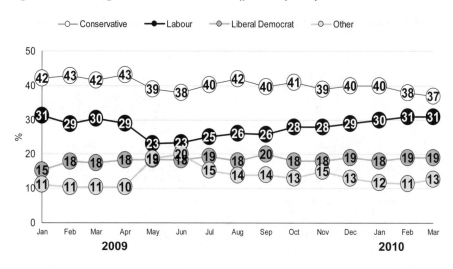

Source: Ipsos MORI analysis of data collected by pollingreport.co.uk
Note: Figures given are the averages of polls conducted each month by the six established polling companies

Both our polling and the results of the European election, a few weeks after the storm broke in the *Telegraph*, suggested that the issue might prove just as damaging to the Tories as to Labour. The public has never seemed convinced by arguments about rotten apples or by one party's MPs being less well-behaved than another's. When asked in a poll we conducted for the BBC just after the expenses scandal broke[68], substantial numbers preferred to spread the blame widely. Two in five said they believed that all (12%) or most (28%) MPs 'use their power for personal gain' and a quarter that all (7%) or most (17%) 'are corrupt'. When asked how MPs spend their time, half the public picked 'furthering personal or career interests' as one of their two or three main activities.[69]

[68] Survey for the BBC: Ipsos MORI interviewed 1,001 GB residents aged 18+ by telephone on 29-31 May 2009.
[69] *Audit of Political Engagement* survey for the Hansard Society: Ipsos MORI interviewed 1,156 GB residents aged 18+ face-to-face, in home, on 13-19 November 2009.

135

Figure 18: Trust in professions to tell the truth, 2009

Q. For each, would you tell me whether you generally trust them to tell the truth or not?

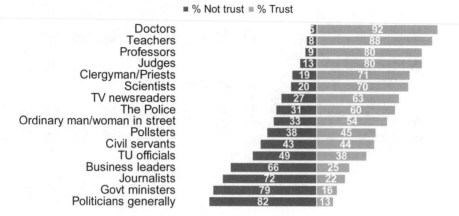

■ % Not trust ■ % Trust

	% Not trust	% Trust
Doctors	5	92
Teachers	8	88
Professors	9	80
Judges	13	80
Clergyman/Priests	19	71
Scientists	20	70
TV newsreaders	27	63
The Police	31	60
Ordinary man/woman in street	33	54
Pollsters	38	45
Civil servants	43	44
TU officials	49	38
Business leaders	66	25
Journalists	72	22
Govt ministers	79	16
Politicians generally	82	13

Base: 2,023 GB residents aged 15+, 4-10 September 2009
Source: Ipsos MORI/Royal College of Physicians

Our September 2009 'veracity' survey demonstrates the escalating damage done by the expenses issue – just a few months earlier at the end of May, with the issue already making headlines, 20% said they would trust 'MPs in general' to tell the truth; by September 'politicians generally' were credible to only 13%. In November, we found (in the Audit of Political Engagement survey for the Hansard Society) that only 22% of the public would be proud if a child of theirs became an MP. (Admittedly, this was notably higher than the 13% who would be proud of a child becoming a tabloid journalist!)[70]

The immediate impact, both in the opinion polls and in the European and local elections held in June 2009, was damage to both major parties, but it was the minor parties rather than the Liberal Democrats that reaped the benefits. The European election in particular showed a dramatic rejection by the voters of all three major parties, the biggest beneficiaries being UKIP: Labour was reduced to a humiliating 16% of the vote, but the

---

[70] *Audit of Political Engagement* survey for the Hansard Society: Ipsos MORI interviewed 1,156 GB residents aged 18+ face-to-face, in home, on 13-19 November 2009.

Tories with less than 28% were hardly happier (Table 33). The most frightening straw in the wind for them was that the swing from Labour to Conservative since 2004 was less than 4%. They knew that they needed to achieve a 7% swing for a majority at the general election; 4% was not nearly good enough.

Table 33: British elections to the European Parliament, 2004 and 2009

Party	2004 %	2009 %	Change	2004 Seats	2009 Seats	Change
Conservative	26.7	27.7	+1.0	27	25	−2
Labour	22.6	15.7	−6.9	19	13	−6
Liberal Democrats	14.9	13.7	−1.2	12	11	−1
UKIP	16.1	16.5	+0.3	12	13	+1
Scottish National Party	1.4	2.1	+0.7	2	2	0
Plaid Cymru	1.0	0.8	−0.1	1	1	0
Green Party	6.3	8.6	+2.4	2	2	0
BNP	4.9	6.2	+1.3	0	2	+2
Others	6.1	8.5	+2.4	0	0	0
Total	100	100		75	69	−6

Source: Results given in House of Commons Library Research Paper 09/53
Note: Figures apply only to Great Britain, not Northern Ireland

It was widely expected before the general election that the expenses saga would influence results here too, but opinions were divided on its likely effects. Would it affect overall support for the main political parties, or would it be purely a constituency effect? If the latter, would it confined to those MPs who stood for re-election or might it even damage the chances of the successors to those who stood down? And would the voters discriminate between the clearly guilty and the more-or-less innocent? Much, of course, would depend on how the opposing candidates chose to direct their campaigning, and on the attitude taken and coverage provided by the local media.

Some commentators foresaw a wider impact, perhaps helping all 'protest' candidates and parties indiscriminately and damaging all incumbent candidates, rather than singling out the MPs who had been entangled in the controversy. This might either boost turnout or damage it. (Would angry voters turn out in droves to throw the rascals out, or stay at home as they lost faith in all politicians equally?) Would it hurt one party more than another, or all parties equally? The announcement shortly before the election of criminal charges to be brought against three MPs (all Labour) and one peer (Conservative) heightened speculation, and reports that they were attempting to avoid a trial by claiming Parliamentary Privilege threw the media, and presumably the voters, into further paroxysms of anger.

Figure 19: Potential impact of the expenses scandal on voting

Q. Suppose at the general election, the candidate for the party you would normally vote for was a sitting MP who had been caught up in the expenses scandal. Which of the following two options would you be most likely to do?

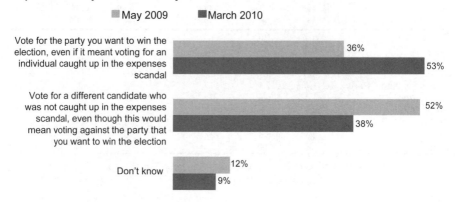

Base: 1,503 GB residents aged 18+, 19-22 March 2010; 1,001 GB residents aged 18+, 29-31 May 2009
Source: Ipsos MORI Political Monitor/BBC

There was little doubt about the depth of the original public reaction: in the BBC survey, 59% said they would support an independent public inquiry to investigate the expenses affair 'no matter how long it takes and how much it costs', and 85% a reform 'so that an independent judicial body scrutinises the activities of MPs, including their expenses and salaries'. And it seemed that there might be a significant impact at the ballot box. More than half the public said they would change their vote rather than support a candidate implicated in the expenses scandal, even if that meant voting against the party they would otherwise support (Figure 19). Even assuming, as we must in such cases, that a question like this concentrating on a single issue much exaggerates its impact on an election where many other considerations are also at work, this was a very high figure: even if only a fifth of that 53% lived up to this threat, it would be enough to swing any marginal constituency.

However, by the time of the general election the issue was a year old, and it is clear that its effect was diminished if not entirely extinguished. By March 2010, the number saying the issue would make them switch their vote was down to 38%, and probably once the election campaign had concentrated minds on the nature of choice to be made between governments, that would have fallen still further.

It clearly was not that the public had become inured to the issue. Polls were still finding a palpable sense of outrage (if perhaps compromised by a shaky grasp of historical context). In a poll for the *Sunday Times* on 25-26 March 2010[71], YouGov told respondents that 'Nick Clegg, the Liberal Democrat leader, said that this is the most corrupt parliament in history', and found that 49% of the public agreed with this description while a (better informed?) 29% disagreed.

But with the immediate fury having faded, maybe it was possible to consider the questions asked by a general election more calmly, and to conclude that complete rejection of all the established parties might not be constructive. ICM found[72] that although 51% of the public agreed that 'Political parties are corrupt', nevertheless most could see some point to them, with only 30% agreeing that 'I want my constituency MP to be independent of political parties' (42% disagreed) and 28% that 'An independent MP would represent me better in Parliament' (41% disagreed).

Another factor which suggested that the scale of any indiscriminate backlash was likely to be limited was a consistent finding of our past investigation into the public's view of politicians, that local MPs are generally much more popular with their own constituents than politicians in general. Although the public have consistently for many years distrusted, and been dissatisfied with the performance of, politicians in general and MPs in particular, we have always found a sharp distinction in their views when asked about their own MP. As Figure 20 shows, the public's trust in their own local MP remained much higher than their trust

---

[71] http://today.yougov.co.uk/sites/today.yougov.co.uk/files/YG-Archives-Pol-STResults-100326.pdf, accessed 12 January 2010.
[72] ICM poll for the Independent Network, 30 April 2010, http://www.icmresearch.co.uk/pdfs/2010_april_independent_candidates_poll.pdf, accessed 13 January 2011.

for 'MPs in general' even as the expenses scandal was breaking (even if the majority of their constituents can't name who they are).

Figure 20: Trust in MPs

Q. I am going to read out some different types of people. Please tell me which you would generally trust to tell the truth and which you wouldn't.

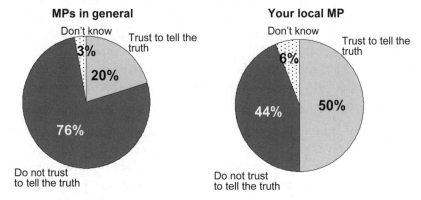

Base: 1,001 GB residents aged 18+, 29-31 May 2009
Source: Ipsos MORI/BBC

Despite the scale of public anger, therefore, it was always likely that the partisan impact on the general election might be limited. But, arguably, the indirect effect was much more damaging to the Conservatives, the issue occupying centre stage in the political game exactly when they needed to be able to take control of the policy agenda and consolidate their lead.

At the time of the European elections, the Tory voting intention lead in the 'general election tomorrow' polls was still big enough for victory. But net satisfaction with David Cameron, which had peaked at +23 in April 2009 (52% satisfied and 29% dissatisfied), fell away again sharply from May onwards, though he staged a partial but brief recovery in the autumn. As Figure 21 shows, this should perhaps not have been unexpected. Opposition leaders find it difficult to maintain a steady level of enthusiasm and Tony Blair had suffered an almost identical dip in his own ratings a year before his eventual election. But Blair's recovery was much more robust than Cameron's, and it may be that Cameron's loss of control of the political narrative at the crucial moment played its part in this.

Figure 21: Net satisfaction with opposition leaders – Blair v Cameron

Q. How satisfied are you with the way Mr Blair/Cameron is doing his job as Leader of the Opposition?

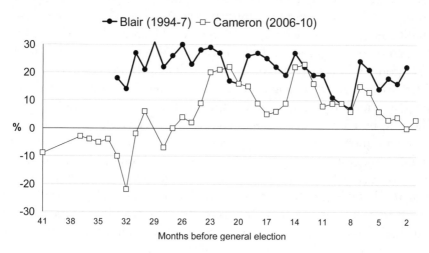

Source: Ipsos MORI
Base: c. 1,000 GB residents aged 18+ in each survey

But the Conservative problem was not simply one of Cameron's slipping ratings. At the same time, Gordon Brown's standing began to recover, narrowing the gap between the two of them. Perhaps it was not all in Cameron's hands, after all?

Targeting the marginals

The second pillar in the Tories' strategy, alongside their aim of improving their national standing, was the hope of outperforming their national swing in the key marginal seats, to which Lord Ashcroft's attention and money had been devoted for a considerable period. This was necessarily a long-term strategy; in fact, changes to the election expenses laws meant that constituency spending was strictly limited from the start of 2010, even before the election date was announced, so they needed to reap any benefit from these extra resources before that restriction came into effect. (Even without Lord Ashcroft's extra help, the Tories would normally expect to have enough money in any winnable marginal to be able spend up to the low legal limits which apply around the election itself.)

At the time of the election, we didn't know for certain which constituencies the Tories were treating as prime targets and which were being left to fend for themselves – this is, naturally enough, a closely guarded secret. But we could at least identify their natural targets, the constituencies where (assuming uniform swing) the result would be closest in a tight election, those which the Tories would probably capture if they reached an overall majority and fail to capture if they didn't. It was in the biggest group of these seats, those being defended by Labour, that we conducted our five-wave polling exercise for Reuters during and shortly before the election campaign. In the event, the Tories did not do significantly better in these constituencies than elsewhere (the results are discussed in more detail below, pages 147–55); our polls proved very revealing in suggesting why this was the case, and found little sign that the Tories had successfully laid the foundations for achieving a better-than-average result here (or, for that matter, that Labour had prepared their defence here unusually successfully). Nor, as some people seem to believe should naturally be the case, are marginal constituencies inherently different in their attitudes from the rest of the country.

This can be most clearly seen by comparing our results in these marginal seats with responses to the same questions asked in our national polls. On key measures, voters in the marginals saw the comparison between Brown and Cameron much as did those in all types of seats, judged the parties very similarly on the key issues, and, critically, few of them seemed aware of the tactical situation in their own constituencies or of the potential importance of their votes. There was no sign that opinion in these constituencies had been impacted in any way by targeted campaigning by the parties.

On views of the policy issues, we found few indications that the marginals were different. As Table 34 shows, their views on the parties' policies on key issues were almost completely in line with national opinions. In each case Labour did a few percentage points better and the Conservatives a few points worse in these key constituencies than nationally, exactly as would be expected given that these constituencies were rather more Labour than average in 2005.[73] Arguably the Conservatives were doing

---

[73] The surveys were conducted in the 57 Labour-held constituencies where the Conservatives needed a swing of between 5% and 9% to capture the seat. Collectively, these constituencies voted

(comparatively) *very* slightly better here than might have been expected, but the difference was at most a small one.

Table 34: Best party on key issues – Marginal Seats

Q. Which party do you think has the best policies on...: the Conservatives, Labour, Liberal Democrats or some other party?

		Con	Lab	LibDem	Other	None	Don't know
Managing the economy							
National 19-22 March	%	29	26	12	4	10	20
Marginals 19-22 March	%	28	29	9	3	10	20
Education							
National 19-22 March	%	29	28	10	3	7	23
Marginals 19-22 March	%	24	32	9	2	7	25
Marginals 16-19 April	%	25	31	17	3	5	19
Healthcare							
National 19-22 March	%	24	33	9	3	8	23
Marginals 19-22 March	%	21	38	6	2	8	25
Marginals 16-19 April	%	26	35	13	4	5	17
Asylum and immigration							
National 19-22 March	%	28	17	9	11	11	24
Marginals 19-22 March	%	25	19	9	10	10	27
Marginals 16-19 April*	%	25	18	20	12	8	19
Crime and anti-social behaviour							
National 19-22 March	%	33	23	8	4	11	22
Marginals 19-22 March	%	27	25	5	3	12	28
Marginals 16-19 April**	%	29	24	12	4	8	22

Source: Ipsos MORI/Reuters
Base: c. 1,000 residents aged 18+ in key marginal seats in each survey/1,503 GB residents aged 18+, March-April 2010
*Asked as 'Asylum' in April   **Asked as 'Crime' in April

Between the pre-campaign and mid-campaign polls the Conservatives made perceptible progress on healthcare, but nothing changed on the other three issues that we re-tested.

We do find a distinction, however, in attitudes towards David Cameron. Four questions comparing the leaders that ran on one of our mid-

---

Conservative 31%, Labour 45%, Liberal Democrat 17% and others 7% in 2005, compared to the national 33%-36%-23%-8% result..

campaign national polls also ran on several waves of the marginals study (Table 35).

Table 35: Leader image – Marginal Seats

Q. In choosing between Gordon Brown, David Cameron or Nick Clegg, which leader do you think…?

		Gordon Brown	David Cameron	Nick Clegg	None	Don't know
…would be best in a crisis?						
Marginals 30 March-5 April	%	41	30	5	11	12
Marginals 16-19 April	%	41	34	12	3	11
Marginals 23-26 April	%	40	33	12	6	10
National 18-20 April	%	40	28	14	8	10
…is most capable?						
Marginals 30 March-5 April	%	37	32	9	10	12
Marginals 16-19 April	%	38	32	16	5	9
Marginals 23-26 April	%	36	33	17	5	10
National 18-20 April	%	33	30	21	7	9
…is most likely to promise anything to win votes?						
Marginals 30 March-5 April	%	33	37	17	5	11
Marginals 16-19 April	%	39	39	10	4	8
Marginals 23-26 April	%	33	37	14	5	11
National 18-20 April	%	36	43	9	4	8
…best understands world problems?						
Marginals 30 March-5 April	%	44	23	7	13	15
Marginals 23-26 April	%	45	23	14	6	11
National 18-20 April	%	45	22	14	8	12

Source: Ipsos MORI/Reuters
Base: c. 1,000 residents aged 18+ in key marginal seats in each survey/1,253 GB residents aged 18+, March-April 2010

Even though the constituencies included were less Conservative than the country as a whole, Cameron's image was significantly stronger here than elsewhere on three of the four measures: a higher proportion than nationally thought he rather than Gordon Brown or Nick Clegg was most capable and would be best in a crisis, and fewer felt he was the most likely to 'promise anything to win votes'. (On being the best at understanding world problems, he was judged much the same in the marginals as elsewhere.)

Nevertheless, despite this boost he still trailed Brown on all four criteria in the marginals as he did across the country. This may be evidence that the

Conservatives had done better in these key constituencies at putting across Cameron's appeal, but the differential was not enough to deliver many extra gains in seats. In fact, these individual aspects of Cameron's image did not seem to translate into the more powerful voting determinants. Despite being less sceptical about these aspects of his ability and character than other voters, those in the marginals were less likely than average to agree that he was ready to be Prime Minister (Table 36).

Table 36: Cameron's readiness to govern – Marginal Seats

Q. On balance do you agree or disagree with the following statements?
'The Conservatives are ready to form the next government/ready to govern'*

	All GB		Key marginals	
	19-22 March %	18-19 April %	30 March-5 April %	23-26 April %
Agree	49	47	46	53
Disagree	41	41	41	38
Neither/don't know	3	4	13	9

'David Cameron is ready to be Prime Minister'

	All GB	Key marginals	
	18-19 April %	30 March-5 April %	23-26 April %
Agree	51	48	46
Disagree	39	40	42
Neither/don't know	2	12	12

Source: Ipsos MORI/*London Evening Standard*/Reuters
Base: c. 1,000 residents aged 18+ in key marginal seats/c. 1,250 GB residents aged 18+ in each survey
*Asked as 'ready to form the next government' in the national poll, 'ready to govern' in the marginals

Other questions revealed that voters in the marginals had a very similar view of the importance of the election result as voters nationally, and very similar proportions claimed to have watched the televised leaders' debates. Nor was there any significant difference in the reported impact of the debates on voting intentions (Table 37), even though earlier targeting of voters in the marginals might perhaps have been expected to have already hardened party support and even though the outstanding feature of the debates – the magnifying of Nick Clegg's credibility – should have been of

145

far less relevance to voters in constituencies like these where the Liberal Democrats had no chance of winning.

Table 37: Reported impact of the debates – Marginal Seats

Q. Which of these statements do you most agree with?

	All GB		Key marginals		
	Debate I	Debate II	Debate I	Debate II	Debate III
	18-20 April %	23 April %	16-19 April %	23-26 April %	30 April-2 May %
The debate has encouraged me to vote for the party I already support	25	32	25	33	26
The debate has encouraged me to switch my vote from one party to another	13	11	14	7	11
The debate made me change from being undecided to choosing one of the parties to vote for	10	6	9	8	9
The debate has put me off voting for any party	1	1	2	1	2
The debate has had no impact on how I intend to vote	46	45	47	47	48
None of these	4	3	3	2	4
Don't know	1	1	1	2	1

Source: Ipsos MORI/*London Evening Standard/News of the World*/Reuters
Base: c. 1,000 residents aged 18+ in key marginal seats/c. 1,250 GB residents aged 18+ in each survey

In fact, the volatility of voting intentions proved very similar in marginal and safer seats, with almost identical proportions in our polls at any given time saying that they might still change their minds on how to vote (Table 38).

Table 38: Volatility of the vote – Marginal Seats

Q. Have you definitely decided to vote for the .. party, or is there a chance you may change your mind before you vote?

	All GB			Key marginals				
	18-19 April %	23 April %	5 May %	19-22 March %	30 March- 5 April %	16-19 April %	23-26 April %	30 April- 2 May %
Definitely decided	50	54	69	52	54	51	53	63
May change mind	49	45	30	46	46	47	46	36
Don't know	1	*	1	2	1	2	1	1

Source: Ipsos MORI/*London Evening Standard/News of the World*/Reuters
Base: c. 1,000 residents aged 18+ in key marginal seats/c. 1,250 GB residents aged 18+ in each survey

How well did the Tories do in the marginals?

At first glance, it might appear that the Tories had at least limited success in their aim of doing better in the marginal seats than nationally: they did better in seats than uniform swing would have predicted, while Labour, the Liberal Democrats and the smaller parties collectively all did worse. Had the national change in the share of the votes applied equally in all seats, the Conservatives would have won only 289 seats (17 less than they did) while Labour would have had 265 (7 more), the LibDems 62 (5 more) and others (in Great Britain) 16 (5 more). The benefit was tangible, if not quite sufficient to overcome the systemic bias and deliver a majority.

It is true that we don't know exactly which seats the Tories targeted and which they ignored, so we can't directly compare the swing in those where Lord Ashcroft's money was spent and those where it was not. But we can see that the extra Tory gains were not concentrated in likely target constituencies: they were scattered much more unpredictably, and a good many seats they would have expected to win slipped through their grasp. Of the seats contested between the Conservatives and Labour, there were 23 Conservative gains in constituencies where the party needed a swing bigger than the 5.0% they achieved nationally; but there were also 9 that would have fallen on a 5.0% swing where Labour hung on. Similarly, they won 9 extra seats over and above the national swing from the LibDems, but not only did they miss 4 they 'should' have won but the LibDems gained 3 seats from them despite the national swing being in the other direction. Labour also did better than the swing would have suggested in seats they contested with the Liberal Democrats, and a few constituencies where the minor parties were in the reckoning also failed to go with the form book.

In fact, the constituency results were (even) less uniform in 2010 than is usual. Perhaps this is most easily shown by the statistical measures: Figure 22 shows the standard deviation[74] of the change in vote share for each of the three major parties across the constituencies they contested in 2001, 2005 and 2010.

As this shows, Labour's change in share was more erratic than that of either of the other two main parties, but Conservative performance was also noticeably more variable than in 2001 or 2005. What this meant was that, taking the two together, the standard deviation of the Lab-Con swing was 4.1, whereas in 2005 it had been 2.6. This variation was enough to dictate that there would be many more seats won in defiance of the national trend than is normally the case, even without the marginals being systematically different from the rest of the country.

This variation was responsible for some dramatic and unexpected results. The Conservatives needed a 10.5% swing from Labour to take Cannock Chase, and took it with a swing of 14.0%, while in Montgomeryshire where only an 11.5% swing would be sufficient to dislodge the well-known LibDem Lembit Opik, they achieved 13.2% (compared to a national LibDem to Conservative swing of just 1.5%). On the other hand, Labour held Birmingham Edgbaston (where the Conservatives needed only a 2.0% swing), Dumfries and Galloway (2.9%), Westminster North (3.3%) and Eltham (3.8%). The Liberal Democrats achieved a coup of by-election proportions in Redcar (victory with a 21.8% swing), and even Labour managed some superficially improbable results, regaining Chesterfield[75]

---

[74] 'Standard deviation' is a calculation used by statisticians to measure the spread of a series of values about their average – in this case, it measures how much the differences in constituency change vary from the overall average change. The higher the standard deviation, the further the individual values or observations tend to be from the average. Here, a standard deviation of 5.1 means that in about two-thirds of all constituencies the change would be within 5.1 percentage points of the average change.

[75] They also regained Blaenau Gwent and Bethnal Green & Bow, less unexpectedly, and notionally gained the former Speaker's seat of Glasgow North East.

and racking up some substantial swings in their favour in London and Scotland even on an otherwise awful night for them.

Figure 22: The scale of variation in constituency results, 2001-10

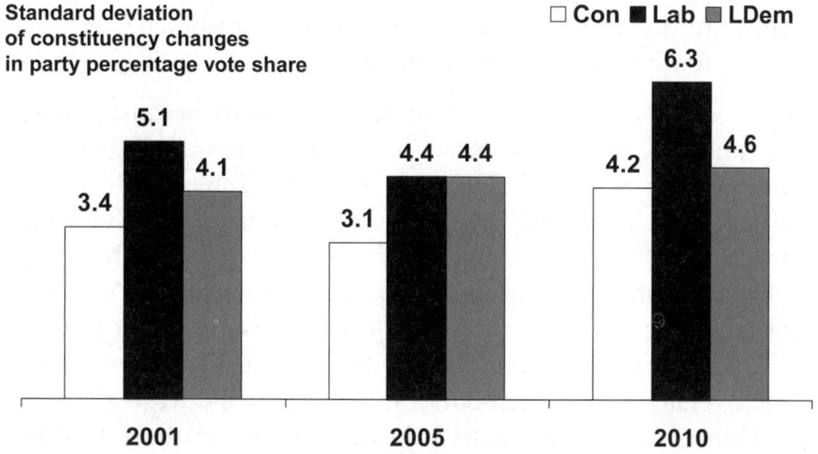

Source: Calculated from election results as published by the House of Commons Library in Research Paper 10/36 (8 July 2010) and official results of earlier elections

Part of this variation from the expected national outcome, however, can be explained purely in terms of regional variations in the vote: if we take into account the regional swings, Labour's performance looks much less erratic. The increased variation in Labour's performance shown in Figure 22 consisted mainly in a dramatically better-than-average performance in London and Scotland: with those two regions ignored, the amount of variation in change of vote share was almost identical for the three parties[76], and only in the case of the Conservatives was their vote share less systematically predictable than in 2005.

We can put this in a less statistical way: if we were to predict the result in each constituency on the basis of a uniform regional swing rather than a national swing, it reduces the net difference from the national result by around half (while not altering the fact that the net discrepancy comprises

[76] Standard deviations were 4.3 for the Tories, 4.5 for Labour and 4.4 for the LibDems.

a great many anomalous individual results, rather than reducing the local variation to a handful of over-performances). But the rest of the Conservative over-performance in seats won seems to have depended on purely random or local rather than systematic factors – not luck as such, since in many cases the local factor may have been the hard work of the constituency party, the quality of the candidate or the performance of their opponents, but not anything that seems obviously attributable to the plans of the national party or of targeting key seats.

We think it worth exploring this point in more detail, because it is clearly of significance not only in understanding what happened in 2010 but what might be possible or sensible in future elections. Table 39 therefore sets out in detail the changes in party vote share in constituencies classified by their tactical situation: this enables us to see precisely whether marginal seats behaved distinctively, and if so how. Because there were a number of different factors operating in the 2010 election, it is important to compare like with like. Most significantly, since the Liberal Democrats increased their vote overall while the Labour vote fell, we would expect differences between Conservative target seats held by Labour and those held by the Liberal Democrats. So we also distinguish between constituencies where the principal battle was between different pairs of parties.

In all seats where Labour stood first and the Conservatives stood second in 2005, Conservative share rose by an average 4.5 percentage points and the average swing from Labour was 5.8%. There was no band of marginals where the performance was substantially better than this – in fact the swing was *lowest* in the critical group where the margin was between 10% and 20% (the seats that would determine if the Conservatives secured an overall majority). This lower swing was because the Labour vote held up better rather than because the Conservative increase was significantly lower, but there was certainly no evidence of a better-than-average performance in the key marginals. There appears to be no sign of a relationship between change in the Conservative share of the vote and marginality in Labour-Conservative marginal seats.

Between the Conservatives and Liberal Democrats, there seems a slightly clearer pattern. As in 2005, there was a big difference between the results in the most marginal seats held by the Conservatives over the Liberal Democrats and those held by the Liberal Democrats over the Conservatives. Each party on average improved its vote share more strongly in the seats it already held, and overall Conservative-held seats swung to the Conservatives while Liberal Democrat seats swung to the Liberal Democrats. However, these averages are distorted by a very high LibDem increase in two seats (Westmorland & Lonsdale and Cheltenham), and in the remaining 8 seats in this group there was on average a small (0.2%) swing to the Conservatives.

Table 39: Vote share changes by constituency type, 2005-10

Constituency type	Number of constit- uencies*	Change in Con vote % share	Change in Lab vote % share	Change in LD vote % share	Lab to Con swing	LDem to Con swing
Average change all seats*	629	+3.8	−6.5	+0.9	5.2	1.5
Average Conservative-2nd seats	264	+4.4	−6.6	+0.4	5.5	2.0
Average Lab 1st Con 2nd	214	+4.5	−7.1	+0.6	5.8	
Average LD 1st Con 2nd	45	+3.7	−4.7	−0.4		2.0
Lab 1st, Con 2nd, margin 0-5%	32	+4.2	−7.7	+1.6	5.9	
Lab 1st, Con 2nd, margin 5-10%	40	+4.9	−7.4	+0.9	6.2	
Lab 1st, Con 2nd, margin 10-15%	34	+4.4	−5.8	−0.9	5.1	
Lab 1st, Con 2nd, margin 15-20%	35	+4.8	−5.6	−0.5	5.2	
Lab 1st, Con 2nd, margin 20-25%	26	+4.4	−7.1	+1.9	5.7	
Lab 1st, Con 2nd, margin 25%+	47	+4.3	−8.3	+0.8	6.3	
Con 1st, LD 2nd, margin 5-10%	9	+4.6	−6.5	+0.2		2.2
Con 1st, LD 2nd, margin 0-5%	8	+5.2	−4.9	−1.7		3.4
LD 1st, Con 2nd, margin 0-5%	10	+2.1	−7.3	+4.8		−1.4
LD 1st, Con 2nd, margin 5-10%	8	+3.8	−5.9	+1.6		1.1
LD 1st, Con 2nd, margin 10-15%	11	+5.4	−4.4	−1.8		3.6
LD 1st, Con 2nd, margin 15-20%	10	+1.1	−3.6	−0.2		0.7
LD 1st, Con 2nd, margin 20-25%	4	+9.9	−4.6	−8.2		9.0
LD 1st, Con 2nd, margin 25%+	2	+3.0	+6.7	−10.7		6.8

Source: Calculated from election results as published by the House of Commons Library in Research Paper 10/36 (8 July 2010)
*Omits Thirsk & Malton, Glasgow NE, Buckingham

It may be easier, though, to get a better grasp of the erratic nature of the constituency results by illustrating it graphically. Figure 23 shows the outcome in the Conservatives first 75 Labour-held target seats (that is, the 75 Labour-held seats that the Conservatives could take with the smallest swing from the 'notional' 2005 result). All these 75 seats would have fallen with a swing of 5% or less, and therefore the Conservatives would expect to capture all of these on the way to an overall majority.

Figure 23: Swing to Conservatives in Labour-held targets 1-75

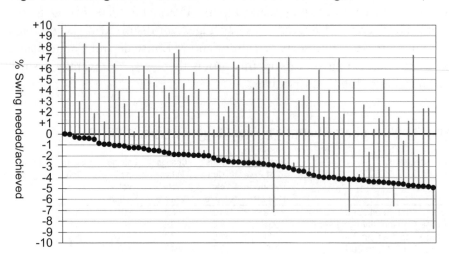

Source: Calculated from election results as published by the House of Commons Library in Research Paper 10/36 (8 July 2010)
Note: Constituencies included are the 75 Labour-held constituencies which would fall to the Conservatives on the smallest swings (from the Rallings & Thrasher 'notional' 2005 results)

Each column on the chart represents one constituency. The circular marker indicates the size of the swing needed to win the constituency – the further below the zero line, the bigger the gap in 2005. The length of the vertical line extending up or down from each circle shows the swing actually achieved, an upwards line being a swing from Labour to Conservative and the few downwards lines being swings in the other direction, from Labour to Conservative. For example, in the leftmost column the swing required is so small that at this scale the marker seems to be on the zero line (this is Gillingham & Rainham, where the Conservatives needed a swing of less than 0.02%), and in the event the swing to the Tories was more than 9%. At the right hand end, target 75 (Ochil & South Perthshire), they needed almost a 5% swing, but in fact Labour managed almost a 4% swing against them. With the chart arranged in this way, the Conservatives capture the seat where the line is long enough to stretch above the zero axis, otherwise they fall short.

The chart shows fairly clearly that there was considerable variation in the swings in these seats but, by the nature of things, it had a comparatively small effect on the number of these seats won since these are the 'low hanging fruit', mostly seats that given a uniform swing the Conservatives would win with plenty of votes to spare and, therefore, not too vulnerable to random fluctuation. As the average swing in seats where Labour was first and the Conservatives second was 5.8%, every one of these seats would have been captured on a uniform swing. Even so, with four seats in the group swinging to Labour and another seven swinging to the Tories but not strongly enough, that makes almost a dozen failures that the Tories needed to make up elsewhere.

Figure 24: Swing to Conservatives in Labour-held targets 76-150

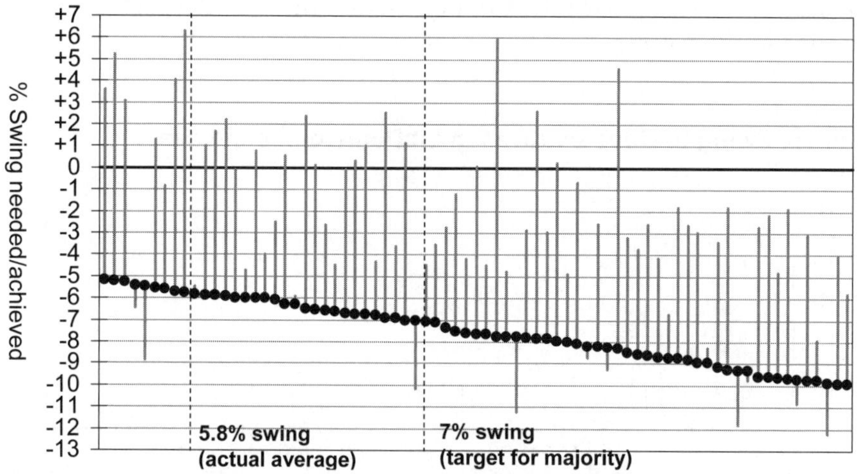

Source: Calculated from election results as published by the House of Commons Library in Research Paper 10/36 (8 July 2010)
Note: Constituencies included are the Labour-held constituencies which would fall to the Conservatives on the 76th to 150th smallest swings (from the Rallings & Thrasher 'notional' 2005 results)

Figure 24 shows exactly the same analysis of the next 75 Labour-held target seats which, neatly, all required a swing of between 5% and 10%. Here we can see the random variation between constituency results having far more effect on which are won and which are lost. The leftmost of the two dotted lines shows the average swing in Labour-Conservative seats – if there had been a perfectly uniform swing, the Conservatives would have won every seat to the left of this and lost every seat to the right. In fact the

153

Tories missed another three of those to the left; on the other hand they picked up a good many to the right of the line.

But the rightmost dotted line shows the 7% swing that was the Conservatives' target – to win an overall majority, they needed to win *every* seat to the left of this line (or pick up one more remote target to compensate for every failure), and do similarly well against the Liberal Democrats. Of course, they fell well short of that.[77]

Finally, to complete the picture, we can look at the Conservative-Liberal Democrat marginals in the same way (Figure 25). In this case, as well as showing the LibDem seats targeted by the Conservatives, we also include the most narrowly-held Conservative seats where the LibDems were the challengers, as Clegg's party had hopes of turning the tables and, indeed, succeeded in three cases.

Figure 25: Swing to Conservatives in LibDem-competing seats

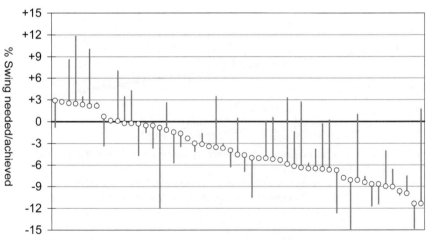

Source: Calculated from election results as published by the House of Commons Library in Research Paper 10/36 (8 July 2010)

---

[77] One Conservative gain from Labour is not shown on the chart: Cannock Chase, gained with a 14% swing, was only target number 157 and therefore off the right-hand edge of the chart.

Again, the results are very erratic – while the average swing from Liberal Democrat to Conservative in all seats where the Conservatives were second to the Liberal Democrats in 2005 was 2.0%, there are very few where the swing was this small – in most it was much larger, but often to the Liberal Democrats rather than against them, so bringing the average down. The variation seems plainly pretty random and it is difficult to discern any pattern except that the Liberal Democrats were unusually successful in many of their most narrowly-held seats, suggesting some successfully-targeted strategic campaigning – but perhaps this, or over-optimism at the course of the campaign, meant they took their eye off the ball and lost a number of what should have been much safer seats to unexpectedly big swings.

Overall, then, we see an erratic picture of constituency results apparently varying fairly randomly. Between the Conservatives and Labour, at least, there are still signs of the traditional underlying uniform swing, but many more constituencies now vary substantially from that pattern than we have tended to expect. But whatever the causes of that variation, it does not seem to be driven by systematically-different swings in constituencies in particular reaches of the list of target seats. If either side's targeting of seats had any effect on their performance, it has been so subtle as to elude us.

Tory standing on the eve of the election

There seemed no logical reason why Gordon Brown should be seeing a recovery in his public image, except perhaps that the expenses scandal was diverting the spotlight from more damaging coverage. In September, the *Sun* – Britain's best-read and most politically-fickle newspaper – had declared for Cameron, after supporting Labour for three elections. In November, Brown had been roughly handled at the Iraq War enquiry, and December's Pre-Budget Review stirred few hearts despite its promise of a tax on bankers' bonuses. Yet, through all this, public satisfaction with Brown's performance as Prime Minister was edging upwards.

Then in the first week of the New Year, the former Cabinet ministers Patricia Hewitt and Geoff Hoon staged a short-lived attempt at a leadership putsch – 'the coup that melted faster than the snow', consigned to history in hours when no other senior figures would publicly back them. Within weeks both had been suspended from the Labour Party when they and a number of other MPs were recorded by undercover reporters touting for lobbying work with promises of the influence they could wield. Soon, also, came Andrew Rawnsley's book, claiming that Brown was a serial bully towards his staff. That, too, made not a scintilla of difference, apparently. Brown rode on.

Meanwhile, the faltering of the Conservative campaign became more obvious. Most memorable was the poster of David Cameron, unveiled in January with the slogans 'We can't go on like this' and 'Year for change'. The *Daily Mail* (of all papers) immediately ran a story suggesting that the picture had been airbrushed[78], and this led to an inventive and sometimes brilliant series of parodies on a website set up for the purpose, mydavidcameron.com, under the title 'Airbrushed for change'. The website (which credited the original poster 'courtesy of the *Daily Mail*') offered the facility to reproduce the original poster but with the user's choice of wording, and many also took the opportunity to manipulate or change altogether the photograph before submitting their offering. Cameron and his campaign were being ridiculed, highly effectively, and the *Daily Mail* kept up the pressure, running a story on the campaign and showing no less than 18 of the best spoofs on the *Mail* website.[79] The mydavidcameron website subsequently gave several other Conservative posters the same treatment (including the ones with the slogan starting 'I've never voted Tory before, but…', which were just asking for trouble!)

The voting intention polls were slow at first to reflect the Tories' weakening grip on the government's throat, but with the turn of the year they suddenly began to narrow. An average 11-point lead in December was down to 10 points in January, with the Tories steady on the psychologically-important 40% but Labour creeping up. Then in February the Tories were down to 38% and Labour up to 31%; and in March the lead was just 6 points.

There were some signs of hope for the Tories in the other indicators. Cameron's satisfaction ratings were similar to those for the victorious

---

[78] 'Meet Dave, the 'airbrushed' poster boy: Tories launch £500,000 pre-election campaign', *Daily Mail*, 5 January 2010, http://www.dailymail.co.uk/news/article-1240734/As-pre-election-campaign-steps-gear-meet-Dave-airbrushed-poster-boy.html, accessed 11 October 2010.

[79] http://www.dailymail.co.uk/news/article-1249616/Airbrushed-change-spoofs-David-Camerons-election-poster-swamp-web.html, accessed 11 October 2010.

campaigns of Margaret Thatcher in 1979 and Blair in 2001 (though lower than Blair's rating in 1997). The public were considerably more satisfied with Cameron than they had been at this stage of the campaign with any party leader who went on to lose the election.

Figure 26: Parties' perceived readiness to govern

Q. To what extent do you agree or disagree that the Conservatives/Labour are ready to form the next Government?

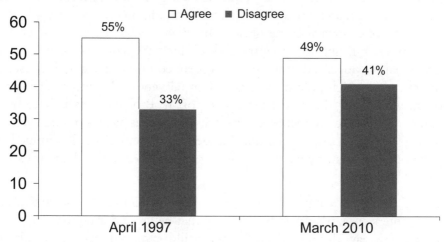

Base: 1,114 GB residents aged 18+, 8 April 1997; 1,503 GB residents aged 18+, 19-22 March 2010
Source: Ipsos MORI Political Monitor

Almost half the public, too, agreed that they felt the Conservatives were ready to form the next government (Figure 26); but it was a less enthusiastic endorsement than Tony Blair had managed in 1997, 14 points lower in the net score (a differential which, if applied to Tony Blair's lead in votes, would leave David Cameron well short of his target).

As we suspected at the time and saw confirmed by events, the Tories had blown it. The winning lead had slipped away. Below the 'magic 40%', the Tories were in trouble. Not because they couldn't beat Labour, but because at best they were unlikely to win big enough to have a sufficient majority to guarantee a full term, and without a good campaign, an overall majority might elude them altogether. It did.

3. The new presidentialism in British politics

Issues or image? Why people vote as they do

So far we have considered the strengths and weaknesses of the parties and their leaders almost entirely in terms of their general image, touching only very lightly on matters related to policy. Yet traditionally, most people tend to think of elections as being decided by 'issues': what are the problems or opportunities facing the country about which the voters care most, and which party's policies do they see as best suited to the challenge? These are the terms in which politicians most often talk about the choice facing the country and how the media tend to report it. Probably this is how most voters would like to feel elections are decided as well – certainly, they usually report their own decisions as being predominantly determined by policies rather than by what they think of the leaders or of the parties as a whole.

Yet of course in reality it is never remotely this simple. In the first place, most voters are not swayed by anything that happens during the election at all. Even today, the majority of voters still maintain long-term loyalty to one or other of the political parties, and short-term factors are very unlikely to shake this. For them, one election is no different from another. Their votes can be predicted a long way in advance, unless a monumentally significant factor or issue intervenes. This is particularly true of Labour and Conservative support. Both parties have a substantial 'core vote'.

It is rather less true of the Liberal Democrats, as it was less true of their centre party predecessors, the Liberals, the relatively short-lived Social Democratic Party (SDP) and the Liberal-SDP Alliance. This has always for many been an 'opt-out' vote for those who are dissatisfied with their traditional party but cannot bring themselves to vote for the opposition, or primarily a protest vote against the two major parties; as the late LSE Professor Hilda Himmelweit described it, 'the dustbin vote'.[80]

---

[80] H Himmelweit, P Humphreys, M Jaeger and M Katz, *How Voters Decide* (London: Academic Press, 1981).

Traditionally, a much lower proportion of Liberal Democrat voters in any election have had much (or any) ideological commitment or long-term loyalty to the party than is the case for either Labour or the Conservatives.

In numerical terms, we can safely say that the Conservatives and Labour both have a substantial 'core vote' which almost nothing will shift, while that for the Liberal Democrats is much smaller and that of the smaller established parties such as the Scottish and Welsh nationalists is in numerical terms tiny, but just as solid. For all these voters, an election campaign is virtually redundant except, perhaps, to remind them to vote at all.

Nevertheless, though the combined 'core vote' is substantial, no party has a big enough permanent support to win elections without finding further votes from elsewhere. In fact the root strength of the two main parties is fairly evenly balanced: we have tended to state it (perhaps a little over simply, but only a little) as being that three in ten voters in the aggregate will (almost) always support the Conservatives, another three in ten Labour, around one-fifth the Liberal Democrats and other smaller parties, leaving between 20% and 25% who are 'floating voters' who hold the balance of power and determine the electoral outcome. Consequently the election campaign is not, after all, redundant, but in reality its effect is concentrated not on the whole electorate but only on a small part of it.

Indeed, given the way the British electoral system works, not even all of these voters, if they do vote, really play much role in determining the result. The majority of constituencies are safe for one party or another, and factors that swing the opinions of the floating voters there will not affect the election outcome – the seat will go to the same party which always wins it. It is only the few floating voters in marginal seats that can change anything by changing their votes: these 'swing' voters will determine not only the outcome but the margin of winning and losing the election, and in a typical British election make up as little as 20% of the electorate in 20% of the constituencies or 4% of the total. A perfectly efficient election campaign would concentrate on winning the votes of this 4% and ignore the other 96% entirely (though such a strategy risks being considered cynical or undemocratic). In practice, though, it turns out that opinion in the marginal constituencies is rarely far from removed from the national trend except when purely local factors intervene. While it makes sense to target the parties' campaigning activities in these key seats, the likelihood is that in policy terms the same promises will enthuse or enrage floating voters across the country, in safe and marginal seats alike and will depend on their perception of where the parties' policies stand on issues salient to them, their image of the leaders and the parties and whether they believe that the party can and will deliver on their promises.

But who are these floating voters, and what do they want? One natural assumption is that since they find it possible to contemplate voting for more than one party they are probably ideologically in the centre-ground rather than at any of the extremes; this assumption naturally encourages the parties themselves to occupy the centre-ground as far as they feel able, and to portray their opponents as extremists. No doubt there is some truth in this.

Nevertheless, we have long known that the bulk of floating voters tend to be distinguished by lower-than-average interest in politics, lower knowledge of politics and by implication, as a result are less equipped than average for sophisticated political reasoning. They may vacillate between the political parties not because they hold an ideologically-intermediate position but because they are not really aware of the ideologies of either of the parties in question and perhaps even of their own. They are sometimes portrayed as carefully reading party manifestos and viewing party election broadcasts, reading newspapers and magazines to help them understand each party under consideration and where its strength and weaknesses lie, and consulting others about their choice as well as searching the internet for guidance on how to exercise their franchise. In fact, in most cases, the opposite is true. The 'floating voter' is less interested in politics, less likely to read any newspaper, less likely to watch political news (let alone party election broadcasts), wouldn't dream of searching the internet (and, by the way, is more likely never to have had access to the internet). On top of all that, he or she is less likely to bother to come to the ballot box to cast a vote.

Should we really believe, then, that these key potential voters who will decide the election are going to do so on the basis of careful weighing against each other of the parties' policy positions on each of the issues that concern them? Clearly not. They will naturally be reliant on their impressions of the parties and of their leaders, into which opinions on policies will feed but which will be affected also by impressions of personality, of competence, of trustworthiness and of an ideological direction with which they can sympathise.

Essential to understanding this process is the concept that voting decisions are not driven by 'facts', but by voters' perceptions of the facts. This can be a very different thing. But in the words of the First Century slave philosopher Epictetus, 'Perceptions are truth, because people believe them'. Emotion plays an important role in this. From the rapturous reception given by the political commentariat to Drew Westen's 2007 book on the subject[81], it would seem that this was news to many of them. But, while the importance of Westen's research and the contribution made by his first-rate analysis should not be played down, it is no more than scientific confirmation and explanation from the psychological perspective of what most competent politicians, and most pollsters, knew or thought they knew already from practical experience.

This is a subject which has been much studied by academics in the last few years. The most recent British Election Study analyses[82] place much importance on 'valence issues' as determinants of voting behaviour, by which they mean issues where the parties are in broad agreement as to the aim to be achieved and hence where perceived competence becomes a more important consideration. They find that attitudes towards the leaders have always been closely associated with voting behaviour, and they explain part of this process in terms of what are called 'heuristic cues', a sort of mental short-cut to decision making. (In other words, the degree to which voters trust David Cameron and the other impressions they have of him help them to make up their minds whether they support or oppose his economic policies.) So voters are being affected by 'image', but not in the superficial sense that critics of modern campaigning like to imply. This is part of the normal reasoning process. The involvement of 'emotion' in political decision-making is not some aberration of the democratically-illiterate, but the normal exercise of intelligence towards rational decision-making that every human being carries out every moment of the day.

---

[81] Drew Westen, *The Political Brain: How People Vote and How to Change their Minds – the Role of Emotion in Deciding the Fate of the Nation* (New York: PublicAffairs, 2007).
[82] Most notably Harold D Clarke, David Sanders, Marianne C Stewart and Paul Whiteley, *Political Choice in Britain* (Oxford: Oxford University Press, 2004).

Although these explanations seem to be being studied much more these days than in the past, and are perhaps more widely accepted, there is nothing particularly new about them. One of us (Bob Worcester) had the task of devising a private polling programme for the Labour Party in the early 1970s, and drew up a detailed model[83] of the way voters decide, to guide the investigations that these polls would make. Based on the work of Abraham Maslow[84], he constructed his political 'hierarchy of human needs', linked to a decision tree analysis of inputs and weights, each of which would help to predict what the people in the polling sample would do in the years leading up to and during a general election.

The model began with the individual elector, and the forces impinging on his or her decision-making processes, determining whether or not the elector will turn out to vote and, if so, which party he or she will vote for. Demographic and family factors are involved, other considerations, issues, direct party and indirect media pressures, and local factors as well. All of these are driven and modified by people's values, which may dictate a party loyalty that none of the other parties can shift or, more rarely, create a permanent floating voter driven by an ideal which does not fit into the traditional left-right dichotomy of British politics and transcends any possibility of party loyalty. But the essential basis of the model was that these factors do not act in isolation – they constantly interact with each other to affect a voter's decision.

The Political Triangle

The central element which emerged from the model, and around which the subsequent polling programme was constructed, was what we came to call the 'Political Triangle', the three interacting aspects of overwhelming importance by which floating voters choose between competing

---

[83] The development of the model is described in more detail in Robert M Worcester, *British Public Opinion: A Guide to the History and Methodology of Political Opinion Polling* (Oxford: Basil Blackwell, 1991), pp 49-50, and also discussed in Robert Worcester & Roger Mortimore, *Explaining Labour's Landslide* (London: Politico's Publishing, 1999), pp 43-8. We applied it to the 2005 election in Robert Worcester, Roger Mortimore and Paul Baines, *Explaining Labour's Landslip* (London: Politico's Publishing, 2005), pp 11-46. It has also demonstrated its continued usefulness for private polling when adapted for MORI's work in other countries in the last few years.

[84] A H Maslow, 'A Theory of Human Motivation', *Psychological Review*, Volume 50, 370-96 (1943).

governments in Britain: (i) their attitudes to the parties themselves; (ii) their impressions of their leaders (as candidates for the premiership); and (iii) their perceived consonance or dissonance with the parties' policies to deal with the issues facing the country. Since 1989, when MORI ceased to conduct Labour's private polls, we have continued to track the same measurements of political opinion as the backbone of our public polling programme for the media.

Figure 27: The Political Triangle©, 2010

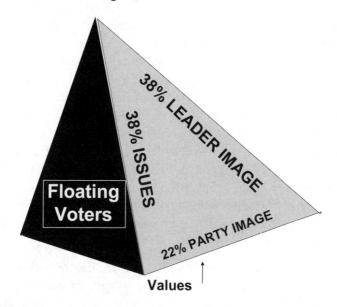

Source: Ipsos MORI
Base: 1,210 GB residents aged 18+ and giving a voting intention

The first question is naturally to establish the relative importance of the three elements, which will change over time with circumstances. This can be achieved in the first instance by asking respondents themselves to judge between the three factors: the percentages shown in our visualisation of the model (Figure 27) are the averages of weights that the prospective voters reported they were giving to each of the three factors in our survey shortly before the start of the 2010 election. They rated the party leaders as being as important as policies in attracting them to the party they currently intended to vote for: on average, they gave 3.8 points out of 10 to each of leaders and policies, and 2.2 points to the party as a whole. (The missing 0.2 is accounted for by 'don't know' answers.)

Asking voters about how they themselves see the relative importance of the three factors gives an important clue to their real importance, and is especially valuable as a trend by which the position in different elections can be directly compared. But this is of course a simplification – people's motives and their reasoning processes are complex, and they are not generally in a position to analyse them objectively. Further, as we have already noted, the factors inevitably impinge on each other to such an extent that is probably unrealistic to suppose that one can be separated from another. The importance of leaders is probably systematically understated by respondents, if only because they will tend to have a much clearer impression of the leaders (and their parties), built up sometimes over a period of years, than they will of the detailed policies, and hence there is more scope for their impressions of the leaders and parties to be unconsciously taken into account as they form their impressions of the parties' policy stances than vice versa. What is more, because it is almost certainly the case that most voters feel they 'should' be deciding on the basis of issues rather than personalities, there is probably a degree of 'social desirability bias' (the process by which survey findings can sometimes be distorted by some respondents giving the answer they think the interviewer expects or that they would like the interviewer to believe rather than the candid truth).

More elaborate surveys, such as the British Election Study, which ask many questions to the same respondents and so can examine in more depth how different opinions are related, can probably dissect more precisely how much influence the various factors have on the choice of the average voter. But for our less ambitious purposes, the political triangle question is adequate for its task. If the relative importance of leaders, parties and policies is changing, we should find an echo of it here.

This theoretical background sets the stage to present the findings in Figure 28, which in some ways are the most important in the whole book towards understanding the 2010 election. This shows the public's reported perception of their voting motivations at each election since we first put the question to them in this way, in 1987. Up to and including the 2005 general election, the pattern was clear and has been since the 1980s. The British public's principal reason for voting for a particular party, they have told us, was because of its policies, then its leader's image and finally the party's image.

Figure 28: The Political Triangle: trends

Q. I want you to think about what it is that most attracted you to the ... party. Some people are attracted mainly by the policies of the party, some by the leaders of the party and some because they identify with the party as a whole. If you had a total of ten points to allocate according to how important each of these was to you, how many points would you allocate to the leaders of the party you intend voting for, how many to its policies, and how many to the party as a whole?

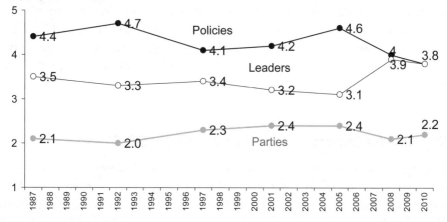

Source: Ipsos MORI
Base: c. 800/1,600 adults in each survey aged 18+ and naming a party. Figures shown are mean scores for each answer.

The 2010 election was different. As can be seen in the graph, it was the first election since we started asking this question at which the public have not given most importance to policies, usually by a wide margin. This time, policies and leaders shared the top spot. But the switch did not come out of the blue (and nor can it be dismissed as a 'rogue' polling result), for we found similar figures earlier in the parliament, in August 2008.

In comparison with the past, many more people considered the image of the party leader as the important determinant in their voting decision, and this rise was for the most part at the expense of the importance that people attached to the policies of the parties. Never before had the rating of leaders come close to that for policies. Certainly, never before had there been a clear gap in favour of leaders rather than policies among any one party's supporters as there was in 2010: those who intended to vote Labour gave 4.0 to leaders (presumably from the other evidence mainly a rejection of David Cameron rather than an endorsement of Gordon Brown), 3.6 to policies and 2.2 to the party as a whole, while Tories gave 3.9 to leaders, 3.7 to policies and 2.2 to the party. Liberal Democrats, however, gave slightly less priority to leaders (3.6) and more to policies (4.0).

The findings presented a further surprise to us, as we expected we would find substantial differences between 'certain' voters and 'floating' voters, yet there was little difference. The importance of leaders was, however, particularly marked among those who read tabloid newspapers (4.15 points on average) and those aged over 55 (4.35 points); broadsheet readers and those aged 18-34 give greater weight to policies in choosing who to vote for.

Why did the importance of policies fall in 2010?

Of course, the dominance of leaders in the 2010 election was evident in much beyond this poll finding, and did not pass the commentators by. But most who discussed it assumed that a pivotal role in this change was played by the introduction of the leaders' debates, and by implication that the concentration on leaders was driven entirely from above, by the campaigning tactics of the parties and the news agendas pursued by the media. This might be reasonably taken as a sign that the 'Presidentialisation' of British politics, much talked about in the past but rarely admitted by the voting public, was now beginning to take hold.

But Figure 28 shows that it is not nearly as simple as that. Our 2010 survey was conducted in February, long before the leaders' debates had further focused voters' attentions on the party leaders; and for that matter the findings are not materially different from those in August 2008, long before the 2010 debates had been agreed or even formally proposed – but not before the beginnings of the economic crisis that transformed and overshadowed the entire issue agenda of the election. The evidence is very clear: Britain was already geared up for a 'presidential' campaign long before the leaders' debates (and in this sense perhaps it could be argued that the debates that the broadcasters had worked so hard to obtain were a symptom of Britain's 'presidential' electoral system and not a contributory cause). Given that we expect responses to the 'political triangle question' to understate the real extent of the influence that impressions of the leaders have on voting behaviour, and given the unquestionable impact that the debates had on the course of the campaign, we can assume that the eventual influence of the leaders on voting was much, much greater than even our February figures suggest.

But if the debates were not the cause, why did the importance of issues slip? Surely for precisely the reasons we have argued in the past[85]: if policies are not in the forefront of the minds of most voters, it is because most issues are not salient to themselves and their families, or because they don't see any differences between the parties on the issues that *are* salient to them, or don't believe that the party if in power could carry out the policy (perhaps because, like the economy, it was felt to be a world-wide problem beyond the capability of any British solution), or believe that it would not carry it out (possibly for political reasons, like the issue of Europe for the Conservatives). In 2010, the issues that mattered most to the voters were ones where they could not adequately distinguish between the parties' policies, or opposed all the options they were being offered, or simply did not trust any of the parties to keep the promises they were making.

Specifically, the economic crisis gradually rose to prominence as the issue of concern dominating all others, and at the same time became an issue on which no party had a clear advantage, on which all the possible policies were unpopular and therefore one which had little role to play in guiding people's voting. On immigration, another policy issue of increasing salience to the public, it was clear that they distrusted all parties and felt that the politicians were evading the subject (as, indeed, they almost certainly were, as this is an issue where the general policy consensus of all parties is completely at odds with the public's instincts.) And more generally, the positions of the parties on most issues have tended to converge in recent years and many of the public have no clear view of their policies.

---

[85] For example in Robert Worcester, Roger Mortimore and Paul Baines, *Explaining Labour's Landslip* (London: Politico's Publishing, 2005), pp 17-19.

The public's broad level of policy illiteracy was well demonstrated in a Populus survey for *The Times* just after the start of the campaign (Table 40). Respondents were asked about eight policies which the various parties had put forward, and in only one case was a majority of the public agreed which party's policy it was. In most cases, voters were almost evenly split on whether the policy was a Conservative or Labour one. But, to be fair to the voters, perhaps part of the difficulty was that the ideological differences between the parties are so small these days that almost of the policies listed might have been proposed by any of them. Little wonder that the parties were finding it hard to gain a clear advantage on any issue.

Table 40: The public's policy (il)literacy

Q I am going to read out some policies that have been proposed by one or other of the political parties during the election campaign so far. Please say in each case which party you think has proposed the policy.

		Lab	Con	Lib Dem	Other	Don't know
A tax break worth £150 a year for married couples and civil partners, paid for by a new tax on banks	%	14	60	6	*	20
Reducing the increase in national insurance contributions currently due to come into effect next year	%	39	35	7	1	19
Allow successful schools, hospitals and police services to take over nearby failing ones to spread best practice	%	29	30	10	*	30
Changing the law so that a two-thirds majority of shareholders would be required to approve the takeover of major British firms, rather than just the simple majority currently required	%	24	24	13	1	39
Fixed term parliaments, so that Prime Ministers no longer have the power to choose the date of general elections	%	19	21	27	1	32
An elected House of Lords	%	34	20	15	1	31
Requiring foreign workers employed in public services to speak fluent English	%	22	40	8	4	26
Doubling the period of paid paternity leave during the first year of a baby's life from 2 weeks to 4 weeks	%	41	22	11	1	25

Source: Populus/*The Times*[86]
Base: 739 GB residents aged 18+, 12 April 2010

---

[86] http://www.populuslimited.com/the-times-the-times-poll-april-2010-120410.html.

Oddly in the circumstances, the public do not necessarily accept their own weak grasp of policy detail. On 19-20 April, just before the second debate, a ComRes poll[87] found that 57% of the public felt they had 'a good understanding of [Gordon Brown's] party's key policies', 56% of David Cameron's and 50% of Nick Clegg's – and each party scored in the region of 80% among those intending to vote for them. But of course this does not invalidate the point. Even if one policy option was far more popular than another, the party advocating it would gain no benefit if their opponents' supporters were mistaken about which party's policy it was, however confidently they held those beliefs.

Probably only time will tell for sure whether the apparent decline of policy issues to lower significance than previously in explaining voting behaviour is part of a long-term process of 'presidentialisation' of British elections, or simply a one-off effect in 2010 dictated by the circumstances of the election. But it is certainly possible to see in the data we collected during the course of the Parliament good reasons to suppose that it was the natural product of the circumstances.

Despite the public's lower-than-normal willingness or ability to engage with the policy issues in 2010, however, we don't believe it is necessarily a sign of a permanent shift towards greater concentration on the leaders. When the public has stopped trusting the promises of any of the parties on the key issues, then issues are unlikely to swing the election. Arguably the key point in reviving the importance of issues will be the extent to which the parties can re-establish trust, and in that public perceptions of the leaders is likely to be vital. But it may be, nevertheless, that trust in the leaders will become a means to an end rather than the end in itself, and that policy differences between the parties will once more come to be seen as the main deciding factor.

The issue agenda in 2010

Of course, the roster of issues which concern the public and which might affect their voting at an election is constantly evolving. We monitor this agenda through the Ipsos MORI Issues Index, a survey normally

---

[87] ComRes poll for ITV News and the *Independent*, http://www.comres.co.uk/systems/file_download.aspx?pg=591&ver=2, accessed 17 January 2011.

conducted monthly, which tracks the changes in the number of Britons citing various issues as among the most important facing the country. The time series is a long one (we first asked these questions in September 1974), and with an unchanged methodology. The questions are asked on an open-ended basis, recording respondents' spontaneous answers without their being prompted by being shown a list or in any other way (though the answers are then categorised from a list that the interviewer sees but the respondent does not). Respondents are asked what is 'the most important issue facing Britain today' followed by the 'other important issues facing Britain today'. The combined responses from these questions (most important issue plus any others) form what we refer to as the Issues Index.

In the short term, there is generally a strong degree of consistency between the public's answers in one month and the next. Nevertheless, over time the Issues Index responses have shown very substantial changes, as the nature of society, politics and people's own concerns change. In the 1970s, inflation and trade unions/strikes tended to be the dominant issues. For most of the 1980s and the early 1990s, it was unemployment, while by the second half of the 1990s, as the political agenda moved to debating the provision of public services, it was generally the NHS/health care that was the issue causing the most widespread concern. Then, after 9/11 and the invasions of Afghanistan and Iraq that eventually followed, defence/foreign affairs and international terrorism were top of the list as often as not for several years. Today, it is the economy, as it has been since September 2008; but before the onset of the current crisis the economy as such had never been the single most cited important issue in thirty years of our polling – though, of course, the previously much-mentioned issues of unemployment and inflation are only facets of the same problem.

But the index can also pick up shorter-lived worries as well as the more permanent shifts in the public mood. In July 1989, perhaps as a result of publicity around CFCs and the holes in the ozone layer, a third (35%) of the public saw pollution/environment as amongst the key issues, higher than any other. For much of 1990, after the introduction of the poll tax, local government was the most important issue, and at the end of that year it was defence/foreign affairs as a result of the Gulf War. In the spring of 2001 it was, briefly, Foot and Mouth Disease. In fact there is generally a close correlation between the appearance of issues near the top of the rankings and the degree of media coverage they receive, and research suggests that the concerns are more driven by, than drivers of, the media agenda, although of course they cannot in any case be entirely independent of each other.

We have, therefore, in the Issues Index a sensitive indicator which we can expect to pick up the signals from the public as to what is worrying them most, and which can probably indicate in advance the issues which might predominate in an impending election. However, experience has shown us that we can't take this for granted, because sometimes the voters feel that the issues that most concern them will not be affected by the outcome of the election – they may not be able to choose between the parties' competing policies, or they may not trust the parties to have either the will or the ability to implant them, or they may simply feel that nothing any government could do would make the situation better or worse. For this reason, we make a separate measurement of the issues that the public believe will be important in their voting.

Evolution of the public's concerns

Four issues tended to predominate among the 'important issues facing the country' between the 2005 election and mid-2008, when concern about the economy suddenly began to take off. Two of these, the NHS and crime, are perennial concerns and consistent election issues – the NHS usually a strength for Labour and crime for the Tories. The other two had risen to prominence more recently: defence/foreign affairs (covering both the situation in Iraq and the wider question of international terrorism), and race relations/immigration/ asylum. These two are clearly related in some respects, and concern about each comes from both ends of the political spectrum and expresses varying and incompatible points of view. But from 2008, and then continually to the election, it was the economy 'first, and the rest nowhere', especially if we include with this issue that of unemployment, which is plainly a different aspect of the same problem.

Figure 29 shows graphically the main results of our monthly polling on the most important issues facing the country during the 2005-10 Parliament. With so many issues vying for first place in the early period, it is perhaps a little too 'busy' to paint an entirely clear picture, but the extraordinary way in which concern about the economy pushed every issue completely off the agenda from the middle of 2008 leaps to the eye. The detailed figures for the twelve leading issues, averaged quarterly, are shown in Table 41.

Figure 29: Most important issues facing Britain, 2005-10

Q. What would you say is the most important issue facing Britain today? What do you see as other important issues facing Britain today?

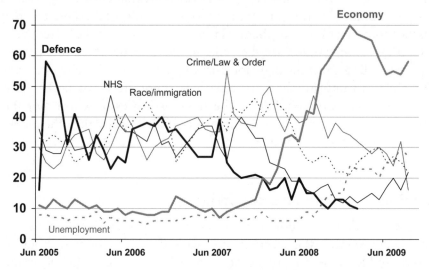

Source: Ipsos MORI Issues Index
Base: c. 1,000 GB residents aged 18+ each month

Several issues were so conspicuous by their absence from the top of the rankings that they also merit comment. Education was still a concern, but much less widespread than it was a few years ago. For one thing, the Liberal Democrats' hypothecated tax support for education was dropped from their manifesto and so from media comment. For an issue that was such a key component in Labour's successful election campaigns in the past to have slipped so far down the public's priorities might well have handicapped the party when the election came.

Euro-scepticism was central to the Conservative general election campaigns in 2001 and 2005, but it has always been a minority concern. In this Parliament, concern about Europe/the EU hit 19% in June 2005, but after that never rose above 7% in any month, not even during the vocal campaigning over the Lisbon Treaty or at the time of the European Parliament elections in 2009. (In mid-campaign of those elections, 21-27 May 2009, just 5% of the British public mentioned Europe, the EU or anything to do with them as one of the most important issues facing the country. In other words, it was always effectively impossible that Europe could be made the focus of a successful election campaign for any party in 2010: it simply is not important enough to enough of the voters.)

Table 41: Most important issues facing Britain today. quarterly averages

Q. What would you say is the most important issue facing Britain today?
Q. What do you see as other important issues facing Britain today?
(Unprompted – combined answers)

	Economy	Unemployment	Inflation/ Prices	Defence / Foreign Affairs	NHS	Crime / Law & Order	Schools / Education	Pollution / Environment	Housing	Pensions/ Soc. Sec.	Race Relations/ Immigration	Taxation
	%	%	%	%	%	%	%	%	%	%	%	%
2005 Q3	11	7	2	53	28	24	20	5	5	9	33	6
2005 Q4	12	7	2	36	32	33	27	6	5	13	28	8
2006 Q1	10	7	2	30	33	30	27	9	6	12	29	7
2006 Q2	9	6	2	25	40	36	24	11	6	14	37	6
2006 Q3	9	6	3	37	34	32	20	10	7	9	42	7
2006 Q4	9	6	4	38	32	33	20	12	7	9	38	9
2007 Q1	14	6	7	36	27	37	22	19	8	8	25	7
2007 Q2	10	8	4	27	37	37	21	12	10	8	38	7
2007 Q3	10	8	4	24	31	48	18	8	10	6	39	7
2007 Q4	12	7	6	21	37	38	20	8	14	6	44	8
2008 Q1	20	7	9	18	27	46	17	8	10	6	43	9
2008 Q2	33	6	18	18	20	38	14	8	13	7	36	10
2008 Q3	46	9	24	14	16	42	12	7	11	4	26	6
2008 Q4	62	15	19	12	14	35	10	6	7	4	24	3
2009 Q1	69	24	13	11	13	33	11	7	7	3	23	2
2009 Q2	59	23	12	9	15	29	13	8	7	4	28	3
2009 Q3	55	28	9	19	18	28	12	7	6	4	26	3
2009 Q4	51	25	10	20	18	25	13	9	5	6	29	3
2010 Q1	52	21	8	17	19	25	17	7	5	6	31	5

Source: Ipsos MORI Political Monitor
Base: c. 2,000-3,000 GB residents aged 18+ each quarter interviewed in monthly surveys

Note too that, despite the attention the issue has received both in the media and from politicians of all parties, the environment remained a top-of-the-mind concern to only a small minority – the apparent perception that the 2009/10 contest was shaping to be Britain's first 'green' election was probably wide of the mark even had the economic downturn not pushed environmental concerns further off the agenda. Although more of the public were prepared to admit the issue as important when prompted, and give at least lip-service to support for policies aimed at tackling global warning and climate change, there must remain a suspicion that votes would still have been lost rather than won by putting concern for the environment above bread-and-butter issues of the economy or public services. David Cameron's earlier appeal to voters to 'Vote Blue, Go Green' may have been important in helping to 'rebrand' the Conservatives when he was newly elected its leader, but this message was little pushed in the general election campaign in 2010. (One symbolic counterbalance to this argument, of course, was the election of Caroline Lucas as the first Green MP.)

The election issue agenda

When we came to ask the public which issues would be very important to them to help decide their vote in the approaching election, we also found the economy at the head of the list, but named by many fewer than were citing it as one of the most important issues facing the country. Table 42 shows the findings, from the survey we conducted in late March 2010. (For the purpose of understanding the ranking of the public's concerns, we have treated the economy and unemployment as a single issue, although they were distinguished and recorded separately when interviewers classified respondents' answers at the time the survey was conducted[88]: it is questionable whether there is a clear distinction in meaning between those who name the economy as important to their vote and those who name unemployment, which may be two different ways of expressing the same thing.)

As well as indicating the issues on which respondents might vote, this survey can be compared with the Issues Index to show which public

---

[88] 32% were coded as mentioning 'the economy' or 'economic management' and 11% as mentioning 'unemployment'.

concerns are absent from the election agenda, those issues that the public considers important nationally yet for one reason or another does not prompt a vote in any particular direction. The most striking point, perhaps, is the paucity of the election issue agenda. Respondents were able to name as many different issues as they felt important, but only five issues (taking the economy and unemployment as one) were named by more than even one in ten of the public. These top five were the economic situation, healthcare, education, asylum/immigration and taxation.

Table 42: The issue agenda: 'very important' election issues

Q. And looking ahead to the next General Election, which, if any, issues do you think will be very important to you in helping you decide which party to vote for?

	All %	Certain to vote %
Economy/unemployment*	40	44
Healthcare/ NHS/ hospitals	26	29
Education/ schools	23	27
Asylum and immigration	14	18
Taxation	12	12
Crime and anti-social behaviour/ law and order	8	9
Benefits	7	7
Pensions	6	7
Care for older/disabled people	7	7
Afghanistan	5	5
Iraq	3	3
Defence	3	4
Protecting the natural environment/ climate change	5	6
Housing	3	2
Public transport/ roads	3	3
Europe/ EU	2	3
Any other issue	17	20
None/don't know/no answer	16	10

Source: Ipsos MORI
Base: 1,503 GB residents aged 18+, 19-22 March 2010
*Combines those mentioning either 'Managing the economy/economic situation' or 'unemployment'

By comparison, there are three issues scoring above 20% and six above 17% in the 'most important issues facing the country' polling for the first quarter of 2010 (Table 41 above), assuming again we take the economy and unemployment combined as a single issue. While it is not safe to make too much of the direct comparison (one survey was conducted by telephone, the other face to face), there is a clear suspicion that many people did not feel that (all) the issues they thought were important helped them decide how to vote.

Nor is the order of priority of issues the same. Most strikingly, crime is outside the top five election issues, mentioned by only one in twelve of the public. This is an issue which was never entirely pushed off the agenda by growing economic concerns: in fact, with a minimum monthly score of 23% it was the most consistently salient of all issues between 2005 and 2010; but it was apparently not an issue on which people felt they would vote. The government's most distinctive contribution in this field, perhaps, was to tackle the subject of anti-social behaviour, to some extent treating it as part of the same issue as crime, and introducing anti-social behaviour orders (ASBOs) in an attempt to control it. The public were simultaneously welcoming and sceptical: in 2005, 82% of adults in England and Wales said they supported the issuing of ASBOs to people responsible for anti-social behaviour, but only 39% believed that they were effective in stopping people from causing anti-social behaviour (although a somewhat higher 53% saw them as effective at 'showing the local community that something is being done' about the issue[89]). So perhaps this was an issue where voters felt the government meant well but was not achieving anything.

Fewer, too, named asylum/immigration as a vote-influencing issue than considered it an important issue facing the country: only the economy trumped it as a general issue of concern, and there was not a single month in the 2005-10 Parliament where it was named as important issue by fewer than one in five of the public, but it was well behind healthcare and education as an issue that might influence voting. Here the problem seems to have been that none of the parties were trusted on the issue, so many of those who cared about it presumably saw no point voting on it.

By contrast, for healthcare and education more of the public were naming them as vote-prompting issues than as among the important issues facing the country. Part of the reason for this, no doubt, will be that these were among the main important issues in previous general election campaigns, and they might therefore more easily come to mind when a respondent is

---

[89] MORI poll, 19-23 May 2005. MORI interviewed 1,857 adult residents in England and Wales.

asked to name his or her vote-determining issues than other issues that
have been less prominent in the past.

But it may also reflect that more of those who find health or education to
be salient issues see a meaningful distinction between the parties' policies
than do those who are concerned about crime or immigration. It seems
clear that many people make a distinction between a pressing national
issue and an election issue – some problems, many seemed to feel, could
not (at that moment) be solved by voting, either because all the parties
were seen as having the same policies or because those who espoused the
more popular policies were not trusted to carry them out. It may be
coincidental that those issues whose election-salience seems to be
strongest are concerned with public services rather than more general
questions of social governance, or that may be a reflection of some wider
perception about the role of politicians and elections. Whichever is the
case, it seems to be of potential significance.

But what does all this mean in terms of party advantage? Overall, we
found that the public's view of the parties' policies coming into the
election was finely balanced: in February, 29% said they thought the
Conservatives had the best policies for the country as a whole and 27%
that Labour did while 16% preferred Liberal Democrat policies; the
remainder picked some other party, no party, or offered no opinion. That
is not unexpected in a close election. But when we look in more detail at
the individual policy spheres we find that, rather than there being a balance
because one party's advantage on one issue is offset by its opponents
being more popular on another, this broad parity applied almost across the
board to the party standings on most of the salient issues.

Figure 30 shows the results when we asked those people who thought
each issue was important which party they believed had the best policies
on that issue.[90] (Again we have taken those naming the economy or
unemployment as a single group – both are included in those asked which
party has the best policies on managing the economy.) On none of the top
three issues did either of the major parties have a decisive lead, and the
Tory lead on taxation, only six points, is not statistically significant. The

---

[90] The 'Best Party' question in each case was asked to the whole sample, but the responses of those
not thinking the issue important are excluded for this analysis, as we are most interested in those
whose votes might be affected by what they think of the issue.

Tories' *did* have a clear lead on asylum/immigration, at least over Labour and the Liberal Democrats, but fewer of the public picked their policy as best than the combined total of those naming some other party, picking no party or saying they didn't know, not an entirely convincing endorsement.

Figure 30: Best party on key issues

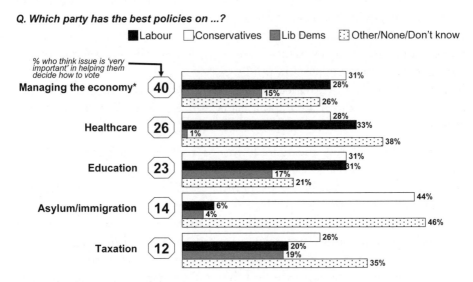

Q. Which party has the best policies on ...?

■ Labour   □ Conservatives   ▒ Lib Dems   ▦ Other/None/Don't know

% who think issue is 'very important' in helping them decide how to vote

Managing the economy* (40)
31%
28%
15%
26%

Healthcare (26)
28%
33%
1%
38%

Education (23)
31%
31%
17%
21%

Asylum/immigration (14)
44%
6%
4%
46%

Taxation (12)
26%
20%
19%
35%

Source: Ipsos MORI Political Monitor
Base: Those thinking each issue was important, from 1,503 GB residents aged 18+ interviewed, 19-22 March 2010
*For 'managing the economy', base includes those naming 'unemployment' as important

Clearly, the implication is that, assuming nothing changed before polling day, there would be a rough balance of power on the issues with none offering a decisive advantage to any party except, perhaps, Tory policy on immigration. (But this was an issue on which the Tories might well have been tempted to soft-pedal given the way it backfired in 2005 in the face of a hostile media reception.) Of course, it would normally be begging the question to assume that nothing would change before polling day. Seizing control of the issue agenda and transforming the voters' perception of party policies is often exactly what much of the election campaign is aimed at achieving. But in 2010, when almost the entire campaign focus was on the leaders, it may have been a safer assumption.

However, we can take the analysis further. To what extent were the issues that people said were important really determinants of their voting intentions? How far did their choices of the best policies on the various issues match up with the party they said they expected they would vote for?

Consider first the issues below first place in the list of priorities. As it happens, these are mostly the issues on which the past few elections have been fought or which the voters at those elections named as important, but which were now pushed out of the spotlight by the economic crisis. Since they were clearly secondary concerns to many voters in 2010, we should not be too surprised if their impact is even less than their ranking on the order of priority suggests – their party preference on health, or education, or crime, might quite reasonably be trumped by a different preference on the more important issue of the economy.

Let us look first at healthcare, second in the list of important issues in 2010, and top in 1997, 2001 and 2005. This was the one mainstream issue where Labour had retained some of the lead it had when Tony Blair was Prime Minister, leading the Conservatives by 9 percentage points among the general public as the party with the best policies. Unfortunately for Labour, the lead was more modest, only 5 points (33% to 28%), among those who picked this as an important issue while 28% of the same group said no party had the best policies or did not know which party had, so this issue too had lost its power for Labour. (In 2001, Labour's lead among those picking the issue as important was 35 points.) About 16% of the public, one in six, said healthcare was important to their vote *and* intended to vote for the party they thought had the best policies on the issue[91]; but we find that as many as 7% despite picking the issue as important named no party as having the best policies, and 5% said the issue was important yet intended to vote *against* the party they felt had the best policies.

---

[91] Those expressing no voting intention are excluded from the analysis altogether – as some of these also expressed policy preferences, their proportions aligning their policy choice with their voting intention would be even lower were they included.

Given that so many with a preference were not intending to vote for the party whose health policies they preferred, we must assume that many of those who *were* voting for the party they felt had the best policies did so only coincidentally. Allowing for this, perhaps 4% of the public and as few as 1% of those 'certain to vote' were really being driven in their voting by their perceptions of health policy – and these were spread between the two main parties, so this issue was failing to 'bite'.

We find a similar story on education, an issue on which Labour enjoyed a substantial advantage throughout the Blair years but where the Conservatives had fought back to parity by 2010, with those believing the issue to be important splitting evenly between the two main parties (31% picking each) as having the best policies. Only a small proportion (4% of the whole public and 3% of those certain to vote) picked education as an important issue without singling out a party as having the best education policies. But again, when we compare the voting intentions of those declaring education's importance with their party preferences on education, those who had a preference and intended to vote that way only narrowly outnumbered those who did not. There was no significant difference between Labour and Conservative in their success at persuading those who preferred their education policy to vote for them, and all the signs are that the issue was a complete electoral stalemate.

But what of immigration and asylum, the issue picked on by some Labour strategists after the election[92] as the one where they crucially failed to connect with the voting public? Certainly, as Figure 30 shows, it was an issue on which Labour started the campaign far behind the Tories, and it is probably true that (on a national level, at least[93]) they failed to make up any significant ground before polling day. It was, as we have seen, perhaps the one 'issue facing the country' apart from the economic crisis on which the biggest proportion of the public had strong feelings. Yet many fewer said

---

[92] For example, Gordon Brown's former pollster Deborah Mattinson, writing in the *Daily Mail*, 'Labour's catastrophic mistake on immigration', 7 August 2010, http://www.dailymail.co.uk/news/article-1301039/Browns-pollster-reveals-Labours-mistake-immigration-cost-power-damaging-democracy.html, accessed 16 February 2011.

[93] Some Labour local campaigns seem to have addressed the issue successfully, as in Barking and Dagenham where Margaret Hodge held her seat with a substantial swing against BNP leader Nick Griffin and where Labour swept all the BNP's councillors out of their wards in the borough elections.

it would be important in helping to decide their vote (only 14% of the public as a whole, and 18% of those who said they were certain to vote, named this as an issue that was important to their vote), and when we look at those that did we can say that the effect was negligible, at least judging by our survey at the end of March.

Taking the public as a whole, we found that half who thought the issue was important intended to vote for a party they felt had the best policies but half did not; of those certain to vote, more were intending to vote against the party with the best policies on the issue, or had no party preference to guide them, than knew which party they preferred and intended to vote for it. Of Labour voters who felt this issue was important, twice as many thought the Tories had the best policy on the issue as thought that Labour did. Put another way, only around two-thirds of those who felt the Tories had the best policy on asylum/immigration, and that this was an issue important to their voting decision, intended to vote Conservative. Neither the Conservatives, nor for that matter the BNP, were gaining significant voting support from the unpopularity of Labour's policy.

This was an issue where the government had lost the public's confidence, if indeed it ever had it, with 72% of the public saying (in our poll for *The Sun* on 31 October- 1 November 2007) that they were dissatisfied with the way the government was dealing with immigration and asylum and 80% disagreeing that 'The government is open and honest about the scale of immigration into Britain'.

Nevertheless, commentators are surely wrong to believe that immigration lost Labour the election or even substantially damaged their chances. It might be argued that with a more popular stance on immigration Labour might have reduced the Tory lead on the issue, but there is no sign that it actually won the Tories significant numbers of votes in any case. (In fact this 38-point Tory lead over Labour on the issue compared to a slightly higher, 41-point, lead in 2005, when it was to a much greater extent a focus of Tory campaigning with their 'It's not racist to oppose immigration' posters – but it didn't stop Labour winning the 2005 election.) If any party could really capture the trust of the electorate on immigration, it might be an entirely different picture, but all parties are a very long way from that (and, for that matter, from securing the voters' total trust on any other issue).

The economy, tax and public spending

However, we still have to address the economy, the one issue we ought to expect to affect voting if any would. Only a minority named managing the economy or unemployment as an issue very important to their vote: 58% of the public as a whole and 57% of those certain to vote did not mention either.[94] Of those that did, they were certainly more likely to be intending to vote for the party they felt had the best policies on managing the economy than for another party, but the relationship was not that strong. The 42% of all adults thinking the issue was important split between 27% who were going to vote for the party they thought had the best policies and 15% who either picked no party's policies as best (7%) or intended to vote against the party they had picked (8%), slightly less than two-to-one. Among those certain to vote the agreement was even lower, 23% aligning their vote with an economic policy preference, 14% voting another way and the remaining 64% not picking it as an important issue or having no preference between the parties' policies.

Given that these influences are not a one-way street, and that it is just as likely that some voters will feel a party has the best policy because they trust that party or its leaders rather than because they have disinterestedly compared the policies, this is a surprisingly weak correlation. Taking the public as a whole, since we have found 15% who say the economy is important yet for some reason intend to vote against the party whose policy they feel is best or cannot pick a party that is best, it is only reasonable to assume that an equal number among those who *are* voting in line with their economic policy preferences are also really driven by some other factor rather than by this policy. That suggests that for only about 12% of the public in total was economic policy the decisive issue on voting choice – and a much lower proportion still (maybe only 2%) of those 'certain to vote', and probably of those who eventually did vote. And, given that this was a policy on which the two main parties stood almost level in terms of the number preferring their policies, and that all parties were successful in converting their own policy-preference-supporters into intending-voters on a roughly equal level, the net effect of

---

[94] As in the previous analyses, we treat 'the economy' and 'unemployment' here as different ways of expressing the same response, but the conclusions are almost identical if we only consider those who gave 'the economy' as an important issue and exclude those who cited 'unemployment'.

the public's perception of party economic policy on the election outcome was almost certainly minuscule.

Of course, for some voters who consider the economy an important election issue it is the government's past record and the current state of the economy as a result that is the determining factor, rather than future policy promises. Perhaps some people voted Labour because they gave Gordon Brown and Alistair Darling credit for avoiding the complete economic meltdown that had looked possible at one point, even if they preferred another party's prescription for the future. Others may have voted Conservative even if they were not necessarily convinced their policies on the economy were the best ones, because they couldn't bring themselves to vote for Labour or Brown as they had been at the helm of the ship when it struck the iceberg.

But this still does not bring us to the root of why the economy was not a decisive election issue. If the issue was so important to so many voters, why did it not drive their voting decision? Why did so many others feel the economy was the most important issue facing the country yet not one that was important in determining their vote at all? And of those who had a preference between the policies of the main parties, was it merely chance that they were almost equal in number or was it that even this group found not very much to choose between the options?

In fact we have been here before, at least in part. At the 1983 election, MORI's private polls for the Labour Party showed that unemployment was seen as the most important issue and that Labour's policies to deal with unemployment were much the most popular. Why, then, did Labour not win that election instead of losing it disastrously? At least partly because the voters thought of it as a world-wide problem at the time of a world-wide recession, and although it was salient to many, and many thought that Labour had the best policies to solve the problem of unemployment and thought Labour would (like) to do something about it, most did not believe that any party could really reduce unemployment and therefore that the issue though important was irrelevant to the electoral choice.

As already noted, for an issue to have an impact it is not sufficient that the voters should see it as important (salience): they must also see a difference between the competing parties with regard to the issue (differentiation), believe that government policy is capable of affecting the situation (without which the policy choice is irrelevant) and be confident that the party whose policies they prefer has the will to implement them if elected.

In 2010, we thought that all of these factors were working against the possibility of economic policy being decisive in the election, and said so in the many opportunities we had on the media and on platforms in answer to the question uppermost in audiences' minds, 'What impact is the financial crisis [as it was almost always put] going to have on the outcome of the election?'.

The economy was overwhelmingly the issue about which the voters were most worried. But many believed that it was a global crisis on which British government policy choices would have no meaningful impact. Others simply rejected all the various policy options being offered, setting an unsolvable policy problem for all parties. Others were either unaware of the policy differences between the parties or did not believe that the pledges would be kept, predicting that governments of all colours would pursue the same policies in office. Many indeed felt the party campaigns were deliberately misleading. (At the opening of the election campaign, a ComRes poll found[95] that 63% of the public agreed that 'Neither Labour nor the Conservatives are being honest about how they would reduce public borrowing'.) Therefore, there was little reason for many of these voters to let party policies on the economy dictate their vote.

Probably the most important of these points is the public's unwillingness to understand or accept that there were differences in the policies the parties would pursue in government. In a poll on 18-20 April, after the differences between the leaders on the issues had already received a considerable airing at the first TV debate, we showed the public a list of four policies and asked whether they thought a Labour or a Conservative government would do each, as well as whether they themselves thought the next government should do so. On three of the four policies – cutting spending on frontline services, increasing income tax and increasing VAT – a clear majority thought both Labour and Conservative governments would act in this way, and a clear majority also thought the next

---

[95] ComRes poll for the *Independent on Sunday* and *Sunday Mirror*, 9-10 April 2010, http://www.comres.co.uk/page1901583313.aspx, accessed 17 January 2011.

government should not. On the fourth option, increasing national insurance, the vast majority thought a Labour government would do so – reasonably enough, as Gordon Brown had just announced he would do exactly that if re-elected. But more also thought the Conservatives would do the same than thought they would not, 47% to 41%, even though David Cameron had made opposition to this 'tax on jobs' the centre of his economic argument in previous days. Again the majority of the public did not want either party to do it.

Figure 31: Economic policies – the gap between desire and expectation

Q. If a Labour/Conservative government is elected after the next General Election do you think it will or will not...?
Q. And do you think the next Government, regardless of which party it is, should or should not...?

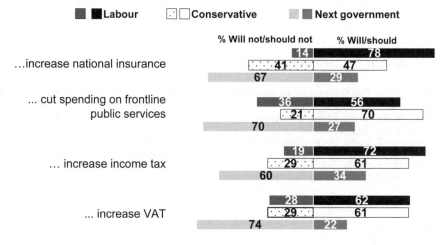

Source: Ipsos MORI
Base: 1,253 GB residents aged 18+, 18-20 April 2010

Perhaps it is hardly surprising then, given these findings, that few of the voters were enthusiastically endorsing either of the parties' economic policies. But in that case what *did* they want? In simple terms, jam today *and* a free lunch tomorrow. Our polling throughout the campaign and in the months before it consistently showed that the public were far less convinced than politicians of all persuasions of the need for urgent, drastic measures to cope with the economic crisis in the first place.

By March 2010, people were almost evenly divided on whether 'There is a real need to cut spending on public services in order to pay off the very high national debt we now have' – 49% agreed and 45% disagreed, but 64% still agreed that 'Making public services more efficient can save enough money to pay off the very high national debt we now have, without damaging services the public receive', hardly changed since November 2009.

Labour might perhaps have had a potential advantage in that their policy of cutting spending more slowly was most nearly in tune with those of the public who saw no need to cut spending at all, and indeed that policy proved twice as popular as the Conservative one of cutting the deficit quickly when we put them to the public, whether or not we told our respondents which party espoused which policy (Table 43). But it seems pretty clear that when we were not reminding them of the party policies, this difference between the policies on offer had not really sunk in.

Table 43: Cut fast or cut slow?

Q. (Version 1) The Conservatives say that the national debt is the greatest threat to the economy and the deficit needs to be cut quickly, starting this year. Labour say that it should not be cut so soon as reducing public spending may stop the economic recovery. Which of these do you think is right?
Q. (Version 2) Some economists say that the national debt is the greatest threat to the economy and the deficit needs to be cut quickly, starting this year. Other economists say that it should not be cut so soon as reducing public spending may stop the economic recovery. Which of these do you think is right?

	Version 1 %	Version 2 %
Cut quickly, starting this year	32	28
Do not cut so soon	56	57
Neither	6	4
Don't know	7	11

Source: Ipsos MORI
Base: Two matched samples of 749 and 754 GB residents aged 18+ each asked one version of the question, 19-22 March 2010

It is natural that voters were reluctant to support painful solutions to a problem they did not fully believe existed. But it may also be that in any case, voters are less susceptible to economic policy arguments for voting than they once were, because they are less convinced that government policy really makes much difference in today's global economy. The same change might apply to the public's willingness to give credit to a government for economic success already achieved (or to vote it out because it was blamed for economic failure).

Figure 32: Economic optimism and Labour voting intention share, 2008-10

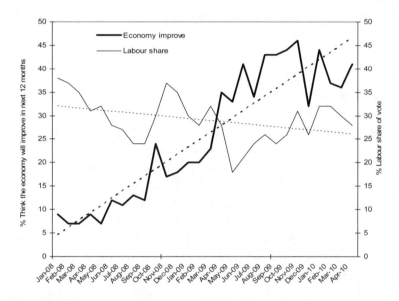

Source: Ipsos MORI Political Monitor
Base: c. 1,000 GB residents aged 18+ in each survey

This is not merely a consequence of the present economic crisis. Arguably, we can see a belief in the government's economic impotence stretching back many years, reflected in the breakdown of the relationship that once existed between support for the governing party and optimism about the future of the economy. In the second half of 2009, in fact, economic optimism had been at a historically high level, yet there was no sign that the government had been benefiting from this in terms of voting intentions. Indeed, from the start of 2008, the trends of economic optimism and Labour voting share were moving in opposite directions, as Figure 32 shows, mapping our monthly economic optimism index (EOI) against Labour's percentage share of voting intentions in the same poll.

However, over the last few months covered by the graph, Labour share tended to rise when the number of optimists was higher, and vice-versa. And this would certainly seem to be the natural scheme of things, since Labour supporters were considerably more optimistic than Conservatives or Liberal Democrats. But the two lines moved in harmony for such a short period that we cannot confidently state that Labour had once more begun to benefit electorally from economic success. And certainly, it proved possible for the government to be defeated despite the EOI having touched its highest-ever levels over the last few months before the election.

This seems odd on the face of it. Received wisdom would seem to be that high levels of economic optimism play an important part in governments being re-elected. But in fact, that received wisdom has not been true for some time, though it seemed to be once. Looking back over the seven elections for which we have data, an interesting pattern emerges. At every general election in our time series when the incumbent government was Conservative (1983, 1987, 1992 and 1997), the index was positive in the last poll before election day; conversely, before 2010 whenever the defending government had been Labour (1979, 2001 and 2005), the index was negative. But, more importantly, there is no consistent relationship between the EOI and the election result – Tony Blair won in 1997 as opposition leader facing a positive EOI, yet also twice won as PM despite a negative EOI that might have been thought to reflect badly on his government. As Figure 33 shows, this completely turns on its head the pattern up to 1992, when a positive EOI saw governments re-elected and a negative one was the precursor of government defeat. So defeat for Gordon Brown was in line with the pattern since 1997, though not with that up to 1992.

But why should the apparently natural link between judgments of the state of the economy and willingness to re-elect the government have broken down? One theory, noting that the break came after the 1992 election, is to attribute the change to 'Black Wednesday'. the day on which sterling fell straight through the floor and out of the European Exchange Rate Mechanism, when the British government found itself less powerful in the international markets than a single American speculator, George Soros. This may have simply convinced British voters that they could no longer reasonably blame their government for its economic failures or, reciprocally, give it credit for any successes. But this explanation is purely speculative, and probably credits public opinion with too much collective rationality, cynicism and a longer-than-realistic folk-memory.

Figure 33: Economic optimism and general election results

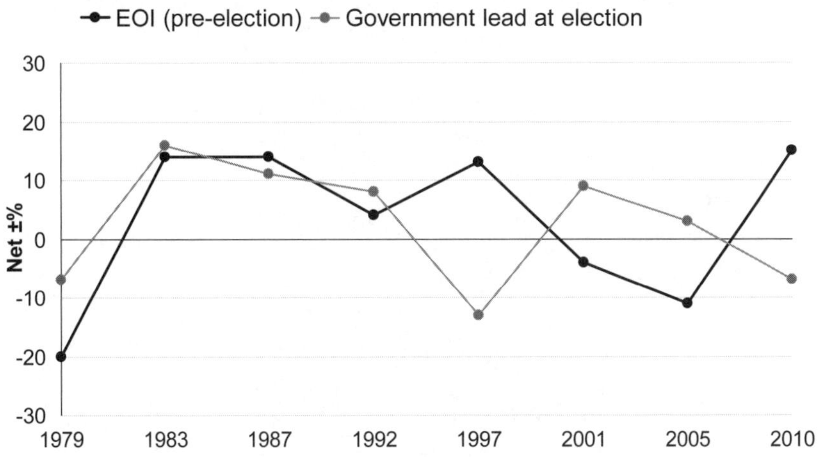

Source: Ipsos MORI
Base: c. 1,000-2,000 GB residents aged 18+ in each survey

An alternative explanation might be that voters are prepared initially to give a government credit for economic success, but once it has lost its credibility is no longer able to recover it. This might plausibly explain why neither in 1997 nor in 2010 could the government marshal the public's economic optimism in its favour sufficiently to gain re-election.

There was, nevertheless, in both cases a clear link between economic optimism and government support in the sense that there was a strong correlation between economic expectations and voting intentions – Conservative voters in 1997 and Labour voters in 2010 were much more likely than average to expect the state of the economy to improve. But given that we cannot tell whether the economic perceptions were drivers of voting intention or whether support for the government bolstered the economic optimism, this does not offer us a clear answer to our question.

At any rate, it seems established that the old habit, whereby a predominant belief among voters that the economy was moving in the right direction

189

was enough to ensure a government's re-election, no longer holds. So, despite having convinced an extraordinarily high proportion of the public that the economy was on the upturn, and despite having a policy to deal with the public spending crisis which was much more popular than that of his Conservative opponents, Gordon Brown could not muster the votes he needed to stay in office. It was plainly not an election at which the issues made the difference.

4. The campaign: how the voters dithered

The tactical battle: overview

Some general elections are a foregone conclusion long before the formal campaign begins but the 2010 general election wasn't one of these. This time no party had a grip on the loyalties of the key floating voters, and so the election campaign was all to play for. That is not always the case. For example, in 1997, there was nothing John Major could do by the time the election date was officially announced that could have pulled a victory out of the electoral bag, and virtually no blunder Tony Blair could have made would have had a powerful enough effect to condemn him to defeat. This campaign was, therefore, different.

The 2010 election campaign started with support for the major parties poised on a knife-edge, where a small swing in one direction or the other could make the difference between Labour survival and a Conservative majority. What was equally important was that the electorate was more volatile than in the past.

For decades now there have been signs that the strength of voters' traditional party loyalties has been being eroded and, during the 2005-10 Parliament, this suddenly blossomed into an unusual degree of instability in the polls. By the time the election was called, the poll numbers seemed to have stabilised, but far more of the public than is usual at this stage of an election were saying they had not yet decided for certain how they would vote. With two-and-a-half weeks to polling day, on 18-19 April 2010, we found a quite extraordinary 49% of those giving a voting intention stating that they might still change their minds. Figure 34 shows the comparison with the poll taken nearest to the same stage of the campaign at every general election since 1983. The number uncertain of their vote at this stage has been steadily rising, from one in six in 1983 to around one in three in 2001 and 2005. But to have half of all voters uncertain so late in the contest really breaks new ground. It meant the voters simply couldn't make up their minds.

Figure 34: Electoral volatility since 1983

Q. Have you definitely decided to vote for the ... party or is there a chance you may change your mind before you vote?

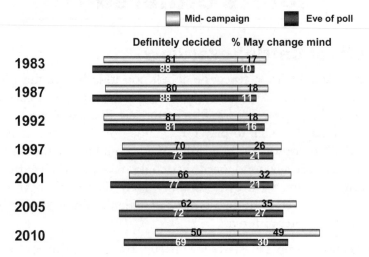

Base: c. 750-1,500 GB residents aged 18+ and giving a voting intention in each survey
Source: Ipsos MORI

Figure 34 also shows how the unusually high level of uncertainty continued until polling day, although by this stage the difference from 2005 was less marked. But three in ten were still not 'definitely decided' even in our final poll, taken the very day before voting. Voters' post-election recollections of their decisions backed this up (see Figure 35). As many as 14% of those who claimed to have voted said they had decided which party to vote for in the final 24 hours, and a further 14% within the preceding week. The corresponding 2005 figures of 10% and 9% were already the highest we had ever found in previous elections.

One reason for such volatility is falling political engagement: far fewer people are committed to a particular party than used to be the case, and lower attention paid to political matters between elections might naturally lead to many of the public feeling less confident of their voting decision when the time came. In many cases, the public were gaining impressions of the candidates or finding information about policies that caused them to switch their support, which in the past would have happened much earlier. But whatever the reason, the potential of the campaign to affect the result in a close election was magnified by the willingness of the voters to be swung in their opinions by events or personalities.

Figure 35: Late decisions on how to vote

Q. When did you decide which party to vote for? Was it before the campaign began, in the first week of the campaign, around the middle, within the last week, or within the last 24 hours?

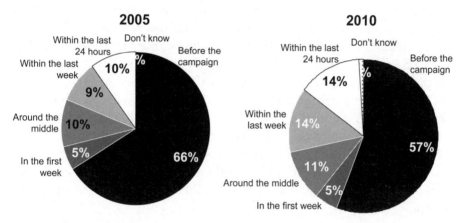

Base: GB residents aged 18+ who said they had voted and named the party (1,399 on 5-10 May 2005, 745 on 12-13 May 2010), 12-13 May 2010
Source: Ipsos MORI Political Monitor

And, moreover, it was evident in advance that there were factors peculiar to the 2010 election which made the result even more unpredictable. For example, the Conservatives' targeted campaigning in the marginal seats (see pages 141–55) made it imperative to keep an eye on the local as well as the national picture, since the latter might give a misleading impression of how many seats the parties could hope to win. Then there was the importance of turnout which, because supporters of some parties tend these days to be more determined to get to the polls than others, might easily be the pivotal factor in the outcome. Turnout always matters, of course, but it is only in the last few elections that significant proportions of those with some preference between the parties have not felt themselves compelled to vote. Looking back at previous elections in modern times, there are none at which it seems clear that turnout had a significant effect in determining which party was the winner. In 2010, however, our polls were suggesting that the difference between everybody with an opinion

193

reaching the polling stations, and only those who were absolutely certain to vote before the campaign started doing so, was the equivalent of a 3% swing, easily enough to tilt the balance.

But above all there was a new wild card in the parties' political marketing armoury: there were to be three televised leaders' debates. We already knew (see Chapter 3) that the public's view of the leaders was likely to be more influential than ever before, with the issues providing a less clear voting prompt than usual. And in the past, even without formal debates, many voters had cited 'the TV debate between the party leaders' as a key factor in their decision. (It was the most mentioned influence in both 2001 and 2005, above other factors such as the views of local candidates, newspapers, and party election broadcasts.) Little wonder, then, that the public expected the debates would have an effect on their vote. Before the election, back in February 2010, three fifths (60%) had said that the debates would be important in helping them decide who to vote for. The audience, at least for the first debate, was set to be massive. It remained to be seen whether after the first hour-and-a-half debate programme anyone other than the political junkies would be there for the rest of the entire four-and-a-half hours.

But assuming that viewers did watch all three debates, could we tell which party was most likely to benefit? No. We had no form, only three runners who had never raced. All three party leaders contesting the debates were new. So the debates were never going to be like Party Election Broadcasts or Prime Minister's Question Time: those are quite literally turn-offs for many people. Would David Cameron be polished? Would Gordon Brown be a champion debater? Would Nick Clegg rise to the occasion, giving the Liberal Democrats an opportunity to shine? We know that most of the public expected Cameron to perform best, but of course this had its perils as well as its advantages: it might mean that he had nothing to gain from a good performance, only from an exceptional performance, and everything to lose should he disappoint. There was only one certainty, and it got far less discussion in advance than it deserved. Giving Clegg a platform on equal terms with Brown and Cameron gave the Liberal Democrats exposure which to date they had only dreamed of. According to Lynton Crosby, the Australian political consultant who worked for Michael

Howard's Tories in the 2005 election, it was a tactical error for the Conservatives to have taken part in the debate in the first place.[96] Nevertheless, it still remained to be seen what Clegg, Cameron and Brown could make of it. At any rate, there was no excuse for being surprised when the debates had a significant effect on the parties' poll standings.

Table 44: Election campaign timeline, 6 April-6 May 2010

Date	Event
Tue 6 Apr	Brown announces the General Election date as 6 May
Wed 7 Apr	Final pre-election Prime Minister's Questions. Senior businesspeople support Conservative national insurance policy
Thu 8 Apr	Labour and the Conservatives are accused of copyright infringement over use of images of Cameron portrayed as TV show detective DCI Gene Hunt from *Ashes to Ashes*
Fri 9 Apr	Labour candidate for Moray, Stuart Maclennan, sacked for disparaging comments about his opponents on Twitter
Mon 12 Apr	Dissolution of Parliament. Labour manifesto launched
Tue 13 Apr	Conservative manifesto launched
Wed 14 Apr	LibDem manifesto launched.
Thu 15 Apr	First leaders' debate, on domestic affairs (ITV, Manchester)
Tue 20 Apr	Close of nominations, new registrations and applications for postal votes
Thu 22 Apr	Second leaders' debate, on foreign affairs (Sky, Bristol)
Wed 28 Apr	'Bigotgate': Brown calls a Rochdale voter a 'bigoted woman' in an unguarded, unscripted moment much to his later embarrassment on Jeremy Vine's Radio 2 show, where he is pictured with his head in his hands
Wed 28 Apr	SNP court action to halt final leaders' debate is thrown out
Thu 29 Apr	Letter from entrepreneurs published in *The Times* warning against a Lib-Lab coalition
Thu 29 Apr	Third leaders' debate, on economic affairs (BBC, Birmingham)
Sat 1 May	The *Guardian* comes out in support of the Liberal Democrats
Sun 2 May	Final TV debates between four main party leaders in Scotland and Wales. The *Daily Telegraph* declares its support for the Conservatives
Mon 3 May	May Day bank holiday
Thu 6 May	Election Day
Tue 11 May	Gordon Brown resigns as Prime Minister: Queen appoints David Cameron

In fact, the major events of the 2010 campaign can be summarised in a few words. The parties launched their manifestoes and held the usual press conferences at which they tried to bend the attention of the media in the direction they hoped would be most beneficial, but all this effort was to little avail. Interest in the campaign revolved almost entirely around the

---

[96] See N Watt and A Stratton, 'TV debate: nervous Tories count cost of Cameron's decision to debate', *The Guardian*, 16 April 2010, http://www.guardian.co.uk/politics/2010/apr/16/tv-debate-nick-clegg-david-cameron, accessed 19 February 2011.

weekly landmarks of the three debates, each on a Thursday evening, leaving just a week before polling day after the final instalment. One other incident, Gordon Brown's inadvertent broadcasting of his disdain for a voter's opinions (the 'Bigotgate' incident – see pages 239–42), gathered a lot of press coverage but is unlikely to have swung many votes.

Table 45 shows the average of the scores recorded by the five pollsters (ComRes, Populus, ICM, YouGov and Angus Reid) that conducted 'Who won?' polls immediately after each of the three debates. While there were some differences in their results, their common finding was that Nick Clegg, the Liberal Democrat leader, was the clear 'winner' of the first debate, and while the next two were rather more inconclusive, Gordon Brown was generally seen as trailing third in each case, although by a smaller margin in the last two debates than most commentators would have expected.

Table 45: Who won the debates?

Average of post-debate poll findings

	First debate	Second debate	Third debate
	%	%	%
David Cameron	23	33	37
Gordon Brown	19	27	26
Nick Clegg	51	31	32

Source: 'Instant' polls published by ComRes, Populus, ICM, YouGov and Angus Reid

The first debate had a dramatic effect on voting intentions (see Figure 36), with Liberal Democrat strength jumping from around 20% to around 30% and remaining there for several days. However, as the debate receded in the public's memory, the voting intention figures for Liberal Democrats began to slowly and steadily trickle away.

Aside from the startling movement in LibDem support, the gap between Labour and the Conservatives barely moved at all. After the first debate, the Liberal Democrats' gain was fractionally more at the Tories' expense than Labour's, so Brown had reeled in the lead from seven points to six points. Between the second and third debates we saw 21 more polls rain down[97], again consistently with the Tories averaging 34%, up a point, Labour at 28%, also up a point, and the LibDems at 29%, down a point.

Figure 36: The course of the campaign – all published polls

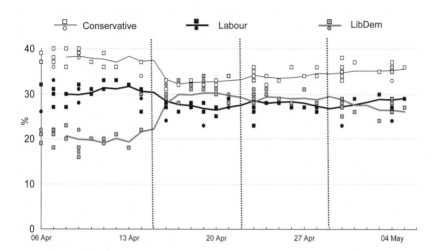

Source: Ipsos MORI analysis of data reported by pollingreport.co.uk.
Note: Polls are plotted at the midpoint of their fieldwork (day after midpoint for polls with an even number of fieldwork days). Graph lines show rolling three-day average of polls by the six established polling companies (square markers; polls from other companies shown with round markers). Dotted lines indicate the three debates.

In the week around the third and final debate, the Tories gained another point to 35%, Labour held at 28% and the LibDems slipped from 29% to 28%. This left the Conservatives with a 5.3% swing, still insufficient to expect a majority on 6 May. Up to this point, with a week to go, there had been nearly 100 polls published and none, not one, had the Tories enjoying a sufficient lead to expect that they would have the 326 seats in the new Parliament necessary to allow them to demand the metaphorical keys to Number 10 Downing Street from the Queen.

But were the Tories doing better than this in their target seats? If they could get, say, a 7.3% swing where it mattered then the 5.3% swing

---

[97] This excludes the Harris/*Metro* poll published between the two debates but with a fieldwork period partly before and partly after the debate.

nationally would be irrelevant, they would still have done enough. Because of this possibility, Reuters commissioned Ipsos MORI to carry out a series of surveys in the 'Battleground Marginals'. However, we found the Tories were doing no better there than anywhere else. Those polls showed a 5.0% swing in some weeks and 5.5% in others, but never with a significant week-on-week movement. Other companies' polls in marginals showed a similar picture, and, when the results were in, we could see that they were right to do so.

By the time polling day came, the Tories and Labour, at least, were back where they had started. All in all, the Liberal Democrats made a net gain in support over the course of the campaign (as they usually do, debates or not), but this was wholly at the expense of the smaller parties. It is unlikely that many of their seats depended on this and there must be a strong suspicion that, despite the potential for the campaign to change everything, in the end it had changed little.

Why? To answer that, we need to look in turn at various aspects of the campaign 'on the ground' and 'in the air', seeing why they failed to swing the weight of the last-minute votes one way or the other, and above all to consider the debates in detail, a matter of interest in themselves. But first we must turn our attention to the third party in the contest, the Liberal Democrats.

The Liberal Democrats enter the story

The Liberal Democrats entered the 2010 election suddenly transformed by the likelihood of a hung Parliament and then by Nick Clegg's performance in the first leadership debate, moving from an irrelevant sideshow to the main pivot on which the election would turn.

The Liberal Democrats, 2005-10

At the 2005 general election, the Liberal Democrats had taken 22.6% of the vote and won 62 seats[98], the highest total they or their predecessors had achieved since David Lloyd George won 158 seats in 1923. But as

---

[98] House of Commons Library Research Paper 05/33, accessed 19 February 2011.

Labour had been returned with a working majority, this allowed the LibDems no share of power, and left them little to do for the next five years except to nurture their strength in local government and the devolved assemblies, and to hope for the occasional by-election or other opportunity that would recall their existence to a largely indifferent public.

Under normal circumstances, many members of the public are barely aware of the Liberal Democrats, even those have voted for them in the past. Consistently over decades, surveys have found that between elections a significantly lower proportion of the public say they voted for the party at the previous election than had actually done so. This does not seem to be because they are consciously reluctant to admit it, rather because some of them actually forget that they did so. We find, too, that when we measure voting intention a good many voters forget the possibility of voting Liberal Democrat unless we draw it to their attention. It is possible to argue that what the Liberal Democrats do between elections hardly matters except to the extent that it leaves them ready for the big push when the moment comes and the broadcasters turn to their stopwatches to make sure every party gets its fair crack of the whip – although this may not be true when they are in government (when the Liberals propped up Labour with the Lib-Lab pact between March 1977 and July 1978, it had a significantly negative effect on their image and vote share at the following election) or are making the big political news (as with the formation of the Liberal-SDP Alliance in the early 1980s). In 2010, the party came to the election with a relatively blank slate, but with its chances significantly affected by two artefacts of the previous five years – its choice of Nick Clegg as leader, and the unusual luxury of having another of its senior figures, Vince Cable, nationally recognised and respected (as a result of his having outperformed both the Chancellor and Shadow Chancellor during the recriminations over the banking collapse and economic crisis).

It had taken the Liberal Democrats two bites of the cherry to pick their standard bearer. When the 2005 leader, Charles Kennedy, was ousted amid accusations of a drinking problem at the start of 2006, the contest pitted probably the best known of the party's other MPs, Simon Hughes, against respected veteran Sir Menzies ('Ming') Campbell and the former *Guardian* economic correspondent and ex-MEP Chris Huhne, who had been in the Commons less than a year. Among the general public (according to an Ipsos MORI survey on 19-23 January 2006), Campbell and Hughes were neck-and-neck (19% and 18% respectively) and Huhne scored only 2% – but, as is the way for the Liberal Democrats, more than half the public answered either 'none of these' or 'don't know', many probably not knowing and perhaps not caring who any of the three were. In the first round of voting, 45% of LibDem party members voted for Ming Campbell, 23% for Simon Hughes and 32% for Chris Huhne. With Hughes eliminated, Ming obtained 58% of the votes and Huhne a respectable 42%. It seemed clearly a vote for a safe pair of hands and a 'unity candidate' not particularly associated with either wing of the party.

Perhaps it was an omen that the party achieved a spectacular success, winning the Dunfermline and West Fife by-election in Gordon Brown's back yard, during the interregnum before Campbell's election, since they achieved no other obvious major victories in the next 18 months. A brief surge in the polls in April 2006 lasted only days, and the LibDems found themselves at a slightly lower rating under Campbell than in the last months of Kennedy's leadership. In May 2007, the LibDems lost more than 250 seats in the local elections and their coalition with Labour lost office in the Scottish Parliament elections. Questions began to be raised over whether or not Campbell was at an inevitable disadvantage when viewed by the public compared to the younger Blair and Cameron. After Brown replaced Blair, and Campbell's bold promise to reduce the basic rate of income tax to 16% made no perceptible leeway for the LibDems, the discontent became more vocal and Campbell resigned on 15 October 2007.

On the polling evidence, the case for replacing Sir Menzies Campbell was not particularly compelling. His satisfaction ratings as leader were steady, with no statistically significant movement at any time in the year up to his resignation: around 45% were consistently unwilling to judge his performance at all, and he had a steady deficit among those who did. It could be argued that these ratings were as much a justification of the desire for a change of leaders as were the Liberal Democrats' lower-than-customary voting intention scores. Yet Paddy Ashdown, who few Liberal Democrats would now consider a failure as leader, was also poorly rated by the public at the start of his leadership, and took more than two years to register his first net positive rating. His ratings after 19 months, the stage at which Campbell resigned, were very similar to Campbell's – 25% satisfied, 33% dissatisfied. Tellingly, once the Liberal Democrats had another new leader in place, there was still no improvement in their voting intention ratings or in their local election vote share, although their new leader reached a mildly positive net score in his leadership ratings after six months.

That new leader was Nick Clegg, MP for Sheffield Hallam, who beat Chris Huhne by the narrowest of margins in a bad-tempered contest (and, reportedly, would have lost had not votes for Huhne been delayed in the Christmas post[99]). But meanwhile, events between the fall of one leader and the election of the next had thrown new light on things. In those few short weeks came the debates over the collapse of Northern Rock and its consequences, and the Liberal Democrats' Treasury spokesman (and acting leader pending the leadership result), Vince Cable, became the darling of the media commentators. He outshone Labour and Conservatives alike in the debates on the banking crisis, and also made his mark over Revenue and Customs' (HMRC) loss of child benefit data and the controversy over proxy donations to the Labour party.

Had Campbell hung on a few weeks longer, the advantages of gravitas over youthful inexperience might have seemed rather more obvious. For that matter, if the leadership election had been a few weeks later, Cable's colleagues would surely have put pressure on him to stand and had he done so, it seems likely he might have won. Whether that would ultimately have helped or hindered the Liberal Democrats is a matter for debate, but it would certainly have made the 2010 election a very different one.

In fact, Cable's impact may have been somewhat exaggerated: the scant polling evidence during his period as acting leader shows little from the public to match the enthusiasm of the media. It is understandable that he should have made no impression on the voting intention figures, since the public knew he was only a stand-in. But when ICM asked which of Brown, Cameron and Cable was 'a competent leader', emphasising that respondents could choose more than one as competent, 43% thought that Cameron was competent and 42% that Brown was, but only 14% said the

---

[99] 'MP Huhne stands by Lib Dem leadership election results', *Southern Daily Echo*, 7 April 2008, http://www.dailyecho.co.uk/news/2175503.mp_huhne_stands_by_lib_dem_leadership_election_r esults/, accessed 19 January 2011.

same of Cable.[100] In 2008, the public rated him well behind Alistair Darling and George Osborne as the best candidate to be Chancellor (26% picked Darling, 20% Osborne and 13% Cable, with 30% saying they didn't know and 8% picking 'none of these').[101] Nevertheless, Cable was regarded as a major asset to the Liberal Democrats as the election approached, and it may well be that the larger parties were more apprehensive about Cable's appearance in a post-budget TV debate against Darling and Osborne than about Clegg's appearance with Brown and Cameron in the three leaders' debates.

The LibDems approached the election with their poll standings around 18% or 19% of the vote. Given the circumstances, this was certainly disappointing. The MPs' expenses scandal that broke in 2009 stirred up huge public hostility to the established parties, and – as Clegg was later to make much of during the leaders' debates – the most serious accusations were all aimed at Labour or Conservative MPs, not at Liberal Democrats. Yet the surge of public opinion was towards support for smaller parties, with the Liberal Democrats benefitting little. In the 2009 European elections, when the protest votes were at their purest, LibDem support was down to 13.7%, behind not only Tories and Labour but also UKIP for the second time in a row. The 'general election tomorrow' polls were not quite that bad for the LibDems, but they couldn't break the 20% ceiling in any of the monthly averages from that point to the start of the election. As Gordon Brown returned from the Palace with confirmation of his chosen election date, the Liberal Democrats still seemed to have an awful lot still to do.

Yet, LibDem prospects were in fact brighter than they had been for many previous elections. On the pre-election consensus of the standing of the parties, stable at 37% for the Conservatives, 31% for Labour, 19% for the Liberal Democrats, neither the Tories nor Labour would be likely to command a majority over all other parties in the House of Commons. Assuming a uniform national swing, the Tories would still be around 30 seats short of the 326 they would need to form a majority. Labour's hole

---

[100] ICM poll for BBC *Newsnight*, 30 November-2 December 2007, http://www.icmresearch.co.uk/pdfs/2007_december_bbc_newsnight_leaders_poll.pdf, accessed 20 January 2011.
[101] ICM poll for the *Guardian*, 18-20 April 2008, http://www.icmresearch.co.uk/pdfs/2008_april_gurdian_april_poll.pdf, accessed 20 January 2011.

would be even deeper, around 60 away from the magic number. Even with their own support sharply down since 2005, a 19% vote share would put the LibDems in the frame to hold the balance of power. Viewed cynically, it was far more important to the Liberal Democrats that they should do nothing to disturb the delicate balance between the two main parties than that they should increase their own support back to or beyond the level achieved in 2005.

It is important to remember that the Liberal Democrats never expected or seriously hoped for outright victory. This was not simply because they are accustomed to finishing in third place in votes. Their vote is much more evenly distributed than that of the two larger parties and this means, under the first-past-the-post system which operates in the UK, that a massive increase in votes across the country would still reap them few seats. Starting with the 62 seats in the House of Commons they notionally held[102], after allowing for the extent of the Tory resurgence at Labour's expense, a uniform 1% swing from all parties in the LibDems' favour taken proportionally from the other parties would actually leave the LibDems as net losers, down to 60 seats. A 2% swing would bring them up to 65. A 6% swing, at which point they would overtake Labour for second place in votes, would still have given them only 83. An 11% swing, ahead of even the Tories in votes and roughly where the most optimistic single poll of the campaign put them, would only get them up to 143 seats. Only if they could push their vote share well past 40%, higher even than the threshold facing the Tories, would an overall majority be likely. That was never going to happen. (Although it's perfectly true that polls regularly find that many people who do not support the Liberal Democrats say they would do so if they thought the party could win – see Table 46. Since they never *do* think the LibDems can win in a general election, this never gets tested in practice despite being proven regularly in by-elections.)

On the other hand, a mass collapse in the number of LibDem seats was never likely either, however many points the party was down nationally on their 2005 standing. Throughout the run-up to the election, commentators and bloggers were consistently feeding poll findings into swingometers and discussing the dozens of seats that this indicated the LibDems were in

---

[102] Allowing for the effect of boundary changes prior to the 2010 general election.

danger of losing. That was nonsense. No swingometer can ever be used without invoking that key caveat 'assuming uniform swing' – depending on the calculations built into the swingometer, the type of swing involved may be different, it might include multiple refinements, regional variations and other bells and whistles, but that assumption in some form still underlies the whole process.

Table 46: If the Liberal Democrats could win...

Q. How would you vote on May 6 if you thought the Liberal Democrats had a significant chance of winning the election nationally?

	Conventional voting intention %	If the Liberal Democrats could win %	Difference
Conservative	33	25	−8
Labour	27	19	−8
Liberal Democrat	31	49	+18
Other	8	6	−2

Source: YouGov/*The Sun*
Base: 1,509 GB residents aged 18+, 18-19 April 2010[103]

All those commentators seemed completely oblivious to the fact, plain as it should be from recent political history, that as far as the Liberal Democrats are concerned, uniform swing is something that happens to other parties. For the most part, LibDems do not win their seats by uniform swing, and they do not lose them by uniform swing. Indeed, on occasion their vote goes up and their number of seats goes down, or vice versa. Liberal Democrat success or failure, far more than for the two larger parties, seems to depend primarily on local campaigning, and while the overall performance of the party nationally is not entirely irrelevant, nor does it dictate the local results.

[103] http://today.yougov.co.uk/sites/today.yougov.co.uk/files/YG-Archives-Pol-SunPossGovts-100419.pdf, accessed 13 January 2011.

How the LibDems were positioned

As the centre party and as one that has not shared power for many years, the Liberal Democrats naturally combine a number of sources of support, catering both for those who actively support their values (whatever they see those as being) and those who are making some form of negative vote, whether a general protest against the whole political establishment or a more tactical vote against one of the major parties. To some extent this requires them to be all things to all men, and it can come as no surprise that the immediate effect of joining a post-election coalition with the Conservatives has been to alienate a significant part of this support. One implication of this, perhaps, is that throughout the election and perhaps for decades before, many of their voters have been misunderstanding the nature of the party which they were supporting, whether it was to suppose that they would not enter government, or that they could not, or that they would only do so in partnership with certain parties. Consequently, events after the election add an extra dimension to any exploration of how the party was seen in advance of the election.

The first point to make is that only a minority of the public, and only a minority of their own supporters, see the Liberal Democrats as purely a protest vote. Two weeks before the election, an ICM poll for the *Guardian* asked whether people agreed that 'They are more a protest vote than a party that stands for things': 42% agreed while 51% disagreed, and among those intending to vote for the party 38% agreed and 62% disagreed.[104]

A separate and sizeable factor is tactical voting. In our eve of poll, 10% of all those giving a voting intention said that the reason for their choice was that 'The party you support has little chance of winning in this constituency so you vote for the ... party to try and keep another party out', and 14% of the remainder said they would switch to a different party if they thought their own party had not much chance of winning. On this evidence, tactical votes made up twice as high a proportion of the Liberal Democrat vote as of the Labour or Conservative vote, and accounted for around one in six of the party's votes. (See Figure 37.)

---

[104] ICM poll for the *Guardian*, 23-25 April 2010, http://www.icmresearch.co.uk/pdfs/2010_apr _guardian_campaign_poll4.pdf, accessed 13 January 2011.

Figure 37: Reported tactical voting by party supported, 2010

Q. You said you have voted for/would vote for/are inclined to support [PARTY]. Which of the following statements comes closest to your reasons for intending to vote for them?

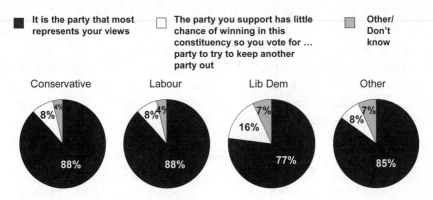

Source: Ipsos MORI/*London Evening Standard*
Base: 925 GB electors giving a voting intention or who had already voted by post, 5 May 2010

This 10% level of tactical voting in our final poll was lower than we found reported earlier in the campaign. In mid-April, 14% said their voting intention was tactical. All other things being equal, we might expect the level of intended tactical voting to increase as the campaign proceeds, as voters move the focus of their attention from the national battle to the local decision that they have to make. But it may be that in 2010 the mid-campaign tactical voters included those who had not yet taken stock of boundary changes that had removed the incentive to continue their tactical voting from previous elections, and it is also not unlikely that the huge shifts in the opinion polls during the campaign changed some voters' perceptions of which parties had a realistic chance of winning their own constituencies.

But we are also forced to wonder how well the public understand tactical voting (or how accurately they are reporting it to us). Why is there such a prevalence of LibDem tactical votes? While the LibDems, being the centre party, can reasonably expect to benefit from both Conservative and Labour tactical votes, this is offset by the fact that there are many fewer constituencies where they have a realistic chance of winning. This was made even clearer to us in our polls of marginal constituencies for Reuters. The 57 constituencies where we polled were all Labour-held Conservative targets and, in virtually all, the Liberal Democrats were in a hopeless third place. Yet we found in our first poll in these marginals after the election was called (16-19 April) that as high a proportion of Liberal Democrats (13%) as of Conservative or Labour supporters said their support was tactical! Furthermore, only 12% of those intending to vote in these constituencies, where tactical voting could be useful, claimed to vote tactically – that compared to 14% in our national poll over the same period. By the time of our final marginals poll, the weekend before the vote, the number saying they were intending to vote tactically was down to 9%, but still almost as high among LibDems as Tories, although Labour was now getting the bulk of the benefit. There must therefore be a clear suspicion that an appreciable proportion of Liberal Democrat support comes from misconceived tactical voting in places where the party cannot win.

Naturally enough, it appears that the protest vote and tactical vote element made up a bigger proportion of Liberal Democrat support at the height of the 2010 election than is the case in 'peacetime', when we would expect they might retain their core support but not that of the discontented who only make their choice of the least-of-many-evils as polling day approaches. In 2007, we found (see Table 47) that one in five of the public felt they shared the party's values and might vote for them. This is considerably more, allowing for current turnouts, than have ever voted for the party at any recent election. At that stage in the parliament, though, we see that four-fifths of those already intending to vote Liberal Democrat explained their choice in terms of shared values.

Of course, we know that political parties' values play a limited role in driving votes. Over the years, we have always found (see Figure 28 on page 165) that voters attribute more importance to parties' policies and to their views of the leaders than to their view of the party as a whole. Although values may influence policies, they do not necessarily dictate them, and any view of Liberal Democrat policies is normally coloured by the perception that they are unlikely to get a chance to implement them. (After 2010, this perception may undergo a change!) In fact, in 2010, Liberal Democrats attributed slightly more importance to policies and slightly less to leaders than Labour and Conservative voters, but were on a par with them in relegating party image firmly to third place.

Table 47: Sympathy with Liberal Democrat values

Q. Which of the following three statements would best describe your attitude to the Liberal Democrats?

	All %	Con %	Lab %	LibDem %
I share their values and will vote for them or would consider doing so	20	12	16	79
I do not share their values but I will vote for them or would consider doing so	12	13	13	14
I would not consider voting for them	39	56	44	5
None of these	20	13	21	2
Don't know	8	6	5	0

Source: Ipsos MORI Political Monitor
Base: 1,004 GB residents aged 18+, 18-23 October 2007

But were those values seen as being in the centre or to the left or the right? It is interesting that among Conservative and Labour supporters who said they might consider voting Liberal Democrat, there was a reasonably even split between those who felt they shared their values and those who did not. Some clearly see the Liberal Democrats as ideologically distinct from their own parties; others, perhaps, see an overlap in values that makes either choice a possible one. There has been a widely-held perception that the Liberal Democrats have positioned themselves as a left-of-centre party, and were well placed to mop up support from disillusioned Labour supporters when the Blair-Brown government finally fell. It is therefore interesting that the proportion of Conservatives who saw the Liberal Democrats as sharing their values and would consider voting for them was only a little lower than the proportion of Labour supporters feeling the same. Whichever way Nick Clegg jumped when finally forced after the election to make a choice, it seems clear that a significant part of the public, including many who eventually voted Liberal Democrat, would be surprised and disillusioned.

All the evidence is that rather more Liberal Democrats tended to the left than felt the opposite, although they did not necessarily see the party in that way. Populus periodically ask respondents in their polls for *The Times* to place themselves and each of the parties on 1 to 10 scale, with '1' being 'very left wing', and '10' being 'very right wing'. In their 2008 poll[105], the public on average placed Labour at 4.82, the Conservatives at 5.91 and the Liberal Democrats at 4.66 – to the left of Labour. But those actually intending to vote Liberal Democrat put the party on 5.18, even though they positioned themselves at 4.88. This might suggest that the party's voters felt slightly left-of-centre but thought the party was a little right-of-centre. However, averages can be misleading, especially as Populus uses an unbalanced scale with four answer categories to the left of centre and five to the right: it might be more revealing to note that 51% of Liberal Democrats gave their own position on the scale as '5' (presumably taking this as being exactly in the centre, though it is not), 18% further to the right of this and 31% to the left. When asked about their party, however, only 36% placed it at '5', 28% to the right and 28% to the left. (What we can't tell from the published figures, unfortunately, is whether those who were on the right themselves felt the party was on the right, or the converse.)

This imbalance was maintained, indeed rather accentuated, right up to polling day. In our final pre-election poll, we asked what voters would prefer to happen in the event of a hung Parliament. Liberal Democrats split 40% to 22% in favour of a Labour-LibDem rather than Conservative-LibDem accommodation (see Table 48), although a third would have preferred the rather more unlikely outcome of all three parties working together.

A different but equally relevant dimension of the ideological views of Liberal Democrats is their attitude to hung Parliaments as such, the only circumstances in which the party can expect a share of power. In our final eve-of-election poll, we found that 30% of the public felt it would be a good thing for the country if no party were to achieve an overall majority, while 55% thought it would be a bad thing. Most Liberal Democrats, reasonably enough, did not agree with this diagnosis but there was a significant proportion who did: 55% thought that no overall majority would be a good thing but 30% said it would be a bad thing. Again, therefore, we find a substantial proportion of the party's voters apparently uneasy at the likely consequences of the vote they were casting. But it

---

[105] http://www.populuslimited.com/the-times-party-conference-poll-2008-070908.html, accessed 21 January 2011

should be borne in mind that Liberal Democrats are by no means unique in this – all parties consist of coalitions of differently minded groups and it is probably a rare and happy voter who can wholeheartedly endorse everything his chosen party stands for.

Table 48: Preferences in a hung parliament

Q. If no party achieves an overall majority, which of these would you prefer?

	All %	Con %	Lab %	Lib Dem %
The Conservatives and Liberal Democrats working together	27	62	*	22
Labour and the Liberal Democrats working together	29	1	65	40
The Conservatives and Labour working together	4	6	7	0
All three main parties working together	33	22	27	35
None of these/other/don't know	8	8	1	9

Source: Ipsos MORI/*London Evening Standard*
Base: 1,216 GB registered electors, 5 May 2010

The debates

The debates were scheduled for three successive Thursday evenings, 15 April, 22 April and 29 April, with the three party leaders going head to head for ninety minutes in each, with just a week left until polling day after the last was done. The three main news broadcasters – BBC, ITV and Sky News – had collaborated in their negotiations with the parties to reach a mutually-acceptable formula, and each was to stage one of the debates, drawing lots to determine the order and the subject matter that each debate would cover.

The parties imposed extremely tight restrictions on the format, no doubt to protect themselves from what they saw as the greatest risks of the process. Although the leaders took questions from a live studio audience, recruited by pollsters ICM to be representative of the electorate, the questions were vetted in advance and the questioners had no opportunity to come back with supplementary points. Even coverage of the audience reaction to the leaders' answers was strictly circumscribed. Each hour-and-a-half concentrated almost exclusively on the interaction between the three leaders and the moderator who was conducting the debate. For this task each broadcaster had selected a respected veteran of political coverage – the redoubtable Alastair Stewart, for ITV, was in the chair for the first debate in Manchester, covering domestic affairs; Sky News staged the second debate, in Bristol, with Adam Boulton in charge and with foreign issues (including defence and immigration) to the fore; and, finally, the media circus arrived in Birmingham where veteran David Dimbleby presided for the BBC over a discussion of economic issues. In each case, however, regardless of the theoretical focus of the debate, the leaders were given substantial freedom to roam over whatever subject matter they chose to bring up.

It was the Liberal Democrats who stood to gain most from the debates. Historically, their voters had made their minds up later than Labour or Conservative supporters. For instance, in 2005, 27% of Liberal Democrats decided to vote within the last week of the campaign, compared with 15% of Labour voters and 14% for the Conservatives. More importantly, Nick Clegg had the opportunity to benefit from sharing the stage with the two 'main' parties on equal terms. A good performance might open the eyes of millions of voters to the possibility of voting for a third alternative.

The ITV Debate in Manchester

On 15 April 2010, for the first time ever in a British general election campaign, the leaders of the main parties in British politics shared a stage – broadcast live on television, radio and the internet – and debated domestic affairs. Everybody was aware that its impact was potentially huge. (Three in five of the public had told us beforehand that the debates would be important in helping them to decide how to vote.) There was perhaps some uncertainty in advance that the size of the audience would do the event justice, but any such doubts proved unfounded: when the official viewing figures were finally collated, it turned out that 9.7 million had been watching[106], which was an exceptionally high figure for any political programme and a respectable audience for any prime-time TV show. Moreover, as polls afterwards confirmed, the debate's impact spread far

---

[106] Figures from the Broadcasters' Audience Research Board (BARB), cited in N Allen, J Bara and J Bartle, 'A Much Debated Campaign' in N Allen and J Bartle (eds), *Britain At The Polls* (London: Sage, 2011), p 183.

beyond those that watched it themselves, with many others seeing news reports or getting other second-hand information on how the leaders had performed.

To analyse each debate for the BBC *News at Ten*, Ipsos MORI recruited a focus group of 36 undecided voters, each watching one of the three leaders, to give their reactions as they watched the debate unfold live. Participants were recruited to achieve a broad demographic mix based on gender, age, social grade and ethnicity as well voting behaviour. We once again partnered with IML, with whom we had pioneered the use of 'people meters' in the 1992 general election, working with the then-youthful Nick Robinson, producing *The Vote Race* which went out every Sunday night during the '92 contest, testing public reaction to the week's media performances by the party leaders and other election performers. Participants again used IML voting pads to record their reactions whilst watching the debate live. Three 'worms' (moving coloured line graphs) – one for each leader – tracked participants' attitudes towards each of the three leaders throughout the debate, identifying the 'high' and 'low' points of their performances according to undecided voters, and illustrating these visually.

This added an element to the subsequent reporting of the highlights of the debate, often lacking when the broadcasters are wholly dependent on their reporters' judgments to pick out key moments. The reactions of our participants were subjective, and – as with any qualitative research – can only be indicative, rather than giving any precise numerical measurement of the public's response to the debates. But in the absence of direct reaction from the studio audience, they offered the best clue to the effect of specific parts of the debates.

There were no major gaffes or triumphs in the first debate. Nick Clegg by consensus won the first debate by a mile. Calm, cool and collected, and certainly self-possessed, he left a good impression with our focus group members as the following comment demonstrates:

> *'I think Clegg just edged it – more personable and on top of that he came across as a bit more light-hearted which politics needs.' (Male)*

No doubt an element in this was that the public in general, and naturally undecided voters (who tend to have lower-than-average interest in politics) in particular, had weaker expectations of Clegg as the following comment indicates:

'I was very surprised by Nick Clegg.' (Female)

The moments when our panel indicated most support for Clegg included his thoughts on immigration (regional quotas in particular), prisons ('colleges of crime'), and his thoughts about the creativity and freedom needed for teachers. On the other hand, people did not rate his views on Britain's nuclear deterrent, Trident, being cut.

Importantly, his ratings increased significantly when he criticised the two larger parties' failure to act on issues such as MPs' expenses and political reform and when he presented himself as removed from the rotten political system. Clegg's position as the third party allowed him to align himself with the voting public and express their frustration at the other two parties: 'the more the two of them attack each other, the more they sound the same'. This sentiment went down well with our focus group:

'I came in undecided, didn't know much about Nick Clegg. I was very impressed by him. He was very specific about what he felt they would do. The other two seemed to concentrate on slagging each other off.' (Female)

However, the debates posed a problem for David Cameron. In an Ipsos MORI poll in February, he had been the overwhelming favourite among the public to perform best in the debates: 53% say they thought Mr Cameron would gain most public support as a result of the debates, compared to 20% for Gordon Brown and 12% for Nick Clegg. Even Labour voters were just as likely to say Mr Cameron would gain most as Mr Brown, 42% for Cameron, 41% for Brown. Three-quarters (74%) of Tory voters and half (51%) of Liberal Democrats also opted for Cameron.

It was the same story in the marginal constituencies. Nearly half, 45%, of people in the key marginal constituencies where Ipsos MORI was polling for Reuters[107] expected Cameron to gain the most public support as a result of the debates; Clegg scored 22% and Gordon Brown lagged at 17%.

---

[107] Defined as those Labour-held constituencies which would be gained by the Tories at a swing between 5 percent and 9 percent.

In the final analysis, Cameron came across as nervous and cautious and, on his opening camera shot, looking like a deer caught in the headlights. Nevertheless, he started the debate strongly on crime and immigration, issues where the Conservatives were already seen by the public as having the best policies. His ratings peaked when he discussed welfare reform to give immigrants less access to benefits. In general, people were potentially receptive to Cameron but not yet fully convinced. Some of our participants gave a positive verdict, others a more negative one:

> *'I thought David Cameron was the stronger candidate – just seemed to make most sense. Think his personality came across better than the other two.' (Male)*

> *'David Cameron was a bit too obsequious. There was a lot about "aren't you wonderful in the army" without actually answering the question.' (Female)*

Brown was also nervous, and surprisingly ponderous, but certainly not impressive, and with a tactical 'I agree with Nick', repeated several times, he came across more as a follower than a leader, and a follower of the new boy on the block Nick Clegg at that. Every time Brown talked about his party's track record the 'worm' went down, and his comments about the future were also apparently overshadowed by people's views on his track record:

> *'It was really a two horse race between Clegg and Cameron, I thought. Gordon Brown came across as very much the grey man. Suppose he's got a record he's got to justify whereas the others don't have that problem.' (Male)*

His mild joke at Cameron's expense (regarding Cameron giving him publicity by picturing his portrait smiling on a Conservative attack poster) did not work particularly well with our audience, and his tendency to smile when under attack made him look nervous or dismissive and did not go down well either. However, he was better received by our test audience near the end of the debate when talking about the need for urgent reform in social care and making it free instead of means-tested. Less popular were his views on policing, the group not responding well to his plans for failing police forces. Neither did they like his comments about investment in the armed forces.

More damagingly, his comments did not seem to resonate with our undecided voters generally:

> *'Gordon Brown didn't seem to put things over well.' (Male)*

'I think Gordon Brown was a bit of a let down.' (Male)

Our research confirmed some of the things one might expect. For example, attacking other leaders and speaking over time did not go down well with our test audience. We also learned that politicians' personal stories failed to resonate. All three party leaders were guilty of attempting the 'folksy charm' typical of American politics to humanise themselves, but none of the leaders benefited when mentioning their family or personal lives – during personal anecdotes, our audience's test ratings either flat-lined or dipped – and stories about meeting members of the public, nurses or war veterans also failed to make any positive impact with the members of our focus groups.

What was noticed by many media commentators was that Nick Clegg made a point of speaking straight into the camera, addressing the audience at home directly, while Cameron and Brown both addressed the chairman or the studio audience, allowing the camera to catch them obliquely, normal practice for a studio interview.[108] It emerged afterwards that Clegg's expert advisers had made a point of telling him to do this while the consultants hired by Labour and the Conservatives had not. Clegg's advisers were right, of course, by facing the camera he came across as sincere, direct and even dynamic.

Ipsos MORI's 'worm' research aimed to identify audience reactions to specific elements and incidents in the debates (and only covering our chosen audience of undecided voters), not to point towards any conclusion about who had won or lost. But several polling organisations were conducting instant reaction polls to ask the public precisely that as soon as the debates were over. By recruiting their samples beforehand they were able to deliver very quick results, in some case reporting their figures only a few minutes after the debates had finished, in time for inclusion in the news bulletins that followed. ComRes, polling for ITV with an automated telephone polling system, took just six minutes from start to finish in polling more than 4,000 viewers after the first debate; ICM used a more conventional telephone polling methodology, while Angus Reid, YouGov and Populus all polled online.

---

[108] See J Chapman, 'Kingmaker Clegg wins TV war of words – and moves Britain even closer to a hung parliament', *Daily Mail*, 16 April 2010, http://www.dailymail.co.uk/news/election/article-1266285/Leaders-debate-Historic-Brown-Cameron-Clegg-lock-horns.html.

The five polls differed slightly over question wordings, and more profoundly over whether their samples should be weighted to match the profile of the whole electorate or only that of debate viewers. Further, some continued polling much longer after the debates than others, so giving different opportunities for their respondents to take in and react to other people's opinions before expressing their own. Nevertheless, all five polls were unanimous, Clegg was the winner. That first election debate ranks in our view as one of the most significant events in the 11 general elections MORI has polled in this country. Certainly, its impact was profound.

Figure 38: The course of the campaign (poll of polls)

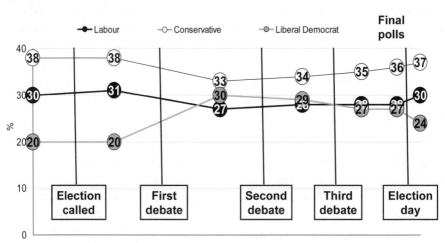

Source: Ipsos MORI analysis of data reported by pollingreport.co.uk.
Note: Figures given are the averages of all polls conducted wholly within each period by the six established polling companies

Whereas the election had been static before the debate, now it was electric. The Liberal Democrats, previously a side show, were now centre stage. Overnight, Nick Clegg had gone from 'Nick Who?' to 'Nick, Wow!'. Between the calling of the election on 6 April and the first debate on 15 April, the polls were in close agreement that the Tories were on around 38%, Labour within touching distance on 31% and the Liberal Democrats out of the race on 20% (See Figure 38). The day after the debate, Liberal Democrat support had risen by half: the average of the polls in the next week, again with very little variation between them, had the Liberal Democrats in second place on 30%, the Tories not far ahead on 33%, and Labour in shock, trailing on only 27% of the vote. Suddenly, the Liberal Democrats were in the running. Prospective voters started listening to Clegg, in a way that LibDems had rarely in living memory been listened to.

Similarly, satisfaction with Nick Clegg increased dramatically. His net satisfaction (the percentage satisfied minus the percentage dissatisfied) increased to +53 from +20 in March. This represented the highest satisfaction score for any leader since Tony Blair's first year as Prime Minister. By contrast, David Cameron's net satisfaction stood at +3, and Gordon Brown's at −24. Nick Clegg was now more popular amongst the general public than Gordon Brown was amongst Labour supporters.

Figure 39: Impact of the first debate (self-assessed by the public)

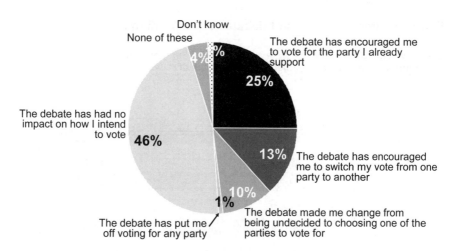

Base: 899 GB residents aged 18+ who said they watched the first debate, 18-19 April 2010
Source: Ipsos MORI Political Monitor

All this came from the debate and from Clegg's triumph being so unexpected. When asked the following weekend, half the public said the debate had had some effect on their voting intention (see Figure 39). For a quarter, it meant they were now intending to vote for a party they had not supported before the debate. One in three people told YouGov that 'I have never voted Liberal Democrat before but I am considering doing so now'.[109]

And yet alert observers were already asking how long Clegg's popularity would last and whether it mattered. Debates have their biggest effect on floating voters who are not already committed to one side or the other and on those who generally take less interest in politics and, therefore, have most to learn about the participants and the issues. But these are also the electors who in the final analysis are less likely to vote at all. It would be a mistake to assume that the first debate provoked a big movement of voters from Labour and the Conservatives to the Liberal Democrats. Comparing our March and April 2010 voting intention polls, it was clear that the big change was an increase in the numbers who were now 'certain' that they would vote. In fact, neither major party had suffered a net loss of voters at all, only of vote share. (See Figure 40.)

Figure 40: Impact of the first debate on poll findings

Q. How would you vote if there were a General Election tomorrow?
('Absolutely certain to vote', projected into millions of votes)

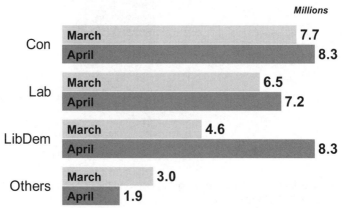

Base: 1,503 GB residents aged 18+, 19-22 March 2010; 1,253 GB residents aged 18+, 18-19 April 2010

Source: Ipsos MORI Political Monitor

---

[109] YouGov poll for the *Sunday Times*, conducted 16-17 April 2010, http://today.yougov.co.uk/sites/today.yougov.co.uk/files/YG-Archives-Pol-STResults-100417.pdf, accessed 13 January 2011.

If these newly enthused Liberal Democrats did not turn out after all, the surge in the polls would do the party no good. The voters themselves, after all, were not convinced that the surge would last. (See Table 49.)

For the moment at least, the Liberal Democrats moved past Labour into second place. Second place in votes was, for the Liberal Democrats, a long way short of second place in seats. In fact, if uniform swing held, Labour in dropping to third place in votes in this way would perversely become the biggest party in terms of seats. While the direct impact of Clegg's win in the first debate was apparently a swing from both Labour and Conservative to Liberal Democrat, its secondary effect was to drop the Labour-to-Conservative swing to 4.5%. Even with a 30% share, the Liberal Democrats would only gain around 40 seats to add to the 63 they currently held. Unless Clegg could surpass himself and add another ten points to the Liberal Democrat share in the remaining three weeks of the campaign, it was the Labour/Conservative battleground seats that would actually determine the outcome of the election. Therefore, it was the swing between the two established major parties that really mattered, and Clegg's surge threatened to put Labour in a position to negotiate. This was no disaster for the Liberal Democrats, of course, for whom the ideal scenario short of being able to form their own government was to achieve maximum freedom to manoeuvre with the possibility of putting either of the other parties into power.

Table 49: Will the LibDem surge last?

Q. As you are probably aware support for the Liberal Democrats has increased sharply since last Thursday's television debate. Do you think this will...?

	%
Prove to be a lasting increase with the Liberal Democrats breaking through and winning many more seats in the coming election	34
Prove to be a 'flash in the pan' with Liberal Democrat support slipping back as their policies come under greater scrutiny	52
Don't know	14

Source: YouGov/*The Sun*
Base: 873 GB residents aged 18+, 19 April 2010[110]

---

[110]   http://today.yougov.co.uk/sites/today.yougov.co.uk/files/YG-Archives-Pol-SunLDsupport-100419.pdf, accessed 13 January 2011

The Sky News Debate in Bristol

The numbers watching the second debate were significantly lower, at only 4.2 million, but not all viewers can receive Sky News and the subject matter may have been the least appealing of the three debates, although the announced subject of foreign affairs was interpreted to include immigration, one of the issues on which voters apparently felt strongest. Maybe, also, the second of the three debates was always likely to draw the lowest audience, having neither the novelty of the first debate nor the immediacy of the last at which all the leaders would in effect make their final appeals for votes.

With expectations high, Clegg performed well again but did not repeat his decisive victory of seven days previously. The post-debate polls found no clear winner, three putting Clegg narrowly ahead and the other two giving the lead to Cameron and, although none put Brown ahead of the other two, he trailed by a much smaller margin than the previous week and was level with Cameron in two of the polls. Meanwhile, our focus groups (including undecided voters only) reacted best to Clegg again, but less decisively so than in the first debate in Manchester.

Brown opened with a personal statement to voters, telling them 'I'm your man'; however, our test audience of floating voters did not agree. Overall, Brown attacked more than the previous week, making several personal sideswipes at both Clegg and Cameron. These personal attacks by Brown, and also those by Cameron, did not play well with our focus groups. Indeed, Brown's worm fell to its lowest as he directly confronted Nick Clegg, telling him to 'get real' on renewing Trident, Britain's nuclear deterrent. His other attacks on Cameron and Clegg, describing both as 'a risk', were also unpopular with our audience. Interestingly, our floating voters did seem more prepared to allow Clegg to attack the other two on their behalf.

As in Manchester, Brown's worm showed little movement when he listed his record of achievements. He scored better when a question about the Papal visit in September allowed him to talk about achievements on human rights and expansion of rights for homosexuals – such as allowing civil partnerships in the UK. His approval ratings also reached a high point when he criticised the country's 'addiction to oil' and declared Britain's need to embrace renewable energy sources.

Cameron's satisfaction line peaked when he talked about immigration, again a repeat of the Manchester reaction: his statements that 'immigration is too high' and 'we need to bring it down' proved very popular. He also scored well when he said that 'Catholics need to act' on the sex scandals (allegations that the Roman Catholic church had failed to act against priests who had committed sexual abuse against minors in several countries) and the need to develop high speed rail in the UK (as it did for Brown when he made a similar point).

However, perhaps most strikingly – and worryingly for the Tories – Cameron's pronouncement in his closing statement that the Conservatives were best placed to 'offer real change' caused his ratings to fall, showing clearly that the undecided voters in our Bristol audience were not accepting the key message of his appeal for support. There was also little movement in the line – positive or negative – when he mentioned the 'Big Society', reflecting indications from other sources that the Tories' had completely failed to convey awareness of their big idea to the voting public.

Perhaps Nick Clegg's most consistently successful theme in the second debate was to argue for the advantages of political co-operation. He dampened fears of what would happen in the event of a hung parliament, reacting to both Labour and Conservative warnings during the campaign of the consequences of an indecisive result, and his ratings shot up when he said that a hung parliament would not mean 'the end of the world' and 'politicians can talk to each other' (what he called the 'new politics'); and he scored another high when he said that it is 'better to work together' to deal with the deficit. His approval ratings also went up when, in his opening statement, he said that 'we should not have invaded Iraq', and when discussing Britain's 'special relationship' with the USA by standing up for Britain, saying that it is not a 'one-way street'. His only significant dips came when on two occasions he welcomed the Pope's visit to the UK in September. In fact, whenever any of the three leaders talked about welcoming the Pope to Britain their ratings fell.

Despite the much lower official viewing figures for the second debate than for the first, three adults in five still reported that they had either watched the debate or the subsequent news coverage, and of these a very similar proportion (45%) felt it had had no effect on how they intended to vote as had said so of the first debate (see Figure 41).

Figure 41: Impact of the second debate (self-assessed by the public)

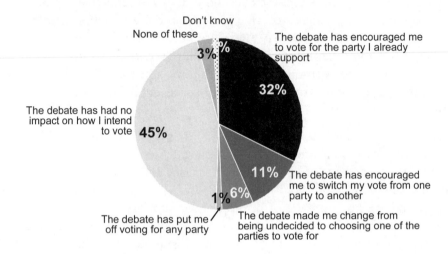

Base: 731 GB residents aged 18+ who said they watched the second debate, 23 April 2010
Source: Ipsos MORI/*News of the World*

However, among the remainder the effect was slightly more than in the previous week to reinforce existing voting intentions rather than to provoke new ones – nevertheless, one in six said it had made them switch parties or change from being undecided to choosing to vote for a party (6%). The effect this time was fairly equal across supporters of different parties, suggesting any real changes were being cancelled out by other voters switching in the opposite direction. Consequently, there were no dramatic moves in voting intentions in the polls that followed, although Labour and the Conservatives may possibly have been gaining slightly from the Liberal Democrats as the impact of Clegg's dramatic debut began to fade.

The BBC Debate in Birmingham

The final debate, staged by the BBC, drew a peak audience of 8.6 million for a confrontation that was to cover the issue judged most important to the election and the country by most of the public and would end with a closing statement from each leader which was in effect their final appeal for votes.

One lesson that our qualitative research with floating voters consistently reiterated was that they do not like the negative politics employed by all three of the leaders. This was never more evident than in David Cameron's closing statement of the final debate: having enjoyed a strong performance throughout the debate, he began his final pitch to the public on a positive note about how important families are, but when he changed tack to criticising the other parties, his audience approval immediately began falling. Of course, we need to bear in mind that the leaders are not only talking to undecided voters in the debates – they are also trying to ensure that their existing supporters get out and vote. Gordon Brown's curious final statement in the last debate clearly flouted the 'stay positive' advice and focused heavily on the risks posed by change, but was probably aimed at galvanising those already sympathetic to Labour.

The 'worm' ratings were at their absolute highest when Cameron spoke on immigration – in particular his mentioning that it is too high and that there is a need to cap it – as well as when both of the opposition leaders spoke about cutting government waste and sacking MPs.

With immigration being raised in each of the three debates, Cameron – whose party the public overwhelmingly think has the best policies on immigration – scored best with our test audience on the issue. Nick Clegg made the most of his standing in the first two debates as an 'outsider' of established politics and his approval ratings went up when he spoke about the 'disgrace' of the expenses scandals. His policy that the public should be allowed to sack MPs between elections was very popular.

Our audiences liked it when both Cameron and Clegg bemoaned the waste in government spending – which is unsurprising, especially given how inefficient many of the general public perceive the government to be, as our polling data has consistently shown.

The post-debate polls once again reported an equivocal verdict, with Cameron ahead of Clegg on average and Brown trailing third in all five polls, but there was no sense that anyone had scored an overwhelming victory or suffered a devastating defeat. If there was any particular significance in the result it was that Cameron, while probably slightly ahead, had not come close to reversing the impact of the first debate when he was toppled from his position as outright frontrunner. There was no immediate movement in the polls – either in reaction to the debate or to the 'Bigotgate' incident of the previous day, which was still stealing some of the headlines – as the parties and leaders entered the finishing straight and the postal voters began to send in their ballot papers.

The campaign away from the debates

Considerably more of the public than usual were convinced that this was an interesting election, perhaps because all three leaders were new to the electorate and the race was perceived by the electorate to be closer than it had been in previous elections.

Our poll question in the post-election Ipsos MORI survey conducted for the *News of the World* (see Table 50), with the advantage of similar data from past elections for comparison, makes much clearer how unusually interesting the public found the 2010 election. Not only did 74% (well above the turnout of 65%) say they had been at least 'fairly interested' in news about the election, but 41% said they had been 'very interested', three times as many as said the same after either the 1992 election (the last one when the contest seemed as close) or the 1997 election (the last to end in a change of government).

Tracking and evaluating communication touchpoints

A research project undertaken by MESH Planning and Cranfield School of Management, the MESH Election Experience Monitor[111], tracked voter sentiment through a real-time experience tracking research programme undertaken amongst a panel of floating voters over the duration of the campaign, and was designed specifically to determine the relative influence of different campaign touchpoints, using real-time text messaging when they encountered a particular touchpoint. Such touchpoints could have included promotional material from a party, direct mail, Internet advertisements, news or radio broadcasts, billboard posters, posters in gardens and even word-of-mouth. It is also worth noting that the parties spent vastly different amounts of money on their campaigns during the

---

[111] This research is reported in more detail in P Baines, E Macdonald, H Wilson and F Blades, 'Measuring Communication Channel Experiences and Their Impact on Voting in the 2010 British General Election', *Journal of Marketing Management*, forthcoming (2011).

election, with the Conservatives spending twice as much as Labour overall and more than three times as much as the Liberal Democrats (see Table 60 on page 249).

Table 50: Interest in election news

Q. Thinking back to the campaign, how interested would you say you were in news about the General Election?

	April 1992 %	29 May 1997 %	9-18 June 2001 %	12-13 May 2010 %
Very interested	13	12	19	41
Fairly interested	39	46	49	34
Not particularly interested	26	27	24	14
Not at all interested	22	14	8	11
Don't know	*	*	*	*

Source: Ipsos MORI
Base (1992-7, 2010): c. 1,000-2,000 GB residents aged 18+; (2001): 1,162 UK (GB and NI) residents aged 18+

By asking about whether or not the experience they encountered made them 'less likely' or 'more likely' to vote for the party mentioned in the communication, it was possible to evaluate the positive and negative persuasiveness of the various touchpoints experienced by the panel of floating voters over the duration of the campaign (see Figure 48 below). The charts demonstrate how the first and last TV debate in the 2010 British general election were so important in persuading floating voters to vote for the Liberal Democrats and Conservatives respectively.

By considering each party's touchpoints and the final vote made by the floating voter respondents, the leaders' debates and the TV news were the touchpoints most frequently encountered. In both cases, these touchpoints were not direct channels to the voter, but were mediated by third parties (the various television news channels). Particularly influential touchpoint experiences for those that voted Conservative included the leaders' debate. However, when Conservatives were the subject of the TV news, it had a seemingly negative effect on Conservative floating voters' voting intentions, and it did so also for those intending to vote for the other two main parties. Party election broadcasts (PEBs) received a mixed response; sometimes received positively as a communication in themselves but then evaluated negatively in terms of their likely effect on voting intention (for example, this was the case for all types of floating voter encountering a Conservative PEB). This result is difficult to explain, although it could be an underdog effect (in contrast Labour floaters encountering a Labour PEB had the opposite effect, an initial negative affect but more positive voting intention).

Figure 42: Labour campaign poster (1)

Posters in all cases, excluding Labour posters seen by floating voters who ended up voting Labour, were negatively received. Labour posters were predominantly negative in tone. For example, Labour's initial poster, crowdsourced online by the party's advertising agency, Saatchi and Saatchi, and designed by Jacob Quagliozzi, a 24 year old Labour supporter from St Albans[112], portrayed Cameron as maverick TV cop, Gene Hunt (from the

---

[112] For more detail, see R Nikkah, 'Labour's Ashes to Ashes Gene Hunt Poster Attack on Tories backfires', *Daily Telegraph*, 3 April 2010, http://www.telegraph.co.uk/news/election-2010/7549905/Labours-Ashes-to-Ashes-Gene-Hunt-poster-attack-on-Tories-backfires.html, accessed 19 February 2011.

television series *Ashes to Ashes*) in an attempt to taint Cameron with the perceived excesses of the Thatcherite 1980s (see Figure 42).

The campaign was widely seen to backfire, not least because the campaign inadvertently portrayed Cameron as 'cool'. The Conservatives responded with their own rebuttal version of the advert with the slogan 'Fire up the Quattro, it's time for a change'.

Figure 43: Labour campaign poster (2)

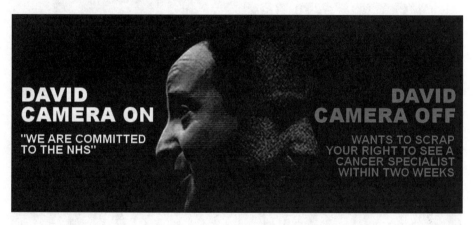

Another Labour campaign poster (see Figure 43) tried to damage Cameron's image in the same way as Labour had tried to do by depicting John Major as two-faced in the 1997 general election. Whilst it probably worked to some extent in 1997, when an unpopular Prime Minister was attacked by a popular new party leader, in 2010 the situation was reversed, with an unpopular Prime Minister attacking a relatively more popular new party leader (although Cameron was much less popular in 2010 than Tony Blair was in 1997).

Conservative posters such as Figure 44, displaying the smiling Brown with seven associated negative messages (for example, 'I doubled the national debt, vote for me'), were described by one panellist in their online diaries as 'positively Orwellian'.

Figure 44: Conservative campaign poster (1)

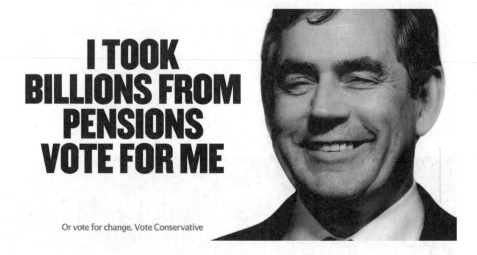

Figure 45: Conservative campaign poster (2)

Although not all Conservative posters had been negative in tone – one at the beginning of the year had the slogan 'I'll cut the deficit, not the NHS' – their campaign posters were. One tried firmly to attach the blame for the economic recession to Brown, by suggesting he would increase the country's indebtedness and directly impact on the voters' pockets by increasing their national insurance contributions (see Figure 45).

The Liberal Democrat posters were also negative in tone. However, they had a much smaller budget to play with and, therefore, had to be much more creative if they were going to cut through the clutter of the other parties' advertising campaigns, particularly that of the Conservatives. Accordingly, they developed a guerrilla marketing campaign focused on the phony Labservative party, an amalgam of the Tory and Labour parties, intended to illustrate the worst features of both. The intention was to portray the Liberal Democrats as above the 'old politics' and able to offer something new and fresh. The campaign, launched by advertising agency Iris, came complete with its own labservative.co.uk website.[113]

Figure 46: Liberal Democrat poster campaign (1)

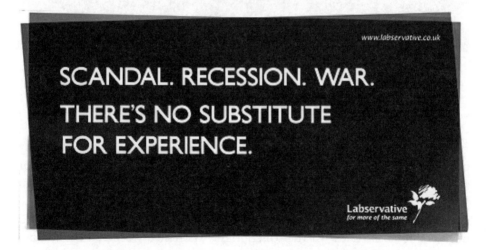

---

[113] For more on the Liberal Democrat's Labservative campaign, see T Sweeney, 'Lib Dems target Labservatives with Guerrilla Advertising Campaign', *Guardian*, 30 March 2010, http://www.guardian.co.uk/media/2010/mar/30/lib-dems-labservatives-guerilla-advertising#, accessed 19 February 2011.

Another poster, also negative in tone, launched by the Liberal Democrats simply re-used an old Conservative poster theme 'Labour's tax bombshell' from its 1992 election campaign, using the slogan 'Tory VAT bombshell' (see Figure 47). The poster was designed to damage the Conservative party's image over its stated intention to raise VAT from 17.5% to 20% once it achieved office.

Figure 47: Liberal Democrat poster campaign (2)

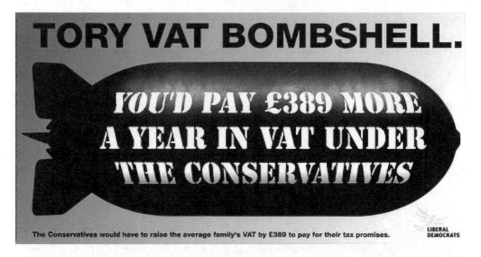

Leaflets, on the other hand, were positively received by both Labour and Conservative floating voters when they received them from both parties. In contrast, the Liberal Democrat floating voters were not particularly persuaded by any party's leaflets. The MESH Political Experience Monitor also indicated, surprisingly, that the Labour party actually benefitted from positively persuasive word of mouth, on average, over the course of the campaign. Figure 48 provides an overview of the overall positive and negative persuasiveness of the touchpoint experiences received by floating voters from the Conservative and Labour parties and the Liberal Democrats, indicating that overall the Labour party's messages were received the most negatively most of the time and the Liberal Democrats' messages received the most positively most of the time. The LibDems enjoyed a positive blip after the first debate and the Conservatives a positive blip after the final debate. Despite the media frenzy, there was little impact on the panel of floating voters' intentions to vote on the day of the 'Bigotgate' gaffe (28 April). The rise in the positive persuasiveness (and decline in negative persuasiveness) associated with Tory messaging from 29 April, is more likely to be a function of Cameron's performance in the final election debate.

Figure 48: Real-time tracking of message persuasiveness

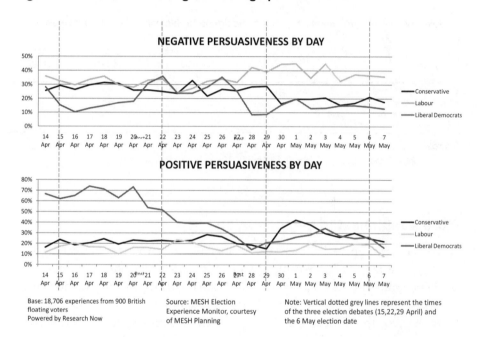

Base: 18,706 experiences from 900 British floating voters
Powered by Research Now

Source: MESH Election Experience Monitor, courtesy of MESH Planning

Note: Vertical dotted grey lines represent the times of the three election debates (15,22,29 April) and the 6 May election date

Source: Paul Baines, 'Political marketing and election campaigning', in J Strömback and S Kiousis (eds), *Political Public Relations: Principles and Applications* (Oxford: Routledge, 2011), pp 115-137.

Overall, the public do not believe they are influenced by negative campaigning. In 2008, we found[114] that 79% agreed that 'I am more likely to trust/believe those politicians who concentrate more on explaining their

---

[114] Survey for the BBC. Ipsos MORI interviewed 1,070 UK (Great Britain and Northern Ireland) residents aged 16+ by telephone on 3-6 January 2008.

own policies than those who concentrate more on attacking other politician's policies' and only 17% disagreed. An ICM/*Guardian* survey, conducted early in the election campaign, found that David Cameron was perceived to be campaigning best for his party, ahead of Nick Clegg and way ahead of Gordon Brown. What is interesting, however, is that all three leaders were perceived to be campaigning well on average (Table 51).

Table 51: Standard of campaigning

Q. How well or badly do you think ... has campaigned for his party over the last week?

	David Cameron %	Gordon Brown %	Nick Clegg %
Very well/quite well	66	45	51
Very badly/quite badly	9	26	13
Neither/Don't know	25	29	36
Net score	+57	+19	+38

Source: ICM/*Guardian*[115]
Base: 1,024 GB residents aged 18+, 9-11 April 2010

More sophisticated segmentation

Key basic segments of the electorate include young voters between 18-34 years of age (about 22% of those who vote, although a higher proportion of those entitled to do so), women (about 51% of the electorate) and older voters (aged 55+, about 41% of voters, significantly over-representing their share of the population). Whilst the Conservatives held a lead with all these main groups, their lead was not sufficiently large to ensure a majority, given the vagaries of the electoral system, with any of these groups and the Liberal Democrat vote was particularly high with young voters (who liked their policies on climate change) and with women. However, the LibDems did not fare so well with older voters, who preferred the Conservatives' policies on immigration and taxation (see Table 52).

---

[115] http://www.icmresearch.co.uk/pdfs/2010_april_guardian_campaign_poll2.pdf, accessed 13 January 2011.

Table 52: Key demographic voter segments in 2010

Group / Proportion of voters***	Young voters (aged 18-34) / 22%	Women /51%	Older voters (aged 55+) / 41%
Key Manifesto Focus/ Commit-ments*	**Labour – Education & employment** 200,000 jobs through Future Jobs Fund: job/training place for young people out of work for 6 months, but benefits cut at 10 months if they refuse a place; anyone unemployed for over 2 years guaranteed work. No stamp duty for first-time buyers on house purchases < £250k for 2 years, paid for by 5% rate on homes worth £1m+. Every young person guaranteed education/training to 18, with 75% going on to higher education or completing an advanced apprenticeship or technician level training, by age 30. Improve citizenship education for young people, free vote in Parliament on voting at age 16. **Conservative – Environment & unemployment** Reduce UK greenhouse gas emissions & increase share of global markets for low carbon technologies. Reduce youth unemployment, reduce the number of children in workless households as part of strategy for tackling poverty & inequality. **LibDem – Employment & education** Scrap arbitrary target of 50% of young people attending university, focus effort on a balance of college education, vocational training & apprenticeships. Strengthen Youth Service by making it statutory, & by encouraging local authorities to provide youth services in partnership with young people & the voluntary sector.	**Labour – Pensions, health & crime** Between now & 2020, the State Pension Age for women will rise to 65 years old. Funding for UN Women's agency doubled. All women will have right, wherever safe, to a homebirth, & every expectant mother will have a named midwife. Maintain women-only services including a Sexual Assault Referral Centre in every area. **Conservative – Pension Age** Review to bring forward the date at which the state pension age starts to rise to 66, although not be sooner than 2016 for men & 2020 for women. **LibDem – Gender Equality** Extend the right to request flexible working to all employees. Introduce fair pay audits for every company with > 100 employees to combat discrimination in pay, e.g. against women. Require name-blind job application forms to reduce sex & race discrimination in employment, initially for every company with > 100 employees.	**Labour – Retirement age, pensions & care** The right to request flexible working for older workers, with an end to default retirement at 65, enabling more people to decide how long they choose to keep working. New National Care Service to ensure free care in the home for those with the greatest care needs & a cap on the costs of residential care so that everyone's homes & savings are protected from care charges after two years in a care home. Re-established link between the Basic State Pension & earnings from 2012; help for ten million people to build up savings through new Personal Pension Accounts. **Conservative – Pensions, benefits & health** Protecting key benefits: the Winter Fuel Allowance, free bus passes, free TV licences & the pension credit. Maintain Attendance Allowance & Disability Living Allowance for the over 65s. Provide a better basic state pension by linking it to earnings in 2012. Make sure no-one is forced to sell their home to pay care home fees. Protect NHS spending so it has the resources to meet people's rising expectations about the quality of care they should receive. **LibDem – Pensions & health** Prioritise dementia research. Restore link between basic state pension & earnings.
Best Party on... **	Education = Lab Unemployment= Lab Climate change = LibDem Crime/ASB= Con	Health = Lab Crime/ASB = Con Education= Lab Unemployment = Lab	Health = Lab Asylum/immigration = Con Taxation = Con Benefits = Lab
Vote***	Con 33%, Lab 31%, LD 29%	Con 36%, Lab 31%, LD 26%	Con 39%, Lab 30%, LD 19%

Sources: *Party Manifestos, **Ipsos MORI Political Monitor (19-22 March 2010), ***Ipsos MORI 2010 general election aggregate estimates of final vote and turnout.

However, to supplement the national and more general picture of basic voter segments, political campaigners are beginning to introduce more powerful and more granular segmentation techniques, many of which have already proved themselves in elections elsewhere, although anecdotal evidence suggests there is still much resistance from traditionalists and other sceptics, particularly in local constituencies. The segmentation technique which has received most coverage is geodemographics, which involves classifying voters on the basis of the characteristics of their neighbourhoods, for direct mail and get-out-the-vote campaigns using telephone canvassing. Geodemographic techniques already have a long pedigree in market research, where they are recognised as a highly effective segmentation tool. Probably the best known of these classifications is Experian's MOSAIC, and both the major parties are reported to have purchased licences to use the MOSAIC database in their campaigning software.[116] MOSAIC combines census data, consumer behaviour and other information to classify neighbourhoods, distinguishing between them down to individual postcode level or even more finely than that. By then uploading local canvass returns, the parties can get a more complete picture of the electorate, allowing them to fine-tune their direct mail and telephone canvassing efforts in different (marginal) constituencies. The Conservatives' software system, MERLIN, provided visibility into all local campaign databases. However, the Labour system – Contact Creator – was even more sophisticated, since it allowed uploading of canvass returns in real–time.[117] How useful geodemographic segmentation and the associated database systems actually are to the parties depends on how they are used in practice. If they are simply used at national level to plan direct mailshots, the chances are that they will be too crude to be useful because national themes may not resonate locally and local know-how is necessary

---

[116] Both parties reportedly had MOSAIC data by the 2005 election, powering the Conservatives' Voter Vault application and the Labour Contact software, according to Patrick Wintour ('Postcode data could decide next election', *Guardian*, 28 December 2004). For its use in the 2010 election see Chris Hastings & Maurice Chittenden, 'Labour hit by cancer leaflet row', *Sunday Times*, 11 April 2010, http://www.timesonline.co.uk/tol/news/politics/article7094308.ece, accessed 6 September 2010, and Benedict Brogan, 'How the charity of a peer's wife will propel Cameron to power', *Daily Telegraph*, 27 January 2010, http://www.telegraph.co.uk/comment/ columnists/benedict-brogan/7086643/How-the-charity-of-a-peers-wife-will-propel-Cameron-to-power.html, accessed 6 September 2010.

[117] See J Fisher, 'Party finance: normal service resumed', in A Geddes and J Tonge (eds), *Britain Votes 2010* (Oxford: Oxford University Press, 2010), pp 193-216.

to craft messages that resonate with local people. Similarly, if they are used at local level but simply to record canvass returns, this is a backward step since it is an expensive method of doing so. On the other hand, when these data are used at local level by competent organisers, combined with effective canvassing and local research so as to accurately link local knowledge – about the voters, the issues about which they are concerned and the best way to communicate with them – with the power of the MOSAIC segmentation which can provide all sorts of lifestyle information, it has the potential to ensure maximum campaigning efficiency, directing scarce resources to the most persuadable people in the most marginal seats, and therefore the best chance of successfully appealing to floating voters yet to make up their minds and to get out the vote for those who have already made up their minds to vote for a particular party.

To demonstrate the possible effectiveness of geodemographic targeting in modern elections, we conducted a simple (and very crude) exercise of matching the 2010 election results at constituency level with the characteristics of the constituencies as measured in the 2001 census. The limitations of this are obvious: not only are we lacking the consumer behaviour data which is an important element in packages such as MOSAIC, but we are relying on census data which was more than nine years old at the time of the election. Nevertheless, it proved astonishingly successful in predicting Conservative and Labour shares of the vote. Using the most straightforward of statistical techniques and only a handful of census variables, we were able to explain 86% of the variation in the Labour vote share and 84% of the variation in the Conservative share.[118] We deliberately refrained from adding extra information such as region, for example. The best single predictor of Conservative share was the percentage of households with two or more cars, which alone accounted for 55% of the variation in the vote[119], while for Labour the best predictor was the proportion of single-parent families, explaining 61% of the variation. This level of predictive accuracy is far greater than we can

---

[118] The analysis used an ordinary least squares linear regression, using a stepwise method to select independent variables from a possible list of 44 variables. The final model for Conservative vote share used 17 predictors and had an R^2 of 0.845; for Labour share, 13 variables and R^2 of 0.856.

[119] However, with extra variables added this variable became less significant, and it was not included in the final 17-predictor model.

manage at the individual level, trying to explain a respondent's voting intentions in an opinion poll on the basis of his or her demographic characteristics.

Canvassing

Whilst canvassing during elections is as old as the hills in its use as a marketing medium and to help parties develop their databases on voters and potential voters for get-out-the-vote efforts, the self-reported level of canvassing was just slightly lower at one in five people than in 2005, and lower than any election since 1979 with the exception of the 2001 general election campaign where Tony Blair's battle against the relatively unpopular William Hague, was a foregone conclusion and when only one in around seven people reported being called on by a representative of a political party.

Figure 49: Reported general election canvassing levels, 1979-2010

Q. During the past few weeks have you been called upon by a representative of any political party?

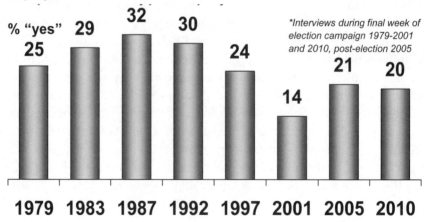

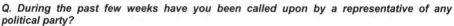
Base: c, 1,000 GB residents aged 18+ in each survey
Source: Ipsos MORI

Nevertheless, all parties spent substantially on canvassing /market research (see Table 60 below), with the Tories spending the most but with the Liberal Democrats outspending the Labour Party. However, it should be noted that self-reported canvassing by the people is might not measure accurately whether or not people have actually been called on, because it is subject to recall and faulty memory can affect a proportion of the answers given (dependent, amongst other factors, on the length of time between the questioning and the canvassing event occurring).

Party election broadcasts

In the 2010 general election, party election broadcasts (PEBs) were largely relegated to the back of the political marketers' toolbox, not least because of the public and media interest in the leaders' debates. Many commentators believe they essentially preach to the converted, a useful tool to raise the morale of one's own supporters but poor at persuading floating voters to change their minds.[120] However, they remain a key means by which parties can speak directly to voters, and in the 2010 election they were released on party websites and on YouTube. Accordingly, PEBs hardly received a mention in the press. As usual, the parties tried to make use of celebrities for endorsement purposes. Labour wheeled out (the voice of) ex-*Doctor Who* David Tennant and actor Sean Pertwee (son of another ex-*Doctor Who*) in their 'The Road Ahead' party election broadcast on 12 April, which attracted an audience of just under 9m viewers across the five main terrestrial networks[121] and Eddie Izzard in the 'Brilliant Britain' PEB. The Conservative PEB, 'What it takes to change a country', broadcast on 19 April, used the opportunity to tackle Clegg's sudden poll surge, apparently scrapping a planned attack on Labour.[122] Cameron used the PEB opportunity to talk about his 'Big Society' idea direct from his back garden, in a pitch aiming to encourage civic community-mindedness devolved and separate from government.

---

[120] For a useful discussion of the expected role of the PEB ahead of the 2010 election, see D Singleton, 'Election 2010: Does the Political Broadcast still matter?', *PR Week*, 16 February 2010, http://www.prweek.com/uk/news/features/984614/Election-2010-Does-political-broadcast-matter/, accessed 20 February 2011.

[121] See J Thompson, 'Party election broadcasts watched by almost 9 million', *New Statesman*, 13 April 2010, http://www.newstatesman.com/broadcast/2010/04/sean-pertwee-party-broadcast, accessed 20 February 2011.

[122] See T Newton Dunn, 'Tories on poll again', *The Sun*, 20 April 2010, http://www.thesun.co.uk/sol/homepage/news/election2010/2939593/Tories-back-on-poll-again.html, accessed 20 February 2011.

Table 53 shows the findings of a research study by the semantic web platform, OpenAmplify, counting internet views and social media reactions to a selection of PEBs by the three main parties. The Conservative 'What it takes to change a country' broadcast received the most internet views and created the biggest social media 'buzz' in volume terms. But, achieving only one social media reaction for every 60 views, it was less engaging in proportional terms than several of the other PEBs. The Liberal Democrats' 13 April PEB, 'Say goodbye to broken promises', had the highest ratio of reactions to views, one for every 36 views of the broadcast.

Table 53: Social media engagement with party election broadcasts

Party	Broadcast	Broadcast Date	Views	Social Media Reactions
Labour	'The Road Ahead'	12 April	53,811	733
Liberal Democrats	'Say Goodbye to Broken Promises'	13 April	30,093	841
Conservatives	'An invitation to join the government of Great Britain'	13 April	59,694	822
Labour	'Brilliant Britain'	15 April	93,669	876
Conservatives	'The Big Society'	19 April	15,955	401
Conservatives	'What it takes to change a country'	19 April	154,282	2,571
Labour	'Our journey'	21 April	9,107	213

N/A=not applicable

Source: Adapted from OpenAmplify, 'UK election: Which party election broadcast created biggest social media buzz?', *netimperative*, 30 April 2010, http://www.netimperative.com/news/2010/april/uk-election-which-party-election-broadcast-created, accessed 20 February 2011.

Campaigning ran far from smoothly for some of the smaller parties. The BNP, found itself served with an injunction by the manufacturers of Marmite after it used an image of their product in an election broadcast in an attempt to mimic the spread's successful 'love it or hate it' strapline. This incident was then cited by the head of the party's online operations, who resigned two days before the election and took down the BNP website, complaining that he had been left 'up the proverbial creek' by the Marmite incident. The following day Bob Bailey, their candidate in Romford and leader of the BNP group on Barking & Dagenham Council, was filmed fighting with an Asian man while out campaigning with the party leader, Nick Griffin.[123]

However, not all viewers want to watch PEBs, intrusive as they are and preceded with an oral warning, 'you are now watching a party election broadcast by the XYZ party'. This was particularly the case with those who had already definitely made up their mind how they would vote who, according to Ipsos MORI polling figures, were more in favour of banning PEBs (17%) than those who had not (13%). Those who said they were tactically voting were considerably more in favour of a ban on PEBs (23%), compared with those who were voting for the party they really supported (14%). Naturally enough, those who watched the first debate in full were less likely to agree there should be a ban on PEBs (11%) than those who neither watched it nor saw any TV news coverage of it (20%), and very few of those who watched the whole debate would ban all TV and radio coverage (5%) or newspaper coverage (7%).

The 'Bigotgate' incident

Perhaps the most outstanding incident of the campaign, arguably the only memorable one, came in Rochdale where Gordon Brown was being filmed canvassing on 28 April. After meeting a pensioner, Gillian Duffy, in the street and defending government policy on immigration, he got back into his car and – not realising that he was still wearing a television lapel microphone – angrily rebuked his advisers for persuading him to talk to 'that bigoted woman'. His gaffe was played across all channels in the next round of news bulletins and when Brown tried to limit the damage by appearing on Jeremy Vine's BBC Radio 2 programme to apologise and explain himself, he was filmed with his head in his hands as he listened to himself. Ironically, although Brown's intemperate remarks had been caused by his being convinced that the original confrontation with Mrs Duffy had been damaging, she had felt that he had responded 'pretty well'

---

[123] Fiona Hamilton, 'BNP man punches Asian on campaign trail as online chief denounces Griffin', *The Times*, 6 May 2010, http://www.timesonline.co.uk/tol/news/politics/article7116654.ece, accessed 18 January 2011.

and said she would be voting Labour before being told of the Prime Minister's subsequent comment.[124]

However, for all the frenzied media coverage of 'Bigotgate' as outlined earlier, there was little sign that it had any real impact on party support. The polls were completely unmoved, and Labour even held their ultra-marginal seat in Rochdale with a swing in their favour from the challenging Liberal Democrats.

In retrospect, this fits a pattern. 'Bigotgate' was only the last in a series of incidents where the press took the opportunity of an apparent gaffe by Brown to launch a vitriolic personal attack. Yet, like all the other potential haymakers before it, the coverage of the Gillian Duffy incident completely failed to land a knockout blow. Within the previous year there had been an attempt to associate Brown with personal culpability in the MPs' expenses scandal (on the grounds that he reimbursed his brother for employing a cleaner for his, Gordon's, London flat), a furore over mis-spellings and poor handwriting in a condolence letter sent to the mother of a soldier killed in Afghanistan, and another storm in a teacup over accusations in a book by Andrew Rawnsley that Brown had bullied staff at 10 Downing Street.

Not one of these incidents did Brown any measurable damage – indeed, the condolence letters and 'Bullygate' both came at a period when his personal poll ratings were slowly improving, and they continued to do so. With the excesses of the tabloid press as much a subject for public condemnation as the inadequacy of politicians, it is not impossible that the main effect was to actually raise sympathy for Brown rather than to harm his standing. Even the *Daily Telegraph*'s chief leader writer felt that in the case of the condolence letters: 'Gordon Brown has emerged ...not as some caricature panto villain but as a decent man with the right instincts trying to do the right thing but fumbling in the process'.[125] And when the founder of the National Bullying Helpline was drawn into backing up the

---

[124] Polly Curtis, 'Gordon Brown calls Labour supporter a "bigoted woman"', *Guardian*, 28 April 2010, http://www.guardian.co.uk/politics/2010/apr/28/gordon-brown-bigoted-woman, accessed 3 February 2011.

[125] David Hughes, '*The Sun* turns Gordon Brown into an object of sympathy, not scorn', *Telegraph* blog, 10 November 2009, http://blogs.telegraph.co.uk/news/davidhughes/100016290/the-sun-turns-gordon-brown-into-an-object-of-sympathy-not-scorn/, accessed 3 February 2011.

Rawnsley claims, apparently breaching the confidentiality of callers to the helpline in the process, it was clear that again there had been a co-ordinated attempt to make political capital out of the accusations against Brown. Tellingly, a YouGov poll in the wake of the bullying accusations found most of the public feeling they were either exaggerated or irrelevant (see Table 54) – the 21% who said that 'Mr Brown's behaviour is outrageous, and he is not fit to be Prime Minister' was probably, if anything, a smaller number than would be normally seize any opportunity to castigate the Prime Minister.

Table 54: 'Bullygate'

Q. There have been reports that Gordon Brown has bullied his own staff. Do you think these reports are...?

	%
Exaggerated – I don't believe Mr Brown has behaved as badly as the reports suggest	43
True – but I'd rather have a Prime Minister who is passionate and sometimes goes over the top, than someone who lacks passion	22
True – Mr Brown's behaviour is outrageous, and he is not fit to be Prime Minister	21
Don't know	14

Source: YouGov/*The Sun*[126]
Base: 807 GB residents aged 18+, 22 February 2010

Polling round the 'Bigotgate' incident pointed to a less clear-cut conclusion. YouGov for the *Sunday Times* found[127] that although two in five (38%) felt that 'It was a trivial incident blown out of proportion that will have no impact on the election', they were outnumbered by the 45% who said 'It was an important incident that said a lot about Gordon Brown's character' – but these votes were strongly in line with voting intentions, Labour voters being overwhelmingly on Brown's side, Conservatives overwhelmingly against him and Liberal Democrats evenly split. Similarly, 55% of Conservatives said the incident worsened their impression of Brown, but only 14% of Labour voters said the same (and 17% of Labour voters felt it had improved their impression of him). This

---

[126] http://today.yougov.co.uk/sites/today.yougov.co.uk/files/YG-Archives-Pol-SunBullying-100222.pdf, accessed 12 January 2011.
[127] Fieldwork 30 April-1 May 2010, http://today.yougov.co.uk/sites/today.yougov.co.uk/files/YG-Archives-Pol-STResults-100501.pdf, accessed 13 January 2011.

is probably a sign that the Duffy affair was only reinforcing voters' opinions on Brown rather than affecting their votes. In fact, ComRes found[128] that 11% of the public claimed 'I have changed my mind about who to vote for because of Gordon Brown calling a voter a 'bigoted woman'', but 13% of those saying they intended to vote Labour said they had changed their mind for this reason, which taken literally would imply the incident was gaining Brown more votes than it was costing him!

Table 55: Is Gordon Brown two-faced?

Q. Generally speaking, do you think Gordon Brown is two-faced?

	All %	Con %	Lab %	LD %
No	23	6	57	24
Yes, but he is no worse than other politicians	53	48	40	61
Yes, and he is worse than other politicians	19	44	1	11
Don't know	5	2	2	5

Source: YouGov/*Sunday Times*[129]
Base: 1,483 GB residents aged 18+, 30 April-1 May 2010

Perhaps more telling, though, is one of YouGov's follow-up questions, on the proposition that Brown's reaction to Duffy revealed him as two-faced (Table 55). Almost half of Conservatives and three-fifths of Liberal Democrats felt that while this characterisation was true, he was 'no worse than other politicians'. So long as this is the way that Britain's voters view their political leaders, no amount of negative campaigning and character assassination is likely to have a strong impact on elections; certainly, the polls showed no movement against Labour in the days immediately following 'Bigotgate', and in the final voting just over a week later Labour's vote share ended two points higher than the polls had found it before he went to Rochdale.

---

[128] ComRes poll for the *Sunday Mirror* and *Independent on Sunday*, http://www.comres.co.uk/page165464813.aspx, accessed 17 January 2011.
[129] http://today.yougov.co.uk/sites/today.yougov.co.uk/files/YG-Archives-Pol-STResults-100501.pdf, accessed 13 January 2011.

The relative (non)influence of online campaigning

The 2010 election failed to be 'Britain's first internet election', as did every previous election which has been confidently predicted to deserve that title since the internet first came into being – unlike the 2008 election in the US, where the medium proved central to Obama's winning campaign and fund-raising drives. We particularly noted the post-election analysis at the website netimperative.com ('Intelligence for digital business'), which flaunted the headline 'Digital election campaign "swayed 40% of voters"' and the facts with which they justified this conclusion:

'Online political campaigning during the General Election influenced the voting intentions of over 4 in 10 of the British public to some degree, according to research commissioned by digital agency Diffusion.

'A survey of over 2,300 people conducted by YouGov, found that 15 per cent of voters stated that the political content they consumed online had either a "fair amount or great deal" of influence on who they decided to vote for on 6th May, more than enough to have changed the outcome of the last election.'[130]

The gap between the 40% claim in the headline and the 15% cited in the second sentence is a pretty conspicuous one. The latter figure, representing the proportion who claimed they had been influenced at least 'a fair amount', is probably the figure which we would normally choose to headline as the most accurate reflection of a similar research finding. But in any case, any survey of the impact of online activity will have measurement problems if the survey is conducted online itself, for obvious reasons – a consideration which YouGov are usually at pains to point out. It is a fair bet that the sort of people who sign up for online panels and take part in regular surveys on political issues on the internet are more likely than the average Briton to take online information sources into account when they are deciding how to vote.

The press

There's always speculation, and usually limited evidence, about the power of the media to influence events. Ever since the claim that 'it was the *Sun*

---

[130] http://www.netimperative.com/news/2010/may/digital-election-campaign-2018swayed-40-of, accessed 21 October 2010.

wot won it' after the 1992 election, and the quick counter-claim by Rupert Murdoch that it did not after all, there has been argument and counter-argument about the role of the media. When it can really count is when there is a close election, and this was never more the case than the election contest in 2010. But what's the evidence for the influence of the press? To answer this question, Table 56 illustrates newspaper readership and voting patterns between 2005 and 2010.

Table 56: Voting by newspaper readership, 2010

| | 2010 vote | | | | | Change since 2005 | | | | Turnout | |
	Con	Lab	LD	Oth	Lead	Con	Lab	LD	Swing (Lab to Con)	2010	Ch.
	%	%	%	%	%	%	%	%	%	%	%
All	37	30	24	10	7	+4	−6	+1	+5.0	65%	+4%
Regular readers of:											
Daily Express	53	19	18	10	35	+5	−9	0	+7.0	67%	−2%
Daily Mail	59	16	16	9	43	+2	−6	+2	+4.0	73%	+4%
Daily Mirror	16	59	17	8	−42	+5	−8	0	+6.5	68%	+5%
Daily Record	12	65	6	17	−54	+5	+10	−10	−2.5	65%	+6%
Daily Telegraph	70	7	18	5	63	+5	−6	+1	+5.5	81%	+4%
The Guardian	9	46	37	8	−37	+2	+3	−4	−0.5	78%	+5%
The Independent	14	32	44	10	−18	+1	−2	0	+1.5	79%	+3%
Daily Star	22	35	20	23	−13	+1	−19	+5	+10.0	43%	−3%
The Sun	43	28	18	10	15	+10	−17	+6	+13.5	57%	+5%
The Times	49	22	24	5	27	+11	−5	−4	+8.0	80%	+9%
None of these	32	31	26	11	2	+5	−6	−1	+5.5	61%	+6%
Quality press*	39	26	28	7	13	+3	−1	−1	+2.0	79%	+5%
All tabloids*	43	30	17	10	13	+5	−10	+2	+7.5	64%	+2%
Mid-market*	57	17	16	10	40	+2	−7	0	+4.5	71%	+2%
Red-top*	30	42	17	11	−12	+7	−12	+3	+9.5	60%	+4%

Includes titles read by too few respondents to be reported separately
Base: 10,211 GB electors, March-May 2010
Source: Ipsos MORI Final Election Aggregate Analysis

The *Sun* is Britain's most widely-read daily newspaper, and also has more of a history of switching its support between the political parties than almost any other national newspaper. It is perhaps, therefore, unsurprising that its support is much sought after by the parties, even if they generally prefer not to admit it. The *Sun* had supported Labour at each of the last three elections, though it made a show of wavering over who to support in 2005 before announcing its decision. This time, though, it officially endorsed the Conservatives as early as 30 September 2009. From then on, it was dedicated to getting Brown out of office and the Tories back in Number Ten. So, in 2010 was it 'the *Sun* wot won it'?

Across the country, there was a 5% swing from Labour to Conservatives between the 2005 and 2010 general election. However, among regular readers of the *Sun* the swing from Labour to Conservative was more than double, a massive 13.5%. In fact their support for Labour dropped 17 points, almost three times as much as the national average, with substantial numbers switching to the Liberal Democrats as well as those who moved to the Tories. As a bonus for the Murdoch millions, readers of *The Times* went from 38% Tory in 2005 to 49%, a swing of 8%.

Yet for all the influence the *Sun* purportedly wields, between 2005 and the time the paper endorsed Cameron, their readers had already swung 12.5% (see Table 57). They had led their newspaper before the word went out that they should vote Tory. The newspaper then simply followed its readership. However, given that the readership had been more Conservative than they eventually turned out to be, what happened to dissipate their support for Cameron's party?

Table 57: Voting intentions of *Sun* readers, 2005-10

	2005 vote %	Jan-Sep 2009 voting intentions %	Jan-Mar 2010 voting intentions %	2010 vote %
All GB adults				
Conservative	33	41	37	37
Labour	36	26	31	30
Liberal Democrat	23	19	19	24
Con lead	−3	+15	+6	+7
Swing from previous		+9.0%	−4.5%	+0.5%
***Sun* readers**				
Conservative	33	42	40	43
Labour	45	29	35	28
Liberal Democrat	12	12	8	18
Con lead	−12	+13	+5	+15
Swing from previous column		+12.5%	−4.0%	+5.0%

Source: Ipsos MORI Election Aggregates and Political Monitor
Base: 17,959 GB residents aged 18+ (including 2,467 *Sun* readers), April-May 2005; 9,051 GB residents aged 18+ (1,243 *Sun* readers), January-September 2009; 4,034 GB residents aged 18+ (488 *Sun* readers), January-March 2010; 10,211 GB residents aged 18+ (988 *Sun* readers), March-May 2010.

It seems that four *Sun* readers in a hundred swung back to Labour between the *Sun*'s declaration for the Tories and early 2010, a very similar reaction to the public as a whole, who swung 4.5% over the same period. But then during the election itself, between 6 April 2010 when the Prime Minister called the election and election day itself, the *Sun*'s readers moved back again towards the Tories, a net swing of five in a hundred, and with support for the Liberal Democrats also more than doubling. Over the same period, the main movement among the public as a whole was also to the LibDems, but with less of the movement still sticking by polling day, and with virtually no movement in the Conservative and Labour share. So, overall, the Conservatives and Liberal Democrats did a little better, and Labour much worse, among *Sun* readers than among the rest of the electorate during the campaign itself.

Over this same period, the *Sun* was delivering a daily hammering to the Labour campaign, its leadership and its focus, while constantly reminding its readers of its support for Cameron. On the first day of the election, 7 April, the photograph dominating the front page was of David Cameron with Big Ben in the background with the headline: 'D-Dave'. On day two of the campaign, they led with 'Brown's a Clown'. Day three had the headline: [Michael] 'Caine: I'll back Tories'. On the following Monday, it was 'Help for kids of heroes' with Cameron's photograph, and so on day after day. Even on the day after the election, the *Sun*'s narrative remained positive with the headline 'Exit Poll puts Tories Ahead' on the banner, and a huge 'Cameron wins the Exit Factor'. The lead story did however also have the sub-head 'But it looks like a hung parliament', relying on the Ipsos MORI/Gfk NOP exit poll which predicted 307 Tory seats, 20 seats short of a majority.

However, did the TV debates act as a countervailing force to the influence of the red top newspapers generally and the *Sun* specifically? Not according to our analysis. Helping to balance the bias, among readers of the *Daily Star*, admittedly from a smaller readership and much less emphasis on election news and comment, before and during the election, while there was a ten percent swing to the Tories among *Star* readers from 2005 to 2010, the *Star*'s readers swung 11% back to Labour during the month long election. And despite the consistent strong support given to Labour by the *Mirror*, between the two elections their readers swung 6.5% to the Conservatives. Overall, the 'red tops' swing between 2005 and 2010 elections was nearly double, 9.5%, the national average, 5%. Among broadsheets 2%, and among the mid-markets, 4.5%.

Of course, many newspaper readers believe themselves to be uninfluenced in their voting choice by their newspaper, and a few even actively disapprove of the fact that the newspapers are reporting the election at all. In our mid-election poll (18-19 April), we found that one in eight of the public, 12%, think there should be a ban on 'all coverage of the election in newspapers'. (See Table 88 on page 316 for the trend table and further discussion).

The media did, however, display a declining interest in each of the successive debates (see Table 58). We know from the 2005 election[131], that the then leaders' debates (which used a different formulae and were individual debates with the anchor rather than debates between leaders) were influential in impacting on how people vote not just because they were broadcast on television but also because who was perceived to have won or lost by the various commentators was widely reported in the press. This resonance effect, of a secondary press influence piggybacking the debate, was probably even more pronounced in 2010, given the fact that there were three debates. However, it is likely that the effect would lessen over time and with each successive debate.

Table 58: Declining media interest in the election debates

Debate	Broadcast	Quality	Midmarket	Popular
First	48	52	47	49
Second	27	25	22	27
Third	24	16	16	17
Various	0	8	16	7
Number	364	151	64	107

Source: Adapted from D Wring and D Deacon, 'Patterns of Press Partisanship in the 2010 General Election', *British Politics*, Volume 5 (2010), 436-54.

According to research undertaken by Loughborough University researchers Dominic Wring and David Deacon (see Table 59), media coverage of the leaders' debates across broadcast, quality, midmarket and

---

[131] See Robert Worcester, Roger Mortimore and Paul Baines, *Explaining Labour's Landslip* (London: Politico's Publishing, 2005).

popular press indicate a clear picture of positive media commentary for Clegg (though with a higher proportion of negative stories in the midmarket and popular press), a negative picture for Gordon Brown (with a more negative picture particularly in the midmarket press), and a largely positive commentary on Cameron in all media (but particularly in the broadcast and midmarket media sectors).

Table 59: Positive/negative media coverage of the leaders

Leader	Evaluation of Story	All	Broad-cast	Quality	Mid-market	Popular
		%	%	%	%	%
Brown	Positive	8	9	6	3	13
	Negative	20	14	14	33	26
	Mixed/unclear/no evaluation	72	77	80	64	61
	Number of cases	389	118	102	63	106
Cameron	Positive	21	15	20	29	23
	Negative	10	4	12	6	15
	Mixed/unclear/no evaluation	70	81	68	65	62
	Number of cases	391	120	103	63	105
Clegg	Positive	38	41	53	34	21
	Negative	8	2	5	11	15
	Mixed/unclear/no evaluation	54	57	42	55	64
	Number of cases	406	126	112	62	106

Source: Adapted from D Wring and D Deacon, 'Patterns of Press Partisanship in the 2010 General Election', *British Politics*, Volume 5 (2010), 436-54.

Party campaign expenditures

The cash-strapped Labour Party (which had higher general administration costs than the other two main parties) found it difficult to raise the necessary campaign funds to fight the election, effectively losing the 2010 election. Labour lost 6.2% of their vote on the previous election and 92 seats. However, considering that they spent around half of what the Conservatives did on the 2010 campaign and only twice the LibDem expenditure (see Table 60), they did not lose sufficiently to allow the Conservatives an outright victory – managing to dent sufficiently the standing of Tory leader, Cameron, or at least create some doubts in the minds of voters.

Whilst the most effective political marketing campaign was probably fought by the Liberal Democrats (who spent particularly highly on transport for get out the vote efforts and market research/canvassing for targeting efforts), they increased their vote share by only 1% nationally and lost five seats. This in itself does not indicate campaign success, but they did, however, succeed in positioning themselves (and Nick Clegg in particular) as a credible coalition partner when the time came to negotiate with the Conservatives, once it became clear that the election result had returned a hung parliament.

Conversely, although the Conservatives won the most seats, they could also be regarded as having lost the political marketing campaign, inefficiently spending considerably more than the other two parties combined, and yet increasing their vote share by only 3.8%, and gaining 97 seats. The Conservatives greater expenditure compared to Labour and the Liberal Democrats on PEBs, advertising and media generally, means it should have dominated the airwaves much more than it actually did. In addition, the Conservatives failed to maintain the lead that they had held in the polls at the end of 2009 through to election day.

Table 60: Party expenditure at the 2010 British general election

	Conservative Party	Labour Party	Liberal Democrats	Totals
A. Party Political Broadcasts	£699,124	£430,028	£152,747	£1,281,899
B. Advertising	£7,532,636	£785,509	£230,482	£8,548,627
C. Unsolicited Material to Electors	£4,779,090	£4,154,985	£3,051,525	£11,985,600
D. Manifesto/ Party Political Documents	£215,869	£345,688	£47,096	£608,653
E. Market Research/ Canvassing	£701,918	£477,911	£496,776	£1,676,605
F. Media	£439,141	£165,997	£147,139	£752,277
G. Transport	£895,018	£291,620	£473,426	£1,660,064
H. Rallies and Other Events	£895,185	£749,334	£87,894	£1,732,413
I. Overheads and General Admin	£524,892	£608,411	£100,508	£1,233,811
Gross Total	**£16,682,873**	**£8,009,483**	**£4,787,593**	**£29,479,949**

Source: Electoral Commission, full details available at www.electoralcommission.org.uk.

5. One year on and the future electoral battle

'Out of power for a generation'

The result of the 2010 general election was a disappointment to many Liberal Democrats. Their share of the vote remained almost the same as in 2005 and their number of MPs actually fell from 62 to 57. In the context of the election campaign and Nick Clegg's impressive performance in the leaders' debates, it is not surprising the party had expected to do better. However, it was not to be, as the exit poll accurately predicted.

The inconclusive election did provide the opportunity for the LibDems to act as 'kingmaker', and after a long weekend of negotiating it was David Cameron and the Conservatives who were supported in a 'full and open coalition' with Britain's third party.

As such, 2010 represented the first time that the LibDems or their predecessor parties have been a formal part of government since 1922, except during the National Government.

In many ways, May 2010 was the highpoint for the Liberal Democrats. Almost immediately after the coalition agreement their public support began to fall away. Within the first few weeks of the new coalition government, around 20% fewer people said they intended to vote Liberal Democrat in 'a general election tomorrow' than cast their votes for the LibDems on 6 May 2010. Perhaps this was always likely to happen as a significant element of Liberal Democrat voters would be aghast at their party getting into bed with the Tories. We don't know, of course, if a similar proportion of other Liberal Democrat voters would have done the same had the party chosen to keep Labour in power. Three times as many Liberal Democrat supporters describe themselves as 'left wing or left of centre' (41%) than 'right wing or right of centre' (13%).[132]

---

[132] Ipsos MORI Political Monitor, November 2010. This measure was asked about those identifying their support for the Liberal Democrats in November 2010 – a much smaller proportion of those

The Governor of the Bank of England's pre-election quip that 'whoever wins this election will be out of power for a whole generation because of how tough the fiscal austerity will have to be'[133] was probably intended as a warning for either the Conservatives or Labour. Yet the evidence since May shows that it is the third party that has suffered the most in its dramatic collapse of popular support as 'the price of election victory'.

The slide in the party's support continued throughout the year so that by mid December we found just one in nine certain voters (11%) said they intended to vote Liberal Democrat – less than half the support they achieved at the general election and their joint lowest rating since October 2007, when the party was temporarily leaderless following the resignation of Sir Menzies Campbell.

We have to go back to July 1995 to find a lower recorded vote share from one of our regular monthly political surveys (then 10% said they intended to vote Liberal Democrat) and to 1990 to find the Liberal Democrats' support regularly below that recorded at the end of 2010.

Polling by other firms confirmed the LibDems' fall from grace. Of the twenty-one published polls conducted in January 2011 all but one had the Liberal Democrats on 10% plus or minus three percentage points (the standard margin of error). Not only are many fewer people telling Ipsos MORI, and other pollsters, that they would vote for the LibDems in an immediate general election, the vast majority of people, according to an ICM survey for the *News of the World*, believed the LibDems will lose votes at the next general election as a result of having formed the coalition with the Conservatives.[134]

It is worth examining in more detail the types of people who moved away from the party after the general election. The drop in support for the LibDems between the general election and January/February 2011 was lowest among the two groups the party were weakest in at the election – among DEs support fell by 6 points (to 11%) and among over 65s it was down by 3 points (to 13%). However, it is the dramatic collapse of the

---

who actually voted in May, presumably therefore excluding a significant many of those so turned off by the Coalition that they'd already switched their party allegiance

[133] See, for example, http://www.independent.co.uk/news/uk/politics/bank-of-england-governor-poll-winner-will-be-out-of-power-for-a-generation-1958867.html.

[134] http://www.icmresearch.co.uk/pdfs/2011_feb_notw_politics_poll.pdf.

party's core young vote that is most striking, down by 20 points since the election, which is double the average decline. By February 2011, therefore, the LibDems were attracting the support of 10% of 18-24 year old voters, which represented just a third of the level of support they managed in May 2010. The Conservatives also suffered among this group with their support falling from 30% at the election to 14%, with most of this change benefitting the Labour party which saw its vote share among 18-24 year olds rise from 31% at the election to 57% by January/February 2011.

Table 61: Change in LibDem support, 2010 election to Jan/Feb 2011

		2010 General Election	January-February 2011	Change
All	%	24	13	-11
Men	%	22	12	-10
Women	%	26	14	-12
18-24	%	30	10	-20
25-34	%	29	18	-11
35-44	%	26	11	-15
45-54	%	26	15	-11
55-64	%	23	12	-11
65+	%	16	13	-3
AB	%	29	17	-12
C1	%	24	14	-10
C2	%	22	10	-12
DE	%	17	11	-6

Source: Ipsos MORI
Base: 1,170 GB residents aged 18+, certain to vote, January / February 2011

The fall in support for the Liberal Democrats was mirrored by the dramatic turnaround in the public's view of its leader, Nick Clegg. For most of his time as party leader, save for his first few months, Clegg was seen as the most popular party leader.[135] From July 2009 onwards he never failed to achieve fewer than four in ten potential voters satisfied with his performance (but usually around a quarter being dissatisfied). As we discussed in Chapter 4, at the height of 'Cleggmania' his ratings shot up even further and at one point two-thirds of the electorate (68%) said they

---

[135] If we take 'net satisfaction' as the indicator, which takes account of the higher proportion of the public saying they don't have an opinion of the third party's leader

were satisfied with his performance. This feat had not been achieved by any party leader since Tony Blair did so in April 1998.

The public were not immediately turned off by the new Deputy Prime Minister. Clegg's average satisfaction rating in Ipsos MORI polls between June and October had him on 49% satisfied. By our November 2010 Political Monitor for Reuters the tide had certainly turned, with fewer than four in ten saying they were satisfied (38%) in both the November and December surveys, falling further to just a third in both our January and February 2011 measures. By this stage he had both the lowest satisfaction and the highest dissatisfaction ratings of any of the three main party leaders. The change in public attitudes towards him from immediately after the general election was substantial, representing a swing of 26.5% from satisfied to dissatisfied.

The following question (Table 62) illustrates the proportion of people that said they liked or disliked either Nick Clegg or the Liberal Democrats when asked in January 2011. This is a question we have asked regularly about the main two parties and their leaders (see Table 17 on page 80 and Table 29 on page 126) but in January 2011 it was the first time we had asked it about the Liberal Democrats.

Table 62: Like Nick Clegg/like the Liberal Democrats, January 2011

Q. Which of these statements comes closest to your views of Nick Clegg and the Liberal Democrat Party?

	%
I like Nick Clegg and I like Liberal Democrat Party	24
I like Nick Clegg but I do not like Liberal Democrat Party	16
I do not like Nick Clegg but I like the Liberal Democrat Party	16
I do not like Nick Clegg and I do not like the Liberal Democrat Party	35
Don't Know	9
Like Nick Clegg	40
Do not like Nick Clegg	51
Like the Liberal Democrat Party	40
Do not like the Liberal Democrat Party	51

Source: Ipsos MORI/Reuters Political Monitor
Base: 1,162 GB residents aged 18+, 21-24 January 2011

A quarter of the public (24%) said they 'like Nick Clegg and like the Liberal Democrat Party', despite the fact that in the same survey only 13%

were intending to vote for the party. Perhaps this evidence shows that there is a deeper level of goodwill towards the LibDems that could be recaptured before the next general election? However, given that as many Conservative (70%) as Liberal Democrat (73%) supporters said they 'like' Nick Clegg, this may simply reflect the Deputy Prime Minister's relatively high approval rating among Tory loyalists, many of whom would not be likely to switch to voting for the LibDems in a general election. But this support could be crucial should the parties agree on a formal or informal electoral pact or alliance in key marginal constituencies under the first-past-the-post electoral system or through second preferences should the country vote in May 2011 to change the electoral system to the Alternative Vote system.

Even so, more of the public at large said they 'do not like Nick Clegg or the Liberal Democrats' and the 'net like' scores for both the leader and the party were both negative at −11. While we do not have any historical data with which to make comparisons, there is a strong case that this net rating is much lower than we would have found before the party went into government. And while the Liberal Democrats might take some comfort in being relatively less despised than the Tories (whose 'net like' score is −19), more people are positive about the Labour party (+3).

Given that the public seem to make little distinction between the Liberal Democrat party and its leader, it could be argued there is little apparent benefit in dropping such a leader, unless they could replace him with someone very popular, and as we write, no one fits that description on the LibDem front benches.

It was always highly likely that the Liberal Democrats' popularity would fall once in government, not least because the responsibility of having to govern means that the party would no longer be able to 'be all things to all men'. The economic and political climate in 2010 was always going to mean difficult decisions on taxation and public services, which few Liberal Democrat voters would have expected their party to be making.

Yet why have the LibDems suffered more than the Tories? Partly this is a reflection of how people see the nature of the Coalition government. In June, 41% thought that the new government was a 'genuine coalition in which decisions are made jointly by the Conservatives and the Liberal Democrats' and 51% felt 'the Conservatives are making most of the decisions in the new government'. By November, many more people felt the Coalition was dominated by the Conservatives (63%) and only a quarter (26%) believed it was a genuine, shared coalition.

The British public are not used to coalition governments and the necessary compromises (or 'broken promises') that these involve. Without doubt the biggest compromise the junior Coalition party has had to make was on retaining and increasing student tuition fees, which saw a considerable backlash from students and many natural LibDem supporters. In a November survey almost two thirds of the public said they believed that the Liberal Democrats were wrong to go back on their pledge to oppose tuition fees (63%), including two in three (68%) of those who said they had voted LibDem in 2010.[136]

(Cameron's) coalition succeeds in 2010

Post election, support for the Conservatives peaked at 40% in our July 2010 poll before falling back, so that by November the honeymoon was over. Labour, now the principal Opposition – with its recently-elected leader, Ed Miliband – was able to take a lead in the voting intentions poll with 39% saying they would vote Labour and 36% Conservative. Yet by our December survey, the parties were effectively level pegging at 38% Conservative and 39% Labour.

Most Conservatives would never have expected to enjoy a honeymoon period like that benefitting New Labour, though fears that soon after the election the public would quickly turn against any public spending cuts or actions to reduce the deficit also turned out to be unfounded. By the end of the year the Tories' support was higher than it had been at the general election in May. So too, of course, was Labour's – up 10 points since the election to 39% support – both essentially at the expense of the Liberal Democrats (down 13 points).

In many ways, 2010 was a good year for the Conservatives. Despite the disappointment of failing to achieve a majority victory at the election, the party formed its first government in 13 years and was able to maintain a

---

[136] See http://today.yougov.co.uk/sites/today.yougov.co.uk/files/YG-Archives-Pol-ST-results-031210_0.pdf.

significant proportion of public support for its decisions after the election. Perhaps most importantly, the new government seemed to have persuaded the public of the need to cut the deficit and to accept the implications of this for public services (at least in the broadest sense). This is illustrated in our November 2010 survey. At the time there were high levels of concern about the impact of cuts on public services - 83% said they were concerned about local public services and 77% about policing as a result of the comprehensive spending review, 44% of adults in full time work said they were very or fairly concerned about being made redundant, and the overwhelming majority (80%) rejected the idea that the private sector would make up for the cuts in public sector jobs. However, in the same survey, more than half of the public (56%) agreed with the statement that 'there is a real need to cut spending on public services in order to pay off the very high national debt we now have'. When we compare public attitudes to this statement from before the election, in March, we find that the 'net agree' score was just +4, but by November it had widened to +23 – a swing of 9.5%.

Other polling also showed that throughout 2010 the public was still broadly in support of the general approach of the new government. In November, for example, an ICM survey for the *Guardian* found that 46% felt the Coalition government is taking the country in 'the right direction' compared with 37% who felt it was going in 'the wrong direction'.[137]

The government therefore survived intact in its first year, claiming to have saved the country from the brink of economic collapse 'like Greece and Ireland' and having reassured the bond markets that Britain had a credible plan to reduce the national debt. The economic data on unemployment and growth also seemed to confirm that the economic recovery could withstand the increased taxes and public expenditure cuts.

However, by the turn of the year and in our January Political Monitor for Reuters, the Tories' support fell decisively. In this survey, Labour had opened up a ten point lead over the Conservatives (42% to 32%). The average voting intention ratings of the major pollsters confirmed the same pattern. In each month between June and December 2010, the average monthly share of support for the Conservatives was 40% plus or minus

---

[137] http://www.icmresearch.co.uk/pdfs/2010_nov_guardian_poll.pdf.

one percentage point; in January this had fallen to 37% (and in 18 of the 21 polls published that month it was below 40%). In February, the average declined another point to 36%. Ipsos MORI's February 2011 survey found 33% intending to vote Conservative and 43% Labour – a ten point gap, exactly the state of the parties in January.

Was this drop just a reaction to the economic data out in January 2011 that showed the economy had contracted in the third quarter of 2010? Perhaps this is part of the explanation. Or perhaps it was a sign that the voters had finally begun to feel the pain (January also saw the rise in VAT to 20%.) It is natural enough that the Tory share should hold up to start with, since the new government was doing what they promised Tory voters they would do. The falling support may, therefore, be the first signs that some of these voters decided that the government's approach was not such a good idea after all, which may come from reading the economic indicators or from beginning to feel the cuts themselves.

A February 2011 YouGov survey found that 57% of the public felt the government's cuts in public services were 'too fast' (up from 44% saying this in October).[138] It is not surprising then that in the same month more than a third of the public (36%) said that they or their family had been affected 'a great deal' or 'a fair amount' by the spending cuts; and perhaps more significantly, double this proportion said they were 'very' or 'fairly' concerned' about the effects of the government's cuts on their family in the next 12 months.[139]

Ipsos MORI's monthly tracking of the country's 'economic optimism' (which has been asked most months since the early 1980s) showed a substantial negative shift between December 2010 and January 2011, and fell further still in February. The 'Economic Optimism Index (EOI) stood at −29 in January 2011 and −37 in February, both ratings being considerably lower than the December 2010 EOI of −12 and a world away from how the public thought of the economy a year earlier in January 2010 (+20). The February 2011 EOI of −37 was the lowest recorded since February 2009.

---

[138] See http://today.yougov.co.uk/sites/today.yougov.co.uk/files/YG-Archives-Pol-ST-results-11-130211.pdf and http://today.yougov.co.uk/sites/today.yougov.co.uk/files/YG-Archives-Pol-Sun-resultsSpendingCuts-211010.pdf.
[139] Ipsos MORI/Reuters Political Monitor, February 2011.

However, we should be careful not to put too much emphasis on the importance of the one economic optimism indicator. It should be remembered, for instance, that public pessimistic about the future state of the economy is not necessarily terminal for a party's electoral fortunes. For most of New Labour's period in office our regular EOI recorded a negative score and the party achieved a landslide election victory in June 2001 despite EOIs of −29 and −22 in March and April of that year; and a comfortable election victory in May 2005 in the context of negative EOIs of −15 and −11 in March and April of that year. The public's generally rosy view of the economy in 1997, in our survey conducted 25-28 April the EOI was +13, did little then to help the Major government avert a landslide disaster the following month.

A more direct measure of how the public view the performance of the government on handling the economy found little change in the public's assessment of the impact of the government's economic policies between October and January, as shown in Table 63.

Table 63: Government policies and the economy

Q. On balance, do you agree or disagree that 'In the long term, this government's policies will improve the state of Britain's economy?'

	November 2009 %	June 2010 %	September 2010 %	October 2010 %	January 2011 %
Agree	40	61	57	48	49
Disagree	54	29	36	39	43
Don't know	6	11	7	13	8
Net agree	**−14**	**+32**	**+21**	**+9**	**+6**

Source: Ipsos MORI/Reuters Political Monitor
Base: c. 600-1,000 GB residents aged 18+ in each survey

In June, roughly twice as many people agreed as disagreed that 'in the long term, this government's policies will improve the state of Britain's economy' (61% to 29%), but support fell most quickly between September and October rather than over the turn of the year. The net result has been that between June 2010 and January 2011 there has been a 13% swing away from confidence in the government's long term economic policy.

Over roughly the same period, there has been a similar swing away from confidence in the government's long term policies for public services, even though the public started off more sceptically. In July 2010, as many people agreed as disagreed that 'in the long term, this government's policies will improve the state of Britain's public services' (45% each), by October half (49%) disagreed and by January almost twice as many disagreed (59%) than agreed (32%). This represents a swing of 13.5% between July and January.

Table 64: Government policies and public services

Q. On balance, do you agree or disagree that 'In the long term, this government's policies will improve the state of Britain's public services?'

	November 2009 %	September 2010 %	October 2010 %	January 2011 %
Agree	38	45	39	32
Disagree	55	45	49	59
Don't know	7	10	12	9
Net agree	−17	0	−10	−27

Source: Ipsos MORI/Reuters Political Monitor
Base: c. 600-1,000 GB residents aged 18+ in each survey

It is perhaps intriguing that several months after the general election, with a new government in power and a seemingly clear determination to cut the country's deficit that, by February 2011, public opinion on the need to cut the deficit was back to where it had been a year earlier. In Ipsos MORI's February Political Monitor, 48% of the public agreed that 'there is a real need to cut spending on public services in order to pay off the very high national debt we have'. In March 2010, 49% of the public agreed also. The headway the new government seemed to have made in convincing more of the public of the need to cut the debt (see page 255) had effectively been wiped out in the first couple of months of 2011.

On non-economic policy, the was little evidence that the Prime Minister's stated vision 'to build a bigger, stronger society' had captured much of the public's attention or enthusiasm since the election.

A YouGov survey for *The Sun* in February 2011 found that just a quarter of the public felt they understood 'very well' (3%) or 'fairly well' (21%)

what the government's Big Society plan is.[140] As shown in Table 65, Ipsos MORI's polling since the election also demonstrated that the public were split on the idea. In February 2011, as many people said it was a good thing (41%) than not (39%), but tellingly the direction of travel from six months earlier was increasing pessimism.

Table 65: The 'Big Society'

Q. The government's plans for creating a Big Society involve giving responsibility to individuals like you to help themselves and their communities, rather than relying on services provided by local authorities or the government. Do you think the government's plans for a Big Society are a good thing or a bad thing for your local area?

	July 2010 %	February 2011 %
Good thing	45	41
Bad thing	35	39
Won't make a difference	12	9
Don't know	8	10
Net good thing	**+10**	**+2**

Source: Ipsos MORI/Reuters Political Monitor
Base: 493 GB residents aged 18+, July 2010; 1,002 GB residents aged 18+, 18-20 February 2011

As well as a different attitude between Labour supporters and those of the government, there was also a significantly different take on the 'Big Society' between Tory and LibDem supporters. Fully two thirds of Tory voters (65%) felt the Big Society was a good thing for their area, but only two in five LibDems (41%) took the same view.

Perhaps just as important, the YouGov/*Sun* poll also highlighted that the vast majority of the public (71%) felt that in practice 'the Big Society will probably not work'. The supporters of all three parties were of the same view about the likely fate of the Prime Minister's 'mission', even if to somewhat different degrees - Labour (87% sceptical), LibDem (79%) and Conservatives (53%).

It is highly likely that the Coalition government's second year may be even tougher than its first. As the public not only hears about, but begins to feel (and worry about), the impact of public service cuts and with the prospect of a sluggish recovery (and perhaps a double dip recession), the

---

[140] See http://today.yougov.co.uk/sites/today.yougov.co.uk/files/YG-Archives-Pol-Sun-BigSociety-150211.pdf.

government will more likely than not be governing against public opinion rather than basking in its support. But this is the case for most democratic governments most of the time.

2010 saw the Coalition government succeed in convincing the electorate that the patient needed to take its medicine to aid its recovery. 2011 and onwards will see the extent to which the patient is prepared to obey the doctors' orders.

David Cameron as Prime Minister

Tony Blair was often described, at least in his first few years as Prime Minister, as 'Teflon Tony' – having the proverbial ability for mud not to stick to him. To what extent can we ascribe a similar quality to Britain's new Prime Minister now that the public have had chance to see his performance in office?

Table 66: Like David Cameron/the Conservative Party, January 2011

Q. Which of these statements comes closest to your views of David Cameron and the Conservative Party?

	January 2010 %	April 2010 %	January 2011 %
I like David Cameron and I like the Conservative Party	27	31	30
I like David Cameron but I do not like the Conservative Party	18	22	17
I do not like David Cameron but I like the Conservative Party	12	7	7
I do not like David Cameron and I do not like the Conservative Party	34	35	39
Don't Know	9	5	7
Like David Cameron	45	53	47
Do not like David Cameron	46	42	46
Like the Conservative Party	39	38	37
Do not like the Conservative Party	52	57	56
NET like Cameron	−1	+11	+1
NET like Conservative Party	−13	−19	−19

Source: Ipsos MORI/Reuters Political Monitor
Base: c, 1,000-1,250 GB residents aged 18+ in each survey

Using our standard four-part 'like him/like his party' question (Table 66), in January 2011, the Prime Minister retained a slender net positive rating

(+1), which included twice as many people who said they 'like David Cameron but do not like the Conservative Party' (17%) than the opposite: 'do not like David Cameron but like the Conservative Party' (7%). True, Cameron's likeability ratings had fallen from earlier in 2010 – in April it stood at +11 – but it was statistically no different from how people viewed him 12 months earlier in January 2010 (−1 'net like').

The Prime Minister also continued to be much more liked than his party (a 20 point gap in 'net like'), even more so than in January 2010 (a 12 point gap). The swing in the 'net like' score for Cameron between January 2010 and January 2011 was 1% to the positive; the swing in the 'net like' score for the Conservative party over the same period was 3% to the negative.

On this evidence, the popularity of the Coalition government in its first year rested more with how the public viewed the Prime Minister (positively) than the main coalition party (negatively). It should also be remembered that the data from the above table was taken from our January 2011 Political Monitor survey, which also saw for the first time more of the public dissatisfied than satisfied in Cameron's performance as Prime Minister, as shown in Table 67.

Table 67: Satisfaction with David Cameron and the Government, 2010-11

Q. Are you satisfied or dissatisfied with the way...
...David Cameron is doing his job as Prime Minister?
...the Government is running the country?

	David Cameron			The Government		
	Satisfied	Dis-satisfied	Net	Satisfied	Dis-satisfied	Net
	%	%	%	%	%	%
May 12-13	51	23	+18	n/a	n/a	
June 18-20	57	26	+31	43	33	+10
July 23-25	55	32	+23	43	40	+3
September 10-12	57	33	+24	43	47	−4
October 15-17	52	37	+15	42	45	−3
November 12-14	46	45	+1	35	55	−20
December 10-12	48	44	+4	38	54	−16
January 21-24	38	52	−14	30	61	−31
February 18-20	39	52	−13	31	60	−29

Source: Ipsos MORI/Reuters Political Monitor
Base: c. 1,000 GB residents aged 18+ in each survey

The Government's honeymoon effectively ended in September, as we measured for the first time more people dissatisfied than satisfied with how it was running the country (43% satisfied and 47% dissatisfied). In spite of this, Cameron managed to retain more fans than detractors until the turn of the year, albeit that by November the public was divided about his performance.

However, Cameron's satisfaction ratings held up favourability against Ed Miliband in 2010. In each of Ipsos MORI's three monthly surveys between October and December more of the public said they were satisfied with Cameron as Prime Minister than Miliband as leader of the Labour Party; and even when we take into account those who express dissatisfaction with the leaders, statistically in all three surveys there was no difference between the two of them. For instance, in December 2010, Cameron's net approval rating was +4 while Miliband's was +1.

Table 68: Image of Miliband, Cameron and Clegg[141]

Q. I am going to read out some things both favourable and unfavourable that have been said about various politicians. Which of these, if any, do you think apply to Ed Miliband/David Cameron/Nick Clegg?

	Ed Miliband %	David Cameron %	Nick Clegg %
A capable leader	26	57	32
Good in a crisis	15	41	24
More honest than most politicians	24	33	27
Understands the problems facing Britain	40	51	45
Rather inexperienced	64	44	65
Out of touch with ordinary people	34	51	43
None of these	5	2	5
Don't know	10	3	5

Source: Ipsos MORI/Reuters Political Monitor
Base: 1,004 GB residents aged 18+, 10-12 December 2010

Further, in examining how the public viewed the two leaders head to head, Cameron was the more popular choice. ICM's October survey for *The Guardian*, conducted 28-29 October, found that more than twice as many people thought Cameron (47%) rather than Miliband (20%) would 'prove

---

[141] This question was asked in a telephone survey and therefore cannot be directly compared with previous leader image questions used earlier, as these were asked using MORI's face-to-face survey where respondents are shown a list of descriptions for each leader separately and asked to select those they think apply.

the most competent Prime Minister'.[142] Of course, the new Labour leader had only then recently been elected so we perhaps should not be surprised by this finding. But another ICM poll conducted early in 2011 (fieldwork 21–23 January) found that while fewer people thought Cameron (38%) would make 'the best Prime Minister' the increase in support to Miliband was slight (25%) and Cameron retained a strong lead.[143]

Table 68 shows the image attributes the public believe applied to each of the three party leaders, when measured in December 2010. As can be seen, Cameron led Miliband on all the positive attributes, in particularly as being seen as 'a capable leader' (31 points difference) and 'good in a crisis' (26 points). However, he was also more likely to be viewed as 'out of touch with ordinary people' (17 points higher than Miliband).

Equalising constituency sizes

Many Tories blame their failure to win an overall majority at the 2010 election on the bias in the electoral system. They are right to do so. In each of the last few general elections, the way the electoral system has translated seats into votes has given Labour a massive advantage – for any given share of the votes, Labour wins many more seats than the Conservatives do. Had Labour had a 7-percentage-point lead in the popular vote in 2010, Gordon Brown would have been returned with a very comfortable majority.

But they are mistaken in the conclusion they have drawn from this. Senior Tories have apparently concluded that an important cause of this bias is that Labour constituencies have fewer voters than Tory ones, and that they can therefore substantially reduce the bias by having the constituency map redrawn with more equally-populated constituencies. As a result, this measure was in the Conservative manifesto, and included as a quid-pro-quo in the Act of Parliament setting up the referendum on the electoral system that had been promised to the Liberal Democrats.[144] Conservative

---

[142] See http://www.icmresearch.co.uk/pdfs/2010_sept_guard_poll.pdf.
[143] See http://www.icmresearch.co.uk/pdfs/2011_jan_guardian_poll.pdf.
[144] They also intend to reduce the number of seats to 600. Far from there being any inherent party advantage in this, the comprehensive boundary review that will be necessary as a result may damage the Tories disproportionately by disrupting the incumbency advantage they could normally expect in all the constituencies they have just gained.

constituencies do have a higher average electorate than Labour's, and it is perfectly true that this is one of the factors involved. But it is by no means the only factor, nor even the most important one. If the Tories believe that they can correct the bias of the system against them simply by equalising constituency sizes they are, from their standpoint, sadly mistaken.

Perhaps we should begin by putting a size on the bias. There are alternative ways of measuring it. One simple way is in terms of votes per seat: in 2010, the Conservatives won one seat for every 34,980 votes they received, 5% more than Labour's 33,359. In fact, this is a rather misleading calculation, because included within it are the normal effects of first-past-the-post in advantaging the largest party. The gap would be much larger if Labour had won, while if the Conservatives had managed a more convincing victory the 'winner's bonus' would have completely offset the bias in the distribution of votes and they would have got more seats per vote than Labour. If we continue to use a single-member constituency system, we have to recognise that the 'winner's bonus' is part of the normal operation of the system and is the winning party's entitlement – the bias we are concerned with here is not affected by that, but involves an inequality in the treatment of the two major parties before the exaggerative effects of first-past-the-post are taken into account. (If we don't like that, then we shall have to consider switching to a more proportional voting system instead[145], and the Liberal Democrats will reasonably point out that the Tories don't have that much to complain about, since the LibDems only got one MP for every 119,933 votes.)

A more useful measure of the size of the bias is one which compares how many seats the parties would have won with the same share of the votes. For 2010, we can either compare the number of seats the Conservatives won with the number that Labour would have won had it been they who had led by 37% to 30%, or we can look at how many seats each party would have won if they had received an equal number of votes. Assuming uniform swing, if Labour had won by this seven-point margin, they would have taken 357 seats, 51 more than the 306 seats the Tories actually won. Had it been a tie, with each party taking 33.4% of the vote, Labour would have 307 seats and the Conservatives 254, an advantage to Labour of 53

---

[145] *Not* the Alternative Vote, which operates in a very similar way to the present first-past-the-post system.

(Figure 50). So it makes little difference which of these two methods we use, but perhaps the latter is a slightly more useful comparison as it shows that while Labour would have been well ahead on an equal split in the votes they would have been short of an overall majority.

Figure 50: Seats to votes: the bias

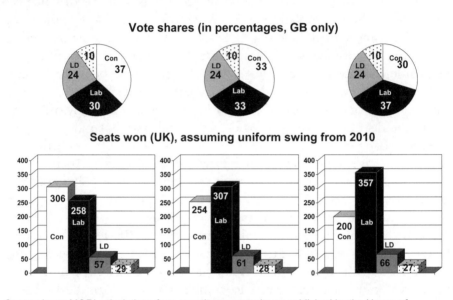

Source: Ipsos MORI calculations from constituency results as published by the House of Commons Library in Research Paper 10/36 (8 July 2010)

But the size of the bias varies from election to election. The system is not always biased towards Labour – in the 1950s and 1960s the tilt was very much the other way. (In 1951, in fact, Labour won most votes and yet the Tories got an overall majority in the House of Commons.) Nevertheless, in recent years it has been consistently the Tories who have been disadvantaged. In the 2005 election the bias to Labour was about 111 seats, double the size it was in the 2010 election. Part of the reason for its having been reduced is the revision of constituency boundaries: according to the Rallings and Thrasher calculations of the result if the 2005 election had been fought on the new boundaries rather than the old[146], the boundary changes reduced the bias from 111 to 96, but this was still big enough that Labour could have won a wafer-thin overall majority while trailing the Tories in votes.

One factor which can change the size of the bias is if the swing in votes from one election to the next is not uniform. Because extra votes in marginal constituencies deliver seats while extra votes in safe seats do not, a party which does better-than-average in the marginals will shift the bias in its favour. Part of the present bias arose in this way, when Labour over-performed in the marginals at the 1997 and 2001 elections, winning more seats than uniform swing would have predicted given its vote share. In 2005, on the other hand, it was the Conservatives who did a little better in the marginal seats, and this eased the bias just a little.

In 2010 this situation was even more complicated. The Tories did not have a systematic advantage in the marginal seats, but there was more apparently random variation in swing than usual so that nevertheless the Tories gained more seats in practice than they would have theoretically won on a simple uniform swing. This cut the bias by another 43 seats.

But where does the bias come from in the first place? Firstly, and this is the point on which the Conservatives have seized, not all constituencies are the same size. As Table 69 shows, the average electorate in the constituencies that the Conservatives won is bigger than that in Labour's – in fact (see the bottom line) there are about 106 electors in every Conservative constituency for every 100 in a Labour one, not an insignificant difference.

Yet this accounts for a relatively small part of the bias. A more significant cause is that turnout is lower in Labour seats than Conservative ones so that Labour can pick up seats more 'cheaply'. If we compare the number of votes actually cast in each constituency (rather than the number available to be cast), there were 118 votes in every Conservative constituency for 100 in every Labour one. This means that by taking the turnout into account as well consistency size, the discrepancy trebles.

---

[146] Colin Rallings & Michael Thrasher, *Media Guide to the New Parliamentary Constituencies* (Plymouth: Local Government Chronicle Elections Centre, 2007)

Table 69: Variation in constituency size and vote

Party winning constituency in 2010	Average electorate 2010	Average total votes 2010	Average votes for winner 2010	Average second place votes 2010
Conservative	72,367	49,440	23,854	14,383
Labour	68,564	41,842	19,383	11,473
Liberal Democrat	69,600	46,944	21,610	16,029
Plaid Cymru	46,316	30,998	11,914	8,147
SNP	58,746	36,831	14,725	11,228
Conservative-to-Labour ratio	1.06	1.18	1.23	1.25

Source: Calculated from election results as given in House of Commons Library Research Paper 10/36 (8 July 2010)

A third factor, also important, is how effectively each party's votes are spread across constituencies. For example, a party needs fewer votes to win if the opposition is split than if it faces a single strong opponent, a factor affected by tactical voting. One measure of this is simply to compare how many votes each party actually needed on average to win its seats, in other words one vote more than its single strongest opponent in each case. Partly because the anti-Labour vote in Labour's seats is more split than the anti-Conservative vote in Conservative seats, we can see that this gives yet a further advantage to Labour. On average, Conservative MPs needed 125 votes to beat their strongest opponent for every 100 that their Labour counterparts needed. On the other hand, this effect was slightly offset because Labour's majorities tended to be a bit bigger than Conservative ones. In other words, they had more unnecessary 'surplus' votes. So if we look at the average number of votes actually cast for each winning MP, Conservatives gained 123 for each 100 cast for Labour victors.

This simple analysis shows why experts expect that only a comparatively small part of the bias will be corrected by the government's plan to equalise constituency sizes.[147] The much bigger cause, differences in

---

[147] In fact there are much more sophisticated methods of dissecting the causes of the bias, which rely on advanced statistical analysis. For a fuller discussion of these complex issues, see Galina Borisyuk, Colin Rallings and Michael Thrasher, 'Parliamentary Constituency Boundary Reviews and Electoral Bias: How Important Are Variations in Constituency Size?', *Parliamentary Affairs,* Volume 63, 4-21 (2010), or Ron Johnston, Iain McLean, Charles Pattie and David Rossiter, 'Can the

turnout, will not be affected by the proposed reform. In fact, it is a natural consequence of Labour being strongest among the demographic groups that are least likely to vote. There is, therefore, an argument that the bias towards Labour is not really as big as it looks. It is probable that of non-voters, many more would vote Labour than would vote Conservative if they did vote. It seems likely that many of them fail to vote only because they know that their vote is not needed, since Labour is sure to win their constituency. If so, then it can be argued that the 'real' Labour support is higher than the share they secure at the polls and that some of the 'extra' seats they win for a given share of the vote merely reflects this.

Nor will changing the boundaries have any effect on the vote distribution (the way that Conservative strength is spread across regions where they fight either Labour or the Liberal Democrats while Labour is strongest where the remaining votes are split between their two opponents), and is unlikely to have much effect on the way tactical voting exacerbates this effect. Only the voters themselves can change this.

Depending on the precise method of calculation, estimates of the contribution of electorate size to the total Conservative-Labour bias differ very slightly, but our own calculations and all those we have seen from academic teams agree that the number of seats involved is in single figures. If this is right, equal constituency sizes would not have taken the Tories even halfway across the gap by which they fell short of an overall majority. It would not even have taken them close enough that a coalition with the DUP was a viable alternative to one with the Liberal Democrats. In other words, the difference in constituency sizes had no material effect on the 2010 election outcome at all.

The Conservatives are right to be worried about the bias in the electoral system, but the changes they have pushed through will not solve the problem. (Nor is it likely to make much difference should the Alternative Vote be adopted: this will use the same constituencies as would be used for a first-past-the-post election, and the bias will probably operate in a very similar way.) We can expect Labour to maintain a very substantial advantage should the votes be close in the next general election.

Boundary Commissions Help the Conservative Party? Constituency Size and Electoral Bias in the United Kingdom', *Political Quarterly*, Volume 80, 479-94 (2009).

Towards 2015?

What do the results of the 2010 general election, and what we know of the public's reaction to the first year of the new Coalition government, mean for the main political parties as we head for the next general election?

First of all, let us assume that the election will be held on 5 May 2015 as expected. If the Coalition government holds – or even if the LibDems split and the Conservatives manage to govern as a minority administration – we have another four years until the next general election. The biggest potential electoral change is the introduction of a new voting system as a result of the referendum in May 2011. At the time of this book going to print (in March 2011) we don't know the outcome of the referendum. A 'Yes' vote, and so a change to the Alternative vote (AV) system, could have a dramatic impact on the parties' strategies and tactics come the general election. If the public reject the new system, we will be on much more familiar ground with the existing first-past-the-vote (FPTP) system.

Politically, a 'No' vote could have even more impact for British politics over the course of the next year or so, putting additional pressure on the LibDem leadership to show some fruits of their coalition with the Conservatives. However, in our opinion, should the public vote to keep FPTP at the referendum, given the LibDems current levels of popularity, it would be almost certain electoral suicide for them to leave the government and try to force an early general election. (Of course, an alternative might be to try to force a change of leader as the 'price' of failure!).

Whether the voting system changes to AV or not, we see very persuasive arguments to suggest that come the 2015 general election, there will be some sort of formal alliance or agreement between the two governing parties (if the grassroots and backbench MPs of the respective parties can stomach it). Even if the Liberal Democrats' poll numbers increase from their current position of barely scraping double digits, it is difficult to see a rebound anywhere close to their performance at the last two general elections. This is particularly so given that, traditionally, a significant proportion their support was based on a protest with the main parties, some of which seems naturally to have drifted to the Labour party, for the time being at least.

Many in the Conservative party should also surely see the potential benefits of continuing the 'marriage of convenience' up to and beyond the next general election. No governing party has increased its share of the vote after a full term in office since 1955. For the Conservatives to be confident enough of being able to 'go it on their own' they would need to do better than in 2010 (even with revised constituency boundaries). Given their experience of double digit opinion poll leads prior to the last general election, will they have the confidence to risk splitting the anti-Labour vote at the next? The combined 'coalition ticket' support at 60% share of the vote at the last general allows for sufficient slippage over the next few years in public support (in Jan/Feb 2011 their combined voting intentions was 46%) for the parties together to feel better placed to take on Labour. And from a purely cynical perspective, it may be that the coalition actually helps the Tories insofar as it seems to be the LibDems that are suffering the most from the unpopular decisions the 'government of the national interest' is making.

Ed Miliband – it's not love at first sight

2010 was clearly a terrible year for the Labour party. Ejected from office after 13 years in government and losing almost 100 seats in the general election, its share of the vote fell below 30% and the party lost almost 5 million voters from its 1997 election landslide.

Ed Miliband was elected leader of the Labour party on 25 September 2010, narrowly defeating his brother, David Miliband, by a 1.3% margin on the support of trade unionists and affiliated societies in the fourth round of their AV system contest, David having won more votes among Labour MPs and MEPs, and Labour members. Four months on from Ed's election as party leader, our January 2011 survey asked a question designed to gauge the popularity of the leader alongside that of his party (see Table 70).

A quarter of the public (25%) said that they 'like Ed Miliband and like the Labour Party' and a further one in nine (11%) said they 'like Ed Miliband but not the Labour Party'. This meant that in total just over a third (36%) of potential voters were positive towards Labour's leader, substantially fewer than those who were not (Miliband's 'net like' score was −15). With the Labour Party's 'net like' rating on +3 it suggests that by the start of 2011 Miliband was not the great asset to the party in the same way that Blair was to Labour from 1994, or Cameron was to the Conservatives from 2006.

Table 70: Like Ed Miliband/like the Labour Party

Q. Which of these statements comes closest to your views of Ed Miliband and the Labour Party?

	%
I like Ed Miliband and I like the Labour Party	25
I like Ed Miliband but I do not like the Labour Party	11
I do not like Ed Miliband but I like the Labour Party	20
I do not like Ed Miliband and I do not like the Labour Party	31
Don't know	13
Like Ed Miliband	36
Do not like Ed Miliband	51
Like the Labour Party	45
Do not like the Labour Party	42

Source: Ipsos MORI Political Monitor
Base: 1,162 GB residents aged 18+, 21-24 January 2011

Perhaps as worrying for the Leader of the Opposition is that fewer people said they like him than said they same about either Nick Clegg (40% like) or David Cameron (47%), although this is affected by the higher percentage who are undecided. If voters at the next general election place as much importance on the leader as they did at the last general election and, as we found with the detailed image of Gordon Brown and David Cameron, that 'likeability' or 'personality' are crucial determinants, then these ratings must surely need to improve if Ed Miliband's hopes of becoming Prime Minister are to be realised.

Yet it is too early to write-off Labour's new, young leader. Miliband's January 2011 ratings are not too far away from the first measure we took of David Cameron when he became Tory leader (in January 2007 his 'net like' score was −8). Cameron's likeability significantly improved over the course of the next 18 months so that, by July 2008, we recorded it as +18 and on the eve of the general election, in April 2010, as +11 (in the same survey Brown's net rating was −23).

But analysis of our longer-term leader likeability trends appears to show that Cameron may have been an exception to the general rule. The worry for Ed Miliband will be that instead of more of the public warming to him the longer he is in the job, a significant proportion have effectively already made up their minds. Miliband's likeability rating in January 2011 is statistically the same as Michael Howard's in April 2005 (−17) − the only time we used this indicator as an image measure during Howard's brief period as Tory leader. (See Table 71.)

Table 71: Like/not like opposition leaders, 1984-2011

		Like leader	Do not like leader	Net like leader
Kinnock (October 1984)	%	51	38	+13
Kinnock (October 1985)	%	52	39	+13
Blair (September 1994)	%	49	24	+25
Blair (January 1996)	%	53	29	+24
Blair (June 1996)	%	52	31	+21
Blair (January 1997)	%	53	35	+18
Hague (June 1997)	%	18	20	−2
Hague (December 1997)	%	24	50	−26
Hague (February 2000)	%	29	50	−21
Hague (June 2000)	%	33	55	−22
Hague (January 2001)	%	30	53	−23
Howard (April 2005)	%	32	49	−17
Cameron (January 2007)	%	36	44	−8
Cameron (July 2008)	%	54	36	+18
Cameron (January 2010)	%	45	46	−1
Cameron (April 2010)	%	53	42	+11
Miliband (January 2011)	%	36	51	−15

Source: Ipsos MORI

For three previous Opposition leaders from Kinnock through Blair to Hague it is striking that at different points during their time as Opposition leader their 'net like' ratings hardly moved. Ed Miliband will be hoping this does not happen to him.

The leader likeability data has only been asked periodically, so our ability to gauge immediate changes in the public's assessment of the leaders' performance is limited. Ipsos MORI's regular leader satisfaction series − asked almost every month since the early 1980s − provides us with a much more robust trend line with which to analyse the early public reaction. In our first measure, conducted within a month of him winning the party leadership between 15–17 October, Miliband began well with twice as many people indicating they were satisfied than dissatisfied (41% to 19%) . In terms of the proportion of the public expressing satisfaction much higher than our first measure of public attitudes towards David Cameron in January 2006 (31% satisfied), or for that matter other previous Tory leaders' initial ratings: Michael Howard (26% satisfied in November 2005), Iain Duncan Smith (15% in September 2001) or William Hague (12% in June 1997). It is also worth noting that while 40% of voters had 'no opinion' either way about Miliband's performance in October 2010 (and presumably a large proportion of these didn't know who he was) this is a lower 'don't know' percentage than has been typical of previous Opposition leaders, including Cameron, 52% (January 2007); Howard, (64%, November 2003); Hague (75%, June 1997) and Blair (50%, August 1994).

Miliband's public approval ratings since that first measure have failed to impress. This is mainly as a result of an increase in how many people say they are dissatisfied with the way he is doing his job. In both our December 2010 and January 2011 surveys, as many people were dissatisfied as satisfied with his performance; by February 2011 those dissatisfied (43%) outnumbered those satisfied (34%). In other words, between October 2010 and February 2011, the proportion of the public dissatisfied with Ed Miliband doubled (from 22% to 43%).

The task facing the Labour Party

The election of Ed Miliband as Labour leader in September 2010 had been widely interpreted as a sign that Labour will now move to the left (whatever that means in the modern context). A quarter of the British public (24%) describe themselves as 'left wing/left of centre' yet many more believe this represents Ed Miliband's politics (44%). However, the 'ideological gap' is not just a problem for the Labour leader. The gap between how many people think David Cameron is 'right wing/right of centre' than would describe themselves as such is even bigger (49% would apply this to Cameron but only 24% to themselves). Indeed, the average gap between self described ideological position (ignoring those who say don't know) are exactly the same for Cameron and Miliband (19 points average difference), though of course for the opposite reasons. Nick Clegg is much more closely aligned to where the public place themselves (average gap is just 4 points).[148]

Lord Ashcroft, in his post-election polling of 'swing voters', captured Labour's problem beautifully. When asked about the effect on their own support, 31% said they would be more likely to go back to supporting the Labour Party if it moved further to the left and 32% said that they would be less likely to do so; the remaining 37% admitted 'I am not sure what is meant by 'moving further to the left'. Almost half the C2DE swing voters picked this last option, the remainder being equally split between being more and less likely to support a left-shifting Labour party. [149]

It is not only in relation to the ideological position of the political parties that the public's attitudes are often internally contradictory, even if this is perhaps truer of floating voters, who are mainly those who have given least consideration to political issues, than of everybody else. Swing voters agree 64% to 36% that 'Private companies should never have any part to play in delivering public services health and education', but disagree 67% to 34% that 'Private schools should be banned so that all children have to go through the state system'. They also agree 77% to 24% that 'Tax relief should be given on private health insurance so as to relieve some of the pressures on the NHS'.[150] Is there a role for the private sector or not? You can't have it both ways.

Despite the loss of office, 2010 was not quite an unmitigated disaster for the Labour party. There are few people who would, at this stage, ask the question 'can Labour ever win again?'. True, the party's share of the vote in the 2010 election was lower than the Tories dismal performance in 1997, but the polling data since then shows that Labour's broader image

---

[148] See Ipsos MORI Political Monitor, October 2010. The average gap is calculated first by working out the difference between the proportion of the public identifying themselves as left wing/left of centre, centre or right wing/right of centre and the proportion believing each of the main party leaders fit into one of these three categories. The total of the differences for each of the categories is summed up and then divided by three for each leader.

[149] Polling by Populus of 2005 Labour voters who did not vote Labour in 2010, for Lord Ashcroft, conducted 3-13 September 2010, http://www.lordashcroft.com/pdf/25092010_swing_voter_tables.pdf, accessed 28 September 2010.

[150] http://www.lordashcroft.com/pdf/25092010_swing_voter_tables.pdf, accessed 28 September 2010.

and potential ability to rebound puts them in a stronger position than that faced by the Conservatives at the end of the last century.

In our January 2011 survey, 45% said they liked the Labour party, which is marginally higher than the 42% who said they did not like it (giving a net score of +3). This is both higher than the Tories' January 2011 rating of −19 (and for that matter the LibDems' −11), and it is also considerably higher than the position of the Tories after their 1997 electoral defeat.[151]

Labour's rebound since the general election has been considerably quicker than that experienced by the Conservatives after 1997. Almost immediately after the election Labour's poll ratings increased from their actual election performance (the monthly average 'poll of polls' showed Labour on 33% in June) and, within a few months, the party was level-pegging with the Conservatives. The 'poll of polls' showed a two-point Tory lead in September and October, a one-point Labour lead in November and the parties both on 40% in December. At the start of 2011, there were clear signs of Labour moving decisively ahead of their main opponents, opening-up a five-point lead (42% to 37%) in the January 'poll of polls' and a seven-point lead in February.

The contrast with the performance of the Conservatives in 1997 is stark. By the end of 1997, MORI found that just over a quarter of the public (26%) intended to vote Conservative in a 'general election tomorrow' – half the proportion (55%) who supported Labour – giving the governing party a massive 29 point lead. It took the Conservatives almost three-and-a-half years to record a lead over Labour in any of our voting intention polls, which eventually came as a reaction to the September 2000 fuel protests (in three separate surveys that month we found a Tory lead of between one and four points) and which, in the end, proved to be a false dawn as confirmed by the results of the 2001 general election. It took the Conservatives more than a decade, two general election defeats and four leaders before they were able to build a consistent polling lead over the government.

---

[151] MORI's tracking data on party advocacy between 1997 and 2005 provides an example of the image problem facing the Conservative party after its heavy 1997 defeat. See http://www.ipsos-mori.com/researchpublications/researcharchive/poll.aspx?oItemId=2387&view=wide.

It is at least arguable that the Labour party is now better placed in terms of its broad appeal than it was in the early 1980s and than were the Conservatives in the late 1990s. Perhaps with the exception of the party's reputation for economic competence, the issues and policies that define the two main political parties are also less marked than before. It is unlikely that come the next general election Labour's manifesto will be described as 'the longest suicide note in history' as was the case in 1983. (Indeed, it appears that it is different parts of the governing coalition that are advocating Britain withdrawing from the European Union and the scrapping of Britain's independent nuclear deterrent!)

However, the events of the last two or three years should also provide a cautionary lesson for Labour. A substantial polling lead in the standard 'general election tomorrow' question is no guarantee of votes in the ballot box. The Tories' regular double-digit poll leads in 2008 and 2009 (on several occasions recording more than 20 points) masked the fact that throughout the last parliament the party never properly 'sealed the deal'.

So where does this leave the Labour party? To answer this we should consider in more detail how the electoral landscape changed in 2010 and the implications of this change for the next five years.

The de-polarisation of British politics

The broad pattern of swing between Labour and the Conservatives was that the swing was biggest among the groups where the Conservatives are traditionally weakest, in other words further flattening out the demographic distinctions between the two parties' support bases, already somewhat eroded by the widening of Labour's appeal when Tony Blair was leader. The young swung more than the old and the working class more than the middle class (with a particularly sharp drop in Labour's support among the C2s); but there was almost no difference between the swing among men and women, with the Tories gaining 4% from each sex while Labour lost 6 points among men and 7 points among women.

Thus, the evolution of the political landscape which began in the 1990s has continued. Britain is less politically-polarised than was the case in 1992. Women are now marginally more supportive of Labour than men, whereas the opposite was once the case (though there has been no movement in the 'gender gap' since 2005). There is effectively no age variation in Labour support, and only a moderate one in Tory support, though their popularity among the retired people is still substantially stronger than that among the working age population.

Table 72: How Britain voted, 2010

	2010 vote					Change since 2005			Lab-Con swing	Turnout	
	Con %	Lab %	LD %	Oth %	Lead %	Con %	Lab %	LD %	%	2010 %	Ch. %
All	37	30	24	10	7	+4	−6	+1	+5.0	65%	+4%
Gender											
Men	38	28	22	12	10	+4	−6	0	+5.0	66%	+4%
Women	36	31	26	8	5	+4	−7	+3	+5.5	64%	+3%
Age											
18-24	30	31	30	9	−1	+2	−7	+4	+4.5	44%	+7%
25-34	35	30	29	7	5	+10	−8	+2	+9.0	55%	+6%
35-44	34	31	26	9	3	+7	−10	+3	+8.5	66%	+5%
45-54	34	28	26	12	6	+3	−7	+1	+5.0	69%	+4%
55-64	38	28	23	12	10	−1	−3	+1	+1.0	73%	+2%
65+	44	31	16	9	13	+3	−4	−2	+3.5	76%	+1%
Social Class											
AB	39	26	29	7	13	+2	−2	0	+2.0	76%	+5%
C1	39	28	24	9	11	+2	−4	+1	+3.0	66%	+4%
C2	37	29	22	12	8	+4	−11	+3	+7.5	58%	0%
DE	31	40	17	12	−9	+6	−8	−1	+7.0	57%	+3%
Housing Tenure											
Owned outright	45	24	21	11	21	+1	−5	+1	+3.0	74%	+3%
Mortgage	36	29	26	9	7	+5	−7	+1	+6.0	66%	+6%
Social renter	24	47	19	11	−23	+8	−8	0	+8.0	55%	+4%
Private renter	35	29	27	9	6	+8	−7	−1	+7.5	55%	+4%

Source: Ipsos MORI General Election Aggregate

Base: 10,211 GB adults aged 18+, 19 March-5 May 2010, weighted to final outcome and turnout

Region

However, one respect in which British voters are moving further apart is geographically. In 2010, Labour actually increased its vote in Scotland, and held most of it in London, while its support collapsed everywhere else.

We might expect Scotland to be different on occasion, with its devolved government, with many of the potential election issues being 'devolved responsibilities' on which the Westminster outcome would not affect

Scotland, with Labour led by a Scottish Prime Minister, and with a fourth major party – the SNP – in the electoral equation and currently in power at Holyrood. Here alone in 2010 Labour increased its share of the vote while the Conservatives made little headway (producing a Conservative to Labour swing of 0.5%) and Liberal Democrat support dropped sharply.

Table 73: Voting by region

	2010 vote						Change since 2005				Swg Lab to Con %
	Con %	Lab %	LD %	Nat %	Oth %	Con lead %	Con %	Lab %	LD %	Nat %	
All GB	37	30	24		10	7	+4	−6	+1		+5.0
East Midlands	41	30	21		8	11	+4	−9	+3		+6.5
Eastern	47	20	24		9	28	+4	−10	+2		+7.0
Greater London	35	37	22		7	−2	+3	−2	0		+2.5
North East	24	44	24		9	−20	+4	−9	+1		+6.5
North West	32	39	22		7	−8	+3	−6	+1		+4.5
Scotland	17	42	19	20	2	−25	+1	+2	−4	+2	−0.5
South East	50	16	26		8	33	+5	−8	+1		+6.5
South West	43	15	35		7	27	+4	−8	+2		+6.0
Wales	26	36	20	11	6	−10	+5	−7	+2	−1	+6.0
West Midlands	40	31	20		9	9	+5	−8	+1		+6.5
Yorks & Humber	33	35	23		9	−2	+4	−9	+2		+6.5

Source: Election results as published by the House of Commons Library in Research Paper 10/36 (8 July 2010).

The Conservatives, though, have never done well in Scotland in recent years and although this result represents a further moving apart, it is not a major surprise that a Conservative-led government could be formed without appreciable support in Scotland. For that matter, half a century ago, it would have seemed improbable that a party could secure a Commons majority while holding no seats in Glasgow; but nobody would rely on that as a harbinger of Tory failure now.

The Conservatives might well have expected a respectable performance in London, given their victory at the Mayoral election in 2008, where they secured 43% of first preference votes for Boris Johnson. Yet Labour won in London in 2010, keeping the swing much lower there than in any other English region;. The Conservative victory nationally came with just 35% of the vote in the capital.

However, it is vital not to interpret the figures as showing Labour doing well in London (or, even less excusably, the Tories doing badly there). The rise in the Tory vote share in London was barely lower than elsewhere; Labour apparently held their losses better than outside the capital, but not because fewer were swinging to the Tories. In 2005, almost certainly as an effect of opposition to the Iraq War and probably concentrated particularly among Asian voters (who are much more concentrated in the capital than in other regions), Labour did unusually badly in parts of London: votes swung to Respect and to the Liberal Democrats in different constituencies, and Labour's vote fell more sharply there than in any other region. So the net swing in 2010 was kept down, almost certainly, by the defectors-to-the-left coming back to Labour even as the centre-ground shifted to the Tories.

The LibDem vote held steady in London, but probably that was also a matter of gaining on the swings what they had lost on the roundabouts. If so, the centre of gravity of LibDem support in London will have moved significantly to the right.

It is also worth highlighting just how badly Labour performed in the South West and South East of England, gaining just 15% and 16% of the vote, respectively. Not only did this performance mean that for every Labour voter in this region approximately three others voted Conservative, but Labour is far from even challenging the LibDems for second place. Indeed, the scale of Labour's unpopularity in the South of England is further illustrated when we consider that the Conservatives actually performed better than this in Scotland (gaining 17% of the vote) though Scotland has only 59 parliamentary seats on offer (the Tories winning just one) while the South East and South West contain 136 (of which Labour won eight).

Class

Perhaps most dramatically, and redefining the whole way in which we need to think about British elections, there is also now almost no pattern of class voting among middle classes (ABs and C1s) and for a sizeable proportion of the working classes (C2s). Only the DEs stand out as somewhat less Tory and much more Labour than the remainder of the electorate. Britain is not yet, perhaps, a classless society but at least its voting is no longer predominantly along class lines.

David Cameron's appeal is wider than was John Major's, reaching further into those groups of the public who are not naturally Tories, but it is also shallower in its hold on the groups that make up the Tory core vote: among the Conservatives' strongest groups – older voters and the middle class – they have lost ground over the last 18 years. Much of this, no doubt, reflects the movement of the political battle to the middle ground, and perhaps Tony Blair's building of a Labour coalition less class-dependent than Neil Kinnock's.

Figure 51: The class shift in Labour's vote, 1992-2010

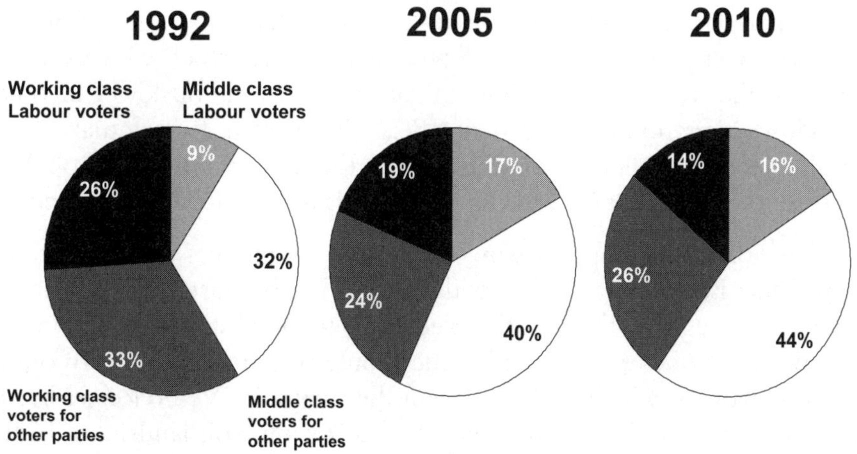

Source: MORI/Ipsos MORI Election Aggregates

As we have already noted (page 116), the class structure in Britain, at least as opinion polls and market researchers measure it, has changed dramatically in the last few decades. When Harold Wilson was Prime Minister, two-thirds of the electorate were working class; now less than half are. The working class are less likely to vote than the middle class, and that differential has widened. But under Tony Blair, Labour successfully appealed to middle class voters as well as to the working class, and secured three separate majorities. When the votes fell away under Gordon Brown, it was Labour's middle class support that proved more resilient, while its working class votes dropped sharply. (See Table 72 above).

The consequence of this, and of the continuing trend towards decreasing class differences in voting, is one that many Labour supporters will find both staggering and shocking. For the first time in history, Labour in 2010 had more middle class voters than working class voters: their 30% total vote share included 14%, just under 4 million voters, who were working class (C2DE) but 16% who were middle class (ABC1), 4.7 million.

This fact is, of course, a matter of controversy in the Labour Party. New Labour's attempt under Tony Blair to reach out to middle class voters, and the changes both in policy and in the ethos of the party necessary to do so, have been resented and sometimes actively opposed by the left.

During the Labour leadership campaign after the election, Ed Balls argued that the party should not subscribe to 'the myth that our biggest challenge is to "win back" middle-income voters. They largely stuck with us at the election while we lost the support of too many people on lower incomes who felt we were no longer on their side.'[152] Ed Miliband's eventual victory was also read as a victory for the left, and a sign that Labour could be expected to move back towards its working class, union-dominated roots.

But Tony Blair's attempt to win middle class votes was both successful and realistic. Labour cannot live without the C1s, because there are simply no longer enough C2DEs in the electorate to build an election-winning vote on them alone (even assuming they could be persuaded to turn out as reliably as ABC1s, which at the moment they cannot). We no longer live in the world in which Clem Attlee and Harold Wilson won landslides. In the 2010 general election, the middle classes made up 60% of all voters (and 56% of the electorate); the working classes were just 40% of voters (and 44% of the electorate). A 'working class party' is doomed to fail – there are just not enough working class voters any more.[153]

---

[152] Ed Balls article in *The Times*, reposted on the Ed Balls for Labour leader blog, http://www.edballs4labour.org/blog/?p=670, accessed 9 August 2010. Balls' campaign team confirmed to the website fullfact.org that 'middle-income' and 'people on lower incomes' were intended as a shorthand for middle class and working class in the normal polling sense.

[153] This point is also made by an analysis of Labour's defeat by a Smith Institute paper in February 2011, see http://www.smith-institute.org.uk/file/Winning%20back%20the%205%20million.pdf.

Towards a more sophisticated approach to class

But, of course, this assumes that the objective occupation-based measure of class used by the opinion polls is the only useful basis for classifying and segmenting the voters on their social status.

The question here is whether class-based appeals and class-based politics make any sense any more. How has the massively class-differentiated voting of only 20 years ago disappeared? Are the class distinctions themselves becoming less meaningful, or simply less closely correlated with voting?

Table 74: Self-assessed social class

Q. Most people say they belong either to the middle class or to the working class. If you had to make a choice, would you call yourself middle class or working class?

	1986 %	1989 %	1996 %	2000 %	2005 %	2008 %
Middle class	28	30	32	35	40	44
Working class	66	67	61	58	57	52
Neither/don't know	5	4	7	7	3	4

Source: Ipsos MORI
Base: c. 600-1,500 GB residents aged 15+/16+/18+

Interestingly, nine people in ten (88%) of the public deny the sometimes argued belief that the class system is no longer extant in Britain, agreeing with the statement that 'There is a class system in Britain'. Cross analysis shows there is no perceptible difference in these attitudes by voting intention.[154]

It is not just the objective definition of social class that has changed over the last three decades. Many more people now describe themselves as middle class, even if a significant proportion of the objectively-defined middle class still think of themselves as working class. In 1986, 28% of the public thought of themselves as middle class, less than half the proportion who considered that they were working class (66%). However, by 2008 the

---

[154] Survey for *Schott's Almanac*. Ipsos MORI interviewed 1,054 GB residents aged 16+ by telephone on 7-9 March 2008.

gap had narrowed considerably so that 44% felt they were middle class and just over half (56%) working class.

While four in ten (40%) of objectively defined middle-class ABC1s consider themselves to be working class, six in ten (61%) say their parents were working class at the time they started primary school. Indeed, 42% of those who now consider themselves middle class think their parents were working class when they were a child – as do two-thirds (63%) of Conservative voters!

Table 75: Self-assessed social class compared to social grade

Q. Most people say they belong either to the middle class or to the working class. If you had to make a choice, would you call yourself middle class or working class?

	All %	ABC1 %	C2DE %	AB %	C1 %	C2 %	DE %
Middle class	44	57	27	68	48	26	28
Working class	52	40	68	30	49	70	66
Neither/don't know	4	3	5	2	3	4	6

Source: Ipsos MORI/*Schott's Almanac*
Base: 1,054 GB residents aged 16+, 7-9 March 2008

There are other discriminators, of course. Some habits or behaviours are so strongly associated with one class or the other that they are better at identifying those who think of themselves as falling into one class or the other than is the market research classification. For example, only 39% of those who say they ever listen to Radio 4 consider themselves 'working class', but 65% of those who never listen to Radio 4 say the same.

The activity we found that most of the public identified as distinctively working class (rather than something that might be done by someone of any class or was more likely to be done by the middle or upper classes) was to travel by bus: 62% said taking the bus would be more likely to be done by a working class person. (52% said the same of having an allotment, 45% of watching *Coronation Street* and 48% of eating in front of the television.)

But if Labour is to rebuild its electoral appeal on a reconstructed class basis, it needs to be sure that the message will be accepted. Certainly, under Tony Blair's leadership, Labour's image as being specifically the party of the working class was weakened. Asked in March 2008 which political party 'best represents the rights of the working class', only 39% picked the Labour Party while 10% picked the Conservative Party. More to the point, 21% said that no party did so, and a further 17% that they didn't know.

Worse, ABC1s (41%) and those who considered themselves 'middle class' (42%) were marginally more likely (41%) to think that Labour was the party representing working class rights than C2DEs (36%) or the self-identified 'working class' (37%). Has New Labour's drive towards the centre ground damaged Labour's class appeal irrevocably? The Conservative Party was slightly more widely identified with representing the rights of the middle classes (by 46% of all adults and 48% of those who considered themselves 'middle class'), but at the same time 19% of adults and 18% of those who consider themselves middle class identified Labour as the best party for the middle classes, so the electoral benefit of middle class identification for the Tories was even lower than that of working class identification for Labour.

Gender

As Figure 52 shows, for the last two general elections men have tended to favour the Conservatives more than women, and nothing much changed in 2010. The Conservatives had a ten point lead over Labour among men (38% vs. 28%) and, had only men voted at the election, Cameron would probably have ended several seats closer to his longed-for overall majority. Conversely, had the franchise been restricted to just women, the Conservatives' lead would have been just five points (36% vs. 31%) and Gordon Brown might still be Prime Minister.

Labour's stronger appeal among women is a relatively new phenomenon. Through the 1970s and 1980s (with the exception of 1987), the Conservatives' lead over Labour was considerably higher among women. New Labour first closed and eventually reversed this pattern, both in the elections it won and in those it lost.

It is the 'gender gap' that always seems to capture the imagination of the media. In 2010, the pre-election commentary was once again widely concerned with the behaviour of 'the women's vote' and the parties' willingness to address 'women's issues', and discovered in the internet community Mumsnet a symbolic embodiment of the political forces for which they were looking.

Figure 52: The gender gap, 1974-2010

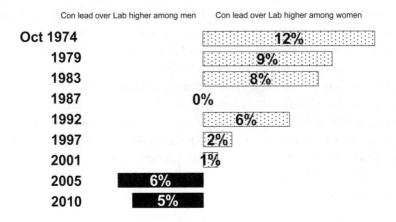

Source: MORI/Ipsos MORI Election Aggregates
'Gender gap' shown is difference between Conservative lead over Labour among men and among women.

Gordon Brown's former pollster, Deborah Mattinson, was quoted[155] as calling Mumsnet 'totemic of the modern mothers who will be the key political battleground at the next election.' But this not unreasonable identification of one key target group quickly became transmuted into such headlines as 'Meet the two Mumsnet founders, the women who could decide the next General Election'.[156] All three party leaders and some other senior figures submitted themselves to interview on Mumsnet during the campaign. It produced numerous deep political insights, such as:

---

[155] Rachel Sylvester, 'This election will be won at the school gate', *The Times*, 17 November 2009, http://www.timesonline.co.uk/tol/comment/columnists/rachel_sylvester/article6919267.ece, accessed 21 October 2010.
[156] *Daily Mirror*, 26 January 2010, http://www.mirror.co.uk/news/top-stories/2010/01/26/britain-s-most-powerful-mums-115875-21995678/, accessed 21 October 2010.

'Biscuitgate: After 24 Hours of Dithering Gordon Brown finally confesses his favourite dunk'.[157]

Table 76: Voting by 'Mumsnetters' (ABC1 women aged 25-44)

	2005 %	2010 %	Change %
Conservative	24	29	+5
Labour	40	34	−6
Liberal Democrat	29	31	+2
Other	7	6	−1
Con lead over Lab	−16	−5	+11

Source: Ipsos MORI Election Aggregates
Base: ABC1 women in GB aged 25-44 (1,965 in 2005; 1,071 in 2010)

In the end, it was Labour who won among the Mumsnet core group (middle-class women aged 25-44, see Table 76), as had been the case in 2005. But probably more relevant is that the changes in vote share among this section were almost identical to the national shifts in the vote, with the overall Labour to Conservative swing being 5.5% – for all the targeting there was no evidence that any party had made much headway in turning this 'key political battleground' to its advantage.

The progress Labour made by February 2011 is shown in Table 77, which shows the main demographic breakdown of the party's ten point lead over the Conservatives. This is derived from aggregating the results of our January and February surveys asking the electorate how they would vote 'in a general election tomorrow'. Of course, there is not going to be a general election tomorrow and as David Cameron learnt to his cost support in opinion polls cannot be relied on to turn into votes at the ballot box.

Nevertheless this analysis provides us with evidence of who, at this stage, is at least prepared to consider switching their support to the Labour party. The swing among men and women is practically the same and the swing by housing tenure is fairly consistent – Labour's support is higher among social renters (60%) than any other demographic group. (If interest rates

---

[157] *Mail on Sunday* headline, 18 October 2009, http://www.dailymail.co.uk/news/article-1221180/Biscuitgate-After-24-hours-dithering-Gordon-Brown-finally-confesses-favourite-dunk.html, accessed 21 October 2009.

rise over the next few months and years, we will be watching with particular attention at those with a mortgage).

Table 77: Change in party support, 2010 election to Jan/Feb 2011

	2010 vote				Jan/Feb 2011				Con-Lab swing
	Con %	Lab %	LD %	Con Lead %	Con %	Lab %	LD %	Con Lead	
All	37	30	24	+7	33	43	13	−10	8.5%
Gender									
Men	38	28	22	+10	35	41	12	−6	8.0%
Women	36	31	26	+5	32	45	14	−13	9.0%
Age									
18-24	30	31	30	−1	14	57	10	−43	21.0%
25-34	35	30	29	+5	25	47	18	−22	13.5%
35-44	34	31	26	+3	40	40	11	0	1.5%
45-54	34	28	26	+6	31	44	15	−13	9.5%
55-64	38	28	23	+10	31	47	12	−16	13.0%
65+	44	31	16	+13	42	35	13	+7	3.0%
Social Class									
AB	39	26	29	+13	37	36	17	+1	6.0%
C1	39	28	24	+11	34	43	14	−9	10.0%
C2	37	29	22	+8	32	46	10	−14	11.0%
DE	31	40	17	−9	27	52	11	−25	8.0%
Housing Tenure									
Owned outright	45	24	21	+21	42	34	13	+8	6.5%
Mortgage	36	29	26	+7	34	44	14	−10	8.5%
Social renter	24	47	19	−23	18	60	7	−42	9.5%
Private renter	35	29	27	+6	27	40	19	−13	9.5%

Source: Ipsos MORI
Base: 10,211 GB adults aged 18+, 19 March-5 May 2010, weighted to final outcome and turnout and 1,230 GB adults aged 18+, January-February 2011, absolutely certain to vote

By February 2011, the Conservatives had lost their lead among all social classes, though they were tied with Labour among ABs (though this group had swung away from the Conservatives less than the others). Labour were ahead by nine points among the electorally crucial C1 voters. Even in its 1997 and 2001 landslides, the party never managed more than a two-percentage-point lead among this group.

The swing from Conservatives to Labour by age confirmed the collapse in support for the coalition among the youngest voters with a massive 21% swing among 18-24 year olds, more than double the overall swing of 8.5%. The policy decisions of the coalition have hurt both parties among this segment of the electorate. Yet, the Conservatives' lead remains among the oldest segment, over 65 year olds.

Appendix 1: Polls and polling

We have written about the theory and principles of polling, why polls are useful and why they should not be banned, how sampling works and the limitations of 'phone(y) polls', 'voodoo polls', 'just a bit of fun' polls and the like in books and articles for nearly forty years. However, in every election there are those new to the game who confidently assert that the bookies are better than the pollsters at predicting elections, and others who purport that their econometric models presented six months before elections are more accurate than eve-of-election polls. Politicians of every stripe also regularly disparage polls by asserting that 'that's not what we are finding on the ground', particularly when the findings of professional pollsters are not helpful to their campaign positioning.

Most of our readers will no doubt be familiar with the way polls are conducted, but others may be new to the field or may be hazy about the exact details. We would therefore like to take our readers step by step through the process of conducting an Ipsos MORI poll, and comment at least briefly on how and why other companies' methods differ. At the same time, we update the record of the success of the polls generally – our own and those of other companies – in the 2010 election as well as the period before it.

The polls in 2010

The Ipsos MORI political team were pleased with the performance of our polls in the 2010 election. Together with GfK NOP, commissioned by the BBC, ITV and Sky, with analysis by a team of political scientists, we produced a near-perfect exit poll prediction for the second election in a row. In addition, our final pre-election poll performed as well as possible within the limits of our trade in 'forecasting' the results. Our polls in marginal constituencies for Reuters gave a consistent story throughout the campaign which demonstrated what was happening in these key seats and was an accurate precursor of the eventual outcome there. This polling in the marginals helped contribute to a wider understanding of the election by indicating how far a national uniform swing was likely to hold (therefore making clearer the implications of the national vote shares which were raining down on the electorate daily). Also, in order to test the effect of the leaders' debates on viewers, the BBC asked us to bring back the 'worm'[158], which measured the reactions of groups of undecided voters, informing viewers and afterwards the commentators on the leaders' debates to help illustrate in depth the strengths and weaknesses of the leaders and their debate performances.

In fact, it was a good election for all the established pollsters. It was the most polled British election ever, with almost a hundred voting intention polls published during the month of the campaign.

Opinion polling is much more difficult under such volatile conditions than in a settled situation where most of the voters have definitely decided how they would vote. As late as a fortnight before polling day, 45% of people who told us which party they intended to vote for said they might, nevertheless, change their minds. (In 1992, the corresponding figure was much lower, at 18%.)

Of the six 'established' pollsters (those that published a final 'predictive' pre-election poll both in 2005 and 2010), all had the Conservatives on between 35% and 37%, all had Labour on 28% or 29% and all had the Liberal Democrats on between 26% and 28% (Table 78).

The average accuracy of the established pollsters was within one point of the Conservative share, two points of the Labour share and one point of the Conservative lead over Labour. On the Liberal Democrats, the discrepancy was slightly larger, but still, on average, within the plus-or-minus three points which is generally quoted as the 'margin of error' for samples of c. 1,000 nationwide.

The results from the 'new boys on the block' were slightly wider: Opinium were within three points for each party, Angus Reid and BMRB somewhat further astray, and none of the three had a better prediction for any of the parties than the average of the established six. The non-BPC result was more mixed, with a very credible forecast from RNB India, to a wildly-out set of findings from an internet newcomer to the game, OnePoll, and also at the margins, the BPIX academics.

---

[158] See page 212 above. The technique, pioneered in this country by MORI and IML, was originally introduced in the 1992 general election in a series of programmes called *The Vote Race* on Sunday evenings, produced by the young Nick Robinson, now the BBC's political editor.

Table 78: Final pre-election polls in 2010

Polling Organisation	Con %	Lab %	LD %	Other %	Con lead %	Method
ComRes	37	28	28	7	+9	Telephone
Harris Interactive	35	29	27	10	+6	Internet
ICM	36	28	26	10	+8	Telephone
Ipsos MORI	36	29	27	8	+7	Telephone
Populus	37	28	27	8	+9	Telephone
YouGov	35	28	28	9	+7	Internet
Established pollsters average	**36**	**28**	**27**	**9**	**+8**	
Angus Reid	36	24	29	11	+12	Internet
Opinium	35	27	26	12	+8	Internet
TNS BMRB	33	27	29	11	+6	Face-to-face
New BPC pollsters average	**35**	**26**	**28**	**11**	**+9**	
BPIX	34	27	30	9	+7	Internet
OnePoll	30	21	32	17	+9	Internet
RNB India	37	28	26	9	+9	Telephone
Non-BPC pollsters average	**34**	**25**	**29**	**12**	**+9**	
Actual Result	**37**	**30**	**24**	**10**	**+7**	

Source: Data from British Polling Council (BPC) and politicalbetting.com

The British Polling Council noted in its post-election press release,

> *While not proving as accurate as the 2005 polls, which were the most accurate predictions ever made of the outcome of a British general election, the polls nevertheless told the main story of the 2010 election — that the Conservatives had established a clear lead. All but one of the nine pollsters came within 2% of the Conservative share, and five were within 1%.*

> *The tendency at past elections for polls to overestimate Labour came to an abrupt end, with every pollster underestimating the Labour share of the vote, though all but one were within 3%. However, every pollster overestimated the Liberal Democrat share of the vote.'*

What the BPC neglected to mention was the most important fact of all, that all of their members' forecasts, accurately as it turned out, called the election 'hung', in that no one party would have an overall majority given the vote shares they were projecting.

Effectively, all six 'established' pollsters collectively and individually 'got it right' within the power of polls to do so. Anything better than being within ±3% is luck. But if you're not lucky, it's not a good business to be in. With no fewer than 14% of those who did vote telling us the week after the election that they decided how they were going to vote 'within the last 24 hours' of the campaign, and given the severe challenges that opinion polls must regularly overcome even in a more sedate election, we believe

292

that overall the performance of the polls, ours included, was better than satisfactory. The results from these various polls were too close to each other for it to be reasonable or useful to draw distinctions between them and note that one was 'better' or 'worse' than another. The others however, did not, with the honourable exception of the Indian firm.

The exit poll

In our 2005 book, we noted the following apropos the exit poll:

> *'On election night, Roy Hattersley and Ken Clarke led a bi-partisan attack on the exit polls, Hatters losing it on ITN and Ken rubbishing the exit poll on the BBC, both dismissing the exit poll seat projection of a 66-seat majority for Labour, saying that "exit polls are always wrong".'*

No, gentlemen, it's politicians that are (almost) always wrong. Exit polls are usually right. Other commentators were however more kind[159]:

> *'Finally, talk up the BBC exit poll. By far the most reliable guide to the outcome of the election is the exit poll carried out by Ipsos MORI for the BBC. That poll, due out at 10pm on May 6, is likely to be more accurate than any other.'*

Just as in the last three elections (see Table 79), the exit poll in 2010 projected the outcome of the election very accurately. The results of the Ipsos MORI/GfK NOP exit poll, commissioned by the BBC, Sky and ITV News, were released at 10 pm on Thursday 6 May. The 10 pm results predicted that the Conservatives would win 307 seats, Labour would win 255 and the Liberal Democrats 59 seats (this was the prediction that was projected onto the side of Big Ben, as well as opening all three of the election results programmes). An hour later, with the final tranche of data returned and processed, the prediction was slightly updated to state that the Conservatives would win 305 seats, Labour would win 255 and the Liberal Democrats would win 61 seats. This prediction was widely ridiculed, but by the time all the votes had been counted we knew that the

---

[159] Toby Young, 'General Election 2010: A bluffer's guide to opinion polls', *Daily Telegraph* blog, 4 May 2010, http://blogs.telegraph.co.uk/news/tobyyoung/100037815/general-election-2010-a-bluffers-guide-to-opinion-polls/, accessed 30 November 2010.

final result was that the Conservatives won 307 seats, Labour won 258 and the LibDems 57.[160]

Table 79: The record of the British exit polls, 1997-2010

Projections of seat numbers for biggest party (Labour to 2005, Conservative 2010)

	MORI for ITV	NOP for BBC	MORI/NOP average	MORI/NOP for BBC & ITV	Election Result
1997	410	429*	419.5		419
2001	417	408	412.5		413
2005				356	356
2010				305	307

*In 1997 the precise NOP projection was not published, but was broadcast as indicating an overall majority of 'about 200'.

One of us was at the ITV election night party at 10 pm, watching the exit poll results projected onto Big Ben, and could hardly believe the results himself and watched the unanimously sceptical coverage. Then, moving on to the BBC's boat party below on the Thames, to a further hail of sceptical comments from the likes of Peter and Dan Snow, and Peter's wife and Dan's mother Ann McMillan, the CBC Bureau Chief. The four of us were standing not ten feet from where Andrew Neil was getting what he apparently regarded as a more authoritative view of how the election was going, from Bruce Forsyth.

For the 2010 Exit Poll, Ipsos MORI and GfK NOP surveyed 17,607 voters at 130 polling stations across Great Britain, phoning back the results at regular intervals throughout the day. The data were processed by the academic team led by Professor John Curtice (currently President of the British Polling Council) who designed the statistical modelling that produced the final prediction. The methodology was essentially the same as in the equally successful exit poll in 2005, which is explained in detail in a paper in the *Journal of the Royal Statistical Society*.[161] To summarise briefly,

---

[160] The broadcasters prefer to class the Speaker's seat as won by the party for which he was previously an MP, and therefore the exit poll figures are calculated on this basis. The figures include Thirsk & Malton, where voting was delayed because of the death of a candidate but whose result was included in the exit poll projection.

[161] John Curtice and David Firth, 'Exit polling in a cold climate: The BBC/ITV experience in Britain in 2005', *Journal of the Royal Statistical Society Series A,* Volume 171, 509–39 (2008).

the final prediction depends on measuring the vote at polling stations in a wide variety of types of constituency, which then makes it possible to build a statistical model which relates differences in the trends to the characteristics of the constituencies. From this, the analysts can infer the probability of each party winning each constituency in the country, and consequently derive a prediction of party seat totals. As far as possible, we conducted the poll in the same polling districts as in 2005, so that a direct measure of vote change since the last election could be taken; but where new sampling points were needed (for example when polling districts had been altered, or to improve the coverage of particular types of constituencies), the polling district we thought most likely to be representative of its constituency was chosen, through a combination of local election voting patterns and census data.[162]

The campaign polls

The final polls and the exit poll were not the only ones conducted during the campaign. For the record, Table 80 shows all of Ipsos MORI's polls from mid-March which included a voting intention measurement.

Also for the record, Tables 81-83 list all the published national voting intention polls that we are aware of between the formal announcement of the election date and the final polls (including a couple by BPIX, who are not affiliated to the British Polling Council). At some elections in the past, the polls from different companies during the campaign have seemed to be telling a different story about the course of the election, but that was not the case this time (other than Angus Reid). Allowing for the unavoidable statistically insignificant fluctuations in single polls, and for the newer companies who started out of line with everyone else but then kept in step throughout the campaign, it was as unanimous a message as we can hope for.

---

[162] Unlike most countries, the UK does not publish voting results at polling district level or even allow it to be published. Therefore any exit poll has to rely on inferring the past voting behaviour of polling districts from external sources, including data from exit polls conducted at the same polling stations at previous elections.

Table 80: Ipsos MORI polls before and during the 2010 election campaign

	Fieldwork dates	Con %	Lab %	LD %	Other %	Con lead over Lab %
National polls						
Ipsos MORI Political Monitor	19-22 March	35	30	21	14	+5
Ipsos MORI Political Monitor	18-19 April	32	28	32	8	+4
Ipsos MORI/News of the World	23 April	36	30	23	11	+6
Ipsos MORI/Evening Standard	5 May	36	29	27	8	+7
Eventual Result	**6 May**	**37**	**30**	**24**	**10**	**+7**
Marginals polls						
Reuters/ Ipsos MORI Poll 1	19-22 March	37	41	11	11	−4
Reuters/ Ipsos MORI Poll 2	30 March-5 April	38	41	11	10	−3
Reuters/ Ipsos MORI Poll 3	16-19 April	32	36	23	9	−4
Reuters/ Ipsos MORI Poll 4	23-26 April	35	38	21	6	−3
Reuters/ Ipsos MORI Poll 5	30 April-2 May	36	36	20	8	0
Eventual Result	**6 May**	**36**	**39**	**16**	**9**	**−3**

Scotland poll		Con %	Lab %	LD %	SNP %	Other %
Ipsos MORI Scottish Public Opinion Monitor	14-17 April	14	36	20	26	4
Eventual Result	**6 May**	**17**	**42**	**19**	**20**	**2**

Source: Ipsos MORI; election results calculated from those published by the House of Commons Library in Research Paper 10/36 (8 July 2010)

It is certainly true that there are significant differences in the methodologies of the polling companies, yet these have not over the past few years caused 'house effects' in the poll findings from the companies with a long track record. This is despite different approaches to drawing a representative sample, and different theories of how to translate the raw data into a voting intention projection allowing for factors such as who might not vote at all and how to treat those who won't say how they will vote. If there is any consistent difference between the results of the six 'established pollsters', it is measured in fractions of a percentage point, far too small to be evident in the outcome of a single poll.[163]

---

[163] There is a clearer case that there is a 'house effect' in the difference between the findings of Angus Reid and the other pollsters. This seems to have been caused not by a difference in the raw data but by Angus Reid's decisions on how to weight their data, which flew in the face of the advice of pollsters with more experience of political polling in Britain. The result was that from their first published poll in the autumn of 2009, Angus Reid showed a significantly lower Labour share than

Table 81: Published voting intention polls before the first debate

Dates of Fieldwork	Size	Pub. Date	Pollster/Client	Con %	Lab %	LD %	Oth %	Gap %
5-6 Apr	1456	7 Apr	YouGov/Sun	40	32	17	11	8
6-7 Apr	1484	8 Apr	YouGov/Sun	37	32	19	12	5
6-7 Apr	2193	7 Apr	Angus Reid/PB	37	26	22	15	11
6-7 Apr	1507	7 Apr	Populus/Times	39	32	21	8	7
7 Apr	1032	10 Apr	ICM/Sunday Telegraph	38	30	21	10	8
7-8 Apr	1626	9 Apr	YouGov/Sun	40	31	18	11	9
7-8 Apr	1012	10 Apr	Harris/D Mail	37	27	22	14	10
8-9 Apr	1527	10 Apr	YouGov/Sun	40	30	20	10	10
9-10 Apr	1001	11 Apr	ComRes/IoS/S Mirror	39	32	16	13	7
9-10 Apr	1431	11 Apr	YouGov/Sunday Times	40	32	18	10	8
9-10 Apr	2051	11 Apr	BPIX/Mail on Sunday	38	31	20	11	7
?	?	11 Apr	OnePoll/The People	37	31	21	11	6
7-13 Apr	1916	15 Apr	TNS BMRB	36	33	22	9	3
9-11 Apr	1024	13 Apr	ICM/Guardian	37	31	20	11	6
8-13 Apr	1523	15 Apr	Harris/Metro	36	27	23	14	9
9-12 Apr	1825	13 Apr	Opinium/Daily Express	39	31	17	13	8
9-12 Apr	2006	14 Apr	Angus Reid/PB	38	28	22	13	10
10-11 Apr	1455	12 Apr	YouGov/Sun	37	31	20	12	6
10-11 Apr	1004	13 Apr	ComRes/Ind/ITV	37	30	20	13	7
11-12 Apr	1493	13 Apr	YouGov/Sun	39	33	20	8	6
11-12 Apr	1002	14 Apr	ComRes/Ind/ITV	36	31	19	14	5
12 Apr	1525	14 Apr	Populus/Times	36	33	21	9	3
12-13 Apr	1583	14 Apr	YouGov/Sun	39	31	20	9	8
12-13 Apr	1001	15 Apr	ComRes/Ind/ITV	35	29	21	15	6
13-14 Apr	1578	15 Apr	YouGov/Sun	41	32	18	9	9
14-15 Apr	1490	16 Apr	YouGov/Sun	37	31	22	10	6
14-15 Apr	1033	18 Apr	ICM/Sunday Telegraph	34	29	27	10	5

Note: Client abbreviations: ES=*London Evening Standard*; Ind=*The Independent*;
IoS=*Independent on Sunday*; NotW=*News of the World*; PB=politicalbetting.com

Not that this has stops some bloggers getting wound up in 'gold standards' about one polling company or another, or holding sometimes arcane and frequently tedious debates about the meaning of small, usually statistically insignificant, shifts in poll findings. Nor does it stop the media from picking out and highlighting the results that favour their editorial stances or from only reporting their own poll results, ignoring other simultaneous poll findings that in some cases contradict their line. Nor could it stop the academic alchemists responding to the media's desire to be able to tell their readers and viewers what will happen in the future, insisting there must be a way of transmuting poll numbers into electoral gold.

the other pollsters; at the election, Angus Reid underestimated Labour's share by 6 percentage points, whereas the established pollsters all underestimated Labour by 1 or 2 points.

Table 82: Polls between the first and third debates

Dates of Fieldwork	Size	Pub. Date	Pollster/Client	Con %	Lab %	LD %	Oth %	Gap %
16 Apr	1290	17 Apr	YouGov/Sun	33	28	30	9	5
14-19 Apr	2062	21 Apr	Harris/Metro	31	26	30	13	5
14-20 Apr	1953	22 Apr	TNS BMRB	34	29	30	7	5
15-17 Apr	3715	18 Apr	OnePoll/The People	27	23	33	17	4
16-17 Apr	1006	18 Apr	ComRes/IoS/S Mirror	31	27	29	13	4
16-17 Apr	2149	18 Apr	BPIX/Mail on Sunday	31	28	32	9	3
16-17 Apr	1490	18 Apr	YouGov/Sunday Times	33	30	29	8	3
16-18 Apr	1024	20 Apr	ICM/Guardian	33	28	30	9	5
16-19 Apr	1957	20 Apr	Opinium/Daily Express	32	26	29	13	6
16-19 Apr	2004	20 Apr	Angus Reid/PB	32	24	32	12	8
17-18 Apr	1433	19 Apr	YouGov/Sun	32	26	33	8	6
17-18 Apr	1003	20 Apr	ComRes/Ind/ITV	32	28	28	12	4
18-19 Apr	1509	20 Apr	YouGov/Sun	33	27	31	9	6
18-19 Apr	1012	21 Apr	ComRes/Ind/ITV	35	26	26	13	9
19-20 Apr	1595	21 Apr	YouGov/Sun	31	26	34	9	5
19-20 Apr	1501	21 Apr	Populus/Times	32	28	31	9	4
19-20 Apr	1953	21 Apr	Angus Reid/PB	32	23	33	12	9
18-20 Apr	1253	21 Apr	Ipsos MORI/ES	32	28	32	8	4
19-20 Apr	1015	22 Apr	ComRes/Ind	35	25	27	13	10
20-21 Apr	1545	22 Apr	YouGov/Sun	33	27	31	9	6
21-22 Apr	1576	23 Apr	YouGov/Sun	34	29	28	9	5
22-23 Apr	1048	24 Apr	Harris/Daily Mail	34	26	29	11	8
20-26 Apr	1678	28 Apr	Harris/Metro	32	25	30	13	7
23 Apr	1381	24 Apr	YouGov/Sun	34	29	29	8	5
23 Apr	1245	25 Apr	Ipsos MORI/NotW	36	30	23	11	6
23 Apr	1020	25 Apr	ICM/Sunday Telegraph	35	26	31	8	9
21-27 Apr	2078	28 Apr	TNS BMRB	34	27	30	9	7
22-24 Apr	2571	25 Apr	OnePoll/The People	32	23	32	13	9
23-24 Apr	1412	25 Apr	YouGov/Sunday Times	35	27	28	9	8
23-24 Apr	2193	25 Apr	BPIX/Mail on Sunday	34	26	30	10	8
23-24 Apr	1006	25 Apr	ComRes/IoS/S Mirror	34	28	29	9	6
23-25 Apr	1031	26 Apr	ICM/Guardian	33	28	30	8	5
23-26 Apr	1942	26 Apr	Opinium/Daily Express	34	25	28	13	9
23-26 Apr	2433	30 Apr	Angus Reid/Economist	33	23	30	14	10
24-25 Apr	1466	26 Apr	YouGov/Sun	34	28	30	8	6
24-25 Apr	1003	26 Apr	ComRes/Ind/ITV	32	28	31	9	4
25-26 Apr	1491	27 Apr	YouGov/Sun	33	28	29	10	5
25-26 Apr	1005	27 Apr	ComRes/Ind/ITV	33	29	29	9	4
25-26 Apr	1005	27 Apr	ICM/Guardian	33	29	29	9	4
26-27 Apr	1006	28 Apr	ComRes/Ind/ITV	36	29	26	9	7
26-27 Apr	1598	28 Apr	YouGov/Sun	33	29	28	10	4
26-27 Apr	1510	29 Apr	Populus/Times	36	27	28	8	9
27-28 Apr	1530	29 Apr	YouGov/Sun	34	27	31	8	7
28-29 Apr	1623	30 Apr	YouGov/Sun	34	27	28	11	7

Note: For client abbreviations see previous table

Table 83: Polls after the third debate

Dates of Fieldwork	Size	Pub. Date	Pollster/Client	Con %	Lab %	LD %	Oth %	Gap %
29-30 Apr	1020	1 May	Harris/Daily Mail	33	24	32	11	9
30 Apr	1412	1 May	YouGov/Sun	34	28	28	10	6
30 Apr	1019	2 May	ICM/Sunday Telegraph	36	29	27	8	7
28 Apr - 4 May	786	5 May	Harris/Metro	36	26	28	10	10
?	?	2 May	OnePoll/The People	30	21	32	17	9
30 Apr - 1 May	1019	2 May	ComRes/IoS/S Mirror	38	28	25	9	10
30 Apr - 1 May	1483	2 May	YouGov/Sunday Times	35	27	28	10	8
30 Apr - 1 May	2136	2 May	BPIX/Mail on Sunday	34	27	30	9	7
30 Apr - 1 May	1874	2 May	Angus Reid/S Express	35	23	29	12	12
30 Apr - 2 May	1026	3 May	ICM/Guardian	33	28	28	12	5
30 Apr - 3 May	1870	4 May	Opinium/Daily Express	33	28	27	12	5
1-2 May	1475	3 May	YouGov/Sun	34	28	29	9	6
1-2 May	1024	3 May	ComRes/Ind/ITV	37	29	26	8	8
2-3 May	1455	4 May	YouGov/Sun	35	28	28	9	7
2-3 May	1024	4 May	ComRes/Ind/ITV	37	29	26	8	8
3-4 May	1461	5 May	YouGov/Sun	35	30	24	11	5

Note: For the final polls, see Table 78.

The near unanimity between the polls during the election was only a continuation of what was happening for most of the period between the 2005 and 2010 elections, when there was a consistent congruence between the polls from companies regularly publishing findings. For example, consider the polls in 2009. Table 84 shows the average findings over the year of ComRes, ICM, Populus, Ipsos MORI and YouGov, the five companies polling monthly who had also polled at the 2005 election – there was a slight divergence of opinion on the strength of 'others', but for the three main parties all five pollsters were within a point of the 'poll of polls'.

Table 84: Average voting intention poll results by company, 2009

	Con %	Lab %	LD %	Other %	Con lead %	Method
Com Res	40	26	19	16	+14	Telephone
ICM	42	28	19	11	+14	Telephone
Populus	40	28	18	14	+12	Telephone
Ipsos MORI	41	26	19	14	+15	Telephone
YouGov	41	28	17	14	+13	Internet
Average	**41**	**27**	**18**	**14**	**+14**	

Source: Polls published by Ipsos MORI, ICM, YouGov, Com Res and Populus.

Between 1 January and 31 December 2009, there were just under 200,000 interviews taken in the 125 polls conducted by the major polling organisations: ComRes (24), ICM (20), Ipsos MORI (13), Populus (13) and YouGov (42) with the occasional entry by BPIX (7), Harris (1), MSI (1) and towards the end of the year, Angus Reid, the Canadian pollster (4). Over the year, nine in every ten published polls (91%) fell within the generally accepted 'margin of error' of plus or minus 3% of the monthly average of all polls. There was slightly greater volatility in the first half of the year with 86% within the average margin, but in the second half 96% were consistently saying the same thing given the 'margin' limits. It is this consistency that has encouraged us in this volume to use the 'poll of polls' throughout to track the course of public opinion, rather than relying on a single poll series.

How is a poll conducted?

It would be remiss of us to write an entire book based upon the finding of opinion polls and not to give some brief explanation, for the benefit of any reader who is not familiar with the subject, of how polls are conducted. The opportunity provided in the last few years to read others' discussions of polls and polling in the blogosphere has made it plain that even among those who take a real interest in the subject and who consider themselves well informed there are some startling misconceptions and misunderstandings. We think, therefore, that it might be a useful service to run through the genesis of a poll from start to finish.

For the most part we will confine ourselves to voting intention polls since they are most relevant to the subject in hand and also among the most complex of political polls, and as the most obvious and relevant case we will take our final pre-election poll as an example. We must also emphasise that we are talking only about Ipsos MORI's polls; other companies use significantly different methods in many respects.

None of Ipsos MORI's polling methodology is secret. Since its founding in 1969 and entry into public opinion polling for the media in 1975, MORI has followed the practice, now adopted by all the major polling organisations, of complete transparency. Initially as the private pollsters for the Labour Party in the 1970 general election and in the two 1974 elections, MORI made it mandatory that all of its clients agreed to MORI's

Terms and Conditions of Contract, which provided for not only sample size and fieldwork dates being made public, but also full question wording, number of sampling points and raw data with full tabulations being available for anyone to inspect.

As (founding) members of the British Polling Council (BPC) we are also obliged to post on our website (www.ipsos-mori.com) details of every poll we publish, including basic details such as question wording, sample size and fieldwork dates, but also the *minutiae* such as details of the weighting applied to the data. But Ipsos MORI's chief principle in the way we publish our political polling data has always been transparency, and we do go much further than our membership of the British Polling Council requires. Although basic computer tables showing the results of our polls broken down in a few simple ways can always be found on our website, we are often able and willing to provide much greater detail on request, to conduct extra analysis or even to hand over the raw data for other researchers to analyse for themselves.

Our surveys usually aim at drawing a representative quota sample of the adult population in Great Britain, in other words not including Northern Ireland; this is always true of our voting intention polls. Our regular political polls are currently conducted by telephone (although often in the past they have been conducted face-to-face, as are many of our non-political surveys today, and occasionally online). We select telephone numbers using 'random digit dialling' (which ensures that we don't leave out people who are not in the phone book). When somebody answers the phone, we select a member of the household to take part in the survey with the help of quotas. These are chosen to ensure that the sample broadly matches the adult population in the distribution of the sexes, of age, of social class and of working status (that is whether the respondent works full-time, part time or not at all), as well as geographical spread. Interviewers may interview anybody within the household who falls within their quota and is willing to be interviewed at that time or within the fieldwork period.

For each poll we interview a fresh sample of between 1,000 and 2,000 respondents. Why this number? All polls are subject to a margin of error, because they are based on interviewing a sample of the public rather than the whole public. All other things being equal, the bigger the size of the sample, the narrower the margin of error (technically called the confidence interval). So the choice of sample size is a trade-off between the greater precision possible with a bigger sample size and the higher cost of conducting extra interviews (and, unfortunately, doubling the sample size and hence the cost only reduces the margin of error by around a third). Traditionally, most opinion polls take a sample size of 1,000 as being a satisfactory compromise, but bigger samples are sometimes useful, especially when it is useful to compare subgroups within the sample (e.g. men against women).

Of course, sceptics often question how a sample of only 1,000 or 2,000 can possibly reflect the opinions of 44 million British adults. The time-honoured answer to this question goes back to the early days of George Gallup, the American who invented modern opinion polling: if you have a large bowl of soup, you don't have to drink the whole bowl to decide if it has too much salt in it – just stir it well, and one spoonful will suffice. Less whimsically, perhaps, most people accept the idea that only a drop of blood is necessary to carry out a blood test. What is important is whether the sample is representative, not how big it is. Knowing how to find a representative sample of the public is one of the most important skills of our job.

The purest way of selecting a sample is 'random' or 'probability' sampling, where the exact probability of any person being selected to take part in the survey is known. In that case, and assuming a perfect response rate, the exact risk of sampling error can be calculated mathematically. The '95% confidence interval' due to sampling variance with a sample of 1,000 respondents is roughly ±3%, meaning that 95% of the time (19 times out of 20) the sample measurement will be within three percentage points of the true measurement for the population being sampled. Although it is a simplification, we normally take this confidence interval as representing the 'margin of error', so that a poll that records the Conservatives as having 40% of the vote is really only stating that the Conservative share is between 37% and 43% – but more likely to be 40%, 39% or 41% than 36% or 37% or 42% or 43%.

In fact, many polls published these days have an effective sample size of less than 1,000, because they are only concerned with the views of that part of the sample who are likely to vote or because they are very heavily weighted, and so the margin of error is correspondingly larger. And even beyond that, we cannot prevent the occasional rogue poll — the one poll in every twenty which probability suggests will be outside the usual margins of error.

Pure random probability sampling is not practical for election opinion polls – apart from any other consideration, it takes a long time to get a sufficiently high response to be reasonably reliable, which would defeat the object of a poll that needs to measure a snapshot of opinion at a single point in time. The 2010 election showed how, on occasion, big swings of opinion in a short period of time during the campaign can make surveys which spread their interviews over many days effectively worthless.[164] Moreover, the confidence interval applies only to error caused solely by sampling variation (the risk of randomly picking the wrong people to interview). In practice we also have to deal with non-response error (e.g. supporters of one party may be more prepared to take part in surveys than of another) and measurement error (i.e. whether we can accurately translate people's answers into predictions of their voting behaviour). Nevertheless, practical experience over many years has shown that well-conducted quota sampling (the method that we use) tends to produce weighted samples with a variance broadly similar to a pure probability (random) sample of the same size, and it is therefore customary to quote confidence limits as if a random sample had been used. Indeed, on several 'real' tests, such as the general elections in the 1970s and the 1975 referendum on membership of the Common Market, the quota samples performed better, not worse, than the random samples.

Having chosen our respondents and persuaded them to take part, we now ask them each of the questions in the poll, read out verbatim by our trained interviewers. (For any of our published polls you can find the full wording of the questionnaire and the order in which the questions were asked on our website.) They will also be asked a series of demographic questions so that we can ensure that the sample is truly representative, and can see how answers vary between different types of voter. In political surveys, the voting intention questions are always the first in the questionnaire (to avoid any risk that answers might be affected by any of

---

[164] At least as opinion polls, whose function is to measure opinion at a single point in time and usually to report the findings quickly. Surveys such as the British Election Study, whose purposes are very different, may be less disadvantaged by spreading interviews over a period of weeks rather than days.

the other questions in the survey). The interviewers use CATI (computer-assisted telephone interviewing) technology, which brings up the questions on a screen in front of them and allows them to key in the response directly. These responses form our unweighted or raw data.

Our final voting intention poll was carried out on the afternoon and evening of Wednesday 5 May, the day before the election. By the cut-off of 9 pm (the latest that research industry rules allow us to make calls), our interviewers had reached their target of 1,200 interviews. We had set quotas on gender, age, work status and social class, and throughout the day the supervisors at the telephone units kept an eye on the numbers that were being successfully interviewed in each of these categories and updated the instructions to the interviewers on which groups they should be particularly targeting. The hardest to find are usually people who work full-time (who are naturally less likely to available on their home numbers during most of our interview period than people who are not working) and the young. The sample is also controlled by region, but this is done automatically by controlling the phone numbers issued to the interviewers. (We don't know *who* will be on the end of a given phone number, but we know *where* it probably is from the exchange number.)

So by 9 o'clock we had the data from 1,216 interviews in the computer, including for example 125 with 18-24 year olds, almost exactly their correct proportion in the adult population. All of these had been asked whether they had already voted by post and, if not, how likely they were to vote, and which party they had voted or intended to vote for. In addition, they had been asked another dozen or so questions about aspects of the election or the personalities, and further questions about themselves – detailed demographics, newspaper readership and so on. We also asked their postcodes, which meant we could work out which constituency they were in and what sort of neighbourhood they lived in, both important to making sure our final sample was an accurate microcosm of the British public.

The next stage is to weight the data to make it fully representative. This is a complicated-sounding process, and the mathematical procedures that are used to achieve it are certainly complex, but the idea is a very simple one. Suppose we were to find that in a sample of 1,000, 550 (55%) of the respondents are men and only 450 (45%) are women. Then, if the views of men and women are different this would give us an inaccurate reading of public opinion, because in the British public as a whole, around 49% of adults are men and 51% are women. But we can correct for this by counting each woman as slightly more than 1 and each man as slightly less than 1, so that the final total works out right. In this case we would count each man as 0.891 (in other words, 49 divided by 55), and each woman as 1.133 (51 divided by 45): that would mean the men in total added up to 490 and the women to 510, the right proportions. With this straightforward example, correcting for only a single factor, the mathematics is simple enough to do with a calculator. However, to combine several factors at once we use a more complicated procedure called rim weighting, and we have to leave it to the computer to calculate the corrections; but the basic principle is the same.

In fact, the effect of demographic weighting is normally very small, since our sampling method ensures that each sample rarely diverges much from the ideal, and it is really only a fine-tuning process. Unweighted figures from any published Ipsos MORI poll are always included in the computer tables available on our website, so you can see how much of a difference it makes. In our final pre-election poll, for example, the 18-24 year olds were weighted up infinitesimally, from 125 to 129 in the final figures.

The standard weighting variables that we use in our political polls are for region, sex, age, social class (occupation), housing tenure, ethnic group, number of cars in the household and working status (including whether respondents work in the public or private sector and whether they are self-employed). However, the design might sometimes be altered if it seems advisable for a particular survey: in particular, an extra weight may be added if it seems that the existing weighting design has failed to correct a sample imbalance. (We did not need to add any extra weights to our final pre-election poll.) Weights are set at national or regional level, and combined by rim-weighting; of course, for polls that cover only part of the public, such as our polls in marginal constituencies for Reuters, the targets we use in our weighting reflect the profile of the audience that we are polling rather than the national profile. Data for both weights and quotas are derived from the Census, from the Registrar-General's population estimates (the official annual updates of the census figures), the Labour Force Survey and the National Readership Survey, as well as from other Ipsos MORI surveys where appropriate.

This weighting process gives us the final figures for almost all of the questions in our survey. However, the final voting intention figures are subject to one further process, since our headline percentages do not include the whole sample. First, we exclude those who are undecided how they would vote, those who say they would not vote at all. Those who won't say, usually only a small number, are also excluded in most of our polls, but in the final pre-election poll as an extra precaution we deal specially with them, as explained below. This leaves us with those who have named one of the parties, and voting intention percentages are always presented on this basis, since it is directly comparable with the way in which election results are normally published. (The numbers who are undecided, say they would not vote or refuse to answer are always given in the full report of the results of a poll on our website.)

In recent years we have adopted a second filter, to cope with the problem of low election turnouts. In the past, when the vast majority of British adults could be relied upon to vote, at least in general elections, we could be reasonably confident that a poll that accurately measured the voting intentions of the electorate would also accurately predict how an election held at that moment would pan out. (As recently as 1992, remember, 78% of the electorate voted.) These days, however, many members of the public are less sure that they will vote, and supporters of the Labour Party are considerably less likely to say they are certain they will vote than are Conservatives. Consequently, there is generally a substantial difference between the party vote shares if you consider the responses of everyone who names a party for which they would vote and if you consider only the people who say they are certain to vote. Our headline voting intention figure has since 2002 been calculated by excluding all those who are not 'absolutely certain to vote'. We measure this by asking our respondents to rate their certainty to vote on a scale from 1 to 10, where '1' means absolutely certain not to vote and '10' means absolutely certain to vote, and only those rating their likelihood of voting at '10' are included.

We believe that the relative proportion of each party's supporters who are 'absolutely certain to vote' is the best indicator of differential turnout, and therefore produces the best indications from a representative sample of how the country will or would vote. (It should be understood that we are not literally suggesting that the '10 out of 10 certain to vote' criterion necessarily identifies exactly those respondents who will vote, that no 10s will fail to vote and that no 8s or 9s will get to the polls, but that this is likely to give us the best approximation of the political profile of those who do vote. This methodology draws on our past experience, notably in the 2001 election, when we over-estimated Labour share and under-estimated abstention. This convinced us that we should use the most stringent turnout filter available.)

Table 85 shows how each of these stages worked out in our final 'prediction' poll – first weighting the data, then excluding those not giving a voting intention, then restricting the figures to those who were certain to vote (or who had already voted). In this case, weighting had only a tiny fine-tuning effect, but the omission of those who are less likely to vote increases the Conservative lead over Labour from 1 percentage point to 6.

Table 85: Calculating the voting 'prediction' in Ipsos MORI's final poll

	Unweighted	Weighted	Exclude undecided/ will not vote	Already voted/ 'Certain to vote'	With refusers
Number					
Conservative	313	308	308	263	303
Labour	289	293	293	218	251
Liberal Democrat	244	242	242	199	229
Other party*	79	86	86	60	69
Undecided	121	113			
Will not vote	50	51			
Refused to say	120	118	*(118)*	*(111)*	
Total	1216	1211	929	740	852
Percentage					
Conservative	26%	25%	33%	36%	36%
Labour	24%	24%	32%	29%	29%
Liberal Democrat	20%	20%	26%	27%	27%
Other party*	6%	7%	9%	8%	8%
Undecided	10%	9%			
Will not vote	4%	4%			
Refused to say	10%	10%			
Total	100%	100%	100%	100%	100%

Source: Ipsos MORI. Figures may not sum exactly to totals because of rounding error.
*Other parties are measured separately in the poll, but combined here for clarity.

For our final 'prediction' poll we retain the option of adding further refinements, not used in our routine polls, if they seem necessary to improve an unsatisfactory sample or otherwise turn our static Wednesday snapshot into a prediction of how people will behave on Thursday. These include exhaustive checking of the sample against a number of different yardsticks to make sure it is really representative of the British public. For instance, we check that the right proportion are in marginal constituencies, that we have correctly represented deprived neighbourhoods, rural against urban areas, and a host of other geo-demographic factors. If we had found an imbalance we could have added extra weights to correct it, but in this case it turned out that we didn't need to.

We also carry out a separate exercise in the hope of detecting any late swing, interviewing a sample of the public on the Tuesday and then calling back some of them on the Wednesday to see if their intentions have changed. Had we found any swing, we would have adjusted our prediction accordingly, as we have sometimes done in the past. This time, however, we found no evidence of any swing in progress, so no adjustment was needed.

The most important extra step, however, is to take account of those people who refused to tell us how they were intending to vote. Away from elections, this is typically a small proportion of the sample and can be safely ignored, but the number always increases substantially immediately before an election, presumably because a lot of people prefer to keep their vote secret once they have finally decided how they are going to cast it. In our 2010 poll, the refusers amounted to 13% of those who were certain they would vote, far too many to ignore in case they came disproportionately from one party or another. However, we can estimate how this group will vote on the basis of the newspapers they choose to read. (Of the things we measure, newspaper readership is one of the most strongly correlated with voting, and even people who don't want to tell us how they will vote don't mind telling us which papers they read.) As the table shows, we can then add the refusers into the final totals, which on this occasion however made no difference whatsoever to the party shares of the vote.

This is not the only way in which a poll sample can be collected and analysed, and some of the other companies prefer to use different methods which they believe are better for one reason or another. Perhaps the best-known and most discussed of these alternative methods is 'political weighting', or weighting by reported past vote, which was introduced in Britain by ICM during the 1992-7 Parliament, and is now used by many of the other polling companies. This is not the place to explore in any detail the arguments around political weighting. Suffice to say that the problem with this approach is that it has been known for decades that respondents do not necessarily report their past vote accurately[165], and we disagree with ICM and the other companies using weighting by reported past vote that we can correctly make allowance for the inaccuracy of their recall. If we could be sure of the correct weighting target – what a genuinely representative sample would say – of course we would adopt it. However, given the real risk that setting the wrong targets would distort rather than correct the findings, we prefer not to use it.

In making our initial decision not to weight by respondent's recall of their past voting, we were conscious that a higher number of people consistently tended to remember voting than actually voted, and that around half the people who voted Liberal in the previous election forgot they did so. Further, when applying recall of past voting to our final polls in the previous four or five elections, in every case the effect of past vote weighting was to make our forecast worse, not better, than the forecast we used at the time (with no weighting by vote recall).

In this context, we must point to the accuracy of our final polls at the 2005 and 2010 general elections (the two elections at which we have used the methodology we now prefer), which measured in the most natural way have surpassed those of our rivals (Table 86).

Of course, the differences between the companies' accuracy shown in the table are minute, and calculated in slightly different ways the order of the 'league table' would be different. But while it would be ridiculous to preen ourselves on this basis or claim to be 'Britain's most accurate pollster', we are certainly not prepared to allow anybody to claim that our methodology is 'obviously inferior' or that we don't know what we are doing.

---

[165] See, for example, HT Himmelweit, MJ Biberian and J Stockdale, 'Memory for past vote: implications of a study of bias in recall', *British Journal of Political Science*, Volume 8, 365-75 (1978).

Table 86: The proof of the pudding

	2005			2010			Aver-age 'error'
	Con %	Lab %	LD %	Con %	Lab %	LD %	
Ipsos MORI	33	38	23	36	29	27	
Harris Interactive	33	38	22	35	29	27	
ICM	32	38	22	36	28	26	
Populus	32	38	21	37	28	27	
YouGov	32	37	24	35	28	28	
ComRes*	31	39	23	37	28	28	
RESULT	**33.2**	**36.2**	**22.6**	**36.9**	**29.7**	**23.6**	
'Error'							
Ipsos MORI	0.2	1.8	0.4	0.9	0.7	3.4	**1.2**
Harris Interactive	0.2	1.8	0.6	1.9	0.7	3.4	**1.4**
ICM	1.2	1.8	0.6	0.9	1.7	2.4	**1.4**
Populus	1.2	1.8	1.6	0.1	1.7	3.4	**1.6**
YouGov	1.2	0.8	1.4	1.9	1.7	4.4	**1.9**
ComRes*	2.2	2.8	0.4	0.1	1.7	4.4	**1.9**

* Note that the final ComRes poll in 2005 was not strictly speaking an eve-of-poll prediction.

How well the polls are reported

In some ways, the reporting of the polls is better than it used to be, and the arrival of 24-hour news and new media has certainly ensured wider and more immediate access to poll findings. Nevertheless, the reporting is still far from perfect and if we are to judge from the comments posted by many regulars on the two main British polling blogs, Polling Report and Political Betting, the level of understanding even among many interested consumers of the polls is lamentably low. Figures are often reported or discussed, even in the mainstream professional media, without regard to statistical significance, far overplaying the importance of meaningless small differences in the figures between different polls. Seat projections are reported as gospel, without any explanation or even mention of necessary caveats and assumptions. Polls are often reported selectively to fit a particular interpretation of events, or headlined in a completely misleading way that is contradicted a few paragraphs into the copy – but how many readers get that far? Worse – and here the media are the victims rather than the perpetrators – occasional poll stories get into circulation that are completely untrue.

'Horserace' voting intention polls are probably the least useful indicator of political mood except in the immediate run-up to an election. A mid-term poll asks about a hypothetical event, an 'election tomorrow' which will not actually take place. Consequently, these measurements may be fragile at best, representing impressions rather than settled opinions, on a subject on which the voters know they have no immediate need to make up their minds. They almost certainly should not be taken literally. They will typically represent a top-of-the-mind judgment on the success of the government, but with very little consideration of the opposition as an alternative. When an election is in the offing the voters put themselves into a new mindset where they more realistically weigh up the alternatives on offer. (When Gordon Brown took over as Prime Minister he received an immediate bounce in his poll ratings, and Labour seemed to be anything up to nine points ahead. Should he call an election, everybody wondered? We cautioned that a lead of this sort didn't mean much. The public was giving him a brief benefit of the doubt, but he could not rely on it lasting, nor on his being able to translate it into a real lead if minds were concentrated by his calling a general election. Sure enough, as soon as the speculation got out of hand and the public began to consider the real possibility of an election in a few weeks time, the lead melted away even quicker than it had developed.)

Incredibly, we still have to repeat time after time, even to experienced politicians and journalists (and even the occasional pollster) who ought to know better, that opinion polls don't, and can't, predict the future. They are only snapshots of public opinion at the moment when the poll is taken. We don't, ahead of the election, ask our respondents how they think they will vote, only how they would vote if the election were tomorrow; our final poll, probably taken the day before the election itself, is the only one that should be viewed in any way as a prediction of the result (and, as noted above, we may need to add extra refinements, and take into account factors that we don't normally include, to turn that final snapshot poll into a prediction). Polls don't, and can't, forecast the result of elections a month or even a week ahead of an election, much less a year ahead. Our function is to make an accurate measurement of what is happening now, not to try to guess what will happen in the future.

On the other hand, if you do want to guess the future then an accurate understanding of what has happened already is a good starting point. So, think of polls as being like a barometer – barometers don't predict the weather; they measure something that is helpful to know if you want to predict the weather. But for that purpose, rather than relying purely on voting intentions the many other measurements that the polls regularly provide may be far more useful in developing an impression of what the future may bring – leaders' satisfaction ratings, important issues, economic outlook, judgment of party policies or image, and many others. To use a football analogy, voting intentions are, at best, the current state of the league tables without any considerations of games in hand, injuries or which teams have the easiest games still to play.

Another of the media's besetting sins is their fixation with reporting the 'lead' rather than the shares for each party, which when combined with a failure to understand or take into account what is meant by 'statistical reliability' causes them to see movements in opinion or a difference between the polls when none exists.

One Sunday a few weeks before the campaign formally began, 7 March, there were three polls published: ICM in the *News of the World*, BPIX in the *Mail on Sunday*, and YouGov in the *Sunday Times*. Misunderstanding of the nature of polls has rarely been better illustrated. ICM reported a 9% Tory lead, YouGov a 5% lead, and BPIX 2%. All reported their poll's finding for the share of each party, the fieldwork dates, all virtually the same, and all on respectable sample sizes of at least 1,000 (Table 87).

Close examination of the findings accurately showed that the three polls' Tory share was 36%, 38% and 40%, i.e. 38% plus or minus two percent, well within the 'margin of error'. The Labour shares were 31%, 33% and 34%, i.e., plus or minus one and one-half percent, and the LibDem shares were 18%, 18% and 17%; 'others' was equally close, 12%, 12% and 11%. In other words, there was no statistically significant difference between them.

Table 87: Polls published on 7 March 2010

Dates of Fieldwork	Sample Size	Pub. Date	Poll/ Client	Con %	Lab %	LD %	Oth %	Gap %
3-4 March	1,005	7 March	ICM/News of the World	40	31	18	11	+9
4-5 March	1,558	7 March	YouGov/Sunday Times	38	33	17	12	+5
4-5 March	5,655	7 March	BPIX/Mail on Sunday	36	34	18	12	+2

Source: Ipsos MORI analysis of figures collected by pollingreport.co.uk

Yet the media without exception, misreported them, because of their practice of reporting the lead and not the share for each party. In every case of the reporting of the three polls' findings, on radio, on television, and in the newspapers, attention was drawn to the discrepancy of the leads, 9%, 5% and 2%, rather than the consistency of the share findings.

Polls in marginal constituencies can be also misunderstood, leading to misinterpretation by the media. In this case, it is essential to understand which marginal constituencies have been included and how the outcome there relates to the outcome nationally. For example, both Ipsos MORI for Reuters and ICM for the *News of the World*[166] concentrated on the Labour-held constituencies which would decide whether the Conservatives could secure an overall majority or not. Naturally, the Liberal Democrats were much weaker in these seats than nationally; and because we centred our sample of constituencies round the 7% swing target that the Tories needed for victory, a dead-level result in our marginals polls was the equivalent of an 11-point Conservative lead nationally. So all these marginal polls, correctly, showed Labour in the lead *across these constituencies*, but it would have been entirely misleading if anyone had reported 'Ipsos MORI (or ICM) shows Labour in the lead'.

However, the Crosby/Textor marginals poll reported in the *Daily Telegraph* on 15 April was conducted in a very different group of marginal seats. Nothing wrong with that, providing the reader is told what it means. But the *Telegraph* headline was 'Conservatives lead in 100 key seats', with a colour graphic showing a 12-point Tory lead.[167] It certainly misled one or two contributors to the blogs, who took this as being in direct contradiction of the latest Ipsos MORI marginals poll. They clearly hadn't read or taken in the fourth paragraph of the article by Andrew Porter, which accurately informed careful readers that in the same seats the Tories were up seven, Labour down five and the LibDems down two since 2005 – a 6% swing, within one percentage point of what all the other polls, national and marginal, were saying in the previous week. But perhaps they were confused by Porter contrasting the poll with a previous poll which had indicated that 'a hung parliament [was] the most likely result', when a

---

166 ICM also did a separate poll in Liberal Democrat target marginals, for the *Guardian*.
167 Andrew Porter, 'Conservatives lead in 100 key seats, Telegraph poll shows', *Daily Telegraph*, 15 April 2010.

6% swing, as found by Crosby/Textor, would also result in a hung Parliament.

But at least *Telegraph* readers arguably had only themselves to blame if they misunderstood. When the otherwise excellent *The Campaign Show* programme on BBC News held up that edition of the *Telegraph* to show the headline and graphic showing a 12-point lead, how many of the viewers would have gone on to chase down the details in the paper? Jon Sopel correctly pointed out that the poll was in the marginals, but the essential point was the swing that the poll indicated, and this was not explained. The attentive viewer would have naturally jumped to the conclusion that something had happened to change the dynamics of the election, yet in fact it was a re-iteration of the same story every other pollster was reporting.

The following day another, not dissimilar, problem arose, causing a brief flap, and indicating how the speed of the modern news cycle and other communications developments are increasing the risks of faulty reporting. In this case, a journalist tweeted topline figures from a ComRes poll, which were assumed to represent national voting intentions and implied a dramatic swing in the state of the election. These figures were picked up and reported by a number of news outlets, and something of a media frenzy ensued. But, in fact, the figures were from a post-debate poll, and represented only the voting intentions of viewers, not of a nationally representative sample. It took some time before correction could catch up with the original story.

If the professionals are this bad at fairly representing poll results and their implications, it becomes harder to criticise the slanted or over-optimistic interpretations of those with a vested interest. All the parties do it, of course, and it may be unfair to single out the Liberal Democrats for an especially blatant example that we noticed, but there is no legitimate excuse for 'The Liberal Democrats are poised to win Edinburgh North & Leith from Labour, according to a new opinion poll published on 2nd April', put out by the constituency party there. (We saw it online[168], but we would guess it was also used in leaflets.) This conclusion was based not on

---

[168] http://northandleithlibdems.org.uk/en/article/2010/063169/first-opinion-poll-following-vince-cable-s-tv-debate-shows-lib-dems-are-poised-to-win, accessed 20 January 2011.

a constituency poll but on extrapolating by uniform swing from a national poll (ICM's for the *Guardian*, as it happens.) Admittedly, the write-up goes on to mention this, but only on the basis that national swing might under-estimate the local swing! ('Since this analysis is based on "national swing", it doesn't take account of five years' intensive campaigning by the Liberal Democrats in the constituency, and the large number of Tory and SNP supporters who are switching to the LibDems to beat Labour this time. Both of these factors could further boost LibDem support in the constituency and their prospects of success.') The Liberal Democrats did not win Edinburgh North & Leith, despite doing even better nationally in the final outcome than that pre-campaign ICM poll was suggesting. Is it unjust to be amused when we see that the piece goes on to quote the candidate talking about 'Labour's dishonest approach'? But boys will be boys, and it is perhaps unrealistic to expect politicians to be as objective and realistic in talking about research findings as we insist (by contractual obligation) that all our paying clients are.

Then there are what we can only assume are direct lies. At every election, but especially at close elections, people start circulating false rumours about poll findings before they are published. With the proliferation of websites and blogs dealing with polls in the last few years, this is easier now than it ever was before. Sometimes, no doubt, this is an honest error; but sometimes it is deliberate. Perhaps it is an attempt to ramp the markets, or to manipulate the political mood; at other times it may simply be 'fishing', trying to get the pollsters to confirm or deny the figures before the due publication time, in breach of their confidentiality agreements with their clients.

In 2010, it started well before the campaign itself. Back in February, Mike Smithson of politicalbetting.com emailed us to check the 'leaked' figures he had been given for our monthly poll. We don't know who fed those figures to Mike, but there was no such leak and no such poll – we didn't even start fieldwork until the following weekend! The following week it happened again, and this time Mike got caught: relying on figures published on another website, he reported entirely incorrect figures for a YouGov poll, showing an apparent movement towards the Conservatives following the Gordon Brown bullying allegations. These figures circulated for several hours. In fact the real poll figures showed no movement at all.

If not the polls, then what?

Why is there so much interest in the 'horserace' polls? Surely because they are the only objective and systematic measurement of something that the public, and the journalists informing that public, want to know. There is clearly a thirst for knowledge about which parties are doing well and which badly, which are ahead and which are behind, which is not being supplied from any other source.

Most of the public (even those who are not interested in what the polls say) oppose banning polls and have done so at all recent general elections; in fact, support for banning polls is significantly lower than it used to be.

Table 88: Banning polls and other election coverage

Q. During an election campaign, do you think there should or should not be a ban on…?

% 'yes, should be ban'	1983 %	1987 %	1992* %	1997 %	2005 %	18-19 April 2010 %
…publication of opinion polls	22	25	36	16	15	17
…party election broadcasts of the election on TV and radio	14	25	n/a	20	14	17
…all coverage of the election on TV and radio	13	24	n/a	15	11	11
…all coverage of the election in newspapers	9	16	n/a	10	10	12
Average	14.5	22.5		15.25	12.5	14.25

Source: Ipsos MORI
Base: c. 1,000 GB residents aged 18+ in each survey
1992 survey was post-election and asked only about opinion polls

In our mid-campaign poll in 2010, we found 17% of the public saying that they thought there should be a ban, a similar proportion to those who would ban party election broadcasts and only about half-as-many-again as the numbers who would ban all television, radio or newspaper coverage of the election. Support for a ban reached 36% in the immediate aftermath of the polls' perceived failure in the 1992 election, suggesting that the public reasonably enough see the case for polling being weaker if it cannot be relied upon to be reasonably accurate, but at the elections since then we have found the numbers advocating a ban to be less than half this level.

Politicians clearly cannot be trusted to assess their own success or failure. Journalists consistently disagree with each other as to the public mood, often led astray by their own opinions. The betting odds may come closer as an indicator, but then they are naturally based on close observation of the polls in the first place. (It is no coincidence that contributors to Mike Smithson's Political Betting blog during elections talk about tomorrow's opinion polls almost without ceasing.) Deterministic predictions which in essence deny any free will to the electorate during an election campaign would raise questions of their own as a substitute for polls. The polls communicate directly with the prospective voters and offer them a voice. Even though the polls are not perfect, provided they are honest and are competently conducted, as we believe has always been the case in Britain, they are better than any of the alternatives.

Increasingly there is a small army of academic psephologists, the folks who study elections, who insist that they are able to combine various factors (including polling trends from their favourite pollsters, measures of economic optimism, historic financial statistics and bats' entrails), saying that they have the magic formula for 'getting the election right' months in advance of polling day. To date, while occasionally close, they have collectively not yet been able to string success together sufficiently to guarantee the riches desired by the media for their headlines and the punters for making their fortune betting on election outcomes.

Nevertheless, there is some sense behind their efforts, since the purpose is not so much to make the polls redundant as to come to a better understanding of the causes of election outcomes – a sociological formula that could predict election results with 80% accuracy, say, would be of value to political scientists even if inferior to polls purely as a means of knowing the exact result in advance. For that matter, a formula that predicts with reasonable accuracy months in advance is useful even if you get a more reliable finding by waiting until the last 24 hours.

Shortly before the 2010 election kicked off in earnest, there was an interesting academic symposium on election forecasting at the University of Manchester.[169] All who attended were participative and attentive, most

---

[169] Most of the papers are available at http://www.dcern.org.uk/documents/ Electoralforecastingfor2010.pdf.

generous in sharing their past failures as well as pointing up their successes (unlike a few of the polling fraternity on some such occasions). The approaches they used were varied – local election results, 'citizen forecasting' (asking the public what result they expect), modelling from previous general election results, and so on. And all of those who ventured to use the models they were presenting to predict the forthcoming election correctly predicted a hung Parliament in some form, a better record than of some of the forecasts on various bases that we have seen in the past; but then, on this occasion, all the forecasts were built on directly measuring public opinion in some form (whether by polling or in election results) rather than some of the predictors we have seen relied upon in the past. Unsurprisingly, it is the public opinion approach which we believe to be the best.

The betting markets

It is often suggested that the betting markets are better predictors of the election result than the opinion polls. Well, for sure, if you are purely interested in prediction then – since the polls don't claim to predict – comparisons at any point except immediately before an election *ought* to come out in the punters' favour. The trouble is, too often they don't.

The bookies have for decades been invited onto TV and radio to confront pollsters in mid election when broadcasters want a dust up to say that they are better forecasters of elections than the pollsters, because their punters are betting real money and are paying close attention. Martin Baxter argued during this election that the bookies' odds are a more accurate measurement than the opinion polls because

> *'Betting markets have the advantage that people are putting their own money at risk, which forces them to think clearly and make use of all possible information available to them.'* [170]

In fact what they are paying attention to is mainly what the polls are saying, hoping to get their bets down before the public generally wakes up to the change in the political weather. For years we sought hard evidence, and finally, in 2010, the technology delivered our wish. Figure 53 shows

---

[170] http://www.electoralcalculus.co.uk/campaign2010.html.

how on Saturday 1 May, as the final week of the campaign began, at 4 pm 'no overall majority' was a firm favourite.

But then that afternoon, the Sunday papers were preparing graphics and writing the text for the poll stories they were publishing the next day. In all, there were six polls published on the Sunday. It is the practice of the Sunday papers to release the findings of their polls on Saturday evening in order to make early radio and television news leads, and no more so than on the Saturday before the general election.

Figure 53: Watch the money watch the polls

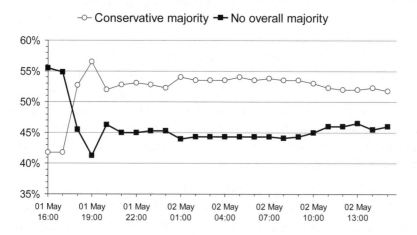

Source: http://odds.bestbetting.com via www.politicalbetting.com

The first poll of the six was released by the paper at 4:30 pm, followed in quick succession by the other five. At least on Bestbetting, the next two hours as one by one the polls were released and reported on the blogosphere and early radio and TV news broadcasts and 'bannered' on Sky, the bets flowed in, with the weight of money being heavily in favour of a Conservative majority. At the first the odds swung round completely, then support for a hung parliament recovered slightly, before settling at a slightly lower level but with a Conservative majority still remaining the clear favourite. In the event, of course, the bookies won. (They always do.) And, of course, betting information is based on the weight of money, not the number betting, which further questions the thesis that the punters (sic) know best.

If anybody still believes the markets predict better than the polls, the betting on election day (as reported on the blog politicalbetting.com[171]) offers a plain counter-argument. Whether led by their own political sympathies, or believing the Conservative conviction that the polls and/or uniform swing were understating David Cameron's chances, the markets over-estimated Conservative and Liberal Democrat prospects while badly understating Labour ones. The main spread betting opening markets on polling day set the spread for Labour's number of seats at 217½-220, 218-223 and 214-219, against the actual outcome of 258. (Uniform swing based on the actual vote shares would have projected 265, while based on the poll-of-polls of the nine BPC companies would have projected 254.) Equally bad were the spreads for the numbers of Liberal Democrat seats (82½-85½, 78-82 and 78-82, compared to the outcome of 57), although this was in line with the 81 that uniform swing would have predicted from the polls' overestimation of the Liberal Democrat vote. True, the markets' overestimation of the Conservative seats was less (spreads of 319½-321, 316-321 and 317-322, result 306) where the polls and uniform swing would have underestimated the number by around 17 seats, but the combined error across the three parties is much higher on the betting than in the polls – and that with the punters able to allow intelligently for non-uniform swing should they wish to do so.

In the same vein, two American academics have comprehensively studied the record of the prediction markets in US Presidential elections. Comparing the Iowa Electronic Market with polls between 1988 and 2004, they find unequivocally that properly analysed and comparing like with like, 'poll-based forecasts outperform vote-share market prices'.[172]

Bizarrely, however, when they undertook a longer-term study the findings were different. They looked at all the available market data on presidential elections since the 19th century, and compared this to the record of the opinion polls since Gallup and his rivals first emerged in 1936. Their findings are somewhat startling: market prices before 1936 were as good at

---

[171] Figures from the post at politicalbetting.com, 13 May 2010, http://www2.politicalbetting.com /index.php/archives/2010/05/13/remember-what-the-markets-were-doing-last-thursday/, retrieved 27 July 2010.
[172] Robert S Erikson and Christopher Wlezien, 'Are Political Markets Really Superior to Polls as Election Predictors?', *Public Opinion Quarterly*, Volume 72 (2008), 190-215.

predicting as the polls have been since 1936; but that the markets have been much less good at predicting in the presence of the polls than in their absence, and that since 1936 the polls have been better predictors than markets.

But they also note, contrary to the assumption that the markets ought to have an advantage before the eve of election because they can include an explicitly predictive element, that

> *'early in the campaign, the polls win the contest. In the modern era, polls provide evidence of who is winning and losing months before the votes are cast. Without polls, it takes more time for the consensus to emerge regarding who will win.'* [173]

We are not quite sure what to make of that! Another recent paper, however, looks at the polls and markets in the 2008 American elections, considering state-level data and including senatorial elections as well as that for President. This finds, more in line with expectations, that

> *'early in the cycle and in not-certain races debiased prediction market-based forecasts provide more accurate probabilities of victory and more information than debiased poll-based forecasts'.* [174]

Voodoo polls and other unspecified sampling methods

Of course, there is no lack of punditry and prognostication around elections which attempts to by-pass serious polling altogether and read the state of play or predict the outcome by less other methods. Sometimes this masquerades as polling yet makes no attempt at representative sampling; sometimes it tries other methods, ignoring altogether the obvious step of asking the voters what they will or would or might do and draws on other indicators.

Some of this is harmless – nobody would object to the marketing exercises by which breweries sell identical beer through pumps decorated with the heads of the party leaders or confectioners sell crisps in differently-

---

[173] Robert S Erikson and Christopher Wlezien, 'Markets vs Polls as predictors', Paper to the Annual Meeting of the American Association for Public Opinion Research, 2009.

[174] David Rothschild, 'Forecasting elections: Comparing prediction markets, polls and their biases', *Public Opinion Quarterly*, Volume 73 (2009), 895-916.

coloured packets, but nor would anyone take it as a serious attempt to predict the election result. Just a bit of fun, as Peter Snow would have said.

But it is less harmless when it is taken seriously, or treated as if it is a serious poll. 'Voodoo poll' data is perhaps the most pernicious form of pseudo-poll, by no means a new phenomenon but far more pervasive in the last few years as easily available software has allowed anybody with a website to carry out an exercise that was once the sole province of those with the equipment to take and tabulate hundreds of phone calls or postcards. Such polls are worse than worthless as a representative measure of public opinion. Without the rigour of sampling or representativeness, they measure nothing more than the views of those who choose to respond, have a connection, or are online at any one point. Yet too often these are reported uncritically, not preceded by any sort of 'health warning'.

Indeed, despite the obvious limitations of self-selecting samples they are still too often not only reported but conducted by otherwise generally-reliable media organisations. The BBC for many years persisted with a voodoo poll for the *Today* programme's Man of the Year award, despite the clearest evidence that vote was being consistently 'stuffed' by the political parties. *Time* magazine was made to look ridiculous by its 'most influential people of the 20th Century' poll on its website (which was swamped with votes for Kemal Atatürk, then swung back by an orchestrated Greek vote for Winston Churchill to stop a Turk winning), yet carries on with similar exercises. (In 2010, another orchestrated campaign had Mir-Hossein Mousavi, the former Iranian Prime Minister defeated in the 2009 Presidential election, voted to the head of its list of the 100 most influential people in the world.)

Of course, neither of these polls or anything like them is liable to have any serious effect on the political narrative. But what are we to make of the ConservativeHome website, for example, which has periodically run a number of polls of its 'Members' panel' over the last few years? We don't know the exact methodology – not being a member of the British Polling Council, ConservativeHome is not obliged to publish it – but this has not stopped both broadcast and print media from treating these polls as serious measurements of Conservative party opinion.

Twitter: the 'wisdom of clouds'?

With every new technology or new application of it comes new possibilities, and it was entirely predictable that from the new media innovations of the past few years would come new attempts at election prediction. At the time of the 2010 election, Twitter was still the latest flavour of the month, so little surprise that there should be an attempt to use it by relating volume of 'tweets' to the election result.

Tweetminster, a website set up to focus specifically on political tweets used over 2 million tweets to make predictions about the election. Their methodology was simple, in the 433 constituencies (of 650) that were represented on Twitter, the candidate with the most mentions on Twitter was predicted to win. In other words, the prediction was based on the volume attention paid to a candidate rather than to any direction of whether people intended to vote for them or not. To calculate the national vote shares they added together the percentage breakdowns of party mentions (by candidate) in each of the 433 seats to form a national vote share prediction.

However, this was billed in advance only as an 'experimental study' using predictive modelling, and *Research World* noted[175] that 'Tweetminster cautions that this exercise is quite different to conventional opinion polling'. In fact, Tweetminster's performance was generally impressive. Its national vote share prediction was in line with the result – and in line with the predictions of most pollsters. (The *Guardian* pointed out that Tweetminster's prediction was 'as accurate as Ipsos MORI and more accurate than YouGov, ComRes, Opinium and Angus Reid'[176]. This followed a similar exercise in Germany at the federal elections in 2009, where the prediction from Twitter mentions was accurate, though less precisely so than that of the opinion polls.[177]) The majority of its constituency predictions also proved accurate: in 69% of seats where each of the main parties had a candidate on Twitter, the most mentioned candidate won, and in 55% of seats where at least one candidate from any

---

[175] *Research World*, May 2010.
[176] http://www.guardian.co.uk/media/pda/2010/may/13/twitter-tweetminster-election.
[177] Andranik Tumasjan, Timm O Sprenger, Philipp G Sandner and Isabell M Welpe, 'Predicting Elections with Twitter: What 140 Characters Reveal about Political Sentiment', http://www.aaai.org/ocs/index.php/ICWSM/ICWSM10/paper/viewFile/1441/1852.

of the three major parties was on Twitter the most mentioned candidate won.

But some individual constituencies point up the fragility of the model – it may be much more obvious who is likely to be the most mentioned candidate than who is likely to win the seat. In Brighton Pavilion this was the Green candidate, Caroline Lucas, and her victory was much touted as a triumph for Tweetminster. But, equally predictably, in Luton South the television personality Esther Rantzen attracted most interest, and therefore most Twitter mentions; however, she did not attract votes to the same degree, and finished with a derisory 4.4% of the vote.

In fact, these weaknesses had already been manifest in earlier attempts to predict elections from Twitter in the USA. In the US presidential election of 2008, Barack Obama's popularity correlated with how frequently his name was mentioned on Twitter. Similarly, during 2009 Carnegie Mellon's Language Technologies Institute tracked political sentiment about President Obama and tracked it against Gallup's daily Presidential approval rating and showed a remarkable closeness. 'Twitter-derived sentiments and the traditional polls reflected declining approval of President Obama's job performance during 2009, with a 72 percent correlation between them.'[178] Unfortunately for this argument, however, it turns out that during the 2008 election mentions of John McCain also correlated positively with Obama's popularity in the polls.[179]

A prime problem with monitoring Twitter and similar phenomena as a tracker of popularity, clearly, is that current methods do not make it possible to accurately track the sentiment or nuances of individual posts. Therefore a simple frequency count of mentions can be misleading: negative news about a candidate might prove just as productive of tweets as positive news. If the Tweetminster model worked reasonably well in the British election, all it goes to show is that the dynamic of the election at the constituency level was more a positive than a negative one, which nobody would confidently promise will necessarily remain true in the future. Of course, we would add further that – for the moment at least – the users of Twitter are a very small and demographically unrepresentative

---

[178] http://www.cmu.edu/news/archive/2010/May/may11_twitterpolls.shtml.
[179] http://news.sciencemag.org/sciencenow/2010/05/twitter-as-good-as-a-telephone-s.html.

sector of the voting public. One German experiment makes the point that 40% of all tweets they looked at were from 4% of the people included – like any crowd, some shout louder and say a lot more than others. Of course, the counterpoint is that these people are the most connected and influential, and may even be setting wider media agendas that affect the general population; but arguably this is only possible in so far as the circles in which the twitterers move reflect the public as a whole. Being able to 'poll' in 433 out of 650 constituencies – not a random selection, of course, but dictated by the technological characteristics of their populations and candidates – is at best a chancy business.

Nevertheless, the further the technology advances towards making it possible to distinguish accurately between the expression of positive and negative sentiments, the more useful it might become as a measurement of public activity and communication during the election campaign. Another company, Lexalytics, tracked online 'sentiment' during the leadership debates, to see who 'won' each one according to positive comments posted online: their findings were broadly in line with the snap reaction measurements from the pollsters. If Twitter, or whatever has replaced Twitter as the fashionable social medium by the time of the next election, could be measured in the same way it could be added to longer-established measurements such as content analysis of the press and broadcasting coverage. But why spend time and effort turning a study that would be interesting and meaningful in its own right into yet another useless voodoo poll?

Appendix 2: Editorial cartoons and the 2010 election

Kent Worcester[180]

Introduction

Historical surveys typically locate the origins of British political cartooning in the Victorian era, when advances in printing, paper production, and periodical distribution facilitated the emergence of mass-circulation illustrated newspapers and magazines.[181] The most famous of these publications, of course, was *Punch*, which was founded in 1841 and which featured cartoons by such eminent figures as Richard Doyle, who illustrated Charles Dickens' Christmas books, J B Handelsman, John Leech, Arthur Rackham, and John Tenniel, who illustrated *Alice in Wonderland*. One of *Punch*'s rivals, an illustrated magazine called *Judy*, featured the comical exploits of Ally Sloper, a work-shy character concocted in the 1860s by Charles Ross and his wife Marie Duval. Ally Sloper was quite possibly the world's first recognizable cartoon icon; his look, antics, and supporting cast provided an influential template for cartoonists seeking to portray urban underclass characters in single- and multi-panel comics. A nineteenth-century Andy Capp, in other words.[182]

But the tradition of political cartooning in Britain arguably dates to the eighteenth and early nineteenth centuries, when artists such as William Hogarth, John Collier, Thomas Rowlandson, James Gillray, and Isaac and his son George Cruickshank fashioned satirical prints that were sold by

---

[180] Kent Worcester is a professor of political science at Marymount Manhattan College, New York. He is the author or co-editor of six books, including *C.L.R. James: A Political Biography* (1996), *The Social Science Research Council, 1923-1998* (2001), *Arguing Comics: Literary Masters on a Popular Medium* (2004), and *A Comics Studies Reader* (2009).

[181] The single most useful resource for the study of modern British cartooning is the British Cartoon Archive, which is located at the University of Kent. The Archive houses over 150,000 original cartoons along with related books, magazines, and newspapers. Their website can be found at http://www.cartoons.ac.uk/.

[182] See Roger Sabin, 'Ally Sloper: The First Comics Superstar?, in Jeet Heer and Kent Worcester (eds), *A Comics Studies Reader* (Jackson, MS: University Press of Mississippi, 2009), pp 177-189.

printshops and displayed in shop windows, taverns, and private homes. The Cambridge historian Vic Gatrell reports that approximately twenty thousand prints were 'published in London between 1770 and 1830, in the golden age of graphic satire.' Of these, roughly 'half of the prints disseminated political news and commentary.' Gatrell suggests that 'most text-trained historians' have overlooked this rich seam of cultural information because they are 'uneasy about using visual evidence.' As he usefully explains:

> 'Visual rhetoric isn't easily reduced to the expository prose historians trade in. Moreover while texts usually explain themselves and tacitly or explicitly refer to each other, images don't always explain their existence. Satirical prints were often deliberately ambiguous, so that deciding on even so simple a question as whether they were 'satirical' may depend on how we choose to spin them. They constructed illusory reality-effects that were filtered through intentions, styles, or market interests remote from the initial observation, or from our easy understanding. On these and like grounds, most historians are wary of visual evidence like this, and feel that words are what they should live by.'[183]

If historians tend to be 'wary of visual evidence,' the same may also be said of political scientists, who sprinkle cartoons into their textbooks, and tape them to their office doors, but rarely concern themselves with the history, craft, and art – what Gatrell calls the 'illusory reality-effects' – of the modern cartoon. Political scientists are not necessarily as text-centric as historians, as they routinely incorporate statistics and data sets into their analyses. But they are perhaps even more reluctant than historians to make systematic use of images and graphics.

As a commercial art form, the history of political cartooning is closely linked to the development of the modern newspaper. But politically-minded cartoons can turn up in all sorts of places, including books, comic books, comic strips, websites, advertisements, and even t-shirts. The most interesting political cartoons are by definition sites of dense visual information. They deploy symbols, icons, lines, shapes, and words to affirm, mock, and complicate the assumptions and boundaries of acceptable political discourse. They draw on established narratives even as they publicize the latest scandals.

---

[183] Vic Gatrell, *City of Laughter: Sex and Satire in Eighteenth-Century London* (London: Walker & Company, 2007), pp 9-11.

Politicians are sometimes infuriated by how they are portrayed by cartoonists. John Major, for example, was reportedly dismayed that Steve Bell drew him wearing underwear over his trousers. At the same time, public figures have been known to purchase original cartoon art in which they appear, even if the imagery itself is unflattering.

Cartoon 1: Martin Rowson, *Guardian*, 19 April 2010[184]

Thanks to Martin Rowson and the *Guardian*

The editorial cartoon is a subset of the political cartoon. The term is used most often to refer to political cartoons that are located outside comic strip sections, as well as to cartoons that appear in politically minded magazines. Editorial cartoons seek to provide topical, reader-friendly outbursts of images and texts that punctuate and enliven the printed page.

---

[184] The cartoons in this chapter are all, of course, reproduced in black and white but, except fot the three by Matt, originally appeared in colour.

Rather than simply matching words with pictures, they can more usefully be understood as complex ensembles of multiple and sometimes contradictory discourses. Newspaper cartoons in particular decorate the page and distract the eye. They encapsulate historical change and transmit coded messages to their readers. Most newspaper cartoons are in black-and-white, but there is no formal reason why this should be so, and the use or absence of colour adds a further dimension to the meaning of specific cartoons.

Ideally, editorial cartoons enjoy a measure of autonomy from the columns of print that surround them. A capable cartoonist can use this space to 'grab people by the lapels, shake them and say, "Don't you understand what's happening?"'[185] As the bitter and occasionally violent protests and economic boycotts over the cartoons published in the Danish newspaper *Jyllands-Posten* in September 2005 made clear, political cartoons can sometimes serve as lighting rods for transnational and even civilisational conflicts.

This appendix is concerned with the contemporary uses and meanings of editorial cartooning in Britain, with an emphasis on newspaper cartoons and the 2010 General Election. With one or two exceptions, virtually all of the country's daily and Sunday newspapers published cartoons during the April-May election period. These appealing graphic commentaries offer a unique perspective on the month-long campaign and how it was filtered through the eyes (and hands) of visually oriented satirists.

The specific focus of the chapter is on cartoons that appeared in the following London-based daily and Sunday newspapers: *The Times*, the *Sunday Times*, the *Independent*, the *Independent on Sunday*, the *Daily Telegraph*, the *Financial Times*, the *Guardian*, the *Observer*, the *Sun*, the *Daily Mirror*, the *Daily Star*, the *Daily Express*, the *Daily Mail*, and the *Mail on Sunday*. The emphasis is on works produced by staff cartoonists rather than occasional contributors.

These publications were not the only periodicals to feature election-related cartoons during this period, of course. Numerous cartoons could be found in the *Scotsman*, the *Glasgow Herald*, and other Scottish (and Welsh)

---

[185] Cartoonist Tom Tomorrow, quoted in Chris Lamb, *Drawn to Extremes: The Use and Abuse of Editorial Cartoons* (New York: Columbia University Press, 2004), pp. 233.

newspapers, as well as in weekly periodicals, such as *Private Eye*, the *New Statesman*, the *Spectator*, the *Economist*, and *Socialist Worker*. A full account of political cartoons and the 2010 General Election would require a broader framework than the one adopted here. The approach taken in this chapter is more selective in its focus, and concentrates on the cartoons (and cartoonists) that were most often read, and more rarely remarked upon, by motivated voters and political figures from across the ideological spectrum.

The campaign

British election campaigns are unusually compact, particularly in comparison to presidential elections in the United States. These campaigns provide a short window during which political cartoonists can help shape the electorate's perceptions of the parties, their leaders, and their programs, as well as the day-to-day issues and controversies that shape and sometimes define the campaign season.

Certain aspects of general election campaigns can be safely predicted in advance, such as the longstanding Tory-Labour rivalry, the ongoing efforts of the Liberal Democrats to cement their status as a major party, and the consequential role of nationalist parties in Scotland and Wales. It can also be assumed that minor parties, such as UKIP, Respect, and the Greens, will use the campaign season to advance their policy agendas, as well as perhaps to win one or more seats. At the same time, each election is inevitably marked by controversies that cannot be anticipated before the campaign commences. Just as military historians refer to the fog of war, political campaigns generate their own thick mist, one that can suddenly and unexpectedly place parties, leaders, and door-to-door campaigners on a spectacularly awkward footing. A stray remark here, a personal scandal there, can turn the most mundane of campaigns into virtual free-for-alls.

As the chapters in this volume show, the 2010 election campaign was a hard-fought process whose outcome was difficult to determine in advance, other than to suggest the likelihood of a hung parliament. As *The Times* reported on its front page at the start of the campaign, the 'formalities between the Prime Minister and the monarch will take only a few minutes but will trigger the most eagerly awaited showdown since Tony Blair swept away 18 years of Conservative rule in 1997.'[186] Or, as a *Daily Mail* banner headline excitedly proclaimed, 'Now the Class War Begins.'[187]

The cartoons

The 2010 General Election provided ample material for columnists, comedians, and cartoonists. Political cartoons can vary enormously, not only in terms of message, style, and formal complexity, but also in terms of size, format, and placement. While some editors seemed to randomly drop single-panel cartoons wherever space needed filling, others made a point of featuring sizable cartoons by well-known artists in high-profile spots, such as adjacent to lead editorials. During the 2010 campaign, several newspapers made a point actively promoting their in-house cartoonists. Journalists may sometimes resent the precious space that is taken up by cartoons, but readers often connect with specific newspapers in part because of the efforts of their favourite cartoonists.

Two of the country's most respected newspaper cartoonists, Steve Bell of the *Guardian*, and Matthew ('Matt') Pritchett of the *Daily Telegraph*, have been canvassing the electoral beat since the Thatcher years. Bell first started working for the *Guardian* in 1981, after contributing cartoons to *Time Out*, *City Limits*, and *The Leveller*. He started attending annual party conferences in the early 1980s, and says that 'after a while you become a bit of a connoisseur, and you get to see how the madness changes.'[188] Pritchett, much better known as 'Matt,' became the *Telegraph*'s pocket cartoonist in 1988. Pritchett's earliest cartoons appeared in the *New Statesman*.[189]

Other prominent political cartoonists in the UK include Peter Brookes (*The Times*), Tim Sanders (the *Independent*), Roger Beale (the *Financial Times*),

---

[186] Roland Watson, 'Let the Race Begin', *The Times*, A1, 6 April 2010.

[187] James Chapman, 'Now the Class War Begins: Labour Targets Cameron's Background', *Daily Mail*, A1, 7 April 2010.

[188] Quoted in Kent Worcester, 'The Steve Bell Interview', *The Comics Journal*, Number 272 (November 2005), p 70.

[189] Matt was awarded an MBE in 2002. He is a four-time winner of the Cartoon Art Trust annual prize. While Bell has yet to receive a political honour, he has been the recipient of no fewer than eight Cartoon Art Trust annual prizes.

Martin Rowson (the *Guardian*), Chris Riddell (the *Observer*), and Stan McMurtry, better known as 'Mac' (the *Daily Mail*).

While the number of female and non-white cartoonists whose work shows up in British newspapers is vanishingly small, the web has provided an important outlet for up-and-coming cartoonists. One of the most impressive of the web-based political cartoonists is Martha Richler, who is known as 'Marf'. Her work appears on the Political Betting website ('Britain's most-read political blog'), and in the *Evening Standard*.[190]

Cartoon 2: Marf, *Political Betting***, 28 September 2009**

*"I wonder if 'The Beast from the East' has
a better ring to it than 'Big Gord'?"*

Thanks to Martha Richler and *Political Betting*

---

[190] See http://www6.politicalbetting.com/index.php/archives/category/marf-cartoons/.

Newspaper cartoons can be distinguished in terms of their political values (implicit or explicit) as well as their intrinsic aesthetic interest. Some cartoonists are skilled at creating beautiful pen-and-ink compositions, but may not offer interesting or strongly held points of view. Others may be fiercely partisan, but lacklustre in terms of visual aesthetics. While some cartoonists use their pens to motivate readers to support a particular party and/or cause, others pride themselves on their changeability. The ideological views expressed by cartoonists can change over time, of course, as bedrock assumptions soften or as prejudices harden. Only a select number of cartoonists are able to consistently generate pieces that are both thought provoking and visually exciting.

In the context of the 2010 General Election, British political cartoonists occupied a spectrum consisting of four main positions: strongly partisan, weakly partisan, unpredictable, and cynical or anti-political. Most, but by no means all, of the cartoonists working for daily newspapers fell into the first three camps.

Strongly partisan cartoonists can be readily placed on the party-political map and use their perch to inspire the faithful. Their appeal is to some extent limited by their predictability, at least for readers who do not subscribe to their point of view. By way of contrast, weakly partisan cartoonists often try the patience of politically committed readers and can be regarded as unreliable by party strategists. Meanwhile, consistently unpredictable cartoonists strive to keep readers off balance, and emphasize the open-mindedness of the cartoonist or the publication or both. Anti-political cartoonists use the medium to cast aspirations on the entire political class. There is usually a link between the ideological affiliation of a specific newspaper, and the cartoonists whose work appears in its pages, but this is not always the case. It is not unknown for socialists to contribute to right-leaning papers and vice versa.

A good example of a strongly partisan cartoonist is provided by the *Daily Mail*'s Mac, who devotes his considerable skills to promoting Conservative policies and mocking the Labour Party. During the election, he often depicted Gordon Brown as an emotional wreck whose departure was both imminent and overdue. A Mac cartoon that appeared on April 6 showed a teary PM at Buckingham Palace being consoled by the Queen. 'From what I can understand,' she tells her husband, 'it's something about May 6th and not wanting to go – more tissues please, Philip...' After the awkward incident in Rochdale, Mac presented a BBC producer on the eve of the final debate, talking into a mobile phone. 'Alright, Prime Minister: I'll tell you how I know you're in the bath sipping whisky and shouting at your plastic duck – you've left your microphone on again.' For his final cartoon before voting day, the *Daily Mail's* top cartoonist drew a picture of a group of men in overalls at a removal company. 'Remember, men. A coalition will bring us three jobs. Brown out, Cameron and Clegg in…now get out there and vote!'

By way of contrast, the *Mail on Sunday* ran cartoons by two long-time *Private Eye* contributors, Michael Heath and Robert Thompson, neither of whose work is as fiercely partisan as Mac's. A representative example is a cartoon by Thompson that appeared on 18 April that showed a cloud of black smoke emanating from a television image of the three leaders in their first debate. As the man explained to his girlfriend, 'The air is full of it and it's going to last for weeks!' This self-consciously anti-political stance is very different in tone from anything that Mac produced during the election.

Another pro-Conservative cartoonist is Paul Thomas, the staff cartoonist for the *Daily Express*. Like Mac, he mainly targeted his polemical fire at the outgoing Prime Minister rather than the Liberal Democrats or the new, right-of-centre Tory leader. To say that Thomas' work is blunt would be an understatement. At the outset of the election, he showed Brown talking to the monarch at the Palace – 'I'll say goodbye to you properly after the election,' she says, as she waves farewell. A subsequent cartoon placed Gordon and Sarah Brown in a television studio. 'Whatever happens, at least we have each other…' the PM says, rather plaintively. 'I've been wanting to have a chat about that,' Sarah Brown responds, with her arms folded. On voting day, the *Express* featured an inky Paul Thomas graphic that portrayed a steamship, the 'S.S. Brown,' running headlong into an iceberg.

A third Tory partisan is Andy Davey, whose work was featured in the mass-circulation *Sun*. In contrast to Mac and Thomas, Davey ridiculed Nick Clegg's Liberal Democrats nearly as often as he attacked the ruling Labour Party. On 15 April, for example, the *Sun* published a Davey cartoon that showed an immature-looking Nick Clegg jumping into the frame while holding a copy of the LibDem Manifesto. 'Us too – look!' he says.

Another *Sun* cartoonist, David Trumble, also poked fun at Nick Clegg. In a cartoon published on 26 April, Trumble portrayed the Liberal Democrat leader as a bike-riding, beret-wearing Frenchman, complete with red wine and garlic. But neither Davey nor Trumble proved as strongly partisan as their counterparts at the *Mail* and *Express*. Davey's response to the election results, published on 7 May, showed all three party leaders sprawled on the ground like exhausted partygoers. A single thought balloon has them thinking the exact same thing: 'Phew! Now what?'

The nearest pro-Labour analogue to the right-leaning views of Mac, Paul Thomas, and Andy Davey was provided by the graphic jibes of Neil Kerber and David Black ('Kerber and Black'), whose razor-thin lines regularly appeared in the *Daily Mirror*. While their artwork is less detailed than Mac or Thomas', it is equally partisan. Two examples should suffice. On 13 April, they depicted David Cameron working with George Osborne on the Tory election manifesto. Cameron says to his colleague, 'How do you spell caviar?' The following day, their single-panel cartoon shows a father reading from a book of fairy tales to his daughter. 'How about this one…it's called 'Tory Manifesto'?' 'Nah, too unrealistic,' says the little girl. As with many of the partisan graphics that appeared in the pro-Conservative press in April-May 2010, not a few of Kerber and Black's cartoons could have appeared during any one of the country's electoral campaigns over the past several decades.

While the *Daily Telegraph* is often seen as the quintessential pro-Tory paper, it features the work of cartoonists who are best characterized as either weakly partisan or unpredictable. Matt, the paper's pocket cartoonist, produced a number of deftly rendered images during the election that made fun of the process rather than left-of-centre personalities or policies. His affable characters are often quite befuddled. 'I've made a string of promises that I can't possibly keep,' says one voter at the doorstep, in a cartoon published on 28 April, as a happy politician walks out the gate. 'Is it me, or does May 6 seem to be getting further away?' asked another voter on 13 April. 'And don't use that reasonable Nick Clegg tone with me,' shouts a middle-aged woman as she argues with her husband (18 April). With Matt, voters rather than politicians are often the punchline.

Cartoon 3: Three Matt cartoons from the *Daily Telegraph*

'While you're talking I'm drawing the audience reaction worm'

'Oh, all right then, take me to Nick Clegg'

Another cartoonist whose work is featured in the *Daily Telegraph* is Christian Adams, who also produces editorial cartoons for the *Sunday Telegraph*. Rather than using his full name, he goes by the name 'Adam'. His work is busier and less cartoony than Matt's, and he probably fits the anti-political label more closely than any other cartoonist who currently works for an up-market daily paper. During the election he generated a procession of images that expressed disgust with all three major parties. For example, on 8 April the *Telegraph* published an Adam cartoon that showed a voter walking out of a living room that was dominated by a large-screen television set with the faces of the three leaders. Two days later, his cartoon depicted Cameron, Brown, and Clegg as members of the infamous Sex Pistols, complete with safety pins and spiky hair. 'God Save Us All' reads the banner behind them.[191] And in a reference to the volcanic ash that grounded flights across much of Europe during the middle of the campaign season, his cartoon on 16 April portrayed the three leaders as smoky figures in the sky, with a caption that read, 'Eruption Smothers Britain.'

---

[191] The Sex Pistols' second single, 'God Save the Queen', was released in 1977 during Queen Elizabeth II's Silver Jubilee.

The most senior of the *Telegraph*'s in-house cartoonists is Nicholas Garland, who is better known as 'Garland'. His pieces for the 2010 election switched back-and-forth between an anti-Labour and an anti-political position. On 27 April, his cartoon depicted all three party leaders as dinosaurs whose world was about to be snuffed out by a meteorite labelled 'debt'. The next day, he drew a map of Britain that showed the three leaders running for their lives as mythical sea monsters labelled 'Debt', 'Crime' 'Unemployment', and 'Cuts' threaten a beleaguered island nation. His portrait of a post-Rochdale Gordon Brown with his foot in his mouth ('Clunking Foot'), which appeared on 29 April, offered a rare Garland image that was aimed exclusively at the Labour leadership, rather than the political class as a whole. The contrast in tone and sensibility between the equivocal cartoons that appeared in the right-leaning *Telegraph*, and those that turned up in the right-leaning *Sun*, *Daily Express*, and *Daily Mail* papers, is striking.

While the *Daily Telegraph* features the work of multiple cartoonists, *The Times* relies almost exclusively on the pen of Peter Brookes, who published his first cartoon in 1968 (in the now-defunct *New Society* magazine) and who has worked on a full-time basis for *The Times* since the early 1990s. A self-identified Labour supporter, he told the paper on the eve of the campaign that 'Cameron glows with privilege...the nose is patrician, almost Roman, and the mouth small. His hair, if not an Eton crop, is certainly very public school – it's got bounce, and you can almost smell the Molton Brown.'[192] According to his biographical entry on the British Cartoon Archive website, journalists at the paper 'adore Peter Brookes'. The political commentator Matthew Parris says, 'Peter can hardly enter the lift at Times House without a colleague rounding on him and demanding in a ho-ho voice: 'And who have you got in your sights for tomorrow, Peter?''[193]

As this anecdote suggests, Brookes' political cartoons can best be described as unpredictable. After all, no one at the *Daily Mail* would have needed to ask whom Mac was going to go after during the 2010 election. It is certainly the case that none of the major parties escape Brookes' satirical

---

[192] 'Peter Brookes Reveals the Tricks of the Cartoonist's Trade', *The Times*, 5 April 2010, www.timesonline.co.uk/tol/news/uk/article7087575.ece.
[193] See www.cartoons.ac.uk/artists/peterbrookes/biography.

grasp. He produced what is arguably one of the finest cartoons published during the entire four-week election, a splendid three-panel strip that appeared on 29 April. In the first panel, Gordon Brown says, 'Bigoted Woman!' In the second panel, Brown clutches at the overhanging word balloon, and in the third panel he jams it into his stomach. It's a simple image, but a powerful one that cleverly plays with the language of comics.

Cartoon 4: Peter Brookes, *The Times*, 28 April 2010

© Peter Brookes/The Times/NI Syndication (2010). Thanks to Peter Brookes and *The Times*.

Another memorable Brookes graphic, published on 5 May, depicts a beleaguered Brown driving the porcelain bus. 'A day to go...almost there...One Last Heave!' Yet for every rude image-text aimed at Labour, Brookes produced at least one anti-Tory cartoon. David Cameron was unlikely to find much succour in Brookes' work, in other words. One of his cartoons, published on 4 May, shows Cameron leaning back in his office chair, with his feet on his desk. Nick Clegg and Vince Cable tell him,

'We want PR!' Cameron smugly replies, 'Super, guys! PR's what I'm all about!' In another cartoon, published on 28 April (see facing page), a rather phony-looking Cameron invites journalists to, 'Ask me about policies!' 'How will you pay for them?' comes the reply. 'Any hung parliament questions?' responds the well-groomed Conservative leader. If the Tories could more or less take the paper's editorial support for granted, the same cannot be said for the *Times'* featured cartoonist.

Perhaps the most distinctive graphic stylist employed by a national paper is Gerald Scarfe, whose scathing single-panel cartoons for the *Sunday Times* invariably ridiculed all three parties. Scarfe is one of Britain's most successful graphic artists. He has worked as a conceptual character artist for Disney, has designed numerous sets for operatic productions, collaborated with the National Portrait Gallery to produce caricatures of famous Britons, including Winston Churchill and Agatha Christie, and was commissioned to create postage stamps in the late 1990s. In 2005, the *Press Gazette* named him one of the country's 40 most influential journalists, an honour he shared with two other cartoonists, Carl Giles ('Giles') and Matt Pritchett. He was appointed Commander of the Order of the British Empire (CBE) in the 2008 Birthday Honours.

The *Sunday Times* ran four Scarfe cartoons during the 2010 election. The first, which appeared on 11 April, shows Gordon Brown dumping household waste on the head of David Cameron, who is standing in front of Number 10. 'The debate begins,' reads the caption. A subsequent cartoon, published on 25 April, placed the three party leaders in the desert, with Clegg leaning over Gordon Brown's prostrate body. 'What about me?' a dazed Cameron asks, as the caption reads, 'Kiss of Life.' A week later, Scarfe depicted the three party leaders as axe-wielding executioners, with John Bull's head on the chopping block ('The Voter's Choice'). Few if any of the country's political cartoonists were as consistently hostile to the choices on offer as the staff artist for the *Sunday Times*.

Two papers with very different audiences – the *Financial Times* and the *Daily Star* – both featured cartoons that could be more aptly described as unpredictable rather than partisan or anti-political. Scott Clissold, who signs his work 'Scott,' has been the *Star*'s editorial cartoonist for nearly a decade. His election cartoons made light-hearted fun of all three leaders. A representative example was his portrait of Nick Clegg with a swollen head (overleaf), which appeared on 27 April. 'The next TV debate better be in widescreen!' says an alarmed member of the public. Similarly, the *Financial Times'* Ingram Pinn took swings at all three party leaders, who were often depicted as squabbling children. The *FT*'s pocket cartoonist, 'Banx' (Jeremy Banks) has an unusually pithy style. His 27 April cartoon shows a middle-aged couple sitting down for tea in front of the telly. 'It's time for change,' says the man. 'Let's see what's on the other channel.'

Cartoon 5: Scott, *Daily Star*, 27 April 2010

Thanks to Scott Clissold and the *Daily Star*

The *Observer*'s Chris Riddell generated two different types of cartoons during the 2010 general election. Under the banner 'Riddell's View' he produced traditional editorial cartoons that featured such familiar archetypes as John Bull and the Grim Reaper. For a 2 May cartoon titled 'The Bungle Book' he portrayed the three leaders as Jungle Book characters: Cameron as Kaa the snake ('Trust in me, just in me…'), Brown as Baloo ('I'll cut the bare necessities…'), and Clegg as King Lowe Louie ('I don't want to be like you-two-oo…'). It was a clever image but oddly affectionate in its portrayal of the three contenders. Riddell also produced rather less conventional comic strips for the paper that busily crammed words and caricatures into a small amount of space. Just before the election, for example, on 2 May, he published a strip titled 'And the winner is…' that showed the party leaders flashing big grins as 'Leonid Nibling, Emeritus Professor of Media Studies at the University of the South Circular' renders irrelevant pronouncements on the state of the campaign. Many readers may assume that the paper keeps two cartoonists on staff, rather than just one.

In their ongoing competition for media-savvy readers, the *Guardian* and the *Independent* both featured numerous cartoons during the election season. While the *Guardian* mainly showcases the work of in-house cartoonists Steve Bell and Martin Rowson, it also publishes sketches and comics by freelance illustrators on occasion. The *Independent*'s staff cartoonists are Dave Brown and Tim Sanders, who supplies the paper's pocket cartoons. The *Independent on Sunday* runs cartoons by Peter Schrank, who also works for the *Economist*. Bell, Rowson, Brown, and Schrank tend to refer to the world of art and nineteenth century illustration more often than their peers at other newspapers, which may speak to the comparative sophistication of their papers' readerships. In keeping with their papers' equivocal editorial policies, the *Guardian* and *Independent* cartoonists can be characterized as weakly partisan or perhaps even unpredictable. Occasionally their work is simply anti-political. Both papers are generally viewed as left-of-centre but they are clearly unreliable from a partisan perspective.

Dave Brown's graphics tend to be dominated by his rather sympathetic caricatures and often feature spacious backgrounds. A typical image, published on 4 May, shows the Conservative leader prematurely opening a bottle of Champagne whose cork bounces around the cartoon frame and threatens to whack Cameron on the head. 'Triumphalism? What triumphalism?' he innocently asks. Two days later, he referenced a James Gillray print by showing Britannia on her deathbed surrounded by three dodgy surgeons – Brown and Clegg, who both wield saws, and Cameron, who carries a menacing scythe. 'Death may decide when Doctors disagree,' reads the caption. While his images often poked fun at Labour and Liberal Democratic leaders, he usually aimed his most pointed attacks at the Tories.

Brown's chastened perspective on the state of British politics is perhaps best summed up by a 21 April cartoon that spotlighted the faces of the three leaders. While Clegg's visage was accompanied by the word 'Soap,' and Brown's by 'Dope,' Cameron was shown swinging from a 'Rope'. Like many left-of-centre voters, Dave Brown was evidently disappointed by the performance of the left-of-centre parties, but at the same time antagonized by the Tories. A similar sense of disenchantment was conveyed by the work of Peter Schrank, whose final cartoon before polling day, published on 2 May, depicted Gordon Brown dangling from a cliff as he unhelpfully punches himself on the head. Many Labour supporters would no doubt have appreciated where Schrank was coming from.

Cartoon 6: Steve Bell, *Guardian*, 30 April 2010

Thanks to Steve Bell and the *Guardian*

The *Guardian* took a reportorial interest in how cartoonists were covering the election, and even ran a feature toward the end of the race where they invited artists and graphic designers to develop their own political poster art. Most of the resulting contributions were more anti-Tory than pro-Labour, with Mark Wallinger's 'David Cameron: Ha Ha Ha' getting straight to the point. In his commentary, Wallinger complained, 'Cameron reminds me of a bar of soap. He has been leader for a long time now and I have no idea what he stands for.'[194] This is likely to have been the attitude of Martin Rowson and his colleague Steve Bell, both of whom ruthlessly mocked the Tory leader as an inflated media darling. Like the *Daily Mail*'s Mac, Rowson used the metaphor of hot air to capture the spirit of the debates, but mostly treated Gordon Brown as a hapless fool rather than a malevolent collectivist.

Perhaps the least flattering portraits of the Conservative leader flowed out of the pen of Steve Bell, who portrayed David Cameron as an empty-headed condom with bugged-out eyes. While his Gordon Brown resembled Toad of Toad Hall, and his Nick Clegg looked like a slick yuppie, Bell's rendition of Cameron was simply derisive. In one memorable graphic he drew Cameron floating above the Battersea Power Station, which was a reference to Pink Floyd's floating pigs. Bell's most potent cartoon from this period parodied the famous Edvard Munch painting 'The Scream.' Published on 7 May, the cartoon showed the three party leaders holding their hands to their open-mouthed faces. 'Oh shit!!!' they shouted in unison. 'We won/lost/drew!' Even readers who did not share Bell's scabrous politics could appreciate his skill at appropriating iconic images on behalf of contemporary political analysis. Fans of newspaper editorial cartooning often look back to a utopian past, when legendary figures like Thomas Rowlandson or David Low walked the earth and plied their trade. American observers are particularly quick to complain about the decline of the newspaper cartoon as an art form and the dearth of opportunities for younger editorial cartoonists.[195] As this chapter shows, however, the editorial cartoon, at least in Britain, is flourishing. This may in fact be a new golden age of the English-language political graphic.

---

[194] Mark Wallinger, untitled contribution, *The Guardian*, A14, 27 April 2010.
[195] For a contrarian view, see Ilan Danjoux, 'Reconsidering the Decline of the Editorial Cartoon', in Kent Worcester (ed.) 'Symposium on the State of the Editorial Cartoon', *PS: Political Science and Politics*, Volume XL (April 2007).

Further reading

Timothy S Benson, *The Cartoon Century: Modern Britain Through the Eyes of its Cartoonists* (New York: Random House, 2007).

Mark Bryant, *Dictionary of Twentieth-Century British Cartoonists and Caricaturists* (Farnham: Ashgate Publishing, 2000).

Vincent Carretta, *George III and the Satirists from Hogarth to Byron* (Athens, GA: University of Georgia Press, 1990).

Diana Donald, *The Age of Caricature: Satirical Prints in the Reign of George III* (London: Paul Mellon Centre for Studies in British Art, 1996).

Vic Gatrell, *City of Laughter: Sex and Satire in Eighteenth-Century London* (London: Walker & Company, 2007).

Paul Gravett and Peter Stanbury, *Great British Comics* (Worthing: Aurum, 2006).

Jeet Heer and Kent Worcester (eds), *A Comics Studies Reader* (Jackson, MS: University Press of Mississippi, 2009).

Jeet Heer and Kent Worcester (eds), *Arguing Comics: Literary Masters on a Popular Medium* (Jackson, MS: University Press of Mississippi, 2004).

Michael Wynn Jones, *The Cartoon History of Britain* (London: Tom Stacey, Ltd., 1971).

Roger Sabin, *Comics, Comix and Graphic Novels: A History of Comic Art* (London: Phaidon Press, 2001).

Helen Walasek (ed), *The Best of Punch Cartoons: 2,000 Humour Classics* (New York: The Overlook Press, 2008).

Kent Worcester, 'Introduction to the Symposium on the State of the Editorial Cartoon', *PS: Political Science and Politics*, Volume XL (April 2007).

Index

10p income tax rate.................................... *See* tax

7/7, 9/11 bombings .... *See* terrorism

Abrams, Mark 3

Adam (Adams, Christian) 336

advertising

  airbrushed posters of Cameron 18, 156

  Conservative posters showing Brown 214, 227–9

  in leadership campaigns 101

  in previous elections 51, 181

  Labour party campaigns............ 18, 62, 226–7

  LibDem campaign.................................229–31

  mock posters.......................................156, 339

  party spending on....................................... 249

  posters...226–30

  See also soundbites and slogans

Afghanistan, War in 5, 41–3, 49

  Brown's condolence letter 240

  salience as election issue....................170, 175

age, and voting/turnout 115–8, 278

  See also older voters, young voters

Al Megrahi, Abdelbaset................................. 133

Alexander, Wendy..70

Alice in Wonderland 326

Alliance Party of Northern Ireland 15

Ally Sloper 326

Alternative Vote ....*See* electoral system

Andy Capp.. 326

Angus Reid (research company)

  post-debate polls 196, 215

  voting intention polls....291–2, 295–300, 323

anti-social behaviour (ASB) 143, 175, 176

armed forces, spending on...............................43

  discussed during leaders' debates 214

Ashcroft, Lord (Michael)

  funding of Conservative campaign in marginal seats.......8, 11, 99, 114, 141, 147

  post-election polling commissioned by ... 275

Ashdown, Paddy... 200

Ashes to Ashes (TV series) 195, 226–7

Asthana, Anushka xv

asylum...*See* immigration

Atatürk, Kemal 322

Atkinson, Simon...xiv

Attlee, Clement......................................99, 282

Attorney General...37

Audit of Political Engagement 135, 136

Bailey, Bob.. 238

Baines, Paul. xiv, 2, 86, 101, 162, 167, 231, 247

Balls, Ed... 134, 282

Bank of England 61, 75, 251

bankers' bonuses, tax on...................... 133, 155

banking crisis

  bail-out of UK banks 50, 70, 75–6

  bail-out of US banks.......................................70

  run on Northern Rock.......... 49–50, 60–1, 75

Banx (Jeremy Banks) 340

Barclays Bank 75

Barking..180

Barking & Dagenham, London Borough 34, 180, 238

Barnard, Salli.. xv

bathplug, reported expenses claim for 134

BBC

  focus group research for.................... 212, 291

  local election vote share estimates 35, 40, 72, 133

  news reports..61

  opinion polls for .... xiii, xiv, 32, 41, 138, 140, 135, 231, 290, 293–4

  staged final leaders' debate . 195, 210–11, 222

  voodoo polls by 322

BBC programmes

  The Campaign Show 314

  News at Ten .... xv, 212

  Newsnight 21, 202

  Today programme 322

  The Vote Race 212

BBC Radio 2.. 195, 239

BBC Radio 4.. 134, 284

Beale, Roger..331

Beckett, Margaret...36

Bell, Steve 331, 341, 342–3

Benedict XVI (The Pope)................*See* religion

benefits, salience as election issue 175

Bentley cars..74

best party on key issues........9–10, 143, 177–81

  in marginal seats 142–3

Bestbetting...319

Bethnal Green & Bow 14, 148

betting markets as election predictors ...318–21

bias in the electoral system 7, 11, 99, 115, 264–9

Big Society.. 110, 221

  party election broadcast about.......... 237, 238

  public attitudes towards 259–60

'Bigotgate' 195, 196, 224, 231, 239–42
   cartoons about 334, 337, 338
bird flu 32
Birmingham Edgbaston 148
'Biscuitgate' 287
Bismarck, Otto von 95
'Black Wednesday' 64, 188
Black, David 335
Blaenau Gwent 14, 31, 73, 148
Blair, Sir Ian 70
Blair, Tony
   attitude to Brown's leadership 71–2
   effect of his premiership on Brown's
     chances 17, 43–9
   events during final term as PM 28–49
   handles death of Diana, Princess of Wales 64
   image as leader, compared to Brown 88–9
   interviewed by police over 'cash for
     honours' 32
   memoirs 31, 77
   public liking for 81–2
   public view of his record 46–7
   satisfaction ratings 44–6, 140–1
   and passim
Blears, Hazel 133
Blunkett, David 31, 35–6, 38
bookmakers 290, 318, 319
Borisyuk, Galina 268
Boulton, Adam 211
boundary changes of constituencies 7
   cause uncertainty for MPs and voters .. 7, 206
   future, to equalise electorates 264–9
   party effect of 7, 11, 14, 111, 267
BPIX 66, 291, 292, 295, 297–300, 312
Braunholtz, Simon xv
Brighton Pavilion 14, 324
British Cartoon Archive 326, 337
British Election Study (BES) 161, 164, 303
British National Party (BNP) ... 13, 14, 34, 130,
   137, 180, 181, 238
   party election broadcast 238
British Polling Council (BPC) 291–2, 294, 295,
   301, 320, 322
Brookes, Peter 331, 337–9
Broughton, Joe xv
Brown, Dave 341–2
Brown, Gordon
   agrees to take part in leaders' debates 10
   and Iraq War 42–3, 69
   bullying allegations 33, 156, 240–1, 315
   condolence letters 240

   cartoons of 331–43
   considers snap election in 2007 .... 8, 49, 65–9
   'control freak' accusations 62
   denies influence of opinion polls 66–7
   depicted in Conservative posters 227
   disadvantaged in personality-based election
     25
   effect on Labour's chances 77–95
   election as leader 57–9
   handling of banking/economic crisis 75–7
   'honeymoon' effect on ratings 46, 59–65,
     67–9
   image in marginal constituencies 144
   in the leaders' debates 25
   leader image 62–3, 71, 79–89, 240–2
   personal attacks on, ineffectual 155, 240–2
   pictured on Conservative posters 214
   political fortunes in office .. 8–10, 49–50, 57–
     77
   portrayed as competent rather than
     charismatic 18
   public dislike of 54–5, 79–82
   record as Chancellor, public view of 51–5
   satisfaction ratings as PM 45, 72, 119–21
   video on YouTube 132
   voting intentions during Blair premiership if
     Brown had been leader 56
   voting intentions if he had stepped down . 94
   and passim
Brown, Sarah 334
Buckingham 110, 111
budgets
   2006 budget 40, 52
   2007 budget 32
bullying allegations against Brown 133, 156,
   240–1, 315
Bury 72
Butler, Sara xiv
Butler, Sir David 112
by-elections, parliamentary
   as predictor of general election result .. 68, 98
   Blaenau Gwent (2006) 14, 31
   Crewe & Nantwich (2008) 70, 73–4, 111
   Dunfermline & West Fife (2006) 31, 200
   Glasgow East (2008) 70
   Haltemprice & Howden (2008) 70
   Liberal Democrat performance in ... 199, 203
   Norwich North (2009) 111, 133
cabinet reshuffles 36, 61, 133
Cable, Vince 19, 61, 69, 199, 201–2
   cartoons of 328, 338–9

Caerphilly..73
Caine, Michael.. 246
Callaghan, James..... xii, 3, 57, 79, 118–22, 124
Cameron, Daniel xv
Cameron, David
    agrees to take part in leaders' debates 10, 122
    airbrushed posters of................................18
    cartoons of 335–43
    coalition negotiations................................6
    election as leader 100–4
    expected to win the leaders' debates....... 213
    fortunes as PM................................ 20, 261–4
    image as leader... 62–3, 71, 82–7, 125, 263–4, 274
    image in marginal constituencies 143–6
    policy decisions................................107–11
    posters depicting 156, 226
    public liking for 54–5, 125–7
    ratings as opposition leader 46, 119–21, 123–5, 140–1, 156–7
    ratings as PM................................261–3
    ratings slip 2009–10 24
    and passim
campaign................................210–49
    impact on floating voters 224–32
    net impact on voting intentions... 197–8, 216
    public satisfaction with, first week 232
    summary of events during 191–7
campaign expenditure................224–5, 248–9
    legal limits on 7–8, 11, 141
Campbell, Sir Menzies ('Ming') ... xi, 31, 41, 61, 62, 78, 84, 199–201, 251
candidates, number of 6–7
Cannock Chase 148, 154
canvassing................ 110, 236–7, 249, 330
    enhanced by geodemographics 234–5
    Gordon Brown in 'Bigotgate' incident 239
    party spending on................................ 249
    reported level of contact 236
care for the elderly, salience as issue 175
Carlton Club................................xii–xiii
Carroll, Liam xv
'cash for honours'.................31, 32, 37–8, 61
Catholic church................................ *See* religion
CATI (computer-assisted telephone
    interviewing) 304
CBC 294
Chancellors of the Exchequer, public
    satisfaction with................................51–3
Cheltenham 151
Chesterfield 148

Chilcot Enquiry into the Iraq War.43, 70, 133, 155
Christian People's Alliance................................130
Christie, Agatha................................339
Churchill, Winston................................61, 322, 339
City Limits 331
civil partnerships 31, 220
Clark, Julia................................xv
Clarke, Charles................................31, 33, 36
Clarke, Harold D................................161
Clarke, Kenneth 52, 102, 103, 293
class
    and turnout 117–8
    changing class profile of party support 26, 277–8, 280–5
    'class warfare' campaigning 73–4, 283–5
    effect on opinions of Cameron 126
    growth of middle class 115–8, 281–2
    self–assessed 283–4
Cleary, Helen xiv
Clegg, Nick
    cartoons of................................328, 334–43
    disliked after election................................ 253–4
    effect of first debate on public image.......216
    election as leader................................201
    image as leader................ 82–7, 263–4
    image in marginal constituencies.......... 143–4
    in the leaders' debates 25
    joins coalition 6
    ratings damaged since joining coalition 20–1, 253
    and passim
climate change 109, 174–5, 232
Clissold, Scott................................*See* Scott
Coalition government (2010–?)
    formation of.................................6, 15, 250
    fortunes since election . 20–1, 250–64, 287–9
    prospects at next election 270–1
coalition governments, rarity of 6
Cobra emergency committee 62
Collier, John................................326
Colville, Kerry 15
Committee on Standards in Public Life
    (CSPL) 36, 37, 38
    Ipsos MORI survey for................................37
Common Market (EEC), referendum on
    (1975) 96, 303
ComRes (research company)
    post-debate polls................196, 215, 314
    voting intention polls30, 66, 291–2, 297–300, 310, 323

other polls........................ 42, 77, 169, 184, 242
Conservative Party 98–157
  campaign expenditure............................248–9
  change of logo and campaign colour 110
  electoral performance 2005–10... 33–5, 40–1,
    71–4, 128–31
  image 89–95, 104–7, 127–8
  internal divisions.................................102, 110
  leadership election (1990) 58
  leadership election (2005) 100–4
  leadership election rules 101–2
  policy programme evolves 107–11
  poor image damages policy credibility..... 108
  public dislike of 54–5, 125–7
  readiness to govern, perceived.................. 157
  scale of task to achieve victory............98–122
  support since forming coalition............255–7
  target seats, performance in.................147–55
  targeting marginals 8, 11-12, 114, 141–55,
    193–4
ConservativeHome (blog)............................. 322
constituency electorates, equalising.........264–9
Contact Creator (Labour campaigning
  software) 234
Cooper, Yvette.. 134
core vote 12, 22, 33, 44–5, 123, 126, 131, 158–
  9, 281
Coronation Street....................................... 284
corrupt, perception that MPs are.........135, 139
Cowling, David...xv
Cranfield University...............................xiv, 224
Crewe & Nantwich 70, 73–4, 111
crime
  discussed during leaders' debates 213–4
  party with best policies on 143
  policies aimed at key groups...................... 233
  salience as political issue 36, 169–77, 179
Crosby, Lynton................................. 130, 194–5
Crosby/Textor (research company)........313–4
Crown Prosecution Service (CPS)........... 37, 61
Cruickshank, George and Isaac 326
Curtice, John .... xv, 294
cuts in public spending... 10, 20, 184–6, 255–7,
  259
Daily Express
  cartoons in 334
  polls for....................................120, 122, 297–9
  voting by readers 244
Daily Mail..................................156, 331
  cartoons in..............................332, 333–4, 337
  polls for..297–9

voting by readers...244
Daily Mirror........................xi, 244, 246, 286, 335
Daily Record, voting by readers of 244
Daily Star................................244, 246, 329, 337
Daily Telegraph..............................74, 195, 240
  cartoons in .... xiv, 331, 335–7
  poll reported in...................................... 313–14
  publication of MPs' expenses claims 9, 28,
    50, 131–5
  voting by readers...244
Darling, Alistair 53, 61, 75, 183, 202
data protection
  HMRC loss of data discs 61,69, 201
databases.. 234, 236
Davey, Andy 334
Davies, Dai... 14
Davis, David 70, 102, 103, 104
Deacon, David 247
debates between leaders 1, 10–11, 194–7, 210–
  24
  Brown at a disadvantage 89
  Cameron expected to win..........................213
  compared with press coverage.............. 246–7
  effect on voting intentions11, 13, 19–20, 24–
    5, 196–8, 216–19, 225
  fail to convince voters of policy differences
    between parties..184
  focus groups during ('the worm')...... 212–15,
    220–1, 223, 291
  impact on voters in marginals............... 145–6
  in newspaper cartoons 334, 339–40, 342
  media coverage... 247–8
  message persuasiveness.......................... 230–1
  polls after..............................196, 215–16, 314
  'presidentialising' effect........................ 166–7
  previous attempts to organise............. 10, 122
  tracking reactions online............................325
  viewers opinions of election coverage......239
  viewing figures......................16, 211, 220, 222
debate, post budget.......................................202
defence policy................................... 109, 211
  salience as political issue 169–77
Democratic Unionists (DUP) 7, 15, 269
demographic changes, effect................... 115–8
Denmark...328
depolarisation of party support ... 26–7, 116–8,
  277–89
Diana, Princess of Wales, death of 49, 64
Dickens, Charles 326
Diffusion (digital agency)...............................243
Dimbleby, David.......................................211

direct mail from parties 101, 224, 234
Dobson, Frank...36
Doctor Who.. 237
Doyle, Richard.. 326
Dromey, Jack 37
duck house, reported expenses claim for ... 134
Duffy, Bobby xiv
Duffy, Gillian...239–42
Dumfries & Galloway.................................... 148
Duncan Smith, Iain................................102, 274
Dunfermline & West Fife 31, 200
Dunwoody, Gwyneth 73
Dunwoody, Tamsin 73
Duval, Marie.. 326
economic determinism of election results 189–
        90, 258
economic optimism index (EOI) 187–90, 257–
        8
Economist, The..............................xv, 298, 330, 341
economy
    Brown gains credit for handling crisis 18–19,
        75–7, 183
    eclipsing other issues 7, 167
    economic crisis since 2008.............. 5, 182–90
    party with best policies on 9–10, 25–6, 27,
        143, 177–8, 182–4, 186
    public doubt depth of crisis........ 25–6, 185–6
    salience as a political issue 169–77, 184–6
    state of, when Brown became PM 53
    support for coalition's policies on 258
Edinburgh North & Leith 314–5
education
    foundation schools...53
    LibDem policy on hypothecated taxes 172
    party with best policies on 143, 177–8, 180
    salience as a political issue143, 172, 173, 175,
        233
    tuition fees 255
'election that never was' ....xii, 8, 49, 65–9
electoral system
    Alternative Vote 16, 269
    bias towards Labour in.......7, 11, 16, 99, 115,
        264–9
    first-past-the-post ....ix, 265
    referendum on 6, 16, 254, 264, 269, 270
    translation of votes into seats...... 23, 99, 203,
        264–9
    See also boundary changes
Eltham.. 148
emotion and voting.. 161

environment as a political issue ..109, 170, 173,
        174–5
Epictetus..161
Erikson, Robert S 320, 321
ethnic minorities
    attitudes to immigration...............................73
    number of minority MPs 15
    See also race relations, immigration
Europe/European Union (EU)
    Conservative policy on...... 109–10, 167, 173,
        277
    European Parliament....................................110
    Lisbon Treaty 61, 173
    proposed EU constitution (2005) 31
    salience as a political issue 172–7
    UK membership of 277
European Economic Community (EEC),
        referendum on (1975) 96, 303
European Parliament elections 18, 68, 123,
        128, 202
    as predictor of general election outcome ... 68
    in 2004 137
    in 2009 .... 9, 50, 133, 135, 136–7, 140, 173
    table of results 137
European People's Party 110
Evening Standard xi
    cartoons in 332
    polls for 122, 145–7, 206, 210, 296–9
Exchange Rate Mechanism (ERM).............. 188
exit poll .... xv, 12, 246, 290, 293–5
    sceptics doubt accuracy of............xiii, 12, 294
expenses claims of MPs 6, 9, 28, 50, 108, 131–
        40, 202
    accusations against Gordon Brown 240
    discussed in leaders' debates 213, 223
    proposed exemption from FOI............ 70, 77
expenses, election..... *See* campaign expenditure
Experian 234
Fannie Mae..75
Financial Times 132, 331, 339–40
Finkelstein, Daniel...73
first-past-the-post.............. *See* electoral system
Firth, David..294
Flanders, Matt...xv
floating voters... 191–3
    decision-making by............................... 162–6
    different opinions to party members.......100,
        123–4
    first to desert unpopular government........44
    research among .. 212–15, 220–1, 223, 224–
        31, 275

low political engagement of...... 160, 218, 275
strategic importance of..... 21–3, 158–61, 235
flooding... 60–1
focus groups, with undecided voters during
  debates 212–15, 220–1, 223, 291
Foot, Michael..98
Foot and Mouth Disease........................61, 170
foreign affairs
  leaders' debate on....................................220–2
  salience as a political issue 169–74
foreign prisoners, uncontrolled release of....31,
  33–6
Forsyth, Bruce.. 294
Fox, Liam..102–4
France, EU referendum 31
Fraser, Christopher 134
Freddie Mac 75
Freedom of Information Act 70, 77, 134
  and MPs' expenses claims..............70, 132
FTSE index 70
G8 summit (2005) 31
Gaitskell, Hugh................................3, 97, 124
Galloway, George...14
Gallup polls (UK)......................28, 96, 97, 124
Gallup Organization (US) 324
Gallup, George 302, 320
Garland, Nicholas 337
Gatrell, Vic 327
gender gap ....*See* women
geodemographics...234–6
get-out-the-vote campaigns 234
Gfk NOP (research company).... xiii, 246, 290,
  293–5
Giles, Carl 339
Gill, Mark..xiv
Gillingham & Rainham 152
Gillray, James...326, 341
Ginsberg, Jodie...xv
Glasgow 61, 70, 151, 279
Glasgow East..70
Glasgow Herald.. 329
Glasgow North East..............................111, 148
global warning 174
Goldsmith, Lord (Peter)....................................37
government, satisfaction with, ratings 72, 119–
  21
GovNet..x
Gosschalk, Brian xiv
Greater London Authority (GLA) 32
Greece 256
Green Party 14, 34, 130, 137, 174, 330

Green, Damian..70
Griffin, Nick 180, 239
Guardian, The............................. 61, 70, 199, 323
  cartoons in 328, 331, 332, 341, 342–3
  polls for ..56, 202, 205, 232, 256, 263, 297–9,
  313, 315
  voting by readers......................................244
Guest, Pete...xv
Gulf War (1991) 64, 170
Gurkhas 70
Hague, William ..xii, 79, 88, 105, 106, 236, 273,
  274
Haltemprice & Howden 70
Handelsman, J B 326
Hansard Society.....................................135, 136
Harman, Harriet..37
Harris Interactive 30, 197, 292, 297, 310
Harris Research poll 97
Hartlepool 73
Hattersley, Roy..293
Hayman, Andy..30
HBOS (bank) 75
healthcare
  party with best policies on...........143, 178–80
  salience as an election issue 169–74
Heath, Edward ....ix, 96, 119, 120, 123
Heath, Michael 334
Helm, Toby...xv
Hermon, Sylvia 15
heuristic cues to voting choice......................161
Hewitt, Patricia.......................31, 33, 133, 155–6
hierarchy of human needs 162
Himmelweit, Hilda.................................. 158, 309
HM Revenue & Customs (HMRC), loss of
  data discs............................61, 69, 201
Hodge, Margaret 180
Hogarth, William.................................... 326, 340
Hogg, Douglas...134
'honeymoon' effect........... See Brown, Gordon
Hoon, Geoff..133, 155–6
House of Commons, reduction in size..........16
House of Lords
  'cash for peerages'.................. 31, 32, 37–8, 61
  Lords Appointments Commission 37
  reform of......................................16, 20, 168
  votes down 42-day detention bill 70
housing as a political issue................... 173, 175
housing tenure and voting..............26, 278, 287
Howard, Michael....xi, 79, 88, 102, 106, 123–4,
  195, 273, 274
Howe, Sir Geoffrey 52

HSBC (bank)..75
Hughes, Simon 199–200
Huhne, Chris..199–201
hung parliament
   betting on..318–9
   Liberal Democrat power in ....ix-x, 13–14, 19
   post-election balance of power .... ix-x, 13–15
   predicted by the polls 1, 19, 198–9, 313–4
   public preferences in case of 209–10
Hunt, Gene (TV character) 195, 226
Hutton Enquiry 38
ICM (research company) 210, 308
   post-debate polls 196, 215
   voting intention polls. 30, 65–6, 97, 251, 292,
     297–300, 310, 312, 313, 315
   other polls by . 56, 108, 139, 201–2, 205, 232,
     256, 263
ID cards 109
IML 212, 291
immigration
   and 'Bigotgate' incident.............................. 239
   discussed during leaders' debates 213–14,
     220–1, 223
   distrust of parties over......5, 14, 33, 167, 176,
     181
   party with best policies on ...109, 143, 177–8,
     180–1
   policies appealing to older voters 232–3
   public attitudes to..................................... 32–3
   salience as a political issue 10, 36, 169–77
income tax .... *See* taxation
indecisiveness of voters...................... 13, 146–7
Independent, The 77, 169, 244, 297–9, 329, 341–
   2
independent candidates 7, 14, 31
   public attitudes to....................................... 139
Independent Network (candidates'
   organisation) 139
Independent on Sunday 42, 184, 242, 297, 341
inflation as a political issue 118, 170, 173
Inglish, Sue xv
inheritance tax...67, 110
   Conservative pledge to restrict............... 8, 61
Institute for Government (IfG)....................xiii
interest in the election 224–5
interest rates 70, 287
internet..160, 211, 238–9
   low impact of online campaigning 243
   Mumsnet...285–7
   opinion polls using..................... 43, 243, 291
   'Smeargate'..70

social media........................... 195, 238, 323–5
   website to mock Cameron poster 156
Iowa Electronic Market 320
Ipsos group 3
Ipsos MORI
   accuracy of polls...........................290–6, 310
   exit polls 293–5
   foundation by merger of MORI and Ipsos
     UK...3–4
   methodology of polls 300–10
   private polls for Labour Party (1969–88).... 3,
     162–3, 183
   and passim
Iran 32
Iraq War......5, 30, 37–8, 41–3, 44, 65, 109, 280
   Brown visits troops 61, 67, 69, 70
   discussed during leaders' debates 221
   enquiry into ....See Chilcot Enquiry
   public support for 41
   salience as election issue 170, 171, 175
Ireland, economic crisis in............................256
Irving, Samantha xv
issues
   importance to election 9, 25–6, 158–90
   important issues in 2010...................... 169–77
   Ipsos MORI Issues Index 169–74
   what gives an issue leverage 25–6, 167
ITV xiii, xiv
   polls for 169, 215, 290, 293–5, 297–9
   staged first leaders' debate...........195, 210–11
Izzard, Eddie 237
jealousy, MP accuses voters of 134
Johnson, Alan...133
Johnson, Boris 70, 71, 93, 129–31, 279
Johnston, Ron 268
Joseph, Rebekah..xv
Journal of the Royal Statistical Society. 294
journalists, public attitudes towards.............136
Jungle Book, The...340
Jury Team x
Jyllands-Posten 329
Keilloh, Graham xiv
Kennedy, Charles...................... xi, 31, 199, 200
Kennedy, John F...10
Kent on Sunday...xiii
Kerber, Neil..335
kettling 70
Kingsmill, David xiv
Kinnock, Neil 80, 106, 122, 273, 281
knowledge, political, of the public ..160, 168–9
Labour Force Survey....................................305

Labour Party
campaign spending....................................248–9
demographic characteristics of voters for..26
electoral performance during 2005–10
    parliament.......... 33–5, 40–1, 71–3, 136–7
fund–raising controversies.............. 36–40, 70
future task....................................274–7, 280–5
image of party...89–95
internal split between Blairites and
    Brownites...47–8, 58
leadership election (2007) 58
leadership election (2010) 271
leadership plots, real or alleged 9, 70
National Executive Committee (NEC) 37
performance in government..................28–77
public liking for 54, 79–82, 271–2
private polls show collapse of Brown
    'honeymoon' 8, 67
private polling for, by MORI (1969–88) 3,
    162–3, 183
Scottish Labour Party....................................70
voting rebellions by Labour MPs ...30, 31, 53
Labserveritve party (Liberal Democrat
    advertising campaign)............................ 229
Lamont, Norman 52
late decisions how to vote................. 13, 192–4
late swing, correcting polls for 308
Latter, Jerry..xiv
law and order ....See crime
Law, Peter..14
Lawson, Nigel 52
leader image..77–89
importance in winning votes 10, 21–3, 25,
    160–7
measurements of 62–3, 71, 82–9, 125
perceptual map of 87
leadership coups, attempted or alleged.... 9, 70,
    155
possible consequences for vote 94
leadership elections 100–2
Conservative Party (1990)............................58
Conservative Party (2005).............. 31, 100–4
Labour Party (2007) 57–9
Labour Party (2010)................................... 271
Liberal Democrats (2006) 31, 199
Liberal Democrats (2007) 61, 201
leaflets, political 101, 230, 314
Leech, John 326
left-right scale, where voters place parties.. 209
Lehman Brothers..75
Leveller, The..331

Levy, Lord (Michael) 31, 37
Lexalytics 325
Liberal Democrats 198–210, 250–5
campaign spending 248–9
disadvantaged by 'first–past–the–post' 99,
    204
fortunes during 2005–10 parliament 40–1,
    198–204
join coalition 6, 15
image of party............... 89–95, 205–9, 253–4
leadership elections................. 6, 31, 199–201
left-right preferences of supporters .. 208–10,
    250
loss of support since joining coalition.. 20–1,
    250–5
low profile 199
power in hung parliament......... 13–14, 202–3
public sympathy with their values 207–8
reasons for supporting.............. 158–9, 205–8
softness of support 13
surge in support after first debate ... 1, 11, 13,
    24–5, 196–8, 216–19, 237
Liberal–SDP Alliance 158, 199
Lib–Lab pact..199
Libya...133
'Like him? Like his party?' 54, 79–81, 125, 126,
    253–4, 272–3
'Like him? Like his policies?'..................... 81–2
Lincoln, Abraham 2
Lisbon Treaty.. 61, 173
Litvinenko, Alexander, murder of.................31
Livingstone, Ken.................70, 71, 78, 129, 130
Lloyd George, David....................................198
Lloyds TSB (bank) 75
loans, secret, to fund Labour Party..............37
local government elections.................... 18, 128
as predictor of general election outcome...68
gains and losses (table)..................................34
in 1995 73
in 2006 ....31, 33–5
in 2007 ....40–1, 200
in 2008 71–3
in 2009 ....133, 136
London Mayor (2004).................................130
London Mayor (2008) 71–2, 129–31, 279
vote shares, national equivalent..................35
Lockerbie bomber released 133
logo of Conservative Party changed............110
London
Labour performance in...............................149
Mayoral election of 2004 130

Mayoral election of 2008 71–2, 129–31, 279
voting at general election 278
London Evening Standard......See *Evening Standard*
Lord Snooty 73
Loughborough University............................ 247
Low, David.. 343
Lucas, Caroline 174, 324
Luton South 324
Mac (Stan McMurtry) 332, 333–4, 337, 343
McAndrew, John...xv
McBride, Damian 70
McCain, John 101, 324
McDonagh, Siobhain......................................70
McDonnell, John..................................... 32, 58
Macintyre, Ben...73
Mackintosh, Charlotte xv
McLean, Iain 268
Maclennan, Stuart.. 195
McMillan, Ann 294
Macmillan, Harold..97
McMurtry, Stan...................................*See* Mac
Mail on Sunday..... 70, 133, 297–9, 312, 329, 334
Major, John
    as Chancellor of the Exchequer..................52
    as leader during Gulf War...........................64
    cartoons of 328
    chaotic government under...........................69
    depicted in Labour posters 227
    drops poll tax...42
    election as Conservative leader 57–8, 97
    image of Conservative Party under 105–6
    loses 1997 election ..... xii, 10, 79, 105–6, 191, 227, 258
    perceived sleaziness of his government. 36–9
    public liking of... 81–2
    wins 1992 election 35, 97, 106, 116–18, 121–2, 281
Manchester, University of............................. 317
Mandelson, Lord (Peter) 98
manifestos...............................160, 195, 233, 335
Marf (Martha Richler)................................... 332
Margesson, George xiv
marginal constituencies 141–55
    best party on key issues polling................. 143
    Conservative targeting of...8, 11–12, 18, 114, 141–55, 193–4
    election results in 17, 24, 147–55, 197–8, 267
    parties outperforming national swing in.. 267
    polls in.... 66–7, 114, 142–7, 197–8, 213, 296, 313–14
    strategic importance of voters in. 22, 159–60

tactical voting in 206–7
volatility of the vote.................................. 146–7
Market Research Society...................................3
Marmite 238
Marr, Andrew 66
Martin, Michael 133
Maslow, Abraham..162
Matt (Matthew Pritchett) ..xiv, 331, 335–6, 339
Mattinson, Deborah 180, 286
media coverage of the election
    effect on salience of political issues 171
    public attitudes towards.............................316
Melvill, Rob...xiv
Menezes, Jean Charles de 30–1
MERLIN (Conservative campaigning
    software)..234
Merthyr Tydfil 73
MESH Planning..224
Metro, polls for 197, 297–9
middle class ....See class
Miliband, David................................61, 70, 271
Miliband, Ed 61, 263–4, 271–4, 282
    election as leader ....
    initial performance as leader 20
Mitchell, Dawn 3
Mludzinski, Tomasz xiv
moat-cleaning (reported expenses claim)....134
Moon, Nick xv
Moray..195
Morgan, Rhodri...78
MORI (Market & Opinion Research
    International) .... *See* Ipsos MORI
Mortimore, Roger .... xiv, 2, 86, 162, 167, 247
MOSAIC 234, 235
most capable PM............. 9, 51, 78, 102, 121–2
Mousavi, Mir-Hossein....................................322
MPs' expenses ....*See* expenses claims of MPs
MPs retiring 6–7
MPs, reduction in numbers 16
Mumsnet.. 285–7
Munch, Edvard 343
Munro, Jonathan..xv
Murdoch, Rupert..............................31, 244, 245
Murphy, Joe xv
Muslims ....*See* religion
mydavidcameron.com 156
Napoleon I..69
National Assembly of Wales............. *See* Welsh
    Assembly
National Audit Office 33
National Bullying Helpline 240

national equivalent vote share estimates........33
National Health Service (NHS) 109
  salience as political issue 169–77
national insurance.......10, 168, 184–5, 195, 229
National Readership Survey 116, 305
negative campaigning............................231, 242
Neil, Andrew.. 294
Netherlands, EU referendum..........................31
New Labour 21, 48, 52–3, 65, 74, 77, 91, 281–2, 284–5
New Society.. 337
New Statesman 237, 330, 331
News at Ten......................See BBC programmes
News of the World.......xv, 82, 146, 147, 222, 296, 297, 312, 313
  polls for..224, 251
newspaper coverage of the election
  coverage of the debates..........................247–8
  coverage by the *Sun*................................234–6
  public attitudes towards 316
newspaper readership
  and reasons for vote choice...................... 166
  and voting.......61, 126, 136, 243–7, 297, 304, 308, 313, 338, 339
NHS...................... *See* National Health Service
Nixon, Richard M 10
Nolan, Fiona xiv
NOP ....*See* Gfk NOP
Norris, Steven.. 130
Northern Ireland 6, 111, 301
  election result in 15
  excluded from most opinion polls 15
Northern Rock (bank) ... 50, 60, 61, 70, 75, 201
Norwich North.......................................111, 133
nuclear deterrent.....................................213, 277
  discussed during leaders' debates 220
Nutt, David 133
Obama, Barack 70, 77, 243, 324
Observer, The .... xv, 103, 332, 340–1
Ochil & South Perthshire 152
older people
  care for elderly, salience as issue............... 175
  policies aimed at 232–3
  See also pensions
Olympic Games.......................................31, 129
O'Neill, Hilary...xv
OnePoll....................................291, 292, 297–9
online campaigning, low impact of 243
OpenAmplify.. 238
Opik, Lembit.. 148
opinion polls 1–4, 290–315

accuracy in 2010..............................290–3, 310
and Brown's decision not to hold an election in 2007 .... 8, 65–7
as predictor of election outcome ...68, 310–12, 317
banning.. 316–7
during the campaign...... 196–7, 216–19, 222, 223–4, 297–300
final pre–election polls.....................12, 290–3
historical highs and lows........... 28, 95–7, 251
hypothetical nature of mid–term polls. 67–9, 95–7, 98, 277, 310–12
in 1992 general election 97, 121–2, 316
methodology.................................... 300–9
post-debate polls.................... 196, 215–6, 314
private polls.......................3, 8, 67–8, 162, 275
public attitudes towards.............................316
reporting of.. 310–15
similarity of results from different companies 29–30, 295–300
transparency... 300–1
weighting 304–6, 308–9
  See also voting intentions, exit poll, and under names of research companies
Opinium 291, 292, 297–9, 323
Osborne, George 93, 202, 335
Page, Ben.. xiv, 65
Palin, Sarah..101
Palmer, Jenny..xv
Parliamentary Privilege..................................138
Parris, Matthew 337
party election broadcasts (PEBs) 225–6, 237–9
  party spending on 249
  public attitudes towards 316
party funding, controversies over........... 36–40
party image........................ 89–95, 104–7, 127–8
  impact on voters 160, 194, 225–6
  importance in winning votes......10, 21–3, 25, 160–6
  perceptual map of 92
party leader..*See* leader
party policies, best *See* best party on key issues
past vote recall, weighting polls by 308–9
Pattie, Charles...268
Paxman, Jeremy...21
pensions...173, 175, 233
  salience as a political issue 173
people meters..212
People, The *(Sunday)*, polls for 297–9
Pertwee, Sean...237
Peskett, Duncan xv

Phillips, Chris xiv
Pierce, Anna xiv
Pink Floyd 343
Pinn, Ingram 340
Plaid Cymru..7, 13, 14, 111, 137, 159, 268, 330
Poland, immigration from 33
police 31, 32, 37, 38, 70, 109
    discussed during leaders' debates 214
    support for government line on terrorism.30
policies
    important issues in 2010 169–77
    party with best .... *See* best party on key issues
    public knowledge of, actual 160, 168
    public knowledge of, perceived 169
'policy-lite' approach.................................... 108
Political Betting (blog) 61, 292, 297, 310, 315,
    317, 319, 320, 332
Political Triangle model of voter behaviour xi–
    xii, 162–6
poll tax (community charge)................... 42, 170
pollution/environment as salient issue170, 173
Pope Benedict XVI........................... *See* religion
population change ...... *See* demographic change
populism 21–2
Populus (research company)
    post-debate polls 196, 215
    voting intention polls..... 30, 65–6, 292, 297–
    300, 310
    other polls by 56, 168, 208–9, 275
pornographic films, inadvertent expenses
    claim for.................................. 134
Porter, Andrew 74, 313
Portillo, Michael 102
postal votes...17
posters .... *See* advertising
Pre-Budget Reports
    November 2008..70
    December 2009 133
    December 2010 155
Prescott, John 31, 32, 33, 36
'presidentialisation' of British politics 25,
    158–90
press... *See* newspapers
Press Gazette, UK..339
Prime Minister, best.........*See* most capable PM
prisoners, foreign.....................................31, 33–6
Pritchett, Matthew................................ *See* Matt
Private Eye.......................................330, 334
private provision of public services............. 275
private schools 275

promises, trust in parties to keep 90–1, 105,
    127, 184–5
public services
    as an election issue.............................5, 176–7
    efficiency savings in.....................................186
    support for coalition's policies on........ 256–7
public spending cuts ....*See* cuts
public transport
    high speed rail..221
    salience as election issue 175
    terrorist attacks on in 2005...................... 30–2
Punch..326
Purnell, James 133
Quagliozzi, Jacob 226
Quick, Bob...70
quota samples 303
race relations, salience as issue.. 32–3, 36, 169–
    74
Rackham, Arthur..326
'rainbow coalition' 15
Rallings, Colin. xv, 7, 14, 34, 35, 111, 152, 153,
    266–7, 268
random samples 303
Rantzen, Esther..324
Rawnsley, Andrew 133, 156, 240, 241
Redcar 148
referendums...6, 16, 31, 270
    on the Common Market (1975).......... 96, 303
    on the electoral system.................................264
Reform Act (1832).. 6
Reform Club 65
regional voting patterns 1, 26, 113, 149, 204,
    278–80, 305
Reid, John..36
religion
    Catholic church 221
    number of Muslim women MPs 15
    papal visit 220
renewable energy..220
Renfrewshire East..17
Research Services Ltd (RSL) 3
Respect (political party)....14, 34, 130, 280, 330
result of the election.........................5–6, 12–15
    comparison with 2005...................................13
    in marginal constituencies 147–55
    seats and votes won.. 5
retirement of MPs...6–7
Reuters, polls for...xv, 114, 142–7, 198, 206–7,
    213, 253, 256–7, 257–9, 261–4, 290, 296,
    313
Riddell, Chris 332, 340–1

Richler, Martha ....*See* Marf
RNB India (research company) 291–3
Roberts, Bob xv
Robinson, Nick 212, 291
Rochdale 195, 239, 240, 242
Roman Catholic church ....*See* religion
Romford 238
Ross, Charles 326
Rossiter, David 268
Rothschild, David 321
Rowden, Gemma xv
Rowlandson, Thomas 326, 343
Rowson, Martin 328, 332, 341, 343
Royal College of Nursing 31
Royal Navy personnel taken hostage 32
Saddam Hussein 31
sampling error 302–3
Sanders, David 161
Sanders, Tim 331, 341
Scarfe, Gerald 339
schools ....*See* education
Schott's Almanac 283–4
Schrank, Peter 341, 342
Scotland 26, 40–1, 195
   Labour performance in 131, 149
   poll in 296
   Scottish Labour Party 70
   voting at general election 278–80
Scotsman, The 329
Scott (Scott Clissold) 339–40
Scottish government 133
Scottish National Party (SNP) ... 7, 13, 14, 37,
   40, 70, 129, 137, 159, 195, 268, 279, 296,
   315, 330
Scottish Parliament ('Holyrood') 32, 70, 279
   election of 2007 ....40–1, 129, 200
Scream, The (painting) 343
second home allowances 132–4
second order elections 98, 128
segmentation 232–6, 283
Sex Pistols 336
Sharkey, John xiii
Sheffield Hallam 201
Sinn Fein 15, 110
Skinner, Gideon xiv
Sky News 319
   exit poll sponsors ....xiii, xiv, 290, 293
   staged second leaders' debate.... 195, 210–11,
   220
sleaze, public perceptions of 37–9
slogans and sound-bites

Airbrushed for change 156
big clunking fist 47
Don't let him take Britain
   back to the 1980s 227
Fire up the Quattro,
   it's time for a change 227
from Stalin to Mr Bean 61, 69
I agree with Nick 214
I'll cut the deficit, not the NHS 229
I've never voted Tory before, but... 156
no time for a novice 62, 70
Not Flash, Just Gordon 18, 62
Tory VAT bombshell 230
Vote Blair, get Brown 51
Vote Blue, go Green 109, 174
We can't go on like this 156
Year for change 156
'Smeargate' 70
Smith Institute 282
Smith, Jacqui 61, 70, 133–4
Smithson, Mike 61, 315, 317
smoking ban 31
Snow, Dan 294
Snow, Peter 294
social care
   discussed during leaders' debates 214
Social Democratic Party (SDP) 158
social desirability bias 164
social grade ....*See* class
social media 195, 238, 323–5
Socialist Worker 330
software, campaigning 234
Sopel, Jon 314
Soros, George 188
Southampton 72
Speaker, change of
   effect on majority in Commons .110–11, 148
   Michael Martin resigns 133
Spectator, The 329
Spelman, Caroline 133
spending (campaign) *See* campaign expenditure
spread betting 320
standard deviation 148
Stationery Office, The 131
Stead, Joe xi
Steen, Anthony 134
Stevenson, Merril xv
Stewart, Alastair 211
Stewart, Marianne C 161
Straw, Jack 31, 36
sub-prime mortgages 61

Sun, The
  cartoons in 334–5
  endorses Conservatives 133, 155, 244–5
  influence on election result 243–6
  polls for 38, 43, 54, 60, 71, 102, 104, 126,
    181, 204, 219, 241, 259–60, 297–9
  voting by readers 244–6
Sunday Mirror 184, 242
Sunday Telegraph 297–9, 336
Sunday Times
  cartoons in 339
  polls for 94, 139, 218, 241–2, 297–9, 312
swing
  'Butler swing' 112
  by various demographic groups 278
  defined 112–13
  in various constituencies 147–55
  possibility of huge swings 95
  swing 1997–2005, 2005–10 compared ... 48–9
  swing needed by Conservatives for an
    overall majority 98–9, 112–15
  See also uniform swing
target seats, Tory performance in 147–55
tax relief on private health insurance 275
taxation
  abolition of 10p rate of income tax 32, 40,
    52–3, 70
  Conservatives as low tax party 110
  expected policies of parties in power ... 184–5
  income tax 10, 52, 70, 184–5, 200
  inheritance tax 8, 61, 67, 110
  party with best policies ... 10, 109, 177–8, 232
  public knowledge of party policies 168
  salience as a political issue 173, 175–7
  tax on bankers' bonuses 133, 155
  Value Added Tax (VAT) 10, 184–5, 230, 257
  See also national insurance
Taylor, Richard 14
telephone canvassing 234
television/radio coverage of the election
  public attitudes towards 316
television news, impact on floating voters . 225
Tennant, David 237
Tenniel, John 326
terrorism
  7/7 bombings in London 31–2
  9/11 attacks in the USA 49, 170
  attacks foiled in June 2007 .... 60, 61
  effect on public opinion 32, 44
  Lockerbie bomber, release of 133
  measures against 30, 32, 70, 109

PMs' ratings boosted by handling 44, 60
  proposed 42-day detention limit 70
  proposed 90-day detention limit 31
  salience as political issue 169–74
Terrorism Act 2006 30
text messaging 224
Thatcher, Margaret
  image of Conservative Party under 105–7
  no 'honeymoon' effect 64
  ousted as leader 29, 97
  public dislike of 80–2
  ratings as leader of opposition 119–20, 157
  refuses TV leaders' debate in 1979 ..... 10, 122
  swing to Tories after she was replaced 97
  victory in 1979 election .... xii, 106–7, 118–22,
    157
Thirsk & Malton 151, 294
Thomas, Paul 334
Thompson, Robert 334
Thrasher, Michael ... xv, 7, 14, 34, 35, 111, 152,
  153, 266–7, 268
Time magazine 322
time of voting decision 13
Time Out 331
Times, The 73, 195, 282, 286,
  cartoons in 331, 337–9
  polls for 56, 168, 208, 297–9
  voting by readers 244–5
Timpson, Edward 73
TNS BMRB (research company) 291, 292, 297,
  298
Tomlinson, Ian 70
Torfaen 73
Townend, Alastair xv
toxic debt 75
trade unions
  members in Labour leadership election ... 271
  strikes as a political issue 170
  UNISON conference boos Hewitt 33
Trident (nuclear weapon) 213
  discussed during leaders' debates 220
Trinidad & Tobago xiv
Trumble, David 335
trust
  in parties' policy promises 90–1, 105, 127,
    171, 184–5
  no party trusted on immigration ... 5, 33, 167,
    181
  professions trusted to tell truth 136
  reliance of voters on trusted politicians 7, 22–
    3, 161

trustworthiness of politicians, perceived. 37–40, 82–4, 135–40, 231–2

tuition fees 255

Turay, Mette .... •.....................xv

Turner, Ruth 32

turnout 16–17, 278

  anticipated effect of expenses scandal 137

  at local government elections 72

  contribution to electoral bias 267–9

  correcting opinion polls for 306

  in local government elections 34

  increasing age and class differential 116–18

  party effect of 72, 115–18, 130, 193

Tweetminster 323, 324

Twitter 195, 323–5

UK Independence Party (UKIP)9, 13, 14, 130, 133, 136, 137, 202, 330

UK Polling Report (blog) 29, 56, 59, 135, 197, 217, 310, 312

Ulster Unionists 15

undecided voters .... *See* floating voters

unemployment

  policies aimed at key voter groups 233

  salience as political issue 9, 118, 169–77, 183, 256

uniform swing 12, 99, 110–15, 142, 204, 320

  deviations from in election results 147–55

  non-uniformity affects electoral bias ...267–8

UNISON (trade union) 31, 33

United States of America

  presidential elections 10, 77, 101, 243, 320–1, 324, 330

  UK 'special relationship' with 221

unpredictability of result 11

valence issues 161

value added tax (VAT) .... See taxation

Viggers, Sir Peter 134

Vine, Jeremy 195, 239

volatility of vote 7–8, 13, 19, 24–5, 77, 95–7, 146–7, 191–4, 300

'voodoo polls' 290, 321–2

Vote Race, The 212, 291

Voter Vault (former Conservative campaigning software) 234

voting intentions

  during 2005–10 parliament (charts) 29, 59, 66, 135

  effect of party policies on 179

  hypothetical, assuming different party leaders 56, 94

mid–term readings should not be taken literally 67-9, 95–7, 277, 310–12

Wales 131, 195, 279

Wallinger, Mark 342–3

websites, party 237, 315

Webster, Paul xv

weighting of opinion polls 304–6, 308–9

Welsh Assembly 32, 40, 129

West, Lyn xv

Westen, Drew 161

Westminster North 148

Westmorland & Lonsdale 151

Whitehead, Toni xv

Whiteley, Paul 161

Wilson, Harold ....ix, 3, 8, 96, 281, 282

'Winter of Discontent' 119, 121

Winterburn, Denis xv

Witney 60, 61

Wlezien, Christopher 320, 321

women

  'gender gap' in voting behaviour 26, 278, 285–7

  lower swing than men during 'Brown bounce' 65

  'mumsnetters' 285–7

  number of female MPs 15

  policies aimed at 232–3

Wooding, David xi

Worcester, Bob 2, 65, 86, 167, 247

  as Labour Party private pollster (1969–88). 3, 98, 162–3

  founder of MORI 3

Worcester, Kent .... xiv, 326, 331

word of mouth campaigning 230

working class .... *See* class

'worm', the .... xiv, 212–15, 220–1, 223, 291

Wring, Dominic 247

Wyre Forest 14

YouGov (research company)

  post-debate polls 196, 215

  voting intention polls30, 65–6, 292, 297–300, 310, 312, 315, 323

  other polls by 43, 56, 94, 139, 204, 217–18, 219, 241–2, 243, 257, 259–60

young voters, policies aimed at 232–3

Young, Toby 293

YouTube 132, 237